The Therapist's Notebook
Homework, Handouts, and Activities
for Use in Psychotherapy

HAWORTH Marriage and the Family
Terry S. Trepper, PhD
Executive Editor

The Therapist's Notebook
Homework, Handouts, and Activities for Use in Psychotherapy

Lorna L. Hecker, PhD
Sharon A. Deacon, MS
and Associates

The Haworth Press
New York • London

The Haworth Press, Inc., 10 Alice Street, Binghamton, NY 13904-1580

Cover design by Marylouise E. Doyle.

Library of Congress Cataloging-in-Publication Data

Hecker, Lorna L.
    The therapist's notebook : homework, handouts, and activities for use in psychotherapy / Lorna L. Hecker, Sharon A. Deacon, and associates.
        p.   cm.
    Includes bibliographical references and index.
    ISBN 0-7890-0400-3
    1. Psychotherapy—Problems, exercises, etc. I. Deacon, Sharon A. II. Title.
RC480.5.H348   1998
616.89′14′076—dc21
                                                                                                          97-26361
                                                                                                          CIP

To my father, who taught me creativity through persistence

—Lorna L. Hecker

To my husband, Bill: King of Creativity, Lord of Laughter,
and as always, Prince with the Golden Heart

—Sharon A. Deacon

CONTENTS

ABOUT THE EDITORS

Lorna L. Hecker, PhD, is Associate Professor of Marriage and Family Therapy in the Department of Behavioral Sciences at Purdue University Calumet in Hammond, Indiana. Also the Clinical Director and Founder of the University's Marriage and Family Therapy Center, she teaches graduate courses in marriage and family therapy, theories of family therapy, gender and culture in family therapy, and professional issues and ethics in family therapy. She also teaches undergraduate courses on human sexuality and marriage and family therapy. She has published articles in the *Journal of Marital and Family Therapy,* the *American Journal of Family Therapy,* and the *Journal of Family Psychotherapy,* and contributed chapters to the book *101 Interventions in Family Therapy* (The Haworth Press, 1993). Some of her most recent work appears in the second edition of *The Family Therapy Sourcebook* (The Guilford Press, 1996). Dr. Hecker presents national training workshops to psychotherapists on working with conflictual couples, and has been a guest on several radio and television programs. She holds Marriage and Family Therapist Certification from the state of Indiana and is an Approved Supervisor and Clinical Member of the American Association for Marriage and Family Therapy.

Sharon A. Deacon, MS, is a graduate student in the Masters Program in Marriage and Family Therapy at Purdue University Calumet in Hammond, Indiana. As a Graduate Teaching Assistant, she teaches introductory psychology courses at Purdue Calumet. She has also held internship positions at the University's Marriage and Family Therapy Center and at Thornton Township Youth Committee in South Holland, Illinois, where she has conducted individual, couple, family, and group therapy. As an undergraduate at the State University of New York at Fredonia, she received the *Psychology Merit Award,* which is given to the most outstanding and promising psychology student, and the *Fredonia Scholars Award,* which recognizes the university's most outstanding student. While at Fredonia, she was a Counselor and Advisor Intern in the Upward Bound Program. In this capacity, she designed and implemented a human sexuality and values course for four local high schools, taught human sexuality to academically challenged and at-risk students, and served as a counselor. Ms. Deacon has published articles in the *American Journal of Family Therapy, Family Therapy,* and *Contemporary Family Therapy.* In addition she has received Purdue University Calumet's *Graduate Research Award* and *The Spotlight on Graduate Research Award.*

Contributors

Stephen A. Anderson, PhD, is a professor in the University of Connecticut's School of Family Studies where he teaches and supervises students in the school's accredited doctoral and master's degree programs in Marriage and Family Therapy. With Dr. Dennis Bagarozzi, he is the co-author of *Personal, Marital, and Family Myths: Theoretical Formulations and Clinical Strategies* and co-editor of *Personal Myths: Psychotherapy Implications.* He is also the co-author (with Ronald Sabatelli) of *Family Interaction: A Multigenerational, Developmental Perspective.*

Mary Anne Armour, MA, EdD, holds a joint appointment as associate professor in the Department of Psychiatry and Behavioral Science and the Department of Family Medicine at Mercer University School of Medicine in Macon, Georgia. She is codirector of the Marriage and Family Therapy Graduate Program within the Department of Psychiatry.

J. Maria Bermúdez, MS, is a doctoral student in the Marriage and Family Therapy Program at Virginia Tech University. She recently received her Master of Science degree in Marriage and Family Therapy from Purdue University Calumet in Hammond, Indiana. For her master's thesis, she surveyed Hispanics nationwide to examine whether differences existed in the way Hispanics described themselves and the ways in which the MFT literature described Hispanic families.

Robert A. Bertolino, MEd, is a Juvenile Justice Coordinator at Youth in Need in St. Charles, Missouri. He is also alPhD candidate in the Marriage and Family Therapy Program at St. Louis University. He is co-author (with Bill O'Hanlon) of the forthcoming book, *Moving On: Brief and Respectful Solutions for Resolving Sexual Abuse* (Wiley), author of the upcoming *Possibility Therapy with Troubled Adolescents* (Wiley), and editor of *An Invitation to Possibility Land: An Intensive Training Seminar with Bill O'Hanlon* (Brunner/Mazel).

Thomas W. Blume, PhD, is an associate professor in the Counseling Department at Oakland University in Rochester, Michigan. He teaches in the Couple and Family Counseling specialization, and maintains a private practice specializing in marital therapy. His Social Role Negotiation approach was developed as an approach to adolescent drug abuse. His current work focuses on marital conflict and parent-adolescent relationships.

Scott W. Browning, PhD, is chair of the Department of Professional Psychology at Chestnut Hill College in Philadelphia, Pennsylvania. Dr. Browning also serves as the Clinical Chair for the Stepfamily Association of America.

Rudy Buckman, EdD, is an outpatient therapist with the Salesmanship Club Youth and Family Centers, Inc. and a faculty member of the Reunion Institute. He is currently being trained in fatherhood by his fourteen-year-old and eleven-month-old sons. His professional interests include the influence of social constructionism/postmodernism on therapy and the theory and practice of narrative and redecision models of therapy.

Kimberly A. Cain, MA, is a master's level psychologist at Family Service and Guidance Center. She has trained in strategic therapy with Dr. Crenshaw and Cloe Madanes.

Thomas D. Carlson, MS, is currently a PhD student in the Family Therapy Program at Iowa State University, Ames, Iowa.

Richard Clements, PhD, is an assistant professor of psychology at Indiana University Northwest in Gary, Indiana.

Hugh Crago, MLitt, MA, was a senior lecturer in counseling, Department of Health Studies, University of New England from 1994 to 1997. He is co-editor of *The Australian and New Zealand Journal of Family Therapy,* and is currently examining historical evidence for differentiation of self within the family since the medieval period.

Maureen Crago, MA, MLitt, is co-editor of *The Australian and New Zealand Journal of Family Therapy.* She is a psychologist registered in New South Wales, Australia, and has a private practice in Armidale, New South Wales.

Wesley B. Crenshaw, PhD, is a licensed psychologist, strategic therapist, and training director at Family Service and Guidance Center of Topeka, Kansas. He is also a regional faculty member of Cloe Madanes' Family Therapy Institute of Washington, DC.

Mary E. Dankoski, MS, earned a master's degree in Marriage and Family Therapy from Purdue University Calumet and is currently pursuing a doctoral degree in marriage and family therapy at Purdue University, West Lafayette, Indiana.

Martin J. Erickson, BS, is a master's candidate in the Marriage and Family Therapy Program at Purdue University Calumet. He is finishing his master's thesis and is interested in Narrative Therapy, values and morals exploitation for therapists, and religion and spirituality issues in therapy.

Mary Forrest, MA, is currently the program director of two programs for the George Gervin Youth Center, a nonprofit organization that services at-risk youths and their families; director of C.H.A.A.N.C.E., a mentoring/tutoring program for at-risk youths ages eight to fourteen; and director of the St. Anthony Residential Home for Pregnant Teens. She is currently working on her doctorate at St. Mary's University in San Antonio, Texas.

Mary L. Franken is professor of family studies at the University of Northern Iowa, Cedar Falls, Iowa.

Steve Gilbertson, MA, LPC, CACIII, is assistant director of Centennial MHC, a community mental health center in eastern Colorado, and specializes in behavioral health services with rural and frontier populations.

Gail Golden, PhD, is a clinical psychologist in private practice in London, Ontario. She is also affiliated with the London Health Sciences Centre and with the departments of psychology and family medicine at the University of Western Ontario.

Tara R. Gootee, BA, is a master's candidate in the Marriage and Family Therapy Program at Purdue University Calumet, Hammond, Indiana, currently working as a teaching assistant in the Department of Behavioral Sciences. She is preparing her master's thesis and is interested in the influences of one's family of origin on the development of sexual values and knowledge.

Cassandra V. Greer, PhD, is an adjunct professor of counseling, University of Missouri–St. Louis and is a family therapist at Incarnate Word Hospital, St. Louis, Missouri.

Patricia E. Gross, PhD, is an assistant professor at the University of Northern Iowa in Cedar Falls, Iowa.

Walter Hartmann is a professor emeritus of psychology, Purdue University Calumet, Hammond, Indiana, a research and religious educator, and an Indiana Mental Health Provider.

Stacy Hernandez, BS, is a master's candidate in the Marriage and Family Therapy Program at Purdue University Calumet, Hammond, Indiana. She is preparing her master's thesis on marital relationships of professional athletes and is also interested in child development.

Miriam R. Hill, MS, is a PhD student in the Marriage and Family Therapy Program of the Department of Child Development and Family Studies at Purdue University, West Lafayette, Indiana.

Susan E. Hutchinson, PhD, ACSW, LMSW-ACP, is an assistant professor and interim chair in the Department of Clinical Social Work at the University of Texas–Pan American in Edinburg.

Brian Jory, PhD, is acting director of the Marriage and Family Therapy Program in the Department of Family Studies at the University of Kentucky in Lexington.

Connie M. Kane, PhD, is an associate professor in the Department of Advanced Studies at California State University, Stanislaus. She also provides family therapy at Family Service Agency in Modesto, California, and is an AAMFT Approved Supervisor.

Liberty Kovacs, PhD, MFCC, is in private practice at the Center for Marriage and Family Therapy, Sacramento, California. She has been a marital therapist for over thirty years. In addition to her private practice she is currently teaching workshops for couples based on her model (and videotape) of the six stages of marriage.

Paul A. Lee, PhD, is a professor of Family Therapy and Counseling at Assembly of God Theological Seminary in Springfield, Missouri. His research interests include parent-adolescent relationships, parenting style, dynamics of healthy families, and military families.

Sid Levine was a clinical social worker for forty-six years, twenty-eight of which were in private practice in Toledo, Ohio. He has recently retired.

Barbara J. Lynch is director of the Marriage and Family Therapy Program at Southern Connecticut State University in New Haven, Connecticut. She is also the clinical director of Marriage and Family Therapy at the Bridge Family Center in West Hartford, Connecticut and maintains a private practice in Old Saybrook, Connecticut.

A. Peter MacLean, MA, PEng, is a doctoral candidate in psychology at Purdue University. His research interests include marital relations, gerontology, and health psychology.

Edward M. Markowski, PhD, is a professor in the Marriage and Family Therapy Program and adjunct professor in the Department of Family Medicine at East Carolina University, Greenville, North Carolina.

J. LeBron McBride, PhD, is coordinator of Behavioral Medicine at the Georgia Baptist Family Practice Residency Program in Morrow, Georgia. He is a clinical member and approved supervisor with the American Association for Marriage and Family Therapy and a Certified Family Life Educator with the National Council of Family Relations. Dr. McBride is the author of the book *Spiritual Crisis: Surviving Trauma to the Soul*, published by The Haworth Press, Inc., and numerous articles.

Stephanie Mueller, MS, is a psychotherapist at Behavioral Health Specialists, Inc., in Norfolk, Nebraska, and also is a recent graduate of the Marriage and Family Therapy Program at the University of Nebraska–Lincoln.

Jan Nealer, PhD, is an adjunct faculty member in the Marriage and Family Therapy Program at the University of New Hampshire, and is clinical program manager at Strafford Psychotherapy and Family Services, Dover, New Hampshire.

William F. Northey Jr., PhD, is an assistant professor of human development and family studies in the Department of Family and Consumer Sciences at Bowling Green State University in Ohio. He is also managing partner of Adolescent Research and Treatment Consultants of Ohio.

Jan Osborn, PhD, LMFT, is a faculty member in the Marriage and Family Therapy Program at Northwestern University. She also maintains a private practice.

David A. Paré, PhD, is a family therapist in Edmonton, Canada. He coordinates the collaborative therapy training at the Lousage Institute, where he maintains a private practice. David publishes and presents widely on Narrative Therapy and is a lecturer at the Alberta campus of Loma Linda University.

Julie A. Reinlasoder Patten, MS, is a family therapist at Onarga Academy's Young Children's Program, which is a residential facility for sexually aggressive youth. She received her master's degree in Marriage and Family Therapy from Northern Illinois University.

Mudita Rastogi, PhD, LMFT, is an assistant professor at the Illinois School of Professional Psychology, Chicago, and is in private practice as an affiliate therapist with the Family Institute at Northwestern University. Her interests include gender, cross-cultural, intergenerational, and adolescent issues.

Daniel J. Reidenberg, PSYD, is a psychotherapist working with adolescents and adults in the locked psychiatric unit of St. Joseph's Hospital in St. Paul, Minnesota. He also maintains a private practice at Birchwood Centers, Inc. in Eden Prairie, Minnesota. Dr. Reidenberg has appeared on several local television stations and frequently conducts workshops and lectures on issues of child abuse and trauma, parenting, adolescents, and drug and alcohol abuse. He is listed in Strathmore's Who's Who Directory and has received two commendations from the Governor of Minnesota for his volunteer work.

Laura Reinke, BA, is a master's candidate in the Marriage and Family Therapy Program at Purdue University Calumet. She is currently preparing her master's thesis on the characteristics and coping strategies of families with autistic children.

Carol Rose is a writer, educator, and counselor who has published in Canadian, American, Danish and Israeli journals. Her poetry collection, *Behind the Blue Gate*, was published by Beach Holme Publishing, Ltd., in 1997. Her articles have appeared in *Healing Voices* (Jossey-Bass), *Living the Changes* (University of Manitoba Press), *The Fifty-Eighth Century* (Jason Aronson), and *Miram's Well* (Biblio Press). She is currently co-editing (with Joan Turner) an anthology of Canadian women's writing titled *Spider Women: A Tapestry of Creativity and Healing*. She teaches courses in Imagination and Healing at the University of Winnipeg's Certificate in Theology program. Carol is the mother of five children.

Eugene Schlossberger, PhD, is an associate professor of philosophy at Purdue University Calumet. He is the author of the book *Moral Responsibility and Persons* (1992, Temple Press) and *The Ethical Engineer* (1994, Temple Press), as well as numerous articles in ethics and philosophy.

Debby Schwarz-Hirschhorn, MS, is a licensed mental health counselor in Florida and is the founder and clinical director of Chabad Family Counseling Services. She is a doctoral candidate in the Marriage and Family Therapy Department at Nova Southeastern University and is also in private practice.

Sherman Benedict Serna, MS, earned a master of science degree in Marital and Family Therapy at Northwestern University and the Family Institute. He is currently a pre-med student at Northwestern University, interested in a career in family medicine.

Catherine E. Ford Sori, MS, is currently a doctoral student in the Marriage and Family Therapy Program at Purdue University, West Lafayette, Indiana, where she teaches adolescent development. She has taught child development as an adjunct faculty member at Purdue University Calumet. She is also a staff therapist at the Samaritan Counseling Center, Munster, Indiana, and has an extensive background in music education.

Marilyn M. Steinberg, BA, is a master's candidate in the Marriage and Family Therapy Program at Purdue University Calumet, Hammond, Indiana. She has been published in journals and books, presented at conferences, and does community service lectures. Her current research interests include common family dynamics found among gang-involved adolescents, which is her master's thesis topic.

Fred E. Stickle, PhD, is a professor and coordinator of the graduate counseling unit at Western Kentucky University in Bowling Green, and also maintains a private practice.

Tracy Todd, PhD, is a licensed marriage and family therapist and president of the Brief Therapy Institute of Denver, Colorado.

Ronn Tyrrell, MS, is a counselor at Family Life Center of Cornerstone Resources.

Dawn Viers, BS, is a master's candidate in Marriage and Family Therapy at Purdue University Calumet, Hammond, Indiana. She is currently working on her master's thesis assessing family relationships and ADHD children. Her research interests include family relationships and child development.

Linda Wark, PhD, is an associate professor and director, Specialization in Marriage and Family Therapy at Northern Illinois University in DeKalb, Illinois. Areas of specialty/expertise include children in family counseling, family therapy supervision and training, and qualitative research.

Joseph L. Wetchler, PhD, is a professor and director of the Marriage and Family Therapy Program within the Department of Behavioral Sciences at Purdue University Calumet. He also maintains a private practice in family therapy.

Daniel J. Wiener, PhD, ABPP, is an associate professor in the Health and Human Service Professions at Central Connecticut State University. He is also the director of Rehearsals for Growth in New York City and is currently in private practice.

Lee M. Williams, PhD, is an assistant professor in the Marriage, Family, and Child Counseling Program at the University of San Diego.

Jill Woodward, MA, LMHP, is in private practice at Associated Psychologists and Counselors in Norfolk and Wayne, Nebraska. She is a doctoral student at the University of South Dakota in Vermillion.

Foreword

There are two types of professional books found on clinicians' bookshelves: those that are *read*, and those that are *used*. (There are also those that are neither read *nor* used, but those are never found in this book series.) *The Therapist's Notebook: Homework, Handouts, and Activities for Use in Psychotherapy* is clearly in the latter category, for this is a book that will be used, and used often.

Lorna Hecker and Sharon Deacon, along with an impressive array of experienced therapists, have authored a compendium of extremely useful activities for the practicing clinician. There are more than fifty detailed homework assignments, in-session handouts, and activities. Each of these has a clearly stated objective, a rationale for use, specific instructions for implementation by the therapist, suggestions for follow-up after the activity has been completed, contraindications, and further readings. And while most psychotherapy books are theory or model-specific, with some activities included to exemplify the *model*, this book highlights the *activities* themselves. The style of the book is also designed for ease of use, employing a larger (8½″ × 11″) page format than is customary in this book series. This will make it easier for clinicians to photocopy the activities for use with clients.

This book can also be used to stimulate the creative processes of therapists. Reading through the interventions, a clinician will certainly think of novel and innovative ways to use them. As I read through the book, I was continually saying to myself, "Hey, I can use that with the 'Smith' family," or "I'll bet if I changed just that one part, I could use that with the 'Jones' couple." I also found myself developing completely new activities to fit certain clients, based on a particular activity I just read.

Although this is often said about new professional books, *The Therapist's Notebook* really *is* appropriate for both students in clinical disciplines and practicing therapists alike. Students will find comfort in the myriad of activities they can use to work with a great variety of presenting problems. But more seasoned professionals will also be pleased to find specific clinical activities all in one place, most of which are theory-neutral and thus applicable for most therapists.

I personally found this book to be one of the most fun, practical, and readable therapy books I have ever encountered. I am extremely proud to have it as part of *Haworth Marriage and the Family*, and am certain it is a book that you will *use* as much as *read*.

Terry S. Trepper, PhD
Executive Editor, Haworth Marriage and the Family;
Professor of Psychology

Preface

The idea for this book grew out of the editors' love for creativity, and because we also believed that therapists can sometimes be so overwhelmed with daily stresses and strains that some of their best therapeutic ideas get lost in diagnosing, setting appointments, writing case notes, and so on. Yet, while therapy has some scientific roots, the delivery of therapy remains largely an art. We created this book in order to help therapists deliver their product in a way that is productive and helps entice clients to take an active role in the process of change.

We were also aware that many therapists who are "in the trenches" seldom get the chance to share what they do in therapy. This book reflects that chance. The homework, handouts, and activities within have been field tested by therapists who indeed have, by trial and error (or sometimes just a fluke), found "what works." We are delighted that so many therapists have shared their work with us.

Probably the most common criticism of a book of this type is that it is a "cookbook approach" to therapy. Trainers complain that students delight in "cookbook interventions" so that they can intervene quickly when they do not know what to do with clients. We are opposed to a "cookbook" approach to therapy ourselves, and believe that each therapist should be firmly guided by their own theory of therapy. Interventions such as the ones in this book should be theory driven. We believe that therapists are adept at taking useful information and adapting it into theory. Some of the chapters in this book will be very clearly theory driven; for example, several chapters are clearly guided by narrative theory. Others, we expect therapists to fit within their theory. For example, the chapter titled "Good Cops and Bad Cops in Parenting" is simply a way to apply behavioral principles in family therapy. Yet, the activity applies these principles in a way that makes reinforcement and punishment readily understandable and accessible to parents, and engages children in a delightful process of assigning their own rewards and punishments. In short, we firmly believe that creativity should not be bound by theory, but should be encouraged by it. We hope this book will encourage therapist creativity and allow therapists (and their clients) to enjoy therapy more fully.

Last, we have run into many psychotherapists of all affiliations who believe they are not creative. For those of you who refuse to give up this "dominant story," you may use the interventions as they are presented. For others, we expect this book to be a springboard from which additional homework, handouts, and activities will be born. Creative ideas beget more creative ideas, and we expect therapists will use this book as a tool to enhance the art form in their work.

ORGANIZATION OF THE BOOK

Because we received so many resources that were devised for a number of specific problems, it would have been impossible to categorize the activities, handouts, and homework assignments by subject. Additionally, since the contributions came from therapists in various fields of specialization, with various theories and degrees, we could not even organize the book according to theory or therapist style. The editors (or Hecker and Decker, as they became known because of one contributor's typo) decided that the best way to organize all of these creative therapeutic aids was by the client population to which they applied. Yet, we must point out that many of these resources can be applied to client populations other than the categorical client group we placed them in.

AUDIENCE

This book is useful to anyone who is practicing any type of therapy. Those in private practice and/or with limited exposure to other therapists' work may welcome this book as a source of ideas and insight into other therapists' styles and work. Experienced clinicians looking for new ideas and trying to develop some of their own may consult this book for inspiration. New therapists and trainees may find this book helpful as they are developing their own ideas about how to intervene with clients. Textbooks often have few specific examples that students can easily implement as they learn to conduct therapy. Supervisors and trainers may use this book as a text for their practicum and skills classes.

Because the contributors of this book come from various regions, professional backgrounds, and theories, the activities, handouts, and homework assignments in this book can be useful to many therapists, in many fields, with various degrees, specializing in different problems. Most of these resources are broad enough to be easily adapted to fit with different styles and theories of therapy.

Acknowledgments

First and foremost, the editors would like to thank all of the contributors who put time and energy into developing their ideas in writing in order to share them with others. If it were not for these creative people, this book would not have been possible.

The editors would also like to gratefully acknowledge the efforts of Pat Geiger, who organized the contributions and kept in contact with all of the contributors. Her organizational skills and efficiency kept the ball rolling. Thanks also to Laurene Lemanski for her help in organizing this manuscript. We cannot forget the unending support of our spouses, Eugene Schlossberger and Bill Deacon, and their patience as we toiled to make this project a reality. It is loved ones' creativity that often inspired us!

We especially want to thank the series editor, Terry Trepper, for his jovial belief that anything is possible (and that we would actually finish this book). He has been a consistent guide and mentor throughout this process.

Last, we would like to thank the people behind the scenes at The Haworth Press, who, in our quest for creativity, were also willing to try different formats and ideas for this book to make it truly *A Therapist's Notebook*. We would especially like to thank Kim Marris, Haworth typesetter, for her extraordinary effort toward quality and consistency in working with a different and challenging format. We hope this conglomeration of creativity will be useful and applicable in your everyday work.

SECTION I:
HOMEWORK, HANDOUTS,
AND ACTIVITIES FOR INDIVIDUALS

The Voodoo Doll Intervention

Sherman Benedict Serna

Type of Contribution: *Homework*

Objective

The voodoo doll intervention is a useful technique for managing and controlling anger and aggressive impulses. The objective of using a voodoo doll is to help the client distinguish between his/her feelings and actions. This intervention enables the client to act out his/her feelings of anger and aggression on the doll rather than on someone else. Therefore, the voodoo doll serves as a safe, alternate outlet or target for a person's feelings of anger or aggression.

Rationale for Use

When working with separating and divorcing couples, as well as couples who present with physical partner abuse, often one or both of the partners has a great deal of difficulty in separating his or her feelings from his/her actions (i.e., feelings of anger and aggression from the actions of battering and physical or verbal abuse). In a sense, feelings of anger and physical/verbal abuse are one in the same for these clients. In addition, many of these clients are unaware of appropriate ways they can experience and express feelings of anger and aggression without having to act them out in harmful, inappropriate ways. The use of a voodoo doll helps a person make the distinction between feelings and behaviors, and specifically helps him/her gain control of his/her anger.

Mr. O presented with difficulty coping with his divorce from his wife. Specifically, this client was experiencing intense feelings of anger and resentment toward his wife for leaving him. Mr. O's divorce represented a tremendous blow to his self-esteem and cultural values. As a result of being overwhelmed by feelings of anger and resentment, Mr. O frequently bad-mouthed his wife in front of his five-year-old daughter. Although he was fully aware of and acknowledged his anger toward his wife, Mr. O did not appear to be aware that he was acting out his anger by bad-mouthing his wife to his daughter. While Mr O. was hesitant at first to act out such an unorthodox intervention, he was motivated by his concern for his daughter, and stated he was willing to try the intervention. The voodoo doll enabled Mr. O to make the distinction between his feelings of anger and resentment, and helped him to stop degrading his ex-wife to his daughter.

With couples presenting with physical abuse, the use of the voodoo doll may also provide the batterer with a distraction, or time out, during which to gain a heightened awareness of feelings. Furthermore, the voodoo doll enables the batterer to experience these feelings of anger without acting them out on his/her partner.

Instructions

The instructions for using the voodoo doll intervention are quite simple and straightforward. In addition to individuals who are separating or divorcing, this intervention may also prove useful with children and adolescents who have difficulty making the distinction between their feelings of anger and aggression, and violent or intimidating behavior.

1. Instruct the client to purchase a voodoo doll and a small needle (toothpicks work especially well, and are safer for children and adolescents). This need not be an authentic voodoo doll, and may be of any size—although smaller dolls are easier to carry around discreetly.
2. Whenever the client experiences feelings of anger or aggression, instruct him/her to act out these feelings on the voodoo doll by stabbing it with the needle.
3. The client should continue stabbing the voodoo doll until he/she has gained sufficient control over the impulse to act out his/her feelings of anger and aggression on others, particularly his/her partner. Acting out these feelings on the voodoo doll enables the client to then interact more appropriately with his/her partner.

Suggestions for Follow-Up

When processing the intervention with a client, it is useful to get feedback on whether the client found the voodoo doll helpful. Follow-up should focus on any change(s) in the client's ability to control and appropriately express feelings of anger and aggression. Exploring any improvements in the client's awareness of his/her feelings is also helpful. Many clients may initially feel silly or embarrassed about using a voodoo doll to help control their anger or aggression, though with time, clients usually grow increasingly comfortable using the voodoo doll.

Contraindications for Activity

When first using this intervention, there may be concern that instructing a client (especially a batterer) to act out his/her anger and aggression on a voodoo doll would only encourage the client to eventually act out similar behavior on his/her partner—that prescribing the use of a voodoo doll is in some way condoning aggressive behavior. However, the use of the voodoo doll is an effective technique for helping clients—including perpetrators of physical abuse—control their anger and make distinctions between feelings and actions. This intervention is obviously not appropriate for all clients. It is conceivable that the use of this intervention by a batterer may place his/her partner at greater risk. This activity is also not suitable for clients who are unable to understand the rationale for using the voodoo doll (e.g., with very young children). This intervention may also prove inappropriate for clients who may find using the voodoo doll offensive (e.g., for religious reasons).

Readings and Resources for the Professional

Fortman, J. (1994). Controlling impulsive expression of anger and aggression. In M. J. Furlong, and D. C. Smith (Eds.), *Anger, hostility, and aggression: Assessment, prevention, and intervention strategies for youth* (pp. 441-471). Brandon, VT: Clinical Psychology Publishing Co., Inc.

Koss-Chioino, J. D. (1995). Traditional and folk approaches among ethnic minorities. In J. F. Aponte, R. Y. Rivers, and J. Wohl (Eds.), *Psychological interventions and cultural diversity* (pp. 145-163). Boston: Allyn & Bacon, Inc.

Zillman, D. (1993). Mental control of angry aggression. In D. M. Wegner, and J. W. Pennebaker (Eds.), *Handbook of mental control* (pp. 370-392). Englewood Cliffs, NJ: Prentice-Hall, Inc.

Bibliotherapy Sources for the Client

Lee, J. H. (1993). *Facing the fire: Experiencing and expressing anger appropriately.* New York: Bantam Books.

McKay, M., Rogers, P. D., and McKay, J. (1989). *When anger hurts: Quieting the storm within*. Oakland, CA: New Harbinger Publications, Inc.

Potter-Efron, R. (1994). *Angry all the time: An emergency guide to anger control.* Oakland, CA: New Harbinger Publications, Inc.

Weisinger, H. (1985). *Dr. Weisinger's anger workout book.* New York: Quill.

Williams, R., and Williams, V. (1993). *Anger kills: Seventeen strategies for controlling the hostility that can harm your health.* New York: Harper Perennial.

Living a New Story:
A Narrative Homework Exercise

David A. Paré

Type of Contribution: *Handout/Homework*

Objective

The handouts in this chapter provide a useful means for adult or adolescent clients in therapy to reflect on the family context of the "obstacle" or problem they are dealing with, and which brings them to therapy. The first handout helps clients to externalize the problem and to trace its history to their family of origin. In so doing, clients gain a view of that problem or obstacle as a particular social construction emerging from a specific cultural context.

The second handout helps clients to move forward by authoring their own "rules for living"—a new story about who they are and how they might live their lives that may contrast in significant ways with the family rules that gave rise to the obstacle in the first place.

Rationale for Use

These exercises are tailored to narratively oriented and related practice which seeks to externalize the problems that persons experience in order to create space for the construction of new meanings and preferred ways of being. According to a narrative worldview, problems can be viewed as socially constructed meanings which emerge from specific cultural contexts. The cultural context which these exercises focus on is the one most often cited as influential in clients' lives: the family of origin.

The homework is designed to be introduced after the therapist has spent some time with the client(s), developing a picture of the current presenting problem or concern. Therapist and client then jointly brainstorm a name for this problem which serves to put some distance between client and problem. This problem is conceived of as the "obstacle" that stands between the client and his or her preferred way of being. Ideally, the obstacle's name should resonate with the informal language of clients, so that depression might be called "the blues," or a woman's derogatory self-talk might be called "The You're-No-Good Story." There are no narrow rules for what the obstacle might be called or how it might be characterized. It is the resonance for the client which is critical.

The homework is founded on the premise that persons come to identify themselves with their problems to the extent that they view *themselves* as problems. In externalizing the problem and tracking a problem's origins, clients come to rediscover the nonproblematic parts of themselves—the personal resources they can use to defy that problem, or at least to form a new and preferred relationship with it.

As clients come to see their obstacles as meanings constructed within specific contexts, they gain a sense of their ability to construct new meanings that are more useful to them at this stage in their lives. The second homework exercise is focused on getting more specific about these preferred meanings. Clients construct the "rules for living" which are more suited to their current values and preferences. In contemporary parlance, clients here construct new meanings after deconstructing the old ones in their lives.

It is important to note that this is not about substituting one rigid story (the obstacle) with a new rigid story (a way around the obstacle), but rather about facilitating a separation of person from problem. For all of us, our "obstacles" shift at different times in our lives, and even from day to day or hour to hour. It may be that in naming and externalizing a particular problem, a client immediately experiences a loosening of its grip on him/her, and the upsurgence of a new "obstacle" to take its place. Life is a changeful process, and so should be any therapy which draws upon narrative ideas and values.

Instructions

Once the problem has been externalized and given a name which resonates for the client(s), the therapist makes the Tracing the Obstacle to Your Family handout available. Clients are encouraged to work with the handout between sessions. Their responses may well become the subject of a subsequent therapeutic conversation.

Handout #2 is used in much the same way as the previous one. It may be helpful to join with clients in naming the "old rules" imbedded in the family stories around the obstacle: for example, "Big boys don't cry," "Wealth is the only measure of success," or "Never forgive yourself for your faults." The handout is self-explanatory and can be completed between sessions.

Suggestions for Follow-Up

Handout #1 is designed to open dialogue. It should be used as a springboard for further conversations between client(s) and therapist. For some clients, it may promote a more in-depth examination of their experience in their families of origin or of their particular issues with one family member. The identification of one obstacle may lead to the uncovering of another obstacle not previously named—in which case the exercise might be repeated, either formally or informally. The primary obstacle that some clients identify may be difficult to locate in their families: for instance, a chronic medical complaint, a negative body image, or a pervasive sense of guilt. In these cases, the exercise helps to trace the obstacle to *other* possible sources such as the body, mass media, or organized religion. In any case, the identification and location of the obstacle creates space to focus on those stories clients have lived, are living now, or can imagine living in the future which are not defined by the obstacle. This is the beginning of "reauthoring" a life.

As clients become clearer on the source of the obstacles they are dealing with, they often feel more prepared to enter into alternative ways of being. The second activity described can be useful to facilitate that process.

Like the first activity, Handout #2 is designed to focus and enrich the dialogue between therapist and client(s). As clients are able to name some of their new rules, the discussion can begin to focus on what habits and support they may need to realize their preferred way of living. Discussion might also center on those factors which might contribute to a "relapse"— a slipping back into the old story, a revisitation of the obstacle.

Contraindications

This activity is only useful when therapist and client have a common understanding about and language for the problem being considered. It is designed primarily to open up dialogue around the history of an externalized problem, and is not intended to lay blame on others for clients' problems. When the family's role in the problem story is identified, the same externalizing process can be used to separate persons from problems, and to entertain the way in which socially constructed beliefs can lead to unhelpful or even destructive behaviors on the part of persons whose *intentions* are most often caring and supportive.

It may be that clients wish to retain some of the "old rules," but to develop a new relationship with them, or to refashion them according to their own values. This activity should not be used for conducting a sort of "purge" of a person's previous ways of being. It may be, too, that for some clients, the world "rule" seems too authoritarian. In those cases, a conversation will usually lead to reinventing of the exercise. Rather than "rules," you might prefer to talk about "wishes," "stories," "values," "dreams," "hopes," or "preferences."

Readings and Resources for the Professional

Epston, D. and White, M. (1992). *Experience, contradiction, narrative and imagination.* Adelaide, Australia: Dulwich Centre Publications.

Freedman, J. and Combs, G. (1996). *Narrative therapy: The social construction of preferred realities.* New York: Norton.

Friedman, S. (Ed.). (1993). *The new language of change: Constructive collaboration in therapy.* New York: Guilford.

Gilligan, S. and Price, R. (Eds.). (1993). *Therapeutic conversations.* New York: Norton.

Hoyt, M. (1994). *Constructive therapies.* New York: The Guilford Press.

Paré, D. A. (1995). Of families and other cultures: The shifting paradigm of family therapy. *Family Process*, 34, pp. 1-9.

Paré, D. A. (1996). Culture and meaning: Expanding the metaphorical repertoire of family therapy. *Family Process*, March 1996.

Parry, A. (1991). A Universe of Stories. *Family Process*, 30, pp. 37-54.

Parry, A. and Doan, R. (1994). *Story re-visions.* New York: Guilford.

Polinghorne, D. E. (1988). *Narrative knowing and the human sciences.* New York: SUNY Press.

White, M. (1995). *Re-authoring lives: Interviews and essays.* Adelaide, Australia: Dulwich Centre Publications.

White, M. and Epston, D. (1990). *Narrative means to therapeutic ends.* New York: W.W. Norton.

Zimmerman, J. L. and Dickerson, V. C. (1994). Using a narrative metaphor: Implications for theory and clinical practice. *Family Process*, 33, 233-245.

HANDOUT #1: TRACING THE OBSTACLE TO YOUR FAMILY

The name I have given the obstacle I am dealing with is

_____ .

By now, you have come up with a name for the obstacle you are dealing with. Though the word or phrase may not completely capture your experience, it probably helps you to focus on some issues you are working on. At least, it puts the issues "out there," where you can see them in your life.

This exercise is designed to help you clarify the family origins of your obstacle. The questions below try to uncover a sense of where the obstacle first arose, how it has affected you in your family, and how you have managed to sidestep it at times. Please give the questions some thought.

• When do you first remember experiencing the obstacle?

• How did your obstacle show itself in your family as you were growing up?

• How does this obstacle fit as part of the "culture" of your extended family?

• Do other family members grapple with the same or similar obstacles?

• What stories were you told about yourself that helped to build this obstacle in your life?

• Which of those stories or ideas about yourself do you still hang on to? In what way do they help to cement the obstacle in place?

• Do you believe the stories now?

• Would you like to replace them with new stories about yourself?

• What qualities does your family see in you that might help you to overcome your obstacle?

• When have you managed to sidestep this obstacle in the past? What story of who you are prevailed in order to make that possible?

• If you feel you have not yet sidestepped the obstacle, can you imagine a situation where you did? Describe the situation to yourself. What or who in that situation supported you in overcoming, avoiding, or escaping from the obstacle?

HANDOUT #2: NEW RULES HANDOUT

In the past few weeks, you have begun to identify how some of the struggles you are now having can be connected to old stories in your families. In some ways, it is as though the family stories were Old Rules that you are beginning to replace with New Rules about how you would like to live your life. This exercise is designed to help you identify those New Rules for Living that are beginning to emerge for you, and perhaps for your families as well. On the black lines below, jot down some of your New Rules in your own words. Do not worry about getting the language "right"—if it feels right to you, it IS right. Use the back of the sheet if you run out of room.

NEW RULES FOR LIVING

1. _____

_____

_____

2. _____

_____

_____

3. _____

_____

_____

4. _____

_____

_____

When "Bad" Is Good:
Reframing for Success

Connie M. Kane

Type of Contribution: *Activity/Homework*

Objective

Clients will identify the positive aspects of personal characteristics that they currently view negatively.

Rationale for Use

Research has shown that people who view themselves positively are generally happier and more successful. Conversely, people with lower self-esteem tend to achieve less and to be more prone to depression. However, self-concept is an individual's *perception* of reality, not reality itself, and every characteristic can be viewed either positively or negatively. For example, someone who gives money to a charitable cause may be seen as kind by one person, and as a "bleeding heart" by another. Since perceptions are learned, not innate, they can be revised. By helping clients to revise their perceptions of themselves to be more positive, we can increase the possibilities for their happiness and success.

For clients who are stuck in taking the most negative view possible about themselves, this exercise can be a helpful experience of reframing. With practice, they can become skilled in challenging their negative judgments to see a positive perspective of the same realities. In time, they can learn to weigh the two perspectives in light of the context, and make a fairer judgment about their own behaviors and characteristics.

Instructions

This intervention includes three components: (1) in-session introduction and practice; (2) client homework; and (3) follow-up.

In-Session Introduction and Practice

If a client is consistently using pejorative terms to describe his or her own behavior or characteristics, first try direct reframe. For example, the client says, "I'm stupid because I let people take advantage of me." A reframe would be, "In other words, you're very generous."

If the client is unable to consider the validity of such a reframe, ask him or her to name someone that he or she admires greatly. Then ask the client to imagine that the admired person is behaving in the very manner that the client has just judged negatively. After giving time for the client to develop that image, ask the client to describe the admired person. Often, clients will see the same behavior in a positive light when performed by someone they admire. If that happens with the client, point it out, confronting the fact that the action is the same, but it received contradictory judgments from the client—a negative judgment for himself or herself and a positive judgment for the person admired. Discuss the client's reasoning and the implications of this for the client's self-concept. Then introduce the homework as indicated below.

If the client does not reverse the judgment of the behavior when attributed to someone the client admires, ask what it is that the client admires about the other person. After you have that answer and have clarified and reflected to be sure you understood correctly, ask how imagining the admired person to be acting like the client affected the client's admiration for the other. Very possibly, the client will say that the imagery did not affect the overall feeling because it was a minor part of what the client sees in the other person. That is your opening—to ask whether there might also be more to the client that needs to be considered in his or her self-evaluation. Suggest that homework might help in this.

Client Homework

Holding the worksheet between both of you, state that every characteristic can be positive as well as negative. Use the examples given or provide your own and check for the client's understanding by asking him or her to think of a situation when a negative judgment would be appropriate and another when the same characteristic might be seen positively. Help the client to do this if needed. Practice with the client until he or she is able to do two examples alone. Then suggest the rest of the exercises in Part I as homework. Read the directions for Part II and be sure the client can generate one set of responses independently. Also assign the rest of the page for homework.

Suggestions for Follow-Up

When the client returns the homework, review it, and work with the client to generate real or hypothetical situations in which the client's behavior might demonstrate each of the characteristics listed. If the client was unable to complete any of the exercises, assist in that effort. Then revisit discussions from previous sessions in which the client's description of his or her own character or behavior was negative. Reevaluate that description now, considering the legitimacy of positive reframes. Continue to practice such deliberate reframing until such time as the client begins offering it spontaneously in his or her own descriptions. Then begin coaching in the generation and selection of appropriate evaluative criteria.

Contraindications

This activity requires ability in abstract thinking, which makes it inappropriate for many children in the elementary levels. It may also be beyond the verbal ability and/or abstraction ability of older children with learning disabilities or lower than average intelligence. Also, when working in multicultural settings, it is important to check for the *clients'* evaluations of their own descriptors to be sure you are not assuming an adjective to be negative that they see as positive, or vice versa. Finally, this is an activity that is intended to facilitate personal growth and, as such, should be limited to personal growth counseling situations.

Readings and Resources for the Professional

Karns, M. (1994). *How to create positive relationships with students: A handbook of group activities and teaching strategies*. Champaign, IL: Research Press.

Morgan, S. R. (1994). *At-risk youth in crises: A team approach in the schools* (Second Edition). Austin, TX: Pro-Ed.

Seligman, M. E. (1995). *The optimistic child*. New York: Houghton-Mifflin.

Vernon, A. (1989). *Thinking, feeling, behaving: An emotional education curriculum for children and adolescents*. Champaign, IL: Research Press.

Bibliotherapy Sources for the Client

Grades 1-6

Robinson, B. (1994). *The best school year ever*. New York: HarperCollins.

Silverstein, S. (1976). *The missing piece*. New York: Macmillan.

Silverstein, S. (1983). *Who wants a cheap rhinoceros?* New York: Macmillan.

Williams, M. (1991). *The velveteen rabbit*. New York: Doubleday.

Grades 7-12

Jamison, K. (1984). *The nibble theory and the kernel of power*. Ramsey, NJ: Paulist Press.

Johnson, H. M. (1986). *How do I love me?* Salem, WI: Scheffield.

Satir, V. (1975). *Self-esteem*. Millbrae, CA: Celestial Arts.

Satir, V. (1976). *Making contact*. Millbrae, CA: Celestial Arts.

It Is All in the Way You Look at It

An Exercise in Positive Thinking

Part I. Every characteristic can be either positive or negative, depending on how you look at it. To be "stubborn" might also mean that you do not give up easily, that you are not a quitter; to be a "clown" could mean that you have a great sense of humor, and so on. For each of the adjectives below, list a positive way to describe the same characteristic.

Negative View	Positive View
silly	playful
bossy	capable of leadership
stingy	
crybaby	
dependent	
chatterbox	
naive	
stuck-up	
greedy	
hot tempered	

Part II. In the first column below, list the negative adjectives that you often use to describe yourself. In the second column, list their positive alternatives.

Negative View	Positive View

4

Addressing the Critical and Supportive Voices Through Art Therapy

Mary Forrest

Type of Contribution: *Activity*

Objective

This activity was devised from one originally developed to facilitate a person's artistic growth, and has been adapted to an art therapy activity format (Diaz, 1983). This activity meets two objectives, the first being to function as a catalyst for broadening a client's perspective about a particular problem or issue. The second objective is to address any mixed emotions the client may feel about the particular problem or issue.

Rationale for Use

This activity can be used compatibly with postmodern family therapy models (e.g., Narrative and Solution-Focused) and can easily be integrated as an activity with more traditional strategic and experiential therapy models. The rationale for this activity is to provide clients with more options for the future through an experiential expression of the problem, as opposed to remaining "stuck" in one narrative/story or with one set of solutions. By experiencing the problem/issue from another angle, the client can become more open to creating new solutions, a new narrative, or to following new directives. The activity literally requires the client to view the problem from a different angle and evaluate the negative points (critical voice) and the positive points (supportive voice) of the new angle/view (Diaz, 1983).

Instructions

If possible, allow for an 80-minute session. At first, the activity may take the full 80 minutes recommended, but as the therapist becomes familiar with the steps, it will be possible for the activity to be completed within the average 50- to 60-minute session. The activity can be viewed as having two parts with eight basic steps. Part I is designed to introduce the client to the experience of art used in therapy, and to viewing the "familiar" from other angles (e.g., the client's signature is a very familiar symbol). Part II is designed to introduce the problem into the art therapy session, and to allow the client to experience the problem/issue differently by viewing the problem literally from another angle. If the session cannot be longer than 50 minutes, then you may want to eliminate Part I (e.g., using the client's name as the first piece of artwork), but this is not recommended.

Part I: Changing the View

1. Make sure the client will be comfortable participating in the activity by discussing what the activity involves and what the process may be like. Obtain consent and trust from the client to begin the activity.
2. Assemble supplies needed prior to beginning of session: colored markers, crayons, watercolors (you can choose the most appropriate), paper (use watercolor paper if using watercolors), and scotch tape.
3. Begin the activity by having the client write or paint his/her name on a piece of paper.
4. Have the client turn the paper *upside down*, and encourage him/her to look at *the shapes* on the paper (*not* the shape of his/her name). Discuss how different his/her name looks upside down by emphasizing how it no longer looks like a name, but like something else. This emphasis "sets the stage" for the client to begin viewing the problem differently and from another angle.
5. Encourage the client to continue drawing or painting based on the shapes he/she sees on the paper.
6. Once the client completes his/her artwork, tape it to an office wall. Then place *two* sheets of paper in front of the client.
7. Have the client label one sheet "Critical Voice" and the other sheet "Supportive Voice" or "Rebuttal." The client can also make up his/her own labels. Just make sure the labels fit the theme of the negative and positive points.
8. Ask the client to contemplate the artwork hanging on the wall. Then ask him/her to write down or list on the Critical Voice paper what the "Critical Voice" would say about the piece on the wall. After the Critical Voice list is complete, ask the client to write down or list on the Supportive Voice paper what the "Supportive Voice" would say in *response* to the Critical Voice's comments.
9. At this point, the client is half-way through the activity. If time is allowed, the therapist may want to discuss with the client his/her experience of the activity and/or any relevant issue(s) brought up by the critical and supportive voices' comments.

Part II: Experiencing the Problem Differently

1. Repeat steps 1 to 3 of Part I. In Step 3, in place of the client's name ask him/her to write or paint the problem/issue currently being discussed in therapy (or one in which he/she feels "stuck").
2. Repeat Steps 4 to 8 of Part I.
3. Tape the Critical Voice list and the Supportive Voice list on both sides of the client's artwork. Discuss with the client his/her experience of the activity and/or any relevant issue(s) brought up by the critical and supportive voices' comments. For example, "Which voice is stronger?"; "Is there a way the problem can be viewed 'upside down' in your life?"; "What other views of the problem could exist?"; "What solutions could be found to solve the problem when it is viewed differently?"; "Do your emotions reflect the feelings for both voices?" This activity can be adapted to fit the therapist's preferred model of therapy and the questions provided are meant only to facilitate the therapist's growth of ideas.

Suggestions for Follow-Up

The therapist can use the remaining time in the session to discuss the positive and negative comments in regard to the client's problem. The therapist can also focus on what it was like for the client to experience the problem differently (i.e., turned upside down). How the therapist discusses the client's experience and the points brought up during the activity will depend on his/her model of therapy. At this point, the client may be more open to discussing other views of the problem or to devising new stories or solutions.

Contradictions

This activity is best utilized with clients ages 16 and older. If the client is not comfortable with experiential therapy or with artistic means of expression then he/she could possibly find this activity uncomfortable and useless. This activity is meant to facilitate options and discussion for the client.

Readings and Resources for the Professional

Diaz, A. (1983). *Freeing the creative spirit: Drawing on the power of art to tap the magic and wisdom within.* San Francisco, CA: Harper.

Gladding, S. T. (1992). *Counseling as an art: The creative arts in counseling.* Alexandria, VA: American Counseling Association.

Jacobs, E. (1992). *Creative counseling techniques: An illustrated guide.* Odessa, FL: Psychological Assessment Resources, Inc.

Parry, A. and Doan, R. E. (1994). *Story re-visions: Narrative therapy in the postmodern world.* New York: Guilford Press.

Rubin, J. A. (Ed.). (1987). *Approaches to art therapy: Theory and technique.* New York: Brunner/Mazel Publishers.

Bibliotherapy Sources for the Client

Diaz, A. (1983). *Freeing the creative spirit: Drawing on the power of art to tap the magic and wisdom within.* San Francisco, CA: Harper.

Patterson, R. B. (1995). *Becoming a modern contemplative: A psychospiritual model for personal growth.* Chicago, IL: Loyola University Press.

5

The Toxic Monster

Sharon A. Deacon

Type of Contribution: *Activity*

Objective

The purpose of this activity is for clients to cognitively make a connection between the stresses in their lives and their psychosomatic symptoms. Once clients are aware of their vulnerabilities to physical symptoms, they can work toward reducing the stresses in their lives, and give up the functions of their symptoms.

Rationale for Use

There is a connection between one's psychological health and one's physical health. When people have psychological problems and/or stresses, it is not uncommon for their bodies to become physically weak and less likely to fight off toxins. People often express their psychological problems through physical symptoms, becoming psychosomatic.

Clients working through difficult issues in therapy may get colds and flus frequently, and have a difficult time "getting healthy." However, clients usually do not connect their physical illness to the emotional stresses they are experiencing. By asking clients to visualize the "toxins" in their lives, the physical symptoms become personified and externalized. Clients can then understand the function and contributing causes of their symptoms, the stress in their lives, and the mind-body connection. At that point, clients are likely to work on resolving their psychological symptoms, and systematically ridding themselves of both concerns at once.

Instructions

Before applying this intervention, the therapist must have evidence that the client's health is suffering. It is important to talk to the client about missed sessions due to illness, the health problems they come into session with, and the physical symptoms they are exhibiting. It is also wise to recommend the client seek medical advice and evaluation first.

The therapist can then propose a discussion on the connection between physical health and mental health. Some psychoeducation is useful here to educate the client about the impact stress can have on one's health. Normalize the client's symptoms, as it is very common for people to be vulnerable to "toxins" while they are in therapy. Therapy is hard work, and it is not unusual to neglect physical health while concentrating intently on mental health.

Begin to define "toxins" as things that bother us, invade our bodies, nag at our well-being, cause us to feel ill, compromise our health, and cause stress in our lives. Then lead the client in the following visualization:

Step 1— Ask the client to close his/her eyes and then lead the client in a progressive relaxation exercise.

Step 2— Read the following visualization scenario, or create a similar one of your own.

Picture yourself walking into your house. Walk through the house into your favorite room in the house. Maybe it is a bedroom, a rec room, the den. Now walk into that room and close the door behind you, so you are alone in the room and have privacy. Find a comfortable place to sit in there. Notice how you are sitting, where your arms are, where your legs are. Notice what you are wearing; something comfortable, perhaps a favorite sweater or pair of jeans, maybe a loose jogging suit?

Does the room have a particular smell? Maybe it smells like cologne or a breeze from outside.

Now listen to any noise around you. Who else is in the house? What are other people doing? What conversations are taking place? Block all noise out now, and just listen to your own breathing.

As you sit there peacefully, the door violently swings open. You look at the door. Standing in the doorway is that toxin that has been bothering you. Take a few minutes and picture what it looks like. Maybe it is a person you know, or an object you are familiar with. Is there a face on the toxin? What color is it? Does it smell? It says something to you. What does it say? Listen closely.

The toxin starts coming closer to you, but this time, you are not afraid. Instead, you feel a surge of energy flow through your entire body. You look to the other side of the room, where you see good things in your life approaching. You see your strength coming back to you. You feel strong, well nourished, and your vitality has returned. You stand up and move toward the toxic monster. As you walk toward it, it retreats back out the door. You close the door, with the toxin on the outside. Now you sit back down, feeling better than you ever have. You take a deep breath and relax.

Slowly, leave that room in your house and come back here to the therapy room. Notice how you are sitting in this chair, and what noise is in this room. As you feel comfortable, open your eyes.

After the client is focused again, ask the client to describe what happened. What did the toxin symbolize? How is that object or person toxic to the client's life? Discuss how the client got strength back and what it would take to push the toxin out of his/her life.

Suggestions for Follow-Up

After the visualization, the client usually has a good idea about what needs to happen for him/her to feel better psychologically and physically. It is then important to make a plan with the client regarding how he/she will rid the symptoms from his/her life. Once clients understand that stresses are impacting their physical health, they are often motivated to work on decreasing stress and resolving the problematic areas of their lives.

Contraindications

This activity is useful with clients who have minor physical symptoms, such as colds, flus, allergies, or headaches. However, it is always important to encourage the client to seek medical attention for their physical problems. This visualization does not qualify as medical treatment, and should not be used as such. Instead, it should be used as an adjunct to medical treatment. It is important to explain to clients that although psychological health and physical health interact, it is necessary to take care of both of them simultaneously, rather than trust one treatment to take care of other symptoms.

Readings and Resources for the Professional

Hunter, M. E. (1994). *Creative scripts for hypnotherapy.* New York: Brunner/Mazel.

Bibliotherapy Sources for the Client

Alman, B. M. and Lambrou, P. (1992). *Self-hypnosis: The complete manual for health and self-change.* New York: Brunner/Mazel.
Davis, M., Eshelman, E. R., and McKay, M. (1988). *The relaxation and stress reduction workbook.* California: New Harbinger Publications.

6

Smush 'Em

Eugene Schlossberger

Type of Contribution: *Activity*

Objective

This activity is designed to aid divorced or divorcing family members process unresolved anger.

Rationale for Use

Divorcing clients often have trouble expressing long-standing anger in safe and socially approved ways. They may instead express anger in a way that fuels rather than purges resentment. This activity normalizes anger, affords a safe vehicle for expressing anger, and turns destructive feelings into a game: past resentments become funny instead of consuming. In addition, feelings of loss can be processed which often lie underneath divorcing clients' anger.

Instructions

The client is instructed to bring a photograph of the ex-spouse to therapy. The therapist asks the client if he or she is willing to take part in an experiment in order to continue to work through feelings from the divorce. The therapist provides ketchup, mustard, mayonaise, soft noodles, and other gooey food items, which are spread out on a large table. The therapist explains that the client is to feel free to "decorate" the picture of the "ex" with the above food items. Some clients may need help in feeling comfortable to deface a picture of their "ex" in such a manner. A client's reluctance may be tied to irrational beliefs such as "one should never grow angry" or the client may still harbor tender feelings toward the ex-spouse. Discussing these feelings and beliefs can aid in divorce recovery.

If the client is able to proceed, the therapist moves to the next step. When everything is set up, the therapist says "ready, set, smush 'em [smush 'er]." The client then has ten minutes to smear the photograph with food items any way he or she wishes. Afterward, the smeared photograph is briefly displayed on a table for the admiration of the client and therapist. Compliment the client on his or her work—"that's a good one—you really smushed him/her up. I love the ketchup on his/her nose." After suitable viewing, the therapist says, "How would you like to see old [name of ex-spouse] go up in smoke?" (At any point, the client may decline to proceed with the activity. Feelings brought about by the activity should be processed and understood within the developmental context in which they arise.) If the client is willing to proceed, the photograph is then ritually burned in an ashtray, and the remains dumped in the trash or somehow symbolically contained.

Suggestions for Follow-Up

This activity, at any stage, may evoke feelings of which the client has been unaware. Normalizing and discussing the feelings is an important part of follow-up on the part of the therapist. Following completion of the activity, clients should be congratulated on their ability to express their anger in a constructive way by playing "smush 'em" [smush 'er].

Contraindications

The activity is contraindicated when clients' anger levels are dangerously high or uncontrolled. Below a safe threshold, the activity turns anger into fun. Above that threshold, it can fuel rage.

Readings and Resources for the Professional

Kaslow, F. (1987). *The dynamics of divorce: A life cycle perspective*. New York: Brunner/ Mazel.
Weiss, R. S. (1975). *Marital separation*. New York: Basic Books.

Bibliotherapy Sources for the Client

Everett, C. and Volgy, E. S. (1994). *Healthy divorce*. San Francisco, CA: Jossey-Bass.
Fisher, B. (1981). *Rebuilding: When your relationship ends*. San Luis Obispo, CA: Impact.
Slepian, J. (1985). *Getting on with it*. New York: Four Winds Press.

7

The Many Roles People Play

Sharon A. Deacon

Type of Contribution: *Activity*

Objective

This activity is designed to help clients realize the many different roles they play, and teach them to use the attributes of these roles in various situations. In doing so, clients learn to approach problems and situations in different ways than usual, perceive problems differently, and change their behavior in order to handle difficult situations in a more adaptive and functional manner.

Rationale for Use

Clients often become stuck and unable to solve problems because they keep trying to do more of the same, ineffective solution. They perceive the problem in only one way, and simply keep repeating the same response to it. Learning about the different roles they play, clients begin to realize that they have many different abilities and attributes that they could utilize to solve their problems. Clients become more flexible in utilizing their strengths throughout various areas of their lives.

Instructions

Begin by providing the client with some paper and writing tools. Ask the client to draw an outline of him- or herself. Next, tell the client to fill in the outline by writing all the roles he or she plays in life. Give the client examples such as daughter, sister, friend, teacher, employee, consultant, mother, wife, in-law, and church member.

Now, one by one, ask the client about each role. The following is a list of sample questions:

- How do you "see" things when you are in that role?
- How comfortable are you in that role?
- What kinds of things do you pay attention to in that role?
- What are your characteristics in that role?
- How do others see you in that role?
- What are your strengths in that role? Your weaknesses?
- What types of problems do you encounter in that role?

Once the client has a good idea about all the attributes and abilities he/she has available to him/her, go back to the problem at hand. Ask the client what role he/she is playing when she/he encounters this problem. What role is he/she in when trying to solve the problem? One by one, ask how he/she would go about solving the problem in the other roles listed. For example, "How would you handle your mother-in-law's criticism of your childrearing if you approached it from your understanding, less reactive, friend role, instead of your daughter-in-law role? Or, how would you react to your angry father if you stepped out of your son role, into your negotiating, adaptable, employee role? Additionally, how would you think about your sister differently if you stepped out of your sibling role, and into your nurturing, fair, mother role?

As the client begins to move in and out of role scenarios, reflect on all the different ways he/she has verbalized for handling his/her problem.

Suggestions for Follow-Up

Usually as the activity progresses, clients start to realize the many ways of viewing the problem and the optional solutions that are available. Take time to generalize what the client has learned to other areas of the client's life. Focus on how clients can use their various roles in alternate situations to broaden their perspective and find new solutions. Continue to refer to these roles throughout therapy as new problems arise. Keep reinforcing the client's abilities to step in and out of all of the roles.

Contraindications

This activity works well when clients' problems are not very severe, but more situational. Clients in crises may respond to this activity after they have stabilized their immediate stress.

This activity may not be successful with clients who are unable to think abstractly, or who have a small, limited number of roles to play, such as young children. It is also important to have some knowledge of clients' roles and moral reasoning before beginning, to prevent the use of dysfunctional roles (such as "criminal" or "abuser") for problem solving.

Readings and Resources for the Professional

Baucom, D. H. and Epstein, N. (1990). *Cognitive-behavioral marital therapy*. New York: Brunner/Mazel, Inc.
deShazer, S. (1988). *Clues: Investigating solutions in brief therapy*. New York: W.W. Norton and Co.

8

Feeling from the Inside Out

Sharon A. Deacon

Type of Contribution: *Activity*

Objective

This activity can be used to help clients understand their behavior. It focuses on teaching clients to recognize the connection of their inside feelings to their outward behavior in order to modify their behavior. This activity is especially helpful for people who have trouble managing or expressing "negative" emotions (e.g., anger, sadness, jealousy, etc.).

Rationale for Use

This activity is used with clients who have a difficult time expressing their feelings, and instead resort to defensive behaviors to protect their vulnerable side. Clients learn to connect their feelings with their behavior and understand how their feelings affect their behavior, and vice versa. In doing so, clients start to take responsibility for their feelings and actions, and modify their defensive behaviors into adaptive, healthy ways of acting.

Instructions

It is important to prepare for this activity by first discussing with the client the circular pattern that exists between our cognitions, behaviors, and emotions, and how each one affects the others.

Have the client to draw an outline of his/her body. Ask the client to identify an emotion he/she has difficulty with, and write that emotion inside the body outline. You may also want to instruct the client to strategically place that feeling in the part of their body they identify with it. For example, clients may feel anger in their tense neck and shoulders or anxiety in their stomach. Using different colored crayons and different printing to symbolically express their feelings can also add to the experience.

Next, ask the client what kind of behaviors he/she engages in when he/she is experiencing that emotion. For example:

Therapist: What do you do when you feel jealous?
   Client: I usually become mad, and give him the silent treatment. Then we usually fight.
Therapist: How do *you* fight?
   Client: I call him names, swear at him, and criticize him.

On the drawing, the client is then instructed to write: "yell, criticize, and swear" on the outside of the body outline. The client then draws an arrow from the inside emotion (jealousy) to the behavior it elicits on the outside (yelling, criticizing). The activity continues until the client has identified all problematic emotions and the behaviors that coincide with them. (It is okay for some emotions and/or behaviors to overlap; they can be depicted as such.)

Once the handout is complete, ask the client to verbally say each of the emotions on the inside. Ask the client, "How would you think/feel about a person feeling all those things?" The client usually responds with some sort of empathetic or sympathetic remarks. Then ask the client to say all the behaviors out loud. Ask the client, "How would you feel about someone who was acting like that?" The client usually responds by showing dislike for the actions. Now, help the client to understand how others perceive him/her when he/she engages in those behaviors, and how he/she might get a better response if the true feelings behind the behaviors were verbalized instead. Encourage and reinforce the client to take responsibility for his/her actions and feelings.

Suggestions for Follow-Up

After the activity has been completed, it will be necessary to help clients learn new, functional ways of expressing their feelings. Some behavior modification strategies may also be necessary. With couples, an activity such as "Feelings Flash Cards" (Chapter 29) may be the next step.

It is important to warn the client that change takes time, and breaking old patterns of reacting can be very difficult. Reinforce each step the client makes toward refraining from defensive behaviors and expressing true, underlying emotions. Along the way, keep reminding the client to take responsibility for his/her actions, and give the client permission to express "negative" feelings in more helpful ways.

Contraindications

This activity may not be appropriate for clients who have very poor self-esteem and/or who are not psychologically stable enough to face their own shortcomings. This activity is also not appropriate in crisis situations, or in groups where the client's vulnerability could be used against him/her (such as with a violent couple or in families with ongoing abuse).

It is important that the client feel comfortable enough with the therapist and anyone else present to be vulnerable. This can be a very emotional experience.

Readings and Resources for the Professional

Baucom, D. H. and Epstein, N. (1990). *Cognitive-behavioral marital therapy.* New York: Brunner/Mazel, Inc.

Greenberg, L. S. and Johnson, S. M. (1988). *Emotionally focused therapy for couples.* New York: Guilford Press.

9

Objects in the Rearview Mirror

Sharon A. Deacon

Type of Contribution: *Handout/Activity*

Objective

The purpose of this activity is for clients to gain insight about how events that have happened in their past can still have an influence on them today. This activity also provides clients with an opportunity to start letting go of some of the problems, feelings, and thoughts they have carried with them from the past.

Rationale for Use

When clients present their problems, they often neglect to understand how their past behaviors have contributed to their current situation and/or "stuckness." Alternately, some clients spend the majority of their time focusing on the past, and are unable to move on with their lives. This activity can help clients to experientially understand and acknowledge how their past is still affecting them. Cognitive interpretations of the past can be modified, and the client can gain a new perspective on life. This activity can be a first step for clients who need to deal with issues from their past that are hindering their growth and future progress. It may also be a first step to altering their lives and the direction in which they are headed.

Instructions

Conduct the following imagery exercise with the client. (This imagery may take up to twenty minutes.) First, lead the client in a progressive relaxation exercise. Then slowly read this story aloud, and ask the client to visualize this scene:

> You are driving down a very long road. It is the road of your life. You are at the wheel. You begin driving at the intersection of five and six years old. Every mile you travel is another year in your life. Some years may pass by quickly, as you speed by. You may choose to travel through other years more slowly, at a lower rate of speed. Put your foot on the gas and begin driving.
>
> Notice, as you travel down this road of life, all the people you are passing at different years, the interactions that you have with the various people, and how these people are interacting with each other. Maybe some run with your car for a few years. Perhaps you

invite some into the car to drive with you, for life. You may leave others behind, while others may pass you by. (Pause.)

Pay attention to the billboards. They depict major events in your life. What events do they advertise? Some may make you laugh, while other advertisements may make you cry. (Pause.) Also, pay attention to the street signs. At what points in your life did you have to yield? Stop? Take a detour? Proceed with caution? Watch for children crossing? Merge or get a green light? (Long pause.)

Stay on your journey, as long as you need to, until you come to the point in the road where you are at now, in your current life. This is probably a construction zone. Take a look into the future. Do you see any billboards ahead of what is to come? Do you see what the road is like ahead? You can probably only see about another mile or two ahead of where you are. Take a good look.

Now sit in the car, and glance to your left. Do you see the rearview mirror? Take a look inside the rear view mirror at all of the things you just passed. What people, places, or events stand out the most? When you have a clear picture, open your eyes.

Once the client has opened his/her eyes, give him/her the handout attached to this activity. Ask the client to draw, or somehow symbolize, what was just seen in the rear view mirror.

Discuss what the client has drawn—the significance and meaning of the drawings. Then, referring to the inscription on the bottom of the mirror ("objects in mirror are closer than they appear"), discuss how events of long ago may still seem to have a great impact on us. It is also helpful to illustrate to clients how they have changed, yet are still reacting to the past event as the people they were then. (For example, talking to a male client about how assertive and confident he is now, yet when he talks about his father's criticism of him, he acts as if it is happening right then and there and he is not using his assertiveness skills.) The intention is to help the client perceive past events through different lenses, or a new perspective. In doing so, the client can begin to acknowledge the impact that past events have, and start to let go of the past.

Suggestions for Follow-Up

Once the client has established the significant past events in his/her life, therapy may progress by focusing on how such events impact the client today, and how change can occur. Cognitive restructuring and rational-emotive interventions are useful here.

This activity can also be referred to throughout therapy. Using the journey metaphor, clients can track their journey through therapy, and discuss the signs and road conditions along the way.

You may want to focus on what clients saw as they looked into the future, since that is their perception of themselves and their lives. The client can spend time thinking about how to prepare for such a future, or how to find a detour in the road to avoid such a future.

Contraindications

This activity is useful with any client who can think abstractly. If a certain client has had much tragedy or turmoil in his/her life, it may be necessary to break the activity down and go "mile by mile." However, even with a client who has been victimized in his/her life, this activity is helpful for highlighting the areas of concern the client has and that are most salient in his/her life. For clients with severe memory problems, this activity may not be as effective.

Readings and Resources for the Professional

Baucom, D. H. and Epstein, N. (1990). *Cognitive-behavioral marital therapy.* New York: Brunner/Mazel, Inc.

Hunter, M. E. (1994). *Creative scripts for hypnotherapy.* New York: Brunner/Mazel, Inc.

Wadeson, H. (1987). *The dynamics of art psychotherapy.* New York: John Wiley and Sons.

Objects in mirror are closer than they appear

34

Through the Eyes of a Child

Sharon A. Deacon

Type of Contribution: *Activity*

Objective

The objective of this visualization activity is to help clients with family-of-origin problems to understand the difference between how they perceived things as children and how they perceive the same things now as adults. For some clients, these two perceptions may be the same, in which case individualization may be a goal of therapy. If a client does perceive the same events differently as a child versus as an adult, the differences can be highlighted and generalized. This activity can also be used as an assessment tool for measuring differentiation of a client from the family-of-origin.

Rationale for Use

Everyone has events in their childhood that probably traumatized them or that they still recall very vividly and about which they become *upset*. For many of us, these past events still have a large impact on who we are today and how we think, feel, and behave. It is quite common to recall these events as they had happened to us as children. Thus, we recall the child's perception of the event, and it is this perception that we carry with us and that affects us. It is difficult to realize that what we experienced as a child was truly scary or hurtful, *for a child*. However, as adults, these events probably are not as intimidating to us.

The purpose of this activity is to help clients change their perspectives of the past. Clients are validated for what happened to them as children, but are then encouraged to take care of themselves and deal with these issues as the adults they now are. In doing so, clients begin to differentiate from their family-of-origin, see new perspectives of events of the past, and learn to be less reactive as adults.

Instructions

Lead the client in a progressive relaxation exercise. Then, read this imagery scenario to the client:

> Picture yourself as an eight-year-old. What do you look like? How are you dressed? What does it feel like to be eight again?
> Now picture yourself at that age, in your favorite place in your parents' home. Take a good look at everything in the room. Maybe you will notice some pictures on the walls,

where the furniture is, what the ceiling looks like, how soft the rug is, or what is reflecting in the windows. Take a good look around that special place.

Take a minute and listen to all of the noise around you in the house. Think about where each member of your family is and what he/she is doing. Do you hear some music, talking, or the television playing? Maybe there is fighting occurring, or maybe no one else is home with you. Listen carefully for a few minutes.

Take a second and notice any scents in the air. Can you smell someone's perfume or cologne? Maybe a pet is nearby. Can you smell the aroma of something cooking in the oven? What type of breeze is blowing into the house? Are the odors pleasant? What do they remind you of? Smell all that you can.

How does it feel to be a small child in a big house? Now, picture yourself walking out of that room and then leaving the house. Take a minute and reflect on what you just experienced.

Now, picture yourself walking into your parents' home three months from today. Is it the same house you lived in as a child? Does it look different? Is the furniture the same? Have pictures changed? Take a second and look up at the ceiling. Does it look as distant as it did when you were a child?

Is anyone in the house? Who is there? What are people doing? Take a minute and listen to the conversations going on. What are people talking about now?

Does your parents' home still smell the same? What does it smell like now? Is anything cooking? Is the family pet still around?

How does it feel to walk into that house as an adult? Do you feel the same way you did when you were a child? How have things changed?

Now, picture yourself saying good-bye to your parents, and leaving their home. Walk down the driveway and take a look back at the house. What kind of feelings do you have? Think about how you see things differently now.

When you are ready, turn and keep walking away from the house. Visualize yourself sitting here. Notice how you are sitting and the noises in this room. Take a deep breath. Open your eyes whenever you are ready.

Once the client has opened his/her eyes, discuss with the client what he/she experienced. Pay close attention to the perceptions of the child versus the adult. Are these perceptions the same? If so, discuss with the client how he/she still sees things through a child's eyes. Are the perceptions different? If so, discuss how the child's and adult's perceptions are different and what has changed to make these perceptions different. It is very important to validate the client's perceptions as a child and as an adult.

In either case, it is also helpful to discuss how our perceptions influence our behavior and interactions with others. Point out how a child would react to his/her parent(s), versus as an adult. Does the client still react like a child to his/her family-of-origin members? How can this be changed?

Suggestions for Follow-Up

This activity can serve as the first step of assessment and intervention with a client who is working on differentiating from his/her family. Along with this activity, it is helpful to construct genograms, and educate the client about transgenerational patterns, reactivity, differentiation, family loyalties, family roles, triangles within the family, and interactional sequences.

This activity can also be used to help clients see events from other people's perspectives. Referring back to the visualization, the therapist can ask the client what his/her mother (or other family member) would have perceived, or what other family members were doing or feeling at that time. Discussing with the client how other family members may have perceived the same scenario differently can help the client broaden his/her view and consider how his/her own behavior affected the rest of the family.

Contraindications

This activity may not be as effective with clients who are unwilling to take responsibility for their own actions as adults. If clients have been abused or severely traumatized as children, therapy should first address these issues before progressing to family-of-origin work.

This activity is meant to be conducted in conjunction with family-of-origin work, and should not be used in a crisis situation.

Readings and Resources for the Professional

Boszormenyi-Nagy, I. and Krasner, B. R. (1986). *Between give and take: A clinical guide to contextual therapy.* New York: Brunner/Mazel, Inc.

Framo, J. L. (1992). *Family of origin therapy.* New York: Brunner/Mazel, Inc.

Kerr, M. E. and Bowen, M. (1988). *Family evaluation.* New York: W.W. Norton and Company.

Williamson, D. S. (1991). *The intimacy paradox: Personal authority in the family system.* New York: Guilford Press.

Bibliotherapy Sources for the Client

Blevins, W. (1993). *Your family, your self: How to analyze your family system to understand yourself, and achieve more satisfying relationships with your loved ones.* California: New Harbinger Publications, Inc.

11

Assisting Clients
in Establishing Personal Boundaries

J. LeBron McBride

Type of Contribution: *Activity/Handout/Homework*

One assignment for clients struggling with boundary issues is visualization of a shield or protective armor in front of them or around them. Often in treatment we have clients who, for various reasons, have not been able to establish clear and protective boundaries in their interpersonal relationships. It may be that they had their boundaries violated and/or destroyed by sexual or physical abuse, or it may be that they come from a very enmeshed family of origin. The characteristic boundaries that others establish developmentally may not be in existence or understood by such persons.

Objective

This homework exercise is a way of making the concept of boundaries more concrete, and should be used in conjunction with a treatment plan. Most persons with very diffuse boundaries are puzzled about the very meaning of the concept of boundaries. Making the concept of boundaries more practical is vital for therapeutic progress. The objective of the visualization of a shield is to begin the process of discovering boundaries for the self. It is easier for a client to initially think of an external boundary such as a shield as he/she moves developmentally toward establishing internal boundaries.

Rationale for Use

The sense of internal disorganization and separation anxiety that clients feel often has to be gradually repaired. The move from an external visualized boundary to the differentiation of the self is a complicated one. However, the establishing of an external visual boundary can be a step in assisting the development of a better sense of inner connectedness and awareness. A better integrated and connected self will in turn be able to establish better and more appropriate boundaries with others.

Instructions

When working with clients who have difficulty establishing and maintaining boundaries, the therapist may attempt to assist them in seeing the association between their emotional pain and, for example, the "verbal darts" of which they may be a target. Talk with them about how the "verbal darts" encounter few barriers to stop them from going into the depths of their being. Discuss how they are totally exposed, and without protection, are like being in a battle with no armor. Gradually developing this analogy with clients' own personal data and problems helps to make it relevant and powerful for them. They often identify very readily with the analogy. The fuzzy issue of boundaries begins to have some level of meaning for them.

At this point, introduce to clients the concept of a protective piece of armor that you want to give them to take from the therapy room. A visualization exercise, such as the one at the end of this chapter, may be used at this point. Next, describe the concept of visualizing a shield that they are to carry in front of them through the week. When persons throw verbal darts, clients are to remember the shield and visualize the darts being deflected. Discuss how that even with a shield, a person can feel a strong jolt from something hitting the shield, even if it stops short of hitting them.

Additionally, the handout in this chapter can be used as a visual aid and as a way to formulate goals for treatment. On the side of the shield labeled "Ways I can use boundaries to protect myself," a client might write: (1) Limit my time when I visit my in-laws; (2) Call rather than go by to see Susan. Under "Ways I have not been using my boundaries to protect myself," the client might write: (1) I have been unable to say "no" for fear of hurting Joe; (2) I have not been assertive about my own needs and wants; (3) I have felt that I don't have the right to ask for space in the relationship. It is important for the therapist to assist clients in stating some of their strengths at the bottom of the handout which they can utilize to set boundaries, such as: I have good insight; I am willing to work hard in therapy; I am ready for change; and so on. Many such clients have difficulty claiming their strengths. Writing down even simple strengths can be a confidence builder for them.

Suggestions for Follow-Up

This simple exercise gives therapists a way to coach some clients about boundaries and assist them in learning how to understand and implement boundaries. However, unless the activity is followed over the course of therapy and used in experiments outside of therapy, its impact is lessened. Therefore, it is important to continue coaching the client and anticipating how the shield can be wielded to assist in limit setting and protection. Have clients tell how the visualization of the shield worked or did not work in various instances. Clients gradually can feel more protection and separation from the intrusions of others.

Boundaries are how we define ourselves as separate from others. They assist us in defining who we are and what we think and feel. They act as protection and give us a defense against intrusions. Therefore, finding ways to operationalize the concept of boundaries for our clients is extremely important. The visualization of a protective shield is one way to accomplish this goal.

Contraindications

The only initial contraindication to this activity is when there is physical danger in the client's relationships; in these cases the first order of priority is establishing client safety. Also, in the absence of additional therapy supports and practical application in day-to-day experiences, visualization to learn boundary maintenance is largely ineffective.

Readings and Resources for the Professional

Briere, J. N. (1992). *Child abuse trauma.* Newbury Park, CA: Sage Publications.

Kaplan, L. J. (1978). *Oneness and separateness from infant to individual.* New York: Simon & Schuster.

Solomon, M. F. (1989). *Narcissism and intimacy.* New York: W.W. Norton & Company, Inc.

Bibliotherapy Sources for the Client

Mason, M. J. (1991). *Making our lives our own.* New York: HarperCollins Publishers.

Peck, S. (1978). *The road less traveled.* New York: Simon & Schuster.

Thoele, S. P. (1991). *The courage to be yourself.* Berkeley, CA: Conari Press.

Visualization Script

I would like for you to relax and visualize or imagine a protective shield that you are able to hold in front of you for protection. When you imagine the shield, what is it like? Of what material is it made? The shield is a barrier or boundary to help keep you safe. First of all, imagine the shield keeping stones thrown at you from actually hitting you.

Picture in your mind stones being thrown at you, as you put up the shield, deflecting the stones to the ground. Imagine feeling the jolt of the stones hitting the shield and then seeing the stones falling near your feet. You are able to survive the onslaught of stones. You feel safer knowing that you have the shield to protect you.

Next, imagine the same shield that you are holding in front of yourself. However, this time instead of stones, painful words in the form of darts and arrows are thrown. Picture someone throwing these words at you. Use your shield to deflect the words just as you would the stones. Visualize the arrows and darts of words falling near your feet. You are able to survive the onslaught of words by putting up your shield.

Now imagine the same shield being used to give you personal space around yourself. You may feel crowded by another person, and the shield is used between you and that person as a boundary to make you feel more comfortable. You feel a sense of peace knowing that you can maintain some personal distance with the shield.

I would like for you to repeat this visualization each day you are in therapy.

Establishing Personal Boundaries:
My Protective Shield

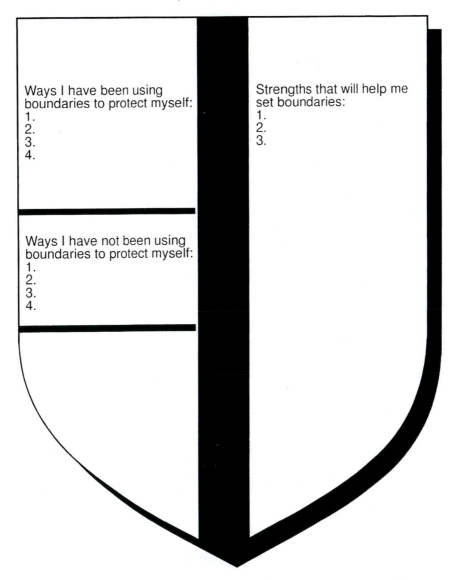

Ways I have been using
boundaries to protect myself:
1.
2.
3.
4.

Strengths that will help me
set boundaries:
1.
2.
3.

Ways I have not been using
boundaries to protect myself:
1.
2.
3.
4.

Use this handout as a way to help formulate the goals you have for setting boundaries by filling in the ways you do and do not use boundaries to protect yourself. Then list some of the strengths you have that will assist you in obtaining these goals.

Sports Talk

Daniel J. Reidenberg

Type of Contribution: *Homework/Handout*

Objective

The purpose of this activity is to help clients better understand the importance of communication, including defining communication skills and how to practice and use communication skills. This is accomplished by the therapist's use of sports metaphors in relation to teaching and practicing communication skills.

Rationale for Use

From the little league field down the street to the Super Bowl, sports bring people together. Sports teach adults and children about challenge and competition, about the importance of practice, about winning gracefully, and how to survive losing. Sports teach people how to work together as a team, how to set limits and boundaries, the importance of having and striving for goals, as well as the importance of following rules. Sports have a universal quality, and can be used as a metaphor to help people communicate better and understand that what may seem to be roadblocks to healing can be viewed differently. Because the language of sports is universal and applies to many situations, this intervention can be used successfully with children, adolescents, adults, couples, and families.

Instructions

If the client is interested in a particular sport or game, he or she can be encouraged to use that sport in this assignment. The client likely knows a great deal of the plays and language of the sport, but has just never thought about it in another way. Used in the therapy setting, the client has an opportunity to view the sport from an entirely different perspective, and may even become more appreciative of something he or she already enjoys.

It is important to determine who or what the client is struggling with in his or her communication; for example, a significant other, family member, co-worker, peer, or perhaps difficulty communicating with all. In some cases, a game such as Ping-Pong works well to illustrate a communication breakdown between two people. For example, in Ping-Pong when the ball is served with an aggressive slam, the opponent may feel powerless to return the serve. This person may be frustrated by missing the ball and feel defeated, or they may feel compelled to return the serve with similar aggression. This style of Ping-Pong returns may approximate a style of verbal battles between people. The therapist can ask clients to choose their favorite sport and draw parallels between the sporting behavior and the client's communication style using metaphors.

In giving the instructions for the assignment, ask the client to write about how Ping-Pong (soccer, tennis, pool, or any other sport they like) is like communicating with a mom, dad, spouse, boss, teammates, or so on. Ask the client to explain what is involved in the game, the number and roles of players, and the techniques or skills a person needs to be successful. If a client is still confused about what he or she is supposed to do, it is helpful to give one or two ideas. For example:

> *Client:* What do you mean? How is Ping-Pong like talking to my parents?
>
> *Therapist:* Let me give you an example. In Ping-Pong, someone has to serve the ball, right? When you and your parents are talking or you sit down to discuss a problem, someone has to start the conversation. That is just like a serve. Here is another example. In Ping-Pong, there are rules that—no matter who is playing or whether it's singles or doubles—everyone must follow. What are the rules you need to follow when trying to communicate and discuss things with your parents? Employees? Siblings?

If clients do not know about rules for conversation, they can be reminded of, for example, their childhood or grade school, when only one person was allowed to speak at a time, and everyone else listened until it was their turn to speak.

Ask clients to be as specific as they can when completing the homework. Explain that they should really put effort into this assignment and think about how they communicate. What seems to work well in their communication? What seems to cause roadblocks in a conversation or discussion? Does he or she end up in arguments or other verbal conflicts and believe the only way is to "win at all costs?" How do they go about winning in a game and in communication? Clients should be encouraged to consider how the game is related to communication patterns.

Finally, it is also helpful to give a minimum length for the assignment, perhaps two pages—front and back, single spaced. While a client's initial response may be, "What? How can you expect me to write two pages on Ping-Pong? That's impossible!" if the client is engaged and putting sincere effort into the therapy, he or she will typically turn in more than the assigned number of pages.

Suggestions for Follow-Up

Therapists should follow up with clients when the assignment is completed by processing the various components of the sport and communication including, but not limited to, the following:

   a. Rules for communication—The therapist should address listening behaviors and communication rules such as talking one at a time, staying present centered, and not engaging in blaming.

   b. Boundaries—Discuss the fairness of the behaviors and rules the clients have.

   c. Net/Center line—Discuss neutral zone topics agreed as part of the general topic being discussed.

   d. Players and coaches—Discuss the roles players have and why each is important; for example, in Ping-Pong there can be two or four players. How does this change the rules and roles for the players?

 e. Ball/paddle/racquet—Discuss differences between people's communication styles (e.g., aggressive versus assertive, dominant versus passive).

 f. Spin on the ball—Discuss how verbal manipulation occurs in what is said, not said, or taken the wrong way.

 g. Time limits—Establish time limits for the game and for fair fighting.

 h. Teams—Address how clients can work together versus against each other.

Clients may need help in understanding the importance of communication. Ask questions such as: "Why is it important to talk to others? Why share your feelings? Why let others know where you are with important issues in your life?" If a client is struggling with friendship issues, comparing how teammates are similar to friends might be useful. For example, a client may talk about how the other players on the team are like friends or family because they have all played together for a long time and they all know a lot about each other. If one player has a problem with another player, the whole team can be affected. Therefore, the other players have to make sure things get worked out, which may be like problem solving in a family among siblings. Another client struggling with trust issues may say that the game is all about having fun and seeing how the players get along. The client may talk about how much he or she can trust team members and the coach. For example, the coach is like a parent who makes sure players make it to practice and the games, and play fair. It is important to trust that the other players will do their jobs and not hurt the team. If there is a problem, the coach is there to help sort things out, just as parents do among their children.

Discussions about what happens in a game without an opponent or opposing team can also help facilitate the discussion of importance of communication. Questions the therapist might ask include: "How is practicing different from playing the actual game?" The therapist can follow up with: "How is it to think about problems or your feelings alone compared to sharing them with someone sitting across from you?" Clients can generally understand this when thinking about how important it is to let their teammates know what is happening and what their playing strategy is, because teammates know that if they do not work together, they will probably not win the game. The same applies to clients' communication with others.

After the client understands the importance of communication, the therapist should begin discussing communication skills with the client. For example, just as it is important to practice in any sport, the same is true for communication. During this processing stage, the therapist will likely have an opportunity to provide the client with feedback about his or her communication styles which may be creating some of the client's problems. For example, assume a client does not make any reference to boundaries in the game in the homework assignment. During the processing and follow-up, the therapist should ask the client about the importance and use of boundaries for the game as well as in communication. It might also be helpful if the therapist can point out when the client has engaged in boundary violations in his or her communication. Given that boundaries are extremely important in communication, and in sports, it would be appropriate to discuss boundaries on the playing field and between people who are attempting to communicate their ideas, values, opinions, and feelings with each other. For example, clients may write about the ball in terms of freedom, and boundaries in terms of how to keep the ball in play.

The sports metaphor can also be helpful for clients who tend to have such great difficulty with communication, they often are unable to participate in conversations at all or very little. When a therapist identifies ways in which the client becomes the ball (or object being used in the game), the client may begin to understand how others are directing his or her life. For example, in football, there are different players who are allowed to do different things to the ball. One person can kick the ball, another person can throw the ball, while another person can catch the ball, and yet others never touch the ball. A client who feels powerless in a relationship might believe a good deal of the communication is taking place around him or her and he or she actually is not getting a word in at all. The sports metaphor can help the client understand how a person might feel he or she is being passed around like a ball and that important issues are being discussed without his or her own thoughts and feelings being heard. At the same time, another client might describe him- or herself as observing from the sidelines and never taking part in the game. In either case, others are communicating for or about the client without his or her input.

It is most important to process with the client whatever issue appears to be most difficult for him/her to overcome, and the sports metaphor may allow the client to deal with that issue in a nonthreatening way. This can be anything, from a particular communication issue such as listening skills or rules for fighting fair, to more broad issues of family dynamics/roles or how to work as a team. For example, suppose the issue is loss or grieving an opportunity for a relationship, a job, etc. If the client is able to discuss losing a game that he or she had been preparing and practicing for, thinking and having feelings about it for days or even longer, suggested follow-up might be to ask the client how he or she would grieve losing the final game in a long awaited series or tournament. Discussing the feelings concerning all aspects of that loss would be important, especially the way in which the client would describe how he or she would continue with his or her life, live with the defeat or loss, and how self-esteem and self-worth will be recaptured, maintained, and/or strengthened.

Here is an example of the homework assignment using the sports metaphor. After writing about the rules of the game, when and where the game was invented, one client wrote that ping pong is like a relationship because people have to give and take. A player can also put a spin on the ball. The other person can take it the wrong way, thinking it is spinning to one side, but it is really spinning to the other. The lines represent a player's own space, his or her own boundaries. The different brands of paddles can mean the different personalities and ways to communicate. If teams play, players need to be there, just like a friend, to support each other. Ping-Pong is like a relationship because there is competition. In teams, players have to take turns and communicate. The ball bounces back and forth just like words and people build or play off what the other person says. In processing the written assignment, verbal manipulation was also discussed. For example, a statement made by the client to a parent was identified as a mixed message (because the parent heard something different than what the client intended). It was then discussed how the original message was exactly opposite of the message the parent received. The client talked about boundaries in terms of what issues were appropriate to talk about with whom and in what setting. Finally the client also talked about the importance of going back and forth with the conversation in order for the game not to end.

Therapists can also role-play with a client, using the game as an analogy or with specific examples from the client's history. It may be useful to assign the client the role of a "referee" or a "spectator" in family meetings or in a group therapy session. This affords the therapist the opportunity to observe interactions of the identified client and other family or group members. Role-plays provide the client with the opportunity to view the game/interaction being played by others as he or she observes, enforces rules, and provides feedback on how positive, confusing, or otherwise the discussion was to watch.

Finally, at times communication can be frustrating, emotional, difficult, and/or painful; however, it can also be exciting, enlightening, and intimate. Therefore, it is important to make sure that the goal is not to win, but rather to play hard, have fun, learn something new, and experience life at its fullest.

Contraindications

When clients have no proclivity or interest in sports, this intervention will not be of interest.

Readings and Resources for the Professional

Berne, E. (1975). *Games people play.* New York: Ballantine Books.

Miller, S., Miller, P. A., Nunnally, E. W., and Wackman, D. B. (1992). *Talking and listening together.* Littleton, CO: Interpersonal Communications Programs.

Potter, S. (1952). *Gamesmanship: How to win without actually cheating.* New York: Penguin Books.

Sports Talk:
Sport Metaphors for Communication

Communication Topic—Boundaries (what is/is not out of bounds in discussion)	
Game	**Possible Metaphor(s)**
Baseball	Foul lines
Football	Sidelines, goal line
Basketball	Foul line, sideline
Golf	Fairway
Soccer	Sidelines
Tennis	Service box, lines for singles vs. doubles

Communication Topic—Neutral zones (net/center line, topics agreed as part of a discussion, but not the main issue)	
Game	**Possible Metaphor(s)**
Football	Line of scrimmage
Tennis	Net
Volleyball	Net
Basketball	Center line
Soccer	Center line
Hockey	Center line

Communication Topic—Time limits	
Game	**Possible Metaphor(s)**
Baseball	Innings (seventh inning stretch)
Football	Quarters, halves, two-minute warning
Basketball	Quarters, halves
Soccer	Halves
Hockey	Periods
Fishing	Open/Closed seasons

Communication Topic—External information (this is the nonverbal information taken in that affects the listener and topic)	
Game	**Possible Metaphor(s)**
Baseball	Pitcher takes in what everyone is doing and decides whether to pitch or throw to first base to get player out
Football	Quarterback watches defense and can change plays
Soccer	Goalie watches all players and directs teammates on free kicks
Golf	Slopes, bunkers, water, etc., that affect which way the ball is hit and lands

Communication Topic—Rules for communication (one person speaks at a time, starts the dialogue)	
Game	**Possible Metaphor(s)**
Baseball	Pitcher starts the play with the pitch
Football	Quarterback starts the play, no one can move until ball is in play
Volleyball	One person serves at a time
Fishing	Catch and release (about sharing in relationships)
Tennis	One person serves at a time

Communication Topic—Roles (who does what)	
Game	**Possible Metaphor(s)**
Baseball	Pitcher, batter, infield, outfield
Football	Lineman, defense, offense, back
Basketball	Guard, forward, center
Soccer	Halfbacks, forward, defense, goalie
Hockey	Goalie, defense, forward, center

Communication Topic—Mediator (person who facilitates or helps discussion/play move along)	
Game	**Possible Metaphor**
Baseball	Umpire
Football	Referee
Basketball	Referee
Soccer	Referee
Hockey	Referee
Tennis	Line judge

Communication Topic—Team vs. individual play (communication between two people or more)	
Game	**Possible Metaphor**
Baseball	Can be used for two or more people/families
Football	Can be used for two or more people/families
Basketball	Can be used for two or more people/families
Soccer	Can be used for two or more people/families
Hockey	Can be used for two or more people/families
Tennis	Can be used for two or four people (singles or doubles)
Ping-Pong	Same as tennis
Volleyball	Can be used for two or more people/families

Communication Topic—Goals (what you want to "shoot for")	
Basketball	Basket/hoop
Football	Touchdown/end zone
Baseball	Run/homeplate
Golf	Hole in one
Soccer	Goal/net

Communication Topic—Communication style (assertive vs. aggressive)	
Game	**Possible Metaphor**
Football	Quarterback sack
Basketball	Playing offensively or defensively (full- or half-court press)
Golf	Sending the ball aggressively is hitting it beyond the cup; assertively is to the cup

Communication Topic—Talking skills (tell people what it is you want/need them to do)	
Game	**Possible Metaphor**
Baseball	First and third base coaches tell a player to run or stay
Football	Quarterback tells players to run a certain play
Basketball	Player bringing the ball down court tells teammates what play to run

Communication Topic—Mixed messages, Verbal manipulation (creates confusion for listener; message sent and intended to mean one thing, received by another meaning something different)	
Game	**Possible Metaphor**
Baseball	Two fielders each telling the other they will catch the ball, or different types of pitches (e.g. knuckleball, fastball, etc.)
Ping-Pong	Top spin, back spin
Basketball	Fake shot, trap play
Golf	Back spin helps control the ball
Fishing	Fly rod and jigs (the rhythm used looks natural to the fish, but actually is manipulating them)
Soccer	Passing the ball to the other team thinking your teammate is there

Communication Topic—Fighting
(need to first define the issue, i.e., get something started)

Game	Possible Metaphor(s)
Baseball	Bunt or hit away (to get person on or advanced)
Football	Kick away or on-side kick, pass, or run
Basketball	Shoot for two or three points
Hockey	Take goalie out for extra player or not

Communication Topic—Inappropriate fight talking
(consequence for inappropriate or unfair comments)

Game	Possible Metaphor(s)
Baseball	Free base for hitting batter
Football	Unsportsman-like conduct, personal foul/free yards or replay of down
Basketball	Personal foul/free throw
Soccer	Unsportsman-like conduct/penalty kick
Hockey	Checking/penalty time-out
Boxing	Low blow/points taken from score card

Communication Topic—Reframing
(viewing/hearing from a different perspective)

Game	Possible Metaphor(s)
Baseball	Catcher has a view of all players; other players do not have that view
Football	Owners in the boxes see the game differently than coaches on the field
Basketball	Coaches look at whole court; players focus on smaller areas
Hockey	Goalies see game coming at them; center or wings see where they want to go

Communication Topic—Paradoxical intervention
(telling someone to do the opposite of what you really want)

Game	Possible Metaphor(s)
Baseball	Fake stealing, then stealing a base
Football	Quarterback sneak

13

Setting Goals and Developing Action Plans

Richard Clements

Type of Contribution: *Handout/Activity*

Objective

This handout/activity has three primary objectives: first, to provide clients with specific suggestions for setting personal goals both inside and outside of therapy; second, to provide clients with suggestions for developing action plans to achieve those goals; and third, to provide clients with a structured method for setting goals and developing action plans.

Rationale for Use

Many therapy clients attempt to set goals for themselves (both inside and outside of therapy), but they often do so in an informal and unsystematic way which limits their ability to achieve their goals. This handout/activity provides clients with a systematic method for setting goals and developing action plans that can greatly enhance their ability to achieve the goals that they set for themselves. Use of this activity in the therapy setting offers several potential benefits, both to the client and to the therapist. The activity will help the client develop skills which will enable him or her to make optimal use of therapy and which will continue to be useful after therapy has been terminated. This activity benefits the therapist by helping him or her to establish a therapeutic alliance with the patient as they collaborate in the goal-setting process and by providing some structure for therapy sessions.

Instructions

This activity works best when the handout found at the end of this chapter is discussed with the client in a therapy session, then given to the client for homework. In that next session, the therapist should discuss with the client the goals and action plans the client has formulated, responding to the client's questions about the process of setting goals and developing action plans, and addressing any difficulties the client experienced in completing the handout. If the client has not effectively utilized the guidelines provided in the handout (i.e., has not set goals that are specific, challenging, measurable, etc.), the therapist can provide suggestions for revising the goals and action plans. A portion of some or all of the subsequent therapy sessions with the client can then be devoted to discussing the client's progress toward the goals he or she has established, how to deal with obstacles standing in the way of goal achievement, etc.

If the therapist wishes, this goal-setting process can also include a component that is tied more directly to the therapy process itself, e.g., when the therapist initially gives the handout to clients to complete, the therapist can assign the clients to set some goals that they would like to accomplish in therapy in addition to goals they are setting for other areas of their lives. In the next session, the therapist and client can discuss these goals for therapy, make any indicated revisions or additions to the therapy goals, and then use the agreed upon goals as a structure for subsequent therapy sessions. This collaborative process can increase the therapeutic alliance and can increase the client's commitment to the therapy process.

Suggestions for Follow-Up

The therapist can, in subsequent therapy sessions, revisit the goals and action plans the client has set in order to respond to problems the client is experiencing in working toward those goals, check on the client's progress toward those goals, and provide positive reinforcement to the client for efforts toward meeting his or her goals. If the therapist has used the handout to collaborate with the client in setting goals for the therapy process itself, those goals can be used to structure the therapy process, with sessions being primarily devoted to working toward the agreed upon goals.

Contraindications: None

Readings and Resources for the Professional

Martin, G. and Pear, J. (1996). *Behavior modification: What it is and how to do it* (Fifth Edition). Upper Saddle River, NJ: Prentice-Hall.

Bibliotherapy Sources for the Client

Watson, D. L. and Tharp, R. G. (1993). *Self-directed behavior: Self-modification for personal adjustment*. Pacific Grove, CA: Brooks/Cole.

Setting Goals and Developing Action Plans

Therapy provides you with an excellent opportunity to examine your goals in life and what you hope to accomplish in the future. Maybe there are some goals that you have had for a long time, but have not made as much progress toward as you would like. Maybe there are some new goals that you would like to set for yourself. This handout is intended to provide you with some guidelines for setting effective goals and some suggestions for developing and implementing systematic plans for achieving those goals.

I. SETTING EFFECTIVE GOALS

Suggestions for setting effective goals include the following:

• *Make your goals as specific and concrete as possible, and include deadlines for achieving the goals.* When setting your goals, consider such questions as What? When? How often? How long? For example, "I want to lose ten pounds by June 1" is a better goal than "I want to lose some weight."

• *Make sure that you can measure progress toward your goal.* Otherwise, you will have no sure way of knowing whether your efforts are yielding any results. An example of a measurable goal is "I want to save $1,000 by the end of this year." This is measurable because it is stated in specific numerical terms (number of dollars). During the year, you can check your progress toward this goal by simply checking the balance in your savings account.

• *Set challenging, but realistic goals.* Setting extremely difficult goals can lead a person to get frustrated and give up on his or her goals; setting extremely easy goals does not lead to significant self-improvement and does not tend to produce a sense of accomplishment or satisfaction. Therefore, the best goals are ones that are challenging (that is, of medium difficulty) and also realistic (achievable, rather than impossible).

• *Choose goals that are truly important to you.* If you set goals that you do not feel are really important or worthwhile, you are unlikely to put in the time and effort needed to achieve those goals.

• *Set goals for a variety of time frames* (for example, you might set daily goals, weekly goals, monthly goals, goals for the year, for the next three years, etc.). The questions listed below are intended to help you do this.

• *Set goals in a variety of life areas* (for example, job/career goals, financial goals, personal growth goals, health/fitness goals, education/training goals, therapy goals, etc.).

• *Avoid setting too many goals at once.* Base the number of goals you set on an assessment of how many goals you can realistically, rather than ideally, pursue. Setting a few goals and making steady progress toward them is better than setting a large number of goals that end up being forgotten or abandoned.

Keep these suggestions in mind as you answer the following questions. (Note: you may want to copy these questions and complete the questions for each of the major areas in which you are setting goals, with one sheet for career goals, one sheet for financial goals, one sheet for personal growth goals, etc.)

1. What is a goal that you would like to accomplish today?
2. What goal(s) would you like to accomplish in the next week?
3. What goal(s) would you like to accomplish in the next month?
4. What goal(s) would you like to accomplish in the next six months?
5. What goal(s) would you like to accomplish in the next year?
6. What goal(s) would you like to accomplish in the next three years?
7. What goal(s) would you like to accomplish in the next five years?
8. What goal(s) would you like to accomplish in the next ten years?
9. What goals would you like to accomplish in this lifetime? A useful way to think about this is to imagine that you are 70 or 80 years old, nearing the end of your life, and that you are reflecting back on your life. At that point, what things would you like to be able to say you have accomplished in your life?

II. DEVELOPING AND IMPLEMENTING ACTION PLANS FOR ACHIEVING YOUR GOALS

After you have set some goals, the next thing you need to do is to develop and implement action plans for achieving those goals. Suggestions for doing this include the following:

• *For each goal, brainstorm methods of achieving that goal.* Brainstorming involves generating as many ideas as you can and writing all of these ideas down as they come to you, no matter how foolish or unrealistic some of the ideas may seem. Do not evaluate or criticize the ideas as they come to you; simply write them down. After you have generated several ideas, THEN you can analyze them and evaluate them. Ask yourself such questions as: "How realistic is this method? What skills/resources/information would I need to put this method into practice? Do I already have those skills and resources and that information? If not, how can I acquire them?" Based on your evaluation of your ideas, choose the method that seems most realistic and most likely to lead to achievement of your goal. (Note: you should also keep your original list of methods for reaching that goal; that way, if the first method you choose does not succeed, you can refer back to your list for other methods you can try.)
• *Complex goals and long-term goals should be broken down into smaller, more manageable steps.* For example, if your goal is to open your own business by the end of this year, you probably need to break that goal down into several smaller, more specific goals, such as saving enough money each month in order to have the amount you will need to start the business by the end of the year, purchasing needed equipment, finding a location for your business, etc.
• *Think of positive reinforcers (rewards) that you can give to yourself for accomplishing steps toward a goal and for accomplishing the goal itself.* Rewarding yourself for achieving individual steps toward a goal keeps you motivated and working toward that goal. Reinforcers can include such things as a nice dinner out, a break period in which you do something you find relaxing, purchasing a small item you have been

wanting, etc. The size of the reinforcer should match, at least approximately, the size of the accomplishment.

• *Write your goals down on note cards, along with the steps you will need to take to achieve them.* Next to each step, write down the reinforcer that you will give yourself for accomplishing that step.

• *Keep your note cards in a place where you will see them frequently.* This will help you to stay focused on your goals.

• *Review your goals on a regular basis (daily, weekly, or whatever time period works well for you), and monitor your progress toward your goals.* One way of doing this would be to check off steps toward a goal on your note cards as you accomplish those steps. Those checkmarks provide a visual sign of your progress and can help you stay motivated with regard to that goal.

• *If the action plan you have developed is not leading to satisfactory progress, consider ways in which you might change that plan to speed up your progress.* You may need to try an entirely new plan. Your original brainstorming list can come in handy here.

• *Share some or all of your goals with a trusted family member, friend, or therapist, if you feel comfortable doing so.* The person you choose should be willing to support your efforts to achieve your goals and encourage you when you are experiencing difficulties. They may also be able to give you additional suggestions for reaching your goals.

• *Keep these suggestions in mind as you write out action plans for accomplishing each of the goals you have set for yourself.*

14

Sculpting for Visual and Kinesthetic Learners

Connie M. Kane

Type of Contribution: *Activity*

Objective

To enhance clients' understanding of the significance of their behavior patterns by working with them visually and kinesthetically.

Rationale for Use

There are three primary modalities through which people learn: visual, auditory, and kinesthetic. Psychotherapy relies heavily on the auditory modality. But for people whose primary learning modality is visual or kinesthetic, talking alone may be ineffective. For that reason, other modalities such as art therapy, play therapy, and family sculpting have been developed. These allow the client to portray his or her feelings, thoughts, and experiences in pictures, in actions, or in static sculptures. The process used in family sculpting can be adapted to small group, couple, or even individual therapy without losing the potential impact. By seeing and/or feeling themselves in action, visual and kinesthetic learners are more likely to recognize the significance of their behavior for themselves and for their relationships. Such awareness is often considered a prerequisite to change.

Instructions

When a client is describing or performing a behavior that you believe to be a manifestation of the primary dynamic in his or her relationship, but talking about it has not brought appreciation of its significance or change in the pattern, sculpting may be an appropriate intervention. Introduce the exercise in a manner similar to this: "I want to ask you to try an exercise that may be more helpful than talking right now. Instead of *telling* me what you said and how you were feeling, see if you can *show* me. Assume a position and a facial expression that gives the message you were trying to give with your words in that situation. That is, if you were creating a sculpture that portrayed that moment in your relationship, show me what the sculpture would look like." The client may need you to assume the position of another party in the relationship if it is individual therapy. If it is conjoint therapy, the client you are addressing can tell the other person what position they would like him or her to assume in the picture.

In either case, after the client has created the sculpture, ask whether he or she is satisfied with the result: "Does this portray the relationship the way you see it?" or, "Does this portray the message you were trying to convey?" When the client answers affirmatively, have him or her stay in that position while you explore the implications. How does this position feel? What does it say about the relationship? How does it fit with his or her goals for the relationship?

Then ask the client to assume another position in the sculpture—one that you or another member of the system were filling—and repeat the exploration of implications from that perspective. If you are working with more than one member of the system, you may wish to have each of them offer their response to their own position before switching roles, or you may wish to have the less empathic person work on every perspective before having the other parties self-disclose.

At the point when a client can say that a behavioral stance does not fit with his or her goals for the relationship, you can begin generating alternatives and establishing strategies to learn new behavioral patterns. It can be helpful then to have clients create new sculptures that represent the desired relationship. This reinforces the goals and serves as an anchor for their daily choices.

Some clients may need help in forming their sculptures initially. You can assist by simply telling them that you would like to show them how this relationship appears to you at this time. Then ask them to assume positions that represent the distribution and use of power, the degree of intimacy, and the clarity and permeability of boundaries. For example, when one person is clearly dominant in the relationship, you might have him or her, in a Satir fashion, stand on a chair while the other person sits on the floor looking up at the first; a blaming relationship might be portrayed by a pointed, accusing finger and a placating one by having the person kneel on the floor in a begging position; indifference might be shown by having one's back turned toward the other, and so on.

Suggestions for Follow-Up

Discuss the implications of the relationship dynamics portrayed. Help clients clarify what they would like to change, and work with clients to portray the preferred relationship in a sculpture. Begin clarifying what is different about this preferred picture from the original one: How do the people interact in this one? How do they feel about themselves? How do they feel about each other? How do they make decisions? What are their expectations of each other? Have the client(s) describe the preferred relationship with as much detail as possible. Consider with him or her the first possible opportunity to implement desired changes, and begin practicing those behaviors in session. In conjoint therapy, facilitate this using actual concerns. In individual therapy, role play can be used to help practice desired change.

Continue to use reminders of this sculpting as needed, asking client(s) to remember how the relationship was and how they want it to be, and having them resume the positions for potency if need be. As other situations or dynamics are described, refer back to these sculptures and ask the client whether they fit and to what degree. Over time, facilitate clients' recognition of interactional *patterns* that impact most of their relationships. As clients solidify behavioral changes in their most significant relationships, check to see if they are generalizing these changes to other relationships, if they want to, and whether they need help in doing so.

Contraindications

This activity requires confidence in the therapist. Do not use it if you are doubtful about its efficacy or unsure of your credibility with the client. Also, be very careful about using this activity with clients involved in abusive relationships. Unless you have a clear and firm agreement from them that there will be no violence and no touching that anyone is uncomfortable with, this activity could be counterproductive. Perpetrators may become abusive and survivors may panic. Even with clear ground rules, there is a need to proceed cautiously with clients involved in abusive relationships. Extra care must be taken to forestall any movement toward abuse and to ensure that the survivor is setting needed boundaries. If that is done, sculpting may be a very effective intervention with both perpetrators and survivors of abuse.

Readings and Resources for the Professional

Constantine, L. L. (1978). Family sculpture and relationship mapping techniques. *Journal of Marriage and Family Counseling, 4*(2), 13-23.

Duhl, F., Kantor, D., and Duhl, B. (1973). Learning space and action in family therapy. In D. Bloch (Ed.), *Techniques of family psychotherapy: A primer* (pp. 47-63). New York: Grune & Stratton.

Hawkins, J. L. and Killorin, E. A. (1979). Family of origin: An Experiential workshop. *American Journal of Family Therapy, 7*(4), 5-17.

Satir, V. (1972). *Peoplemaking*. Palo Alto, CA: Science & Behavior.

Bibliotherapy Sources for the Client

*Since the process of sculpting suggested here can be applied to *any* relationship dynamic, client readings would need to be selected based on the dynamics or issues being addressed. The following books provide food for thought on numerous facets of life and relationships.

Anonymous. (1994). *The Aesop for children*. New York: Scholastic, Inc.

Canfield, J., Hansen, M. V., and Wentworth, D. V. (1995). *Chicken soup for the soul*. Deerfield Beach, FL: Health Communications, Inc.

Canfield, J. and Hansen, M. V. (1995). *A 2nd helping of chicken soup for the soul*. Deerfield Beach, FL: Health Communications, Inc.

Satir, V. (1976). *Making contact*. Millbrae, CA: Celestial Arts.

15

Conscientious Activities for Compulsive Clients

Hugh Crago
Maureen Crago

Type of Contribution: *Homework/Activity*

The following chapter details a number of sequenced interventions that are particularly useful in working with clients whose personality style is obsessional, and who exhibit mild to moderate (nonpsychotic) levels of obsessive compulsive disorder. The interventions could equally be classed as "homework" or as "activities," and though separate, are governed by the same broad objectives, rationales, and contraindications for use. Accordingly, all the latter have been summarized in the introductory material, with details specific to any given activity mentioned in the relevent section.

Objective

The "obsessional personality" was one of the earliest neurotic styles to be delineated. The style is clear-cut and easily recognizable, even when it is not characterized by out-of-control obsessive-compulsive behavior. It is precisely this consistency in the "conscientious" (Oldham and Morris, 1990) person's approach to life and the predictability of his/her underlying emotional issues that allows us to devise interventions that are widely applicable. However, this does not mean that specific interventions can simply be transferred unmodified from one client's situation to another. It is more a question of creatively meshing the individual client's personal style and issues with appropriate, broad categories of intervention. All of the following activities were originally devised for particular clients who are in particular situations. Much highly individualized "joining" took place before the interventions were employed. Obsessional clients are, on the whole, comfortable with working slowly. There is no need to rush into intervention until a solid alliance has been built. Tolerance of the client's obsession with often irrelevant detail, a willingness not to push for underlying emotion, allowing the client to remain in control of the interview, and giving priority to kinesthetic language and metaphors as opposed to visually derived language are all factors vital in creating such an alliance. Note the way that "easier" and more individual/symptom-focused tasks precede more challenging, relationship/feeling-focused tasks. The final step with such clients is often to persuade them to express feelings directly to significant others, usually parents. Once the obsessional client has reached this stage, he or she is well on the way to a less emotionally constrained, more spontaneous, and less ritual-bound lifestyle.

Rationale for Use

Obsessional clients usually seek help because they feel out of control of their symptoms (compulsive checking, handwashing, cleaning, and other behaviors which Rapoport [1989] sees as "vestigial grooming rituals"). Often, they have lived with such rituals for years, but are unable to tolerate them when they escalate to higher levels of frequency or intensity, usually in response to some stressful life event. It has been our experience that moderate, but egodystonic levels of compulsive behavior are in fact amenable to nonbiological intervention, at least in the short term, and sometimes in the long term as well. It seems particularly important in the case of young clients, where the symptoms may not yet have gained a strong hold, to allow young clients to leave therapy feeling that they are equipped with tactics that have given them control now, and will work again in the future.

Instructions

Obsessive clients do not appreciate being told straight out that their rituals are under their control. Interventions to master compulsions must thus tread a fine line between asserting total control (which would leave the sufferer feeling blamed and not heard) and denying any control at all (which would leave the sufferer feeling that drug therapy is the only hope). Several of the examples that follow leave the area of control deliberately ambiguous. It is possible to "frame" a control-oriented intervention with an initial assertion of lack of control, or alternatively, for the therapist to take on the lack of control, asserting the client's right to prove him/her wrong.

Framing Comment 1

I think this checking thing is really not something that you can change much, but you can probably make just a little bit of difference. Would you be interested in seeing whether the latter is the case? You realize, of course, that simply tinkering with your checking will not solve the problem, and you probably will not feel any better about it. But if we begin by just gaining precise information on your checking, at least it will tell us what we are up against.

Observation tasks may involve charting, logging, measuring, and generally being "more obsessional than the obsessive." Clients normally take them very seriously—at least until they become impatient with "imposed" behavior that is so like their own, and begin to find themselves becoming less cooperative. Such tasks give a "baseline" (as behavioral techniques prescribe), but more important, they tell the client that his/her routines are important, and to not devalue them by attempting to argue them away or reduce their place in his/her life.

Once observation has been carried out, a good next step is:

Varying the Number of Times a Ritual Is Performed

Activity 1. The technique of "plusing and minusing" (Crago, 1995) can be useful in restoring to the client an initial sense of control, without panicking him/her at the thought that the compulsions may have to be given up. The therapist simply suggests to the client that, having established a baseline number of handwashes, checks, etc., for any given occasion, he/she *adds one or deletes one* from that number, according to a regular schedule. The exact details of the schedule probably do not matter at all—what does matter is the fact that the client is acting purposefully upon the ritual, and testing out his/her ability to take charge of it, while not abandoning it. (Check carefully if the client feels alarmed that adding might make the rituals worse, or that deleting might be a concealed way of "taking them away" from him/her).

The addition and deletion of the number of times a ritual is performed can be an ongoing intervention, varied from week to week. In time, it can give way to other tasks, more directly related to the underlying emotional issues.

Varying the Content of Rituals

It is much easier for clients to contemplate *varying the content of a ritual* than giving it up completely, and under the guise of altering the content, the therapist can often introduce a gradually deepening awareness of feelings "by the back door."

Activity 2. For example, a checking client who makes lists might be asked to list all the feelings he/she had in the minutes preceding his compulsion to check that the door was locked or if the bed was made properly. Since obsessional clients normally are unaware of any link between feelings and rituals, it is important to give the client permission to find no actual feelings, but simply to invent plausible ones that he/she *may* have had.

Activity 3. Clients who are somewhat more comfortable with feelings can be asked to list all the times they have ever felt angry in their lives and to arrange these lists in order, from the easiest to think about to the hardest to think about. Confronting tasks of this type require a longer interval between sessions (three weeks or more), so that clients have a chance to live with the task for a while, and to begin to draw their own conclusions from the new experience.

Varying the Medium or Form of a Ritual

The obsessional person's tendency is to be unaware of visual imagery. Associating painting tasks with rituals, or substituting the former for the latter, is a powerful way of creating external visual images related to the original feelings.

Activity 4. We deliberately asked a client who was a fairly concrete, literal-minded person, to "paint" his list items, using proper paints rather than felt-tipped markers, pencils, or pens. Instructions were:

> Do not worry if you think you are a lousy artist; this is not a test of your artistic skill. In fact, no one needs to see your painted list but yourself. You can really have lots of fun with this list. If you feel like painting a purple lawnmower you can! Give yourself plenty of space on your paper to do a nice big picture for each item. Maybe this task will sound silly to you, but if you think about it, it is no more silly than doing your regular list, and it will give you a chance to bring your new ability to enjoy yourself right into the list making part of yourself.

Activity 4.1. The client was then moved to constructing his next list (made every Friday, to bind the client's anxiety about the weekend) by thinking of the images on the last one, rather than by first thinking of items, and picturing them only later.

Activity 4.2. Eventually, he was asked to paint feelings directly, using any colors he wished, except black (the color he associated with feeling depressed and hopeless).

Moving from Rituals to Feelings

It can be extremely useful to obsessional clients to verbally express their *acceptance* of their own feelings, rather than fighting against them, or feeling that the therapist is asking them to alter the feelings.

Activity 5. "Every time you feel yourself tightening those chest muscles, say out loud to yourself, 'I'm tightening my chest so I don't have to feel anything.' There is no need to say anything more than that, but be sure to say it every time you tighten up. You might like to notice if any particular thoughts come into your mind after you have said it. Make a note of them if you like." Similarly, clients can be given nonthreatening exercises in the acceptance of the positive feelings they normally suppress:

Activity 5.1. "Whenever you feel *proud or affectionate* during the next week, you are to go into another room (if you are with other people at the time) and quietly say the words, "Gee, I feel proud of you" or whatever. Do not say them out loud so others can hear. This is just for you, so you can get a little more comfortable with hearing how the words sound *at the time.*

Activity 5.2. A later, more demanding step in this progression would be to ask the client to articulate disturbing feelings directly to "safe" family members, linking past trauma with present ritual:

> At least twice before we see you again, when you find yourself checking on your kids to make sure they have not lost or mislaid anything, you are to say to them that the reason you feel a need to check to see nothing is missing is that when you were a boy you lost some very valuable, precious things. Explain to your children, even if they are too young to understand fully, that you know they are good and careful kids, but that the checking up is something that you need to do to reassure yourself, because of the precious things you lost in your own childhood. You may not find it easy to carry out this task, but we think it might be very healing for you if you give it a go. You will also be doing something important for your children at the same time. (What this client had "lost" in childhood was actually his father, who had left his mother when the client was about twelve.)

From Rituals to Spontaneity

Obsessional clients are typically extremely governed by habits and unspontaneous in every aspect of their daily lives. Others around them may have more potential for spontaneity, and so it is often important to work through them to alter the wider context of "habit" that surrounds the client's rituals. The notion that spontaneity need not be threatening can thus be introduced in a safe way. It is far harder to maintain a ritual when the context itself is freer and less governed by rules.

Activity 6. In cases where the clients are young, their parents can be encouraged to suggest spontaneous outings to break a fixed weekend routine. The young client need not see this as having anything to do with therapy, or with "problems." With adult clients, spouses or partners will often cooperate with suggestions to spontaneously vary their routines, and for some of them this will be the first time for years that they have "bucked the system" that has arisen around the obsessional partner. Clients themselves can be asked to measure their anxiety levels carefully when indulging in any activity that departs from normal routine.

Readings and Resources for the Professional

Freud's classic case study of the Rat Man (1909) set the pattern for psychoanalytic thinking on the dynamics of obsessionality. The most extensive specialized treatment of the subject is probably Salzman's (1988). Shapiro's chapter in *Neurotic Styles* (1965) offers clear, practical discussion for the clinician. Oldham and Morris' 1990 humanization of DSM III-R is particularly valuable for its conceptualization of the strengths of the obsessional style and its provision of many "positive reframes" for potentially dysfunctional behavior. Rapoport (1989) presents a case for OCD as a purely biological phenomenon. Useful systemic approaches to OCD can be found in Hafner (1992) and Welfare (1993).

Bibliotherapy Sources for the Client

Obsessional clients love to read about others like themselves; they realize that they are not alone, and that their problems may be solvable. Rapoport (1989) is a source of such stories, although her faith in a biomedical approach to the condition may undermine a client's growing belief in his/her ability to control the behavior. Oldham and Morris' *Personality Self-Portrait* (1990), now unfortunately out of print, helps clients to get their problems into proportion; the section on Obsessive Compulsive Personality Disorder (pp. 77-78), with its talk of genetic predisposition, should probably be handed to clients only after careful consideration of the risks and benefits that might be involved. Mallinger and de Wyze's *Too Perfect* (1993) is a self-help title devoted specifically to the obsessional personality. Novels of obsessionality can be double-edged tools for clients who themselves resembling the protagonists governed who are by ritual (Crago, 1995). For literate adults, perhaps Kafka's celebrated short stories "The Burrow" (1931) and "Metamorphosis" (1916) are best, because they vividly portray ritualistic and obsessional behavior in allegorical form, allowing clients to identify at a semi-unconscious level rather than having their noses rubbed in a fictional "mirror" of their own miseries.

REFERENCES

American Psychiatric Association. (1994). *Diagnostic and Statistical Manual of Mental Disorders: DSM-IV.*

Crago, H. (1995). "The Anxious Boys' Newsletter." *Australian and New Zealand Journal of Family Therapy, 16*(1), 29-37.

Freud, S. (1909). "Notes Upon a Case of Obsessional Neurosis." In A. Richards, (ed.), *The Pelican Freud Library, Case Histories II.* (Vol 9). Hammondsworth: Penguin Books.

Hafner, J. (1992). "Anxiety Disorder in Family Therapy." *Australian and New Zealand Journal of Family Therapy, 13*(2), 99-104.

Mallinger, A. and de Wyze, J. (1993). *Too Perfect.* New York: Thorsons/Harper/Collins.

Oldham, J. and Morris, L. (1990). *Personality Self-Portrait: Why You Think, Work, Love and Act the Way You Do.* New York: Bantam Books.

Rapoport, J. (1989). *The Boy Who Couldn't Stop Washing: The Experience and Treatment of Obsessive Compulsive Disorder.* New York: Dutton.

Salzman, L. (1988). *The Obsessive Personality.* New York: Science House.

Schapiro, D. (1965). *Neurotic Styles.* New York: Basic Books.

Welfare, A. (1993). "Systemic Approaches in the Treatment of Obsessive-Compulsive Disorder." *Australian and New Zealand Journal of Family Therapy, 14*(3), 137-144.

16

Breaking the Cycle
Between Being Passive and Aggressive

Lee M. Williams

Type of Contribution: *Handout*

Objective

This handout is intended to help clients recognize that they may be caught in a vicious cycle between being passive and aggressive. The handout advocates assertiveness as an appropriate alternative to being passive or aggressive.

Rationale for Use

Clients frequently struggle with anger and conflict in their relationships. In some cases, individuals may avoid dealing with issues out of a fear of creating conflict in their relationships. Eventually the accumulated resentment over several unaddressed issues increases to the point where the individual finally releases the built-up anger. Unfortunately, the buildup in anger and resentment over several issues often leads to an expression of anger that is generally inappropriate and excessive to the triggering event. For example, the individual may verbally attack or threaten to leave the relationship. In less frequent cases, the individual may even become physically aggressive (see contraindications). The individual's embarrassment or guilt over what was said or what happened during the blow-up leads the individual to resume a passive or conflict-avoidant stance. Thus, the cycle begins over again.

Many clients are unaware of being locked into this pattern. Therefore, the purpose of the handout is to illustrate for these individuals how their extreme approaches to dealing with anger create a vicious cycle. Being appropriately assertive is then offered as an alternative to break the vicious cycle. Clients who previously may have been reluctant to be assertive for fear of creating conflict now see assertiveness as an effective means of avoiding or dealing with conflict because it breaks the cycle.

Instructions

Once the therapist believes the client follows the pattern described in the handout, he or she can go over the handout with the client. As an alternative, the therapist can draw the illustration on a board and describe the key concepts verbally to the client. When describing the cycle, it is generally best to describe the passive or conflict-avoidant end of the continuum first, and then discuss how the buildup of anger and resentment leads to some individuals becoming quite upset. The therapist can then describe how individuals often feel guilty for things they said or did when upset, or are bothered by the conflict that it generated. As a result, these individuals decide that the best approach is to just to let things go rather than make an issue of everything. The therapist then emphasizes that this only perpetuates the cycle happening all over again.

A good approach is to describe the cycle to the individual without personalizing it, and then ask the client if the pattern fits him/her. If the client agrees that the cycle fits his or her situation, the therapist can then introduce the idea that the way to break this cycle is to learn how to be appropriately assertive. Being appropriately assertive is visually drawn as being in the middle of the continuum to differentiate it between the two extremes of being either passive or aggressive.

Assertiveness is described as being different from passivity because the individual is encouraged to stand up for issues that are important. Assertiveness is distinguished from being aggressive because the individual uses constructive and appropriate means of raising the concerns, which in turn is less likely to create defensiveness and aggression. This later point is important because many individuals have difficulty distinguishing between being assertive and being aggressive. It is frequently helpful to tell clients that one reason being aggressive is ineffective is that others tune in to how the message is being delivered, rather than the concern or need that is being expressed.

Suggestions for Follow-Up

Presenting the concepts either verbally or through the handout is generally an effective catalyst for encouraging individuals to practice assertiveness. However, the therapist may need to teach the individuals important tips or skills in being assertive. For example, clients may need help in clarifying which issues they can ignore and which ones require that they assert themselves. In other words, clients may need help in assessing which battles they should choose to fight, and which ones to ignore. Clients may also need to be taught how to use "I statements" to own their feelings and to communicate their needs in a less defensive manner. Role-playing may also help clients practice and become more comfortable being assertive outside of the sessions.

Contraindications

The therapist needs to be careful in assessing whether the cycle is indeed present, particularly when the individual has a history of being physically aggressive. This activity would be contraindicated in cases where physical aggression or battering is used to control one's partner. In these cases, the therapist would need to be careful not mistake the batterer's cycle with the conflict-avoidant, aggressive cycle. Individuals for which this activity is most appropriate are generally best characterized by their passivity and conflict-avoidant nature rather than their aggressiveness.

The therapist also needs to carefully assess the role of alcohol in the cycle to determine whether the activity is indicated or contraindicated. Alcohol may lower an individual's inhibitions and lead him/her to say or do things that he would normally not. The activity would be contraindicated if the therapist determined that the conflict was caused primarily by lower inhibitions due to alcohol or other substance abuse. In some cases, the therapist may conclude that the cycle is indeed present, but alcohol is also a contributing factor. In this case, the activity would be appropriate to use, but would also require the therapist to discuss the role that alcohol plays in the cycle.

Readings and Resources for the Professional and the Client

Lerner, H. G. (1985). *The dance of anger.* New York: Perennial Library.

Breaking the Cycle Between
Being Passive and Aggressive

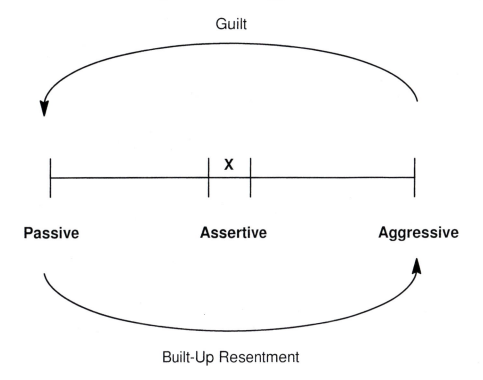

Cycle:

1. Being passive leads to a buildup of anger and resentment.
2. Buildup of anger and resentment eventually leads to a blowup.
3. Blowup causes conflict in relationship.
4. Individual feels guilty for things said or done during the blowup.
5. Individual decides to hold things in again to avoid conflict.

Being assertive breaks the cycle:

1. Being assertive means standing up for issues that are important to you, rather than not saying or doing anything. Being passive is problematic, because you cannot always count on others to know your needs.
2. Being assertive means being appropriate in terms of how you bring up the issues or concerns. Being aggressive is ineffective because others focus on how angry you are rather than on the legitimate need you are trying to express.

17

The Power of Homework
in Survivors' Groups

Jan Osborn

Type of Contribution: *Homework*

Many therapists work regularly with survivors of childhood sexual abuse. While a great deal of survivors' work has been done in individual, couple, and family contexts, group therapy can be a vital adjunct to these modalities. The group setting offers a sense of community through which experience can be shared and shame reduced. Because this sense of community takes time to develop, and because the nature of the work is so difficult, homework assignments can assist with this process. The assignments are structured, affording a boundary around the depth of work to be done. Assignments which are less likely to induce shame are done earlier in the course of treatment. Members usually feel comfortable sharing these exercises with the group, which helps the members bond in common experience. As members become more comfortable with each other and with the process, the assignments can be more difficult in nature.

Which assignments will be given to each group is in itself constantly in process. Some of the homework assignments used with clients include:

- writing about a time when they felt safe
- describing and creating a safe place
- listing present coping mechanisms (a sample list is given), including what these give and what they cost
- outlining healthier ways of coping
- drawing pictures of family-of-origin members and coloring them in relation to the emotions they most often express
- structural maps of the family of origin and the family of procreation
- "the story" (members spend many sessions discussing what it will be like to write the story of their life including the abuse)
- letters to perpetrators
- letters to others (such as mothers who are nonoffending spouses, etc.)
- collages of how clients see themselves, how others see them, and how they would like to see themselves.

What follows are some of the exercises given routinely to group members.

HOMEWORK ACTIVITY TO INCREASE CLIENT BOUNDARIES

Because the violation of boundaries is the nature of trauma, many survivors find it difficult to clearly define their boundaries and to act in a manner which maintains them. Many feel unworthy to have boundaries.

Objective and Rationale for Use

The objective of the following exercise is to give permission to one's self to have boundaries which are clearly defined, and the permission to assert them. The exercise uses Native American medicine. The medicine is anything that brings personal power, strength, and understanding and is the constant living of life in a way that brings healing to Mother Earth and all her creatures. The animals are believed to relay messages of healing to anyone astute enough to observe their lessons on how to live. This exercise draws on the medicine of the armadillo. "Armadillo wears its armor on its back, its medicine a part of its body. Its boundaries of safety are a part of its total being." The armadillo says:

> Armor all my boundaries.
> Teach me my shields
> Reflect all the hurt
> So I will not yield.

The armadillo suggests that it is a gift to the self to create boundaries, setting up what you are willing to experience (Sams and Carson, 1988).

Instructions and Follow-Up

The description of the armadillo is read to the group. The group is then told that if they would like to partake in an exercise to ward off being invaded, they may call on the medicine of the armadillo by creating a similar shield. They are then instructed to make a circle on a piece of paper and see it as a medicine shield. Participants are instructed to write all the things that they desire to have in the body of the shield. All things which bring joy should be included. This sets up boundaries that allow only these chosen experiences to be a part of life, and become a shield to ward off the things that are undesirable. The shield reflects what they are and what they will do to ward others on an unconscious level. Outside of the shield, experiences which may be acceptable by "invitation only" should be placed.

If the exercise is done during group time, adequate time must be left to discuss feelings which arose during the exercise. Because of limited time, feelings that were experienced by participating in the exercise should be addressed, not descriptions of each shield. The exercise can be used as homework, allowing time for two to three shields to be more closely examined during each group session.

Contraindication

Clients must be able to work in metaphor; thus, thought-disordered clients may need to be excluded. The therapist must also be mindful that when giving exercises as homework to a group, s/he may receive more calls from clients during the week than usual because of what such exercises stimulate in the clients. Therefore, such assignments should not be given at times when the therapist will be unavailable.

HOMEWORK ACTIVITY TO ASSIST CLIENTS IN OVERCOMING DEPRESSION

Objection and Rationale for Use

Other assignments come directly out of a member's experience in group. The following is a description of one such exercise. As one survivors group was in the process of discussing what it would be like to write and tell their stories, two members voiced concern that they were afraid that they would slip back into their depression if they wrote their stories, particularly the parts which included the abuse. This fear was preventing them from moving forward. Both were given the assignment of writing about (or drawing) what it is like to go into the depression. They were asked to describe in detail what they know about this place.

The idea behind writing about or drawing the depression is to assist the client in facing it head-on, thus, hopefully being less fearful of it, and possibly even gaining some control over it. When depression is so closely linked to content, it may be a way of coping that is more comfortable than looking at more painful issues. (This is not meant to negate the biological aspects, but meant more as an adjunct to them). When clients draw or write about the depressed place, they can sometimes change their negative view of it, and see the activity as a coping mechanism. For some, the activity is comforting; thus, they feel more control over their depressed place.

Instructions and Follow-Up

The client is simply asked to write about or draw the depressed place and bring it to group the following week. The therapists should also be available during the week, as powerful feelings may surface when doing the assignment. Processing what it was like to do the assignment and share it with the group is as important as the homework itself.

Contraindications

The client must be able to work in metaphor; thus, thought-disordered clients may need to be excluded. Additionally, clients who are actively suicidal should not be given the homework at first. Once the assignment has been done, however, it is a very helpful tool in assessing how far into a depressive episode a client is, including assessing for suicidal tendencies.

Readings and Resources for the Professional

Alexander, P. and Follette, V. (1988). Personal constructs in the group treatment of incest. In R. Neimeyer and G. Neimeyer (Eds.), *Personal construct therapy casebook*. New York: Springer.

Alexander, P., Neimeyer, R., Follette, V., Moore, M., and Harter, S. (1989). A comparison of group treatments of women sexually abused as children. *Journal of Consulting and Clinical Psychology, 57*, 479-483.

Blume, S. (1990). *Secret survivors*. New York: Wiley.

Briere, J. (1989). *Therapy for adults molested as children*. New York: Springer.

Courtois, C. (1988). *Healing the incest wound*. New York: Norton.

Dolan, Y. (1991). *Resolving sexual abuse*. New York: Norton.

Figley, C. (1985). *Trauma and it wake: The study of treatment of post-traumatic stress disorder*. New York: Brunner/Mazel.

Finkelhor, D. (1984). *Child sexual abuse: New theory and research*. Beverly Hills: Sage.

Gelinas, D. (1983). The persiting negative effects of incest. *Psychiatry, 46*, 312-332.

Gil, E. (1988). *Treatment of adult survivors of childhood sexual abuse*. Walnut Creek, CA: Launch Press.

Herman, J. and Schatzow, E. (1984). Time-limited group therapy for women with a history of incest. *International Journal of Group Psychotherapy, 34*, 605-616.

Maltz, W. (1988). Identifying and treating the sexual repercussions of incest: A couples therapy approach. *Journal of Sex and Marital Therapy, 14*, 145-163.

Maltz, W. and Holman, B. (1987). *Incest and sexuality*. Lexington, MA: Lexington Books.

Osborn, J. L. (1995). Incest. In D. M. Busby (Ed.), *The impact of violence on the family: Treatment approaches for therapists and other professionals working with families*. Allyn and Bacon: New York.

Russell, D. (1986). *The secret trauma*. New York: Basic Books.

Trepper, T. and Barrett, M. (1989). *Systemic treatment of incest*. New York: Brunner/Mazel.

Bibliotherapy Sources for the Client

Bass, E. and Davis L. (1988). *The courage to heal: A guide for women survivors of child sexual abuse*. New York: Harper and Row.

Bronson, C. (1989). *Growing through the pain*. Englewood Cliffs, NJ: Prentice-Hall.

Davis, L. (1990). *The courage to heal workbook: For women and men survivors of child sexual abuse*. New York: Harper and Row.

Dinsmore, C. (1991). *From surviving to thriving*. Albany, NY: State University of New York Press.

Gil, E. (1983). *Outgrowing the pain: A book for and about adults abused as children*. San Francisco: Launch press.

Poston, C. and Lidon, K. (1989). *Reclaiming our lives: Hope for adult survivors of incest*. Boston: Little Brown.

Rush, F. (1980). *The best kept secret*. Englewood Cliffs, NJ: Prentice-Hall.

White, L. (1988). *The obsidian mirror: An adult healing from incest*. Seattle: Seal Press.

REFERENCE

Sams, J. and Carson, D. (1988). *Medicine cards: The discovery of power through the ways of animals*. Santa Fe, NM: Bear and Co.

18

A "Magic" Aid for Hypnosis
and Suggestion in Crisis Management

Walter Hartmann
Gail Golden

Type of Contribution: *Activity*

Objective

Within the context of crisis management, combined with suggestions for relaxation and stress management, the present authors have found it useful to give small, smooth, or textured "magic" stones to some clients. The transfer of this type of object is, of course, not a therapeutic treatment in and of itself, but it can be meaningful to the client when it occurs in the context of an appropriate therapeutic relationship. While the technique may be related to the hypnotic process, it does not necessarily require formal hypnotic induction procedures. This "magic" tool, then, is an aid to carrying out suggestions. It obviously does not *do* anything in and by itself. The pebble is always a supplement to suggestion—a tool to focus attention, to distract from noxious perceptions, and to enhance "belief and trust" (see e.g., Kroger, 1963; Munro, 1908). The tool and its transfer appear to help meet the commonly observed need for something tangible in complex situations—the need for ritual to symbolize and embody our perceptions and understandings of difficult and abstract processes.

It may be said that by suggestion, with or without formal hypnotic procedure, we invite, teach, or persuade our clients to use their potentials in fuller, more effective, novel, and surprising ways. Suggestions to clients such as, "feel your arm becoming heavy," or instructions to lower sympathetic nervous system activity or to focus away from pain are at times helped and enhanced by the suggestions to "rub your pain into the stone," and "as you feel the weight and texture of the pebble, you will find yourself feeling more relaxed."

This can be conceptualized as enlisting primary process thinking and feeling, in the sense that "magic" can be referred to the infantile stage of development, in which the entire universe seems under the magic control of the infant. It may be said that here is a concrete example of "regression in the service of the ego" (Gill and Brenman, 1959; Kris, 1952). This aspect may be particularly effective in the peculiar hypnotherapist-client relationship, where hypnosis facilitates both transference and countertransference (Orne, 1965).

A further conceptualization also suggests itself. For better or for worse, there is a kind of power in and of the therapist. The therapist's presentation of a tangible object in the manner of

Note: This contribution was adapted, with permission from the publisher, from the following source:
Hartman, W. and Golden, G. A. (1990). A "magic" aid for hypnosis and suggestion in crisis management: A brief communication. *International Journal of Clinical and Experimental Hypnosis, 38*(3), 157-161.

the "magic" tool, as used by the present authors, suggests a kind of transfer of such power. Recall the badge of the office (e.g., the scepter, mace, robe, etc.) with which power is conferred and transferred in different settings.

The "magic" object as described by the present authors seems to have something in common with the "transitional object," as discussed for example by Brown and Fromm (1986, pp. 300-301). The "transitional object" however, is created by the infant to represent the power and protection of the mother, and it is used to eventually develop the child's own sense of power (Stevenson, 1954). The "magic" object, as described in the present chapter, is created by the therapist to represent the client's power, and it is not a developmental tool.

In summary, the "magic" tool is conceptualized parsimoniously as the symbol of a kind of power transfer in the context of a therapeutic relationship where primary process feelings are utilized.

Rationale for Use

This activity can be used to aid in crisis managment sessions with clients. The present authors (Hartmann and Golden) recently asked themselves how they had arrived at this technique; they had not been taught it, read about it, or heard of any reference to it. The first author had taken it for granted, and the second author had picked it up from him. A number of ideas and experiences seemed to make this technique an obvious part of certain hypnotic-suggestive situations.

Objects have, of course, shown up in the history of hypnosis—from Mesmer's rods (d'Es-lon, 1784/1965), to de Puysegur's tree (Shor, 1979), to the venerable swinging watches, proverbial crystal balls, etc. None of these, however, were carried away by the subject. In addition, there is a lengthy history of the magic amulet, used to ward off evil, to concentrate powers, etc. The rabbis fought with indifferent success against the *mezuzah* (the capsule containing scriptual passages as an amulet which is affixed to the doorposts of Jewish homes) (see Singer, 1904, Vol. viii). The name or names of God are used as powerful magic in popular Jewish tradition, as in the legend of the Golem of Prague (see Singer, 1904, Vol. vi). In other religions, holy water, saints' images, crosses, etc., have been used in a similar manner. In addition, "primitive" religions abound with magic and magical objects (Wedeck, 1956).

The rabbit's foot, the beloved's scarf, and other such charms are "magic" objects in many stories, as well as in real life. Recall, for instance, the war movies in which the heroic pilot lost or mislaid his lucky charm, took off without it, and invariably crashed. In an example from real life, about forty-five years ago, the first author gave a small pendant to a friend. Almost immediately, she was rushed off to a hospital with serious pneumonia, and she held the pendant tightly. It turned out that the little trinket had meant quite a lot to her, and she had made use of it during the crisis of her hospitalization. She has the pendant to this day, and has a special kind of attachment to it. The worry beads of the Middle East, or in a popular way, the "touchstones" rather solemnly advertised as a kind of tranquilizer, are other examples of this sort.

These instances are among the ideas and events which made the "magic" tool obvious to the present authors as a technique to aid with suggestions. We view our "magic" pebble as a kind of talisman.

Instructions

When clients are in crisis, therapists may find it useful to aid them in managing the crisis by giving them a small stone to rub to help them get through the crisis. In the clinical setting, the "magic" tool may be introduced in various ways. A typical form is the one below as used by the second author:

> I have a special gimmick that I have used sometimes when I am going to face a situation that makes me especially nervous. Interested? (The client invariably is.) This is a "magic" stone (smiling, ironically). You can use it to help you relax. Take it in your hand and feel it. (The pebble is handed over.) You can feel its smoothness. If you hold the stone and rub it, you will find it will help you relax. As you concentrate on the stone, on how it feels in your hand, on the weight and texture, you will feel your muscles relaxing; and as you get more relaxed, you will feel more able to cope. There is really nothing special about this stone—you can see I have a whole jar of them (therapist points). It is just a nice, smooth stone. But you can use it to help you relax. I do not know if it will work for you, but I have used it a number of times, and it has been a big help. Want to keep it and see if you can make it work for you? (In some cases, the therapist asks for the stone to be returned.)

No client has ever refused; rather, clients have appeared to be impressed, delighted, amused, and relieved.

Any smooth or interestingly textured pebble is used, such as those which can be found in many Oriental gift stores. Interesting pebbles can be picked up at a lake or seashore. Other small, manipulatable objects would also be appropriate.

Examples from Crisis Management Cases

In a school, which the first author (W. H.) happened to be visiting as a parent, an eight-year old girl fell and broke her ankle. The author was permitted to see the girl, who lay in an empty room while she was waiting for the ambulance. Naturally, she was in a panic and pain. To initiate the interaction, she was given a pebble and invited to "really feel it," to "rub the pain into the stone." These suggestions were successful; the youngster calmed down and talked quietly. She was carried off to the ambulance clutching the stone. It was reported later that she continued making use of the pebble in the hospital, with marked effect on her tolerance of procedures.

The first author witnessed a car crash, and found a mother and child in one auto, both unhurt, but of course, upset. The child, a girl about six years old, was in real distress. Again, quiet suggestions that "everything is all right" and "you and Mommy are fine" were coupled with giving the child a pebble "to rub the pain and fear into." The child's panic subsided as the stone was clutched and rubbed.

The first author teaches a number of his clients relaxation techniques and stress management using hypnotic procedures. In some cases, posthypnotic suggestion or self-hypnosis is not completely effective. Indeed, some clients have asked if there is an extra aid they could have. When such clients were provided with a pebble to aid them, the suggestions almost always became more effective.

In instances of helping clients to cope with the pain and discomfort of surgery (e.g., abdominal, dental, and orthopedic), the first author has used stones as a means to help the client focus on benign stimuli and to distract the client from noxious ones. In most instances, this proved effective as judged by the clients' demeanor, pre- and postoperative, and the clients' reports on the perception of pain and discomfort.

In one of the second author's (G. G.) cases, a crisis occurred after about eight sessions of therapy. At a quickly scheduled emergency session, the client appeared depressed, hopeless, and self-accusatory; she hinted at suicide. In the context of this client's history, the second author decided against recommending hospitalization, in order to avoid the client's interpretation that she was indeed "crazy" and a hopeless case. The author handed her own personal stone to the client and explained that it might help her to remain calm and handle tense situations, as it had done for the therapist. The author asked that the stone be returned at the next scheduled session, two days later. The client walked out, clutching the stone as if it were a lifeline. When she returned, the crisis had passed. The client gave the pebble back, saying, "It was really magic." The emotional tone of this postcrisis session was much deeper than in previous ones. While clearly the "success" here cannot be ascribed entirely to the "magic" stone, making the stone available offered a focus to the client to help herself through the crisis.

Contraindications

There are three inter-related factors militating against indiscriminate use:

1. As discussed, the therapist-client relationship is subtle and requires special care. Especially true with hypnosis and suggestion, feelings and perceptions of power and power relations, and of dependency, as between therapist and client, need careful handling. The present authors suggest that the "dangers of hypnosis," so widely discussed, are in fact the dangers inherent in many human relationships, which often take place unconsciously in a context of expectations, goals, assumptions, needs, and perceptions. In situations involving hypnosis and suggestion, in particular, dangers can arise from a "power trip" the therapist may consciously or unconsciously be engaged in, and/or be perceived as being engaged in (Hartmann, 1986; Orne, 1965). The "magic" pebble may lend itself to a therapist's engaging in "one-upmanship"; the ritualistic presentation of the "magic" tool can arouse counterproductive feelings in relation to power and dependency.

   In view of the considerable emotional load potentially inherent in the transfer of the "magic" tool, the therapist can make light of the tool, and stress that they, too, have used it. Thus, it is implied first, that when the client uses the pebble and makes it work, he/she "has power"; and second, that the "powerful" therapist also can be anxious, fearful, and troubled. Asking for the stone to be returned will add to its "power" in some cases; in others, the outright gift will add to the ambiance.
2. The "magic" stone procedure could lend itself to the irresponsible, "lazy" use of attempting to produce therapeutic effects with the stone alone, rather than providing the kind of evaluation and support needed. Interpersonal, therapeutic skills and attitudes are vital; they cannot be replaced by some gadgetry—however helpful it may be as an occasional supplementary tool.
3. Even with all precautions taken, the client may ascribe effects of hypnosis and suggestion to the stone, probably subconsciously; thus, an undesirable dependency on the tool may be created, and loss, or possible experienced ineffectiveness, may obviate any therapeutic effects to be achieved.

The therapist can use the procedure described here in three types of situations: (1) in crisis situations, when there is no time to teach relaxation conventionally (as in the above examples involving accidents); (2) for medical or surgical procedures, when the therapist cannot be present during a traumatic stress situation; and (3) as an extra "boost" in certain cases, to help the therapist's instructions to be effective (as in the second author's examples above). Finally, it should be remembered that the aim of all therapeutic efforts—including transfer of a concrete object—is to potentiate, to empower the client, and to increase the client's ability to cope.

REFERENCES

Brown, D. P. and Fromm, E. (1986). *Hypnotherapy and hypnoanalysis*. Hillsdale, NJ: Erlbaum.

d'Eslon, C. (1965). Observations on the two reports of the commissioners named by the king investigate animal magnetism. In R.E. Shor and M.T. Orne (Eds.), *The nature of hypnosis*, pp. 8-20. New York: Holt, Rinehart & Winston. (Original Publication as *Observations sur les deux rapports de mm. les Commissaires nommes par Sa Majeste, pour l'examen du Magnetisme animal*. (1784) (D. Chval, Trans.). Paris: Clousier.

Gill, M. M. and Brenman, M. (1959). *Hypnosis and related states: Psychoanalytic studies in regression*. New York: International Universities Press.

Good News Bible. (1976). New York: American Bible Society

Hartmann, W. A. (1986). A note on dangers in hypnosis. Paper presented at the 102nd Annual Meeting of Indiana Academy of Science, Indianapolis, Indiana, November, 1986.

Holy Scriptures. (1952). Philadelphia: Jewish Publication Society.

Jerusalem Bible. (1971). Garden City, NY: Doubleday.

Kris, E. (1952). *Psychoanalytic explorations in art*. New York: International Universities Press.

Kroger, W. S. (1963). *Clinical and experimental hypnosis*. Philadelphia: Lippincott.

Luther, M. (1936). *Die Heilige Schrift. (The Holy Scripture.)* Berlin: Britische und Auslandische Bibelsgesellschaft.

Munro, H. S. (1908). *Suggestive therapeutics, applied hypnotism, and psychic science*. St. Louis: Mosby.

Orne, M. T. (1965). Undesirable effects of hypnosis: The determinants and management. *International Journal of Clinical and Experimental Hypnosis, 13,* 226-227.

Shor, R. E., (1979). The fundamental problem in hypnosis research as viewed from historical perspectives. In E. Fromm and R.E. Shor (Eds.), *Hypnosis: Developments in research and new perspectives*, pp. 14-41. New York: Aldine.

Singer, I. (Ed.). (1904). *The Jewish encyclopedia*. (Vols. 7 and 8). New York: Funk & Wagnalls.

Stevenson, O. (1954). The first treasured possession. *Psychoanalytic Study of the Child, 9,* 199-217.

The Holy Bible. (1935). (King James Version) London: Collins.

The Torah. (1976) Philadelphia: PA: Jewish Publication Society of America.

Wedeck, H. E. (1956). *Treasury of Witchcraft*. New York: Philosophical Library.

Wohlgemut, I. and Bleighrode, I. (Trans.) (1936). *Die Funf Bucher Moses. (The Five Books of Moses.)* J. Frankfurt. M: Lehrberger.

SECTION II:
HOMEWORK, HANDOUTS,
AND ACTIVITIES FOR COUPLES

19

Assertiveness Homework for Couples

A. Peter MacLean

Type of Contribution: Homework/Handout

Objective

In order to help couples master the assertiveness skills they have been learning in session, they are instructed to apply the following A-B-C Model of Assertiveness as homework in role-plays and in vivo situations. These role-plays involve both actual and ideal behaviors. Through the practice of genuinely expressing one's feelings and needs—while recognizing the rights of one's partner—couples learn to resolve disputes in a positive way that facilitates greater intimacy.

Rationale for Use

Greenberg and Johnson (1988) describe the marital relationship as providing "the opportunity for interdependence, the chance to have one's feelings and needs respected, and the opportunity to be the most important person to a significant other. This type of relationship between adults promotes trust, intimacy, disclosure, and the expression of intense feelings" (p. 3). Marital relationships are often complementary in nature (Hendrix, 1988), and this is frequently evident in couples' communication patterns. For example, a nonassertive person in a marriage will often only express frustration to major annoyances whereas an aggressive partner may lack patience and tend to become upset and angry too often. This type of relationship will clearly develop communication problems with respect to having each partner's needs met. One approach to resolving this type of problematic relationship is to adhere to the wise maxim, Aristotle's Golden Mean. That is, find and follow a middle road between the interpersonal extremes of nonassertive and aggressive behavior. That middle road is assertiveness, the expression of one's feelings and needs in an empathic way.

The focus of the present intervention is on helping couples become more assertive with each other. This intervention has effectively been employed in individual as well as group couples therapy.

Instructions

Prior to having clients actually do homework assignments, it is important in assertiveness training that they learn certain fundamental principles of human interactions and, in particular, the language of assertiveness. For example, a basic component of assertiveness training involves teaching clients to differentiate between the three basic types of behavior on the assertiveness continuum: (1) nonassertion (an individual allows others to violate one's rights); (2) assertion (standing up for one's own rights without denying the rights of others); and (3) aggression (lacking empathy and patience, and often infringing on the rights and dignity of others) (Jakubowski and Lange, 1978; Alberti and Emmons, 1982). In addition, clients learn about the eleven "Basic Assertive Rights" that all humans have (see Appendix A; it is given as a handout to each partner as a component of the psychoeducational learning process in couples assertiveness training). They include, for example, the right to be treated with respect, the right to experience and express your feelings, and the right to ask for what you want (Jakubowski and Lange, 1978).

After the basics are learned, it is time for couples to apply these important principles in their interactions. An insightful yet simple model of assertiveness was proposed by Heisler and Shipley (1976), the A-B-C Model of Assertive Behavior. This strategy consists of the following three steps. After being the recipient of an offending behavior by another person, Step A involves briefly telling this individual how you feel using "I . . . " statements (e.g., "I feel embarassed and a bit upset because you were impatient with me just now in front of our friends."). Step B is an empathic statement (and, with friends, is also supportive—see Appendix B) that considers the feelings of the offending individual and enhances the chances that the message being sent will be received (e.g., "I still think you meant well and were probably just in a hurry."). Step C is a request for behavior change in which the individual expresses his/her need that the offending behavior not occur again (e.g., "I need you not to criticize me in front of our friends again in the future. Can you try not to do that?"). (Please refer to Appendix B, a second handout given to clients which provides examples of appropriate [i.e., assertive] and inappropriate [i.e., nonassertive and aggressive] behavior.)

Clinical experience has shown that nonassertive partners need to practice more on the A and C parts of the model (i.e., readily expressing their feelings and needs), whereas aggressive individuals must concentrate more on part B, consciously focusing on seeing their partner's perspective. In addition, a very important concept in all assertiveness work is that of "appropriate assertiveness." This idea is nicely embodied within the A-B-C Model in that respect for others is evident with the inclusion of a focus on empathy.

Before couples apply the ABC model for homework, it is first important that they fully understand and can properly apply it in session with the therapist present to act as a guide. The therapist has the couple role-play a recent frustrating interaction or fight (the "actual" situation, i.e., their usual nonassertive and/or aggressive behavior). After this is completed, they share their reactions to this role-play with each other. Next, the therapist has the couple each identify their respective assertive rights (see Appendix A), and explicitly describe how they should "ideally" act (i.e., assertively) according to the A-B-C Model of Assertive Behavior. This is followed by the couple role-playing their former interaction, but this time in an assertive way following the Heisler and Shipley (1976) model. In addition, videotaping "actual" and "ideal" behavior has proven effective as a learning tool in giving clients immediate feedback on their interactions.

Finally, it is important to discuss with the couple their feelings about how this assertive interaction compares with their earlier nonassertive and/or aggressive role-play. Typically couples will express mixed emotions. That is, although they typically feel pleased with their new style of interacting and report more positive (and fewer negative) emotions toward their partner, they nonetheless express anxiety about the novelty of this new mode of behavior. It is therefore important to state clearly that learning to act assertively is like learning any new skill in that a person must go through two general phases: (1) an initial anxious stage when he/she is trying to integrate unfamiliar ways of behaving assertively, and (2) an automatic phase in which assertive behavior has become a natural way of interacting with others and which only comes with consistent practice. This information is usually helpful in motivating clients to practice the assertiveness skills they have been learning.

Assertiveness homework with couples initially involves having them do more of the role-plays that they have been introduced to in session. For at least one to two weeks, they should include both "actual" and "ideal" role-plays of any negative interactions they experience. This practice will help to reinforce the distinction between the three types of assertive behavior and, as assertiveness becomes more natural, they can decrease the rehearsal of their dysfunctional "actual" behavior. In addition, keeping an ongoing diary of these interactions is strongly encouraged.

For homework, the couple should be encouraged to bring in "success stories" of in vivo situations where they have acted assertively despite initial feelings of anxiety. When assertive behavior is becoming more automatic, the therapist will typically observe greater independence and interdependence in the couple as well as higher levels of trust, intimacy, and expression of intense feelings. Preparations for termination can then begin.

Suggestions for Follow-Up

Perhaps the most important factor necessary for maintaining a couple's gains in acting assertively and avoiding backsliding into old problematic behaviors is for them to adopt a disciplined attitude of tolerating some "short-term pain for long-term gain." That is, this perspective will allow the couple to recognize that, with time and practice, their initial anxiety and awkwardness associated with acting assertively will be replaced with interpersonal confidence and enhanced relationship satisfaction. Clients need to embrace every chance they have to practice being assertive using the A-B-C Model as a guide not only with their partners, but in all of their interpersonal situations. Furthermore, continuing to keep a brief log of assertive interactions is important, especially before these new adaptive behaviors have progressed to the stage of being automatic. This record keeping will help prevent backsliding and will aid the client in identifying ways in which s/he did not act as assertively as a particular situation called for, which should facilitate more assertive behavior in a similar future situation.

In more difficult assertive situations, it is often a good idea beforehand to visualize oneself in the particular interaction acting in an assertive way. In addition, by practicing hypothetical role-plays of upcoming stressful interactions, clients have reported success and greater confidence in their interpersonal ability to act assertively.

Contraindications

Like all types of couples therapy, a commitment to the process of change must be evident in both partners. Thus, the active practice of the A-B-C Model of Assertiveness as a homework tool for enhancing dyadic satisfaction is not likely to be effective unless both partners are committed first to the relationship, and also to personal growth as well as the process of therapeutic change. (This commitment is of particular importance in maintaining the gains made in therapy after the sessions have finished.) A history of partner abuse in the relationship would therefore be a contraindication for this homework activity. In addition, if one partner is psychotic, an active alcoholic, or a drug abuser, these problems should be addressed prior to attempting to facilitate assertive behavior and thus dyadic adjustment. Because of the potential dangers associated with only one spouse learning to be more assertive (e.g., risk of increased wife abuse by an aggressive husband), it is recommended, when possible, that both partners conjointly engage in developing an assertive lifestyle—whether in individual or group couples therapy.

Readings and Resources for the Professional

Alberti, R. E. and Emmons, M. L. (1974/1982). *Your perfect right.* San Luis Obispo, CA: Impact.

Gambrill, E. D. and Richey, C. A. (1975). An assertiveness inventory for use in assessment and research. *Behavior Therapy, 6,* 550-561.

Greenberg, L. S. and Johnson, S. M. (1988). *Emotionally focused therapy for couples.* New York: The Guilford Press.

Heisler, G. and Shipley, R. H. (1976). The ABC Model of Assertive Behavior. *Behavior Therapy, 8,* 509-512.

Hendrix, H. (1988). *Getting the love you want: A guide for couples.* New York: Harper Perennial.

Jakubowski, P. and Lange, A. J. (1978). *The assertive option: Your rights and responsibilities.* Champaign, IL: Research Press Co.

Lange, A. J. and Jakubowski, P. (1976). *Responsible assertive behavior: Cognitive/behavioral procedures for trainers.* Champaign, IL: Research Press Co.

Wolpe, J. (1973). *The practice of behavior therapy.* New York: Pergamon Press.

Bibliotherapy Sources for the Client

Alberti, R. E. and Emmons, M. L. (1974/1982). *Your perfect right.* San Luis Obispo, CA: Impact.

Heisler, G. and Shipley, R. H. (1976). The ABC Model of Assertive Behavior. *Behavior Therapy, 8,* 509-512.

Hendrix, H. (1988). *Getting the love you want: A guide for couples.* New York: Harper Perennial.

Jakubowski, P. and Lange, A. J. (1978). *The assertive option: Your rights and responsibilities.* Champaign, IL: Research Press Co.

Appendix A:
Basic Assertive Rights

As a person, you hold the following rights:

1. The right to act in ways that promote your dignity and self-respect as long as others' rights are not violated in the process
2. The right to be treated with respect
3. The right to say "No" and not feel guilty
4. The right to experience and express your feelings
5. The right to take time to slow down and think
6. The right to change your mind
7. The right to ask for what you want
8. The right to do less than you are humanly capable of doing
9. The right to ask for information
10. The right to make mistakes
11. The right to feel good about yourself

Source: Jakubowski, P. and Lange, A. J. (1978). *The assertive option: Your rights and responsibilities*. Champaign, IL: Research Press Co., 80-81.

Appendix B:
Examples of A-B-C Model

Step A - *Expression of feelings.*

For example, "I feel. . . . (e.g., hurt, offended, angry, etc.) about . . . (identify *specific* behavior that triggered your response)."

Note: This initial statement emphasizes your *current mood*, which is often a response to an offending behavior by another person, as well as the *particular behavior* of the other person that you are reacting to.

Step B - *Statement reflecting empathy for the other person's point of view.*

a) If offender is a *friend* (e.g., your spouse), use (i) and (ii):
i) a warm, *supportive statement* is offered; e.g., "You know I love you" or "I know you mean well"; and
ii) an *empathic statement* is given about the presumed feelings or motivations of the offending person; e.g., "You don't seem to be your usual upbeat self today"; "It looks like you're feeling pressured right now."
b) If offender is a *stranger,* use only an empathic statement (i.e., ii—above), since being supportive would appear presumptive and likely would not be genuine.

Step C - *Request for change in the other person's behavior.*

For example, "I would appreciate if you would stop . . . (identify the offending behavior); Please don't do . . . (offending behavior) again in the future."

Example of Appropriate Assertive Response (Steps A, B, and C) - Partner 2

Partner 1 - is late for lunch because he/she was talking with a colleague at work.

Partner 2 - "I'm upset that you're late for lunch (A). "I know you value your job and are trying to get ahead in your career (B - i and ii). However, I need you to be on time when we set up appointments together (C)."

Note: "I statements" are evident throughout this appropriately assertive response (3 times), and although the listener's point of view is acknowledged (B), the speaker is firm (and specific) about what his/her feelings and needs are (A and C). The probable outcome is that Partner 2's feelings and needs were listened to and will be better met in the future.

Examples of Two Inappropriate Responses - Partner 2

(1) *Nonassertive Response*
Partner 2 suppresses his/her feelings and pretends there is nothing bothering him/her.

Note: Here, Partner 2 is not expressing his/her negative feelings (A) and not asking to be treated with more respect in the future (C). Consequently, the partner's feelings and needs are being placed ahead of his/her own feelings and needs and, in this sense, Partner 2 is being too empathic (B).

(2) *Aggressive Response*
    Partner 2 angrily responds:
      "You're so inconsiderate. You're never on time and couldn't care less about me."

Note: Partner 2 is *overexpressing* his/her feelings and needs (A and C), using "You statements" and therefore is *not* being empathic, i.e., considering that there may be acceptable circumstances that explain Partner 1's lateness (B). The likely result is that Partner 1 will feel hurt and alienated, and could respond in a similarly aggressive way, thus creating even greater emotional distance.

20

Productive Dialoguing with Couples

Susan E. Hutchinson

Type of Contribution: *Activity/Handout*

Objective

This activity is used with couples in session and is continued in the home environment. The objective is to interrupt ineffective dialogue between couples and introduce methods of constructive communication. It also helps the couple clarify important emotional needs of one another, and offers explanations and rationales for behaviors that often provide impetus for conflicts.

Rationale for Use

This activity is beneficial when the primary problem is one of communication. Often couples get "stuck" in miscommunications and misperceptions and cannot proceed toward greater intimacy. Ineffective communication patterns may translate into malintent which exacerbates problems in the relationship. A communications model is indicated when each partner possesses abilities to communicate clearly and rationally, is able to have insight into problems, and is willing/able to listen to the other and attend to emotional needs. Clearly, the couple needs to have well-developed verbal skills. The ability to accurately interpret meta-messages in communication is crucial. The therapist serves as a model of effective communication. The underlying theory is communication-interactive, transactional, with important concepts being metacommunication, "double-bind" communication, and family homeostasis. Emphasis is on improved communication skills/patterns to enhance couple/family functioning.

Instructions

On one 3″ × 5″ card, each partner writes a sentence, phrase, and/or a description of a situation that commonly occurs during negative interactions between the couple. Examples include: "I really dislike it when you use the words 'always' and 'never,'" "I wish you wouldn't criticize me in front of people," or "Whenever we argue, you usually leave the room instead of talking it out." A different sentence, phrase, or situation is written on each card. The therapist requests that the couple write eight 3″ × 5″ cards each. Alternately, the therapist can give the couple sentence lead-in cards to fill in, such as those on the attached handout. These cards are to be completed during the course of one week in preparation for the first session using the cards. The couple brings these cards to the session; and the activity begins.

Each partner holds her/his cards and the therapist asks the couple to prioritize the cards in order of most distressing to least distressing. After ordering, one partner initiates the discussion by reading her/his most distressing card. The individual (talking partner) reads what is printed on the card and stops talking. The other partner (listening partner) has an opportunity to comment. Following these comments, the talking partner explains how she/he would prefer her partner to respond. Desired responses may be actions and/or words. At that point, there is another opportunity for the listening partner to respond. There may be discussion by the couple and the therapist, with suggestions/comments regarding improved responses. After discussion, in which the talking partner clarifies how she/he wishes the other partner to respond, the listening partner agrees to a change (or discussion continues), and the talking partner writes the preferred action/verbal response on the other side of the 3″ × 5″ card. The roles are then switched, and the first listening partner speaks from one of her/his cards. The process is repeated until all cards are discussed. Appropriate responses are agreed upon by the couple and are noted in writing on the reverse sides of the cards. The couple keeps these cards at home for easy reference when such instances occur, and respond according to that which is written on the card. Example:

> *Wife reads the following from one of her cards:* "I hate it when you are on the phone with your mother and you end up telling her some important news before you tell me."
>
> *Husband:* "I don't mean to do that, but sometimes it just happens. I always tell you anyway; so it's no big deal."
>
> *Wife:* "Well, it is to me, because when you do that, it makes me feel as if you want to share more with you mother than with me, or that it's more important that you inform her about stuff before me."
>
> *Husband:* "No! That's not it at all. In fact, I usually tell you first, but sometimes my mother happens to call before I've had a chance to tell you, that's all."
>
> *Wife:* "I understand you may not plan it that way, but it hurts me when it happens and I wish you'd be sure to tell me stuff first."
>
> *Husband:* "Do you mean I have to tell you *everything* first?"
>
> *Wife:* "At least the important things."
>
> *Husband:* "Yeah, but how do I know what you consider important?"
>
> *Wife:* "You know, things that have to do with our family. I want to be informed first."

Similar clarification may continue until the husband understands his wife's issue clearly. At that point, the wife writes the desired behavior on the reverse side of her card.

A second example includes the husband reading from one of his cards:

> *Husband:* "It really puts me off when you say 'Honey, I need to talk to you'."
>
> *Wife:* "Why?"
>
> *Husband:* "Because I get scared that it means we are going to argue."
>
> *Wife:* "I'm just trying to get your attention so we can have a discussion."
>
> *Husband:* "Well, could you wait until we have had a chance to relax and have dinner?"
>
> *Wife:* "Yes."
>
> *Husband:* "Then, I wish you'd say something like, 'Honey, do you have about thirty minutes to talk with me about something my boss told me at work today?' You know, like give me a time frame and let me know right away what this is about, so I feel less anxious."

After such discussion, the husband writes on the back of his card an example of how they both agreed the wife would initiate requests for "talks."

Rationale for this activity includes gaining awareness by the couple of behavioral and verbal interactions that may appear negative, troublesome, or destructive to the relationship. This activity also allows for a good deal of specifics, so that it is clear what each partner prefers. An explanation of how/why a particular statement or behavior is problematic is ascertained by the couple, thus improving mutual understanding of wants, needs, and intentions. The activity interrupts nonproductive patterns of communication and minimizes misunderstandings which, if not clarified, lead to resentment and distrust.

Suggestions for Follow-Up

The couple takes the cards home and practices with them until the desired responses become routine. Additional cards are composed on an ongoing basis, as issues arise. The cards are discussed for the first time in the presence of the therapist, to provide opportunities for mediation between the couple if disagreements occur regarding contentions and/or desired responses. Changes in responses are processed with the couple during each therapy session. Communication patterns often reveal traditional gender role assignments that may prove detrimental to the couple's functioning. The therapist must take note of role inequities and begin work with the couple regarding awareness of such expectations.

Contraindications

The communication model is not effective with couples who lack negotiating skills or adequate verbal skills. Each partner needs to be cognitively oriented, realistic, and evidence the ability and willingness to follow through with the use of the cards in the home setting when appropriate.

Suggested Readings and Resources for the Professional

Nelson, J. C. (1986). Communication theory and social work treatment. In F. J. Turner (Ed.), *Social work treatment: Interlocking theoretical approaches* (Third Edition). (pp. 219-244). New York: The Free Press.

Watzlawick, P., Beavin, J., and Jackson, D. (1967). *The pragmatics of human communication.* New York: Norton.

Bibliotherapy Sources for the Client

Coates, J. (1986). *Women, men, and language.* London: Longman.

Tannen, D. (1986). *That's not what I meant!* New York: William Morrow.

Tannen, D. (1990). *You just don't understand.* New York: William Morrow.

Productive Dialoguing Cards

I really dislike it when . . .	What bothers me most is . . .
I wish you would stop . . .	Whenever we argue, it hurts me when you . . .
When I need to talk, I often feel unable to because . . .	I really get anxious when . . .
It frustrates me when . . .	One thing I need more of from you is . . .
One thing I really resent is . . .	I get very angry when you . . .
I wish you would . . .	What do you mean when you say/ request that I . . .
Sometimes I have a problem . . .	The most difficult thing for me to say is . . .

At times, I have trouble expressing my feelings because . . .	If I could request one change in our communication, it would be . . .
The biggest fear I have when I talk to you is . . .	The most hurtful thing to me is . . .
I am afraid our fights will turn out like . . .	One thing I need to change is . . .
I want us to work on . . .	I think we need to improve our . . .

21

Constructive Communication

Lorna L. Hecker

Type of Contribution: *Activity/Handout*

Objective

The objective of this activity and handout is to aid the therapist in educating clients about basic constructive communication skills.

Rationale for Use

This activity can be used with individuals or couples, and can also be modified for use with families to facilitate positive communication.

Instructions

The therapist can use this activity with couples, individuals, or families to teach communication skills. The therapist first educates the family about effective and constructive communication. The brief lecture on communication can begin with:

> Let's suppose I have a fight with my husband, and during the heat of the argument, I put my fist through the wall. Do you think that he gets the point that I am mad? Yes, he does, so the communication is *effective*, it gets my point across. But is it *constructive*? That is, do you think this type of communication is good for the relationship? No, not really. So there are two parts to communication—getting your point across, but doing it in a way that is good for your relationship. So we want to learn to communicate in a way that is both effective and constructive.

The therapist then asks clients if they are interested in learning new ways to communicate. If they are, move on to a lesson on how to communicate in "I statements." This can be introduced in the following way:

> When we are learning new ways to communicate, it is sometimes useful to have a template to learn how to communicate differently. Often we communicate in a blaming way or in a way where we end up feeling not listened to by others. "I statements" can be useful in learning a new way to communicate with others. "I statements" are when you state your feelings, and describe the behavior the other person is doing that you would

like to see change (or do more of). "I statements" can be awkward to learn, just as it is awkward to learn to ride a bicycle for the first time. But this type of new communication can become comfortable once you practice it a bit. In addition, just to warn you, when people are in conflict, if you can pull yourself out of an argument one out of ten times to try something new or different, that is pretty good. It is very difficult to try new communication during arguments, so you may want to start using "I statements" when you are not upset or angry, and later build up to their use during conflict.

The attached handout on "I statements" is given to clients to keep so they can see the structure of an "I statement" on a daily basis. Clients who are part of a couple or family are then instructed to practice "I statements" in session; individual clients can role-play "I statements" with the therapist. The therapist then structures the clients to begin the use of "I statements" while at the same time teaching the client's partner or family members in how to respond to "I statements." This structuring in session is very important to clients using this procedure correctly outside of session. Clients often make "you statements" and have difficulty asking for what they want instead of the problematic behavior. The therapist acts as a coach in this process. This coaching, for example with a couple, may go something like this:

Therapist: Bob, I want you to practice an "I statement" with Keisha. Think of what it is you would like to communicate.

    Bob: "OK. Keisha, you really make me angry when . . ."

Therapist: "No, try again. 'I feel angry when . . .' "

    Bob: "Oh, Keisha, I feel angry when you show up late for dinner."

Therapist: "Good, now let's go to the second part of the I statement what would you like instead? Fill in the sentence, 'and I would like . . .' "

    Bob: "And I would like you to be more timely when showing up for dinner."

  Keisha: "But I can't help it! I just lose track of time at work."

Therapist: "No, Keisha, I want you to repeat what you heard Bob say."

  Keisha: "OK, he said he's upset when I am late to dinner."

Therapist: "And what would he like instead?"

  Keisha: "For me to show up on time."

Therapist: "Bob, did Keisha hear you correctly? Is that what you said?"

    Bob: "Yeah, that's it."

The therapist's job is to help keep the communication constructive by blocking negative interactions, and keep the clients on task to stating and listening to "I statements." Often, people have difficulty identifying their feelings; thus, a feeling chart is provided below as a handout.

Additional instructions to clients regarding constructive communication can also be added in the therapy session such as:

- Clearly, name the issue that's bothering you. What specific behavior would you like to see changed?
- Choose a good time for communication to be received.
- Assume a win/win stance, rather than a win/lose stance.
- Call "time-out" if communication becomes destructive.
- Actively listen to the other person.
- Check back on your request to be sure the other person heard you correctly.

Suggestions for Follow-Up

The therapist should assign the clients to practice "I statements," and report back to the therapist the successes and problem areas with the assignment. As suggested, "I statements" are more difficult to use in conflict and clients may need help from the therapist to role-play appropriate, constructive communication.

Contraindications

This activity is contraindicated for highly conflictual couples. Conflict needs to be diffused prior to the application of educational assignments in order for them to be effective.

Readings and Resources for the Professional

Hanna, S. B. (1995). *Person to person: Positive relationships don't just happen.* Englewood Cliffs, NJ: Prentice-Hall.

Bibliotherapy Sources for the Client

Smith, M. (1985). *When I say no, I feel guilty.* Toronto: Bantam.
Tannen, D. (1986). *That's not what I meant! How conversational style makes or breaks your relations with others.* New York: William Morrow & Co.

"I" Statements

"I" Statements . . . .

I feel (<u>emotion</u>) when (<u>behavior</u>)

and I would like (<u>behavioral request</u>).

Examples:

I feel (irritated) when (socks are left on the floor), and I would like you to pick up yours socks each day.

or

I feel (glad) when (I see you have taken the trash out), and I would like (to thank you).

104

Feeling Words

What is a feeling? Examples of feeling words . . .

afraid	delighted	grouchy
aggressive	demure	happy
angry	determined	hurt
anguished	despondent	idiotic
curious	disapproving	indifferent
anxious	disappointed	insecure
blah	distressed	joyful
blissful	ecstatic	mad
blue	enraged	pained
bored	envious	perplexed
calm	exasperated	proud
cautious	exhausted	regretful
concentrating	fearful	relaxed
confident	frightened	sad
confused	frustrated	satisfied
crushed	grief-stricken	secure

shocked
shy
suspicious
threatened
tranquil
undecided
wonderful

22

The Tug-of-War

Sharon A. Deacon

Type of Contribution: *Activity*

Objective

The objective of this activity is to help clients examine the various aspects of the problems they bring to therapy, weigh the alternatives, and find a solution to a decision which prompts an internal tug-of-war for the client.

Rationale for Use

This activity is helpful for clients who are having trouble making a decision, or are caught in between various alternatives. Many times clients have difficulty balancing two opposing messages inside themselves. One side says "Do this," and the other side says "No, don't, because. . . . " Clients often have various solutions available to them, but find disadvantages to each choice. This activity helps clients to see all of their options, and how to get around the hindrances that prevent them from choosing any of the solutions.

Instructions

The first step is defining the problem as concretely and specifically as possible. Next, ask the client to draw an outline of him/herself in the middle of a piece of paper. On the top of the paper, instruct the client to write the problem. On the left side of the paper, the client is to list all the possible solutions to the problem (silly and nonsensical ideas are okay, too). On the right side of the paper, the client is to list the disadvantages, or reasons why each solution is unacceptable. Then, tell the client to draw a line, through the body outline, connecting the solution with the disadvantage. The client now has multiple tugs-of-war happening.

Ask the client how it feels to be tangled up in all of these battles. Note to the client that it is difficult to even see the person through all the lines. Discuss feelings of being trapped, behind a hurdle, unable to cut loose.

Now, ask the client to list the various ways that tugs-of-war are ended. Include such ideas as: one side wins, a stalemate, someone cuts the rope, one side give-up or collapses from exhaustion, one side adds more players, or time runs out. Then, strategically apply such solutions to the tugs-of-war going on inside the person.

Some examples are listed to illustrate solutions:

- A child who is afraid to talk to his teacher about his failing grade (left side) because of fear and embarrassment (right side) may choose to add more members (solution) by asking his parents to come along and talk to the teacher with him.

- A woman who is afraid to tell her husband that she lost her job (left side) because he may be angry (right side) may choose to cut the rope (solution) by finding a new job first.
- A man who regrets having an affair (left side) may be afraid to tell his partner because she may leave him (right side), thus he chooses a stalemate (solution) by deciding to not tell her and never do it again.
- A couple who is angry about their child's choice of friends may want to forbid the child to see these friends (left side), but are afraid that the child will rebel, and that they will destroy the trust that exists (right side). They choose to give up the battle (solution) by choosing another alternative on the list.

As each connecting rope breaks, the client can symbolically erase (or put a slash through) the tug-of-war, ending an inside battle. In the end, the client is left with a solution that is the least objectionable, or a few solutions that can be carried out together.

Suggestions for Follow-Up

Once the client has decided on a solution, the therapist may need to help the client iron out any remaining details. It is also important to reinforce the client's creative problem-solving abilities. The therapist should monitor the client's implementation of the solution, and be ready to help the client accept any of the consequences that may result.

Contraindications

Although this activity may be somewhat frustrating with clients who "yes, but" solutions, it can be effective if both parties continue working at it. There is a whole side of the paper the client can devote to the "buts. . . ." This activity may not be helpful for clients who are in crisis situations, and are unable to think clearly and make decisions for themselves. Clients who have difficulty thinking abstractly or hypothetically may not be very successful with this activity.

23

The 80/20 Principle in Marital Therapy

Paul A. Lee

Type of Contribution: *Activity/Handout*

Objective

The purpose of the activity is to motivate clients to take personal responsibility for making progress in their marital relationship by improving their attitudes, beliefs, expectations, and behavior. Clients in the following scenarios may find this intervention useful:

1. A client who feels trapped, helpless, and powerless to change an unsatisfactory relationship
2. A client who has tended to interact with his/her spouse in a reactive mode
3. A client with low self-esteem and low internal locus of control
4. A client whose spouse refuses to enter therapy

Rationale for Use

It is important to begin therapy with the belief that clients can change the quality of their marital relationship by improving their attitudes, beliefs, expectations, and behavior, thereby changing the quality of their marital relationship. Most problems can be solved. Dysfunctional relationships can be improved. The 80/20 principle is a strategy for understanding problematic marital relationships and helping a client take responsibility for making changes and improving his/her relationship.

The 80/20 principle, sometimes referred to as "Pareto's Law," is attributed to Vilfredo Pareto, a nineteenth century Italian economist. The principle states that in a large number of items, 80 percent of the value of the items is in 20 percent or less of the items. For example, 80 percent of a teacher's problems will be caused by 20 percent of the students. Or, in therapy, 80 percent of the therapist's success is likely to come from 20 percent or less of the therapist's efforts.

Clients are amazed when they learn how much control they have over their own behavior and feelings. Often, there is a mistaken belief a client has very little control because of the "inappropriate" behavior of his/her spouse. I suggest that it appears the 80/20 principle is working in marriage and unfortunately, the couple's using it to work against themselves.

In problematic marital relationships, the 80/20 principle works as follows:

1. Spouses assume that 80 percent of their behavior (verbal, emotional, etc.) is "caused/determined" by the uncooperative partner. This leaves only 20 percent of their behavior

under their control. Thus, they feel the way they do (depressed, angry, etc.) and react the way they do because of the uncooperative spouse's inappropriate behavior.

2. Each spouse assumes that 80 percent of his/her marital bliss will come from the other. This leaves each spouse responsible for only 20 percent of his/her own satisfaction. (Both beliefs are examples of linear, nonsystemic thinking.)

Instructions

The therapist suggests to clients that their math is correct (20% + 80% = 100%). What is needed is to reverse the percentages and use the formula to work in their favor instead of letting it work against them: Determine to take responsibility for consciously choosing 80 percent of their behavior themselves (verbal, nonverbal, emotional) and allow their spouse to influence only 20 percent of their behavior.

Therapeutic Purposes

1. This activity helps clients to get out of the "blame game." Clients are unlikely to make significant changes in their marital relationship as long as they blame their spouse for their unhappiness and how they are feeling and behaving.

2. The activity empowers the client to get out of the role of "victim." Victimhood is always disempowering. A victim is saying "someone has done or is doing something bad to me and I can not change it." As a nonvictim and more active participant, clients begin to change themselves and their relationships.

3. It encourages clients to live more consciously and responsibly in all of their life roles and responsibilities. Clients who tend to live reactively in their spousal relationship are usually hoping that their spouse will take care of them, i.e., make them happy. A major tenet of adulthood and maturity is that each person is responsible for self and how satisfied or happy one is going to be with life. Will Rogers was right when he said that each person is about as happy as they decide they want to be.

4. Clients understand that they are primarily responsible for the quality of their marital relationship and their level of marital happiness and life satisfaction. What goes on within the client or "between the client's ears" is far more important than the spouse's behavior. Clients' attitudes, beliefs, expectations, self-image, developmental level, personal life orientation, and previous experiences may be far more important in determining their marital satisfaction than their spouse's behavior. In fact, clients' attitudes, expectations, etc., will determine how their spouses' behavior is perceived and interpreted.

5. Clients are more in control. By taking greater responsibility for all of life, clients begin to take greater responsibility for their marital relationship. As they begin to change, grow, and become increasingly differentiated personally, they influence/change the quality of their marital relationship. Or, in a worst case scenario, they will at least change how their relationship is perceived and can take responsibility for staying in or leaving a problematic relationship.

Assumptions

1. I cannot change my spouse's behavior unless she/he is willing to change.
2. My spouse cannot cause/determine my behavior, feelings, etc., unless I permit it.

3. I can choose/control/change my behavior, feelings, etc.
4. I cannot be solely responsible for my marital relationship but, I can have a major influence on my relationship by focusing on my own behavior, attitudes, expectations, etc.
5. As I change my behavior and attitudes, my marital relationship (marital system) changes.

Contraindications for Use

1. If a client is in an abusive relationship, the top priority should be to end the abuse. If necessary, this may mean that the client has to take responsibility for leaving the relationship.
2. This activity is less helpful with clients who are taking an appropriate level of responsibility for their relationships, but need help in skill development; e.g., improving communication or conflict resolution.

Readings and Resources for the Professional and the Client

Beavers, W. R. (1985). *Successful marriage: A family systems approach to couples therapy.* New York: W. W. Norton.

Branden, N. (1996). *Taking responsibility: Self-reliance and the accountable life.* New York: Simon & Schuster.

McGinnis, A. L. (1990). *The power of optimism.* San Francisco: Harper & Row.

Nelson-Jones, R. (1984). *Personal responsibility counseling and therapy: An integrative approach.* San Francisco: Harper & Row.

Seligman, M. E. P. (1990). *Learned optimism: How to change your mind and your life.* New York: Pocket Books.

THE 80/20 PRINCIPLE IN MARITAL RELATIONSHIPS, MARITAL QUALITY, AND SATISFACTION

Problematic Relationship

80%	Your Spouse's Behavior, Attitudes, Beliefs, Communication, etc.
20%	Your Own Negative Attitudes Belief's, Expecations, Self-Image, Developmental Level, Personal Life Orientation, Previous Experiences.

Healthy Relationship

80%	Your Own Positive/Optimistic Attitudes, Beliefs, Behavior, Expectations, Self-Image, Developmental Level, Personal Life Orientation, Previous Experiences
20%	Your Spouse's Behavior, Attitudes, Beliefs, Communication, etc.

24

A Couple's Ordeal of Sorrow

Wesley B. Crenshaw
Kimberly A. Cain

Type of Contribution: *Homework/Activity*

Objective

This homework assignment is used when a couple presents with severe relational dysfunction stemming from the wife's unfortunate history with men. This typically includes childhood abuse or abandonment by the primary male attachment figure, and at least one romantic relationship in which abuse or infidelity occurred. What makes this a unique moment in the life of the woman, and this technique possible, is that she has become involved with a caring and functional man. Unfortunately, with a lifetime of bad history with men, the wife has become conditioned to problematic response sets which may include unprovoked physical assault, unsupported accusations of infidelity, aversion to sexual contact *after* marriage, juxtaposed with sexual promiscuity before, and so on. The objective of this activity is to reignite a husband's compassion and empathy for his wife's difficult past while reorienting the wife toward the comparative benevolence of her husband. From a theoretical standpoint, the activity is based on Jay Haley's (1984) "ordeal therapy." Rooted in the work of Milton Erickson, Haley's approach placed an unusual spin on traditional behaviorism by offering the client a consequence so aversive that he or she would surrender the symptom to avoid it.

The approach might also work with couples in which the man has had successive bad relationships, but the authors are only familiar with the gender assignments portrayed herein. Further, since the intervention relies heavily upon cultural stereotypes typical to such cases, it might not work "in reverse," that is, with a rescuing wife and victimized husband, nor has it been tested in such cases. For convenience, from herein, the couple will be referred to as if they are married, though the strategy works equally well with unmarried couples.

Rationale for Use

In the tradition of Chauvin, husbands in such cases tend to be "rescuers." The relationships often begin around a theme of the "strong man" protecting an afflicted and abused woman—sometimes even helping her leave the abuser's home. But once he has secured the woman's fate, the White Knight finds the tables turned, as maladaptive learnings from her previous relationships reemerge. He presents as bewildered and frustrated by forces outside his control, and feels blamed for his wife's anger and resentment, when he thought he was the one man in her life who was kindly and caring. In worst cases, the husband actually begins to assume negative behaviors reminiscent of the wife's past relationships, thus completing a self-fulfilling prophecy, and forcing the couple to the edge of separation, and into therapy.

Instructions

1. The therapist queries the husband's knowledge of the wife's history with men and the extent to which she is willing to share it. Some wives have discussed extensively their past mistreatment, while others have disclosed very little.

2. The therapist expresses compassion and empathy for the woman, and notes the tragedy of growing up with poor male role models and/or living in abusive relationships. This show of empathy is itself important in depathologizing the woman and increasing her husband's sense of compassion. The therapist openly hypothesizes that childhood experiences of abuse or abandonment have made it difficult for the woman to choose good romantic partners *in the past*. This is then contrasted with her selection of the current husband who is framed as a comparatively good influence.

3. The therapist asks the husband if he has ever thought about *why* the things men have done to his wife are so wrong. The husband will usually make a fairly generic response, noting that people should not treat one another this way, that boys are taught from a young age not to hit girls, that sex abuse is perverse, that marital vows are sacred, and so on. The therapist ratifies each of these ideas, and goes on to note that such acts were wrong because they hurt the woman's heart. The therapist suggests that in our society, men are supposed to treat women with respect and dignity, and that when they choose to physically, sexually, or emotionally abuse a woman, it damages her spiritually. She is then left to recover without the aid of a strong and caring man to serve as a father, partner, or friend. Be careful to fit this idea into the client's own sense of spirituality and gender roles. In very traditional families, the husband's role is to take care of the wife. In very religious homes, proper treatment of women is required by the Bible, Koran, Torah, etc. In more feminist homes, women and men (girls and fathers.) are supposed to have a spiritual partnership, and such mistreatment violates the implicit agreement between them for this type of partnership.

4. The therapist asks how the husband has tried to help the wife deal with her past. A variety of behaviors may be reported from listening to her troubles to fighting her perpetrator(s). The therapist expresses concern if these attempts are unfortunate (e.g., violent or illegal), but shows empathy for each failed effort. Metaphors of positive rescuing may be suggested consistent with the image of a White Knight rescuing a woman in need. Though a remarkably sexist cliché, such couples often like this metaphor a great deal and find it quite reflective of their own experience. Consistent with the strategic approach, the therapist uses the energy of the couple in supporting such questionable myths to move beyond them.

5. The therapist suggests the possibility that the husband must find other, more powerful ways to show the wife how men conduct themselves with "dignity and honor." The therapist asks the husband if he is willing to do whatever it takes to help his wife become released from her terrible past. This "blind" acceptance is a critical step in any ordeal, and requires that the therapist have a very good rapport with the husband as well as his trust (Haley, 1984). To set the client at ease, the therapist may explain that the assignment will not be illegal, immoral, expensive, or time consuming—but neither will it be easy.

6. The therapist sets a trigger for the intervention, which may occur every time the husband is threatened, attacked, interrogated as to his fidelity, and so on. When there are no natural triggers, just a nebulous dissatisfaction with the relationship, the wife may be asked to discuss with the husband at some given interval one terrible thing a man has done to her in the past. However, this is a much less desirable option, as it creates a quid pro quo contract which is not naturalistic and thus, easily thwarted.

7. The therapist asks that at every trigger point in the coming week, the husband apologize to the wife sincerely and honestly *on behalf of all men.* It is vital that the husband understand he is apologizing *for what others have done.* If there are things in his own past for which he should apologize, then that should be undertaken separately, prior to this intervention. This directive will usually evoke resistance, which nearly always comes from the wife. This is actually a very good sign, as it suggests that the activity will work as an ordeal. The therapist insists on the importance of the husband's apology as a way to heal the past, and notes that he bears a kind of collective shame for what other men have done to the woman.

8. The couple is asked to practice the directive in session, allowing the therapist to see how well the couple understands the activity, and to observe its outcome.

CASE STUDY

The following transcript illustrates the approach in a case in which the wife was quite verbally abusive to the husband, accused him of infidelity, and used sexual relations as a tool of manipulation. The session was conducted by Ms. Cain and supervised by Dr. Crenshaw behind the one-way mirror. While the intervention did not "solve" the case, it did elevate the therapeutic dialog, engage an uncontrollable couple, calm and empower the husband, and gently encourage the wife to deal with the sex abuse issues that permeated her life. It also led the husband to reveal and apologize for his own misbehavior.

Ms. Cain: Sarah, tell me in about two sentences how you feel men have treated you.

Sarah: Like shit! How about two words? Like shit.

Ms. Cain: Ron, when you hear your wife say that, how do you feel?

Ron: I feel like I'm takin' the rap for those sons of bitches.

Ms. Cain: But how do you feel? I understand that's kind of frustrating for you. How does it feel to know that your wife has been hurt the way she has by other men?

Ron: It makes me feel sad for her. It makes me want to help her get over her demons so she can live a happier life, you know . . . and not have to worry about that kind of stuff all the time. Let it go or whatever she needs to do to be a happier person.

Sarah: I have to have a good example first. You're that man. I chose you. I put stock in you.

Ms. Cain: And you still have some stock in Ron, huh?

Sarah: Yeah, but I got slapped upside the head with it too. . . . I just thought you'd be that one.

Ron: Well, dear, I'm not the *perfect* one.

Sarah: God, there's not a perfect person in the world.

Ms. Cain: She's not really asking for that. Actually, you're a pretty good guy.

Sarah: Yeah, I'm not gonna fight that, believe me. I just felt like you'd be the person to understand me and try to meet me halfway. . . . You know, I wasn't born hating men. I was born innocent just like everybody else. The things that you go through teach you that.

Ms. Cain: Ron, you're kinda lucky. She picked one man in this world to trust and that's you. And thank God for that, 'cause you're a great guy and you can help her. Part of your problem is that you didn't really know how, and now we're going to help you figure out what Sarah really needs. You're gonna be her knight in shining armor.

Sarah: (laughs) Oh wow, are you gonna come ride up on a big white horse!?

Ron: But you've got to let me in the door, dear!

Sarah: You know that's hard for me. I can't help that the door has slammed down a lot. It was wide open for you to take advantage . . . and you didn't. Now you want to open it, and yeah, it's hard for me to let you in 'cause once I get hurt, I don't let people do it to me again.

Ms. Cain: Ron, what do you know about the extent to which other men have hurt Sarah?

Ron: I don't know . . . her dad leavin' her when she was six months old . . . and then her mom married a drunk that molested her.

Sarah: For all the right reasons! She didn't marry him knowing that was going to happen! You know, I can't differentiate between that either, because I protect my mother in many ways, and to a certain point, my stepdad. I won't let Ron hate my stepdad, 'cause he didn't do nothin' to Ron. (turns to Ron) So I can't deal with you and your feelings toward him or the decisions my mom made; I'll stand behind them.

Ms. Cain: What Ron needs to understand is the *extent* to which it hurt you. Can you tell him about the extent? We're not talking about the situation or the people, but what the pain was like. What did losing your dad and being molested do to your heart?

Sarah: It broke it. But I need to solve that on my own—Ron doesn't need to know about it. I mean, he wants to go with me. I can't deal with that on top of things I need to get off my chest.

Ms. Cain: We can't really get into that right now. Let's just talk about the hurt.

Sarah: Growing up without a dad or somebody that you feel loves you unconditionally. Maybe that's where the hurt came from.

Ms. Cain: (to Ron) You know, this whole situation kind of gets hard and confusing because Sarah has, in a way, been set up by other men. She has been hurt and you know, Ron, that holds you somewhat responsible to help your wife get over some of the pain that she feels. Would you be willing to help her do that . . . to do whatever it takes? It's not going to be easy.

Ron: Help her get over the pain? Yes, I want to do that. I mean, that's my goal.

Ms. Cain: So that's something that you would really be dedicated to and would take very seriously? (Ron nods). Sarah would you be willing to tell Ron one thing per day about what other men have done to hurt you?

Sarah: I do, don't I? When he tells me I hate men, I tell him why. Now, wait. Are we going to get to the sexual abuse thing? 'Cause I'm not getting into that. He can't go there.

Ms. Cain: No I'm not asking about that. I'm going to have you do something Sarah, and in doing it, I want you to focus on *other men,* because it's easy for you to revert to Ron and say "*you* do that and *you* do this"—in this exercise, its your job is to say what *other* men did to you. It can be any other men in your life. Once a day, I want you to tell him something, from now until the next time you guys come back. And at that time, Ron, I want you to apologize for what they've done to hurt your wife. I want you to apologize for what *other men* have done. I want to apologize on behalf of all those men—and I want it to be sincere.

Ron: Any way I want to?

Ms. Cain: Any way you want to put it, as long as it is sincere.

Ron: Can you give me an example?

Ms. Cain role plays the apology very nicely. So effective is the intervention, that Sarah actually becomes emotional—almost imagining Ms. Cain to be a good substitute for the real perpetrator. Using a nice Ericksonian induction, Ms. Cain continues:

Ms. Cain: Maybe it's a good thing to do this whenever you feel comfortable, maybe you'd want to set a time in the morning and you'll spend twenty minutes talking about the one thing that other men have done to hurt you.

Sarah: (smiles) You got into an awful lot when you married me didn't you? You poor thing.

Ron: I don't think that.

Ms. Cain: Ron, you're bearing a symbol. You are a man in all of this. You are bearing the responsibility for other men and the pain that they have caused, and you are doing it in a way this time that you can help Sarah get over it. You are apologizing for what they've done to hurt her. I know you hurt inside because of the way that they've treated her and you have an opportunity to talk about that now and apologize for them. I want you to try once before we leave, so it's not confusing. I want you to practice looking at your wife and making an apology for what other men have done. Its kind of hard, I know, but you can do it. I have a lot of faith in you or I wouldn't make you go through this . . . 'cause it's serious. Take her hand and tell her.

Ron: Sarah, I apologize for the way men have been to you and the wrong things they've done. I don't want to be in that group. I want to be there for you. I don't want you to ever be hurt like that again by any man—including me.

Sarah: I don't want to be hurt either . . . 'cause it sucks. (turns to Ms. Cain) Oh! You know what?!, I forgot to tell you. I went to go to work this morning, and he'd used sidewalk chalk to put this big old heart on the driveway and it said "Be my Valentine!"

Ms. Cain: Oh my gosh! So he's improving. That's great.

Contraindications

It is vital that this intervention be used only when the therapist is convinced that the husband is a benevolent man. To determine this, the therapist must query him in private as to his feelings for the wife, whether he is considering having affairs, whether he has ever committed physical violence or infidelity against any woman, and whether he has problems with substance abuse. If any of these variables are present, this approach *may* be contraindicated. On the other hand, it can be used successfully when the husband's poor conduct is in the distant past and unrelated to the present marriage. Further, the intervention actually tends to direct the husband toward his own apology for wrongful acts, even when these have not come out before, so it may serve a specific function even when the husband has been improper at times.

Conclusion

The intervention works on two levels. Given her history, the afflicted woman has a right to be angry at men. By taking on the shame of her abuse, the husband has shown her an act of courage and commitment and offered to bear some of the burden with her. A man who is willing to apologize on behalf of people he despises, in order to alleviate the pain of a woman, is fulfilling a romantic notion of honor and dignity that usually lies at the core of such relationships. The intervention also works at a more subtle level—that of the ordeal. When the wife attacks, ignores, or accuses her husband of infidelity, she is *implicitly* blaming him for things he did not do. The ordeal of apology and sorrow makes this blame explicit by asking the husband to take responsibility for the shameful treatment of his wife—even as he has been her primary male supporter. The usual result is that the wife realizes her husband is not to blame for her pain and that she should separate his actions from those of other men. In this way, the explicit ordeal becomes aversive to the woman, and she surrenders the implicit blame in order to end it. This is illustrated in the case study when the wife suddenly mentions the "chalk heart," having never before acknowledged any efforts on the part of the husband. This sudden turn of events is predictable, as the wife desperately tries to rescue the husband from the therapeutic ordeal, and in doing so, finally ratifies his attempts to care for her.

Generally, the therapist restrains quick change, suggesting that the couple continue the task for a few weeks to help the woman become fully released from her past. Of course, the therapist continues working with the clients to improve other aspects of the marriage—something which is easier once the anger and tension has been dissipated.

Resources and Readings for the Professional

Haley, J. (1984). *Ordeal therapy.* San Francisco: Jossey-Bass.
Madanes, C. (1990). *Sex, love, and violence.* New York: Norton.
Madanes, C. (1995). *The violence of men.* San Francisco: Jossey-Bass.

25

The Use of Controlled Punishment and Ritual in Couples Therapy

Barbara J. Lynch

Type of Contribution: *Activity*

Objective

Couples who come into therapy with amorphous symptoms often reveal later in treatment that there has been a traumatic event that occurred in the past and that has lingered as a significant disturbance to intimacy. No amount of "talk therapy" or insight seems to allow these couples to move past the point of emotional treachery. This activity is designed to allow these couples a vehicle for putting the past to rest in a way that allows them to continue their relationship without resentment, revenge, or continual pain.

Rationale for Use

There is an almost natural tendency to desire a commensurate retaliation for an injury inflicted on the person by another. The injury has the potential for greater harm when it is committed by an intimate partner in the context of a significant relationship. Therefore it follows that the grievance merits greater reprisal under these conditions. It appears that the "eye-for-an-eye" principle is in full operation in couple systems. However, when this dynamic is left in the hands of the couple alone, there is a tendency for one partner to avenge the hurt out of proportion to the initial act. There is no "getting-even"; instead it appears that paying off the old score means hurting the partner more than the individual has been hurt; "just desserts" is interpreted as inflicting more pain than was given. When this dynamic comes under the control of the therapist who makes the covert need for vengeance a function of just consequences for hurtful behavior, the original act can be managed in such a manner that closure is realized, and the couple can proceed with their relationship unencumbered.

Instructions

The use of this technique is both sensitive and serious. A thorough exploration of the initial act is required prior to encouraging the couple to devise an appropriate punishment or ritual. Drawing from numerous couples seen in private practices and at the Family Clinic at Southern Connecticut State University, it seems as if the two major acts that couples seem to believe merit revenge are extramarital affairs and abortions instituted as a means of birth control within the couple system. Both acts, when viewed as a betrayal, are ones that contaminate a couple system to the degree that, when left unattended, can result in an impasse or the (unnecessary) end of the relationship.

In the case of abortion, it is usually an act that at the time it was decided, was a mutual decision, validly made, and contextually appropriate. It is only in the aftermath of the act, often far into the future that the full effect of the act is experienced as a "punishable crime." An example illustrates this.

Doris and Jack, both in their early thirties, had been married eight years. Doris was four months pregnant with their first child. The couple had entered therapy because Doris' obstetrician was concerned because she appeared to be depressed and was considering divorce. In response to an inquiry about problems between the couple, Jack replied first saying, "I don't know what's bothering her. I thought everything was fine. We moved into our dream house last year, business is doing well, we're going to have our first baby. I don't know what's going on." At that point, he turned to his wife. "Please tell me what's wrong," he pleaded. "Whatever it is, I'll fix it. I love you. I want us to be married forever."

In response, Doris turned to him, "You can't fix it. I just don't want to be married to you anymore!"

"Why?" he asked passionately, "Give me a reason, any reason. Please."

Instead of responding, Doris closed down verbally, her posture rigidly emphasizing her closed position. Probes and explorations in the remainder of the session were fruitless and with some reluctance from Doris, who claimed that there was not anything that could be changed, another appointment was scheduled. Two more exploratory sessions were also non-productive. Finally in the fourth session, the mystery was solved as a result of the nagging question, "Why now?" which was made operational through a therapist statement, "I was wondering if there was any significance to this time of the year for either of you, an anniversary of any event from your past."

Jack replied first. "No," he said thoughtfully. "Nothing important has happened to us at this time of year." Turning to his wife, he continued, "Nope, not for me. What about you, honey?"

Doris turned on him with a fury that was in direct contrast to the passive posture she had been displaying previously. Her outburst was surprising. "I can't believe it," she began, addressing her husband. "How can you be so insensitive, how could you forget? This is my *second* pregnancy. Six months ago today, exactly, our son would have been seven if he had been allowed to be born. Instead, I had an abortion because *you* said it was too soon to begin a family!"

Jack looked at her with horror. "Oh no! That's what this is all about? I thought that was finished a long time ago. We *both* agreed that it was too soon—not just me! We wanted to have a secure foundation before we had kids. I can't believe you are blaming me."

With these floodgates opened, two more sessions were centered on the expression of resentments and long-buried emotions. However cathartic this might have been, there was no basic change in positions. By the end of the sixth session, it was clear that the impending divorce was Doris' punishment of Jack for being the force behind the decision to "kill" (her word) their baby and, at the same time, she was abandoning him in a way that was a metaphor for his abandonment of her and their potential son seven years ago. The therapist's assessment was that the abortion was a valid issue, and therapy was now aimed at a way to authentically bury the past without another casualty. The therapist attended to the couple's general theme of punishment and retribution, and presented them with two choices, stressing that the outcome of their relationship rested in their ability to follow through on one of two possibilities.

It was at this point that the "activity" was introduced. The couple was presented with two options. One was to devise and follow through on a ritual that would allow them both to work together to completely lay the aborted child to rest. The alternative was to conjointly devise a punishment or act of retribution which would exactly match Doris' conception of the enormity of the deed in such a way that no residue would intrude on their lives. The process of this activity followed these steps:

1. Identification of the trigger act or event around which resentment is focused.
2. Presentation of ritual and retribution options to couple for choice.
3. Monitoring the process of either ritual or retribution.

Vital in this activity is an exact understanding of the crucial aspects of both rituals and retribution. The "rules of ritual" are adapted from *Rituals in Families and Family Therapy* (1988), edited by Evan Imber-Black, Janine Roberts, and Richard Whitney.

1. The ritual must have a distinct purpose. What it should accomplish, commemorate, or celebrate should be clearly articulated.
2. The ritual must contain symbolic behavior or symbolic articles relevant to the task to be accomplished.
3. A detailed plan should be devised that includes time, place, repetition, actions, dress, food, props, scripts if necessary, and other vital details. The meaning of each aspect of the plan should be clear and understood by the couple.
4. An aspect of the ritual should be able to become more "public," e.g., a notice in the newspaper, a gathering of extended family or friends, etc.

If retribution is determined the most effective means of ending the impasse, it is important to adhere strictly to the following "retribution rules."

1. Fit—the punishment should be commensurate with the precipitating event.
2. Match—the punishment should be of the same nature and (symbolic) meaning as the precipitator, a logical consequence.
3. Impact—the punishment must be experienced by the perpetrator as emotionally painful or depriving to the same extent as the original act.
4. Outcome—the parties involved must feel finished; the "debt has been paid," and there is no outstanding emotional residue on either side. The ultimate goal of the punishment is to achieve relationship repair.

There are three other important aspects to consider when this method is used. First, the "perpetrator" does not have to feel as if the punishment is deserved. However, the agreement must be that the punished person will not punish the punisher. Next, there must be a commitment to an absence of physical harm and an agreement from both persons that the punishment is a fit and a match. Finally there must be an agreement that the punishment "settles the score," and no "getting even" for the punishment will be forthcoming. Doris and Jack decided a ritual would be the most productive means to end the impasse. The couple devised a courageous and collaborative ritual that included a cleric who assisted them in devising a funeral service. The couple selected a casket, bought a burial plot, and arranged for music and flowers. In their final session, after the service had been completed, they both reported that they had fully shared in the emotional pain that went with the act. Jack claimed that he had been carrying around a core of pain that he had not realized was present. The impasse was gone and they were able to continue their relationship greatly enhanced.

When couples are left to their own devices, they occasionally instigate a punishment that continues the destruction of the relationship, rather than one that allows for relationship repair. Meg's husband confessed to her that he had ended an affair of two years. He wanted to be recommitted to the marriage without any secrets coming between them; however, Meg felt betrayed both by his actions and by the confession, complaining that if it was over, there was no need for her to have knowledge. The "double betrayal" was a definite burden to the relationship, and Meg decided that the only way she could possibly go on with the marriage was to even the score.

She set about to have an affair, planning on making it a brief sexual encounter that she would then reveal to Mike, her husband, when it was over. She chose a man carefully, one with whom she could be intimate without falling in love or losing control. The affair lasted about six months, and when she believed it was no longer necessary, she ended it and confessed to Mike. He was devastated by her betrayal, and discovered that he was so filled with disgust, that he opted to end the marriage. Meg, of course, was astonished. She could not understand how he could operate with such different expectations for her than he practiced himself. What Meg believed would be the only salvation for her to remain married, her attempt to equalize the relationship, failed, and the marriage ended. If this couple had negotiated the terms of retaliation, this might not have been the outcome.

Martin and Rose were a couple that attempted to negotiate their hurt with the help of a therapist. Martin made a major, nonreturnable purchase for their home, thinking that he had the backing and approval of his wife. She, on the other hand, believed completely that he had acted mostly independently, and had left her out of a very important decision that she would have to live with for a long time. In exploring the problem, it was deemed impossible to facilitate the couple reaching a shared reality where both were equally responsible. It was also apparently futile to attempt to have Rose accept both Martin's action and the purchase.

The stalemate was eroding their relationship to the point that Rose claimed that Martin must make a choice between the purchase or the marriage. While this is an extreme position, it did illustrate the depth of betrayal felt by Rose. The therapist agreed that the purchase, being a major addition to the structure of their home, was going to be a visible reminder of their process. There was also an agreement that if the marriage was important, Rose and Martin together might find a means to neutralize the destructive aspects of the action. Rose's first suggestion was that they should sell the house and start over. Martin argued that the financial loss would be too great. Rose retaliated by informing Martin that the terms of the divorce would be financially greater. There were several other attempts on both individuals' parts to make up for the "mistake." (Martin suggested a European vacation as a peace offering, which Rose rejected.) After several sessions of negotiating, Martin suggested that he discard, give away, something of great importance to him that would make him feel as hurt and devastated as he believed Rose was feeling. Claiming that Rose knew what was important to him, he left it up to her as to what would be a commensurate punishment. For the first time, Rose seemed to relax. It was as if she had finally regained some of the control she believed had been taken from her by Martin. Her initial reply was to give up his firstborn grandson (the child born to a daughter from his former marriage), but she quickly laughed and said that she would give it serious thought.

Martin spent a week in suspense, admirably not giving Rose any hints. She finally decided that if he were to sell one of his treasured antiques and designate the money for something they would purchase together, she would feel vindicated. She retained the privilege of determining which of the treasures would be sold, ensuring that it would be something that she knew he would genuinely regret no longer having in his possession. Martin was visibly shaken. He began to protest, but stopped when he felt the impact of Rose's determination. The terms were negotiated in one session, and the painful process of losing a treasure was begun. Rose reported that she now believed that Martin fully recognized the depth of her feeling, and she respected his following through without being "nasty." Martin said that he would forever be careful to be sure that he was fully aware of Rose's need to be included in decisions, and his tendency to make assumptions in the process of getting something he wanted. The couple left therapy equally hurt and equally satisfied with an addition to their house and the absence of a treasure. The marriage was not only intact, it was greatly improved. An unnecessary disaster had been averted.

In the cases described, the choice between ritual or retaliation emerged from the content and process of the sessions. At times, it may be more important to present the couple with the task of discussing the options and deciding which would best achieve closure. The therapist should focus on supporting and encouraging a full discussion prior to a decision. The therapist can be most effective in reflecting back to the couple any uncovered areas, prolonging the discussion, and reiterating the terms of both options without being committed to either choice. Once a path is chosen, the therapist functions in the position of a coach or referee with the added duty of assuring that underlying relationship issues receive attention.

Suggestions for Follow-Up

The natural conclusion that is achieved in the process of finalizing the ritual or retribution task eliminates formal follow-up procedures. The impasse has been resolved, and the couple can continue their relationship with the potential for future success.

Contraindications

The couple is always in charge of the process, and since the decision to use either activity is entirely within their control, there should be no contraindications. The therapist may voice reluctance to the couple using either method as a means of ensuring that the couple is completely engaged in this course of treatment.

Readings and Resources for the Professional

Black E. I., Roberts J., and Whitney R. (1988). *Rituals in families and family therapy.* New York: Norton.

26

The Empathy Expansion Procedure:
A Method of Assisting Couples
in Healing from Traumatic Incidents

Scott W. Browning

Type of Contribution: *Activity*

Objective

The following chapter has been designed to assist couples as a part of marital/relationship therapy. Specifically, this activity helps couples who are trapped by a few hurtful incidents that can not be forgiven because one member believes that a sincere and empathic apology has never been offered.

Rationale for Use

It is very common to find that as a couple begins to explain their reason(s) for seeking therapy, certain incidents are mentioned that elicit strong reactions from the couple. The reaction highlights that one member remains hurt about the past event, while the other is trying to express some regret about the transgression. Often the offending party recognizes that he or she did do something that was hurtful, but this person simply cannot grasp why the hurt is so extreme. The person who feels slighted or offended does not believe his or her reaction is extreme; on the contrary, she or he has become increasingly frustrated that his or her partner does not seem to understand the hurt generated by the incident in question. When the effect of the incident and corresponding hurt creates an impasse in the couple's ability to relate to one another, this intervention can often pave the way for an empathic, and accepted, apology.

The main objective of the exercise is to help one person truly apologize to another. The irony is that in most cases, if the couple really does continue to have, in essence, positive feelings about each other, they are utterly perplexed by the impasse that is dominating their feelings toward one another. The impasse seems so illogical. They often both know that neither wants this hurt to have such power, and usually some regret has been sincerely stated. The missing piece, however, is capable of keeping the couple completely stuck; that piece is empathy. People need to know that their own felt hurt is acknowledged. There is something uniquely unsatisfying when an apology is only the means to an end, rather than a heartfelt recognition of wrongdoing.

This process is made even more complex by the fact that most people who have wronged another usually did not intend to have that effect. In fact, in some cases, there was no malice whatsoever. For example, in one case, the wife expressed genuine hurt over a garment worn by her husband, to be specific, a sweater-vest. At first glance, such a reaction seems bizarre, but upon further investigation, the depth of the hurt could not have been more clear. The story unfolded that early in Jane and Sam's relationship, and also only a year in recovery from substance abuse, they were going to a dance sponsored by Narcotics Anonymous. Jane reported that she had not been to a dance sober in her whole life, and was giddy at the prospect, as well as desiring to "do it right." So she bought a nice dress, shoes, and all the accoutrements of a fine evening out. She got ready for Sam's arrival, and was waiting anxiously at the window. Sam drove up and stepped out of his car wearing a clean shirt, pants, comfortable shoes, and a green sweater-vest. He did not look bad, he simply looked one step above casual.

During a session, Sam stated that he was sorry for not dressing up in a fashion that would have matched Jane's effort. Both Jane and I believed that he really did wish he had dressed better for that occasion, but he clearly did not know why Jane was so hurt, or why she wished him to never wear this sweater-vest again. This aspect of Jane's hurt and desires seemed excessive. I asked Sam to sit and close his eyes. I asked him to "become" Jane, to live that day as she had three years ago. Sam began to describe the day's events, the shopping, dressing, the excitement. He, as Jane, viewed the scene from her front window, felt the feelings of anticipation. "My first real date, my first real boyfriend, this is my prom. . . ." And then suddenly seeing Sam emerge from his car, looking casual, wearing a sweater-vest rather than a jacket and tie. "Oh God, what a fool I am." Sam said the words out loud that Jane had felt. At that moment, he opened his eyes, began to cry, and told Jane how very sorry he was.

Instructions

1. Determine a prominent hurt experienced by a member of the couple.

2. Evaluate if the hurt stated is the best example of a hurt to move into the forefront for the purpose of the procedure. As in all clinical work, it is always best to use an intervention that will work. A great intervention is useless if the implementation is flawed. For that reason, utilize the following criteria in choosing the best example of hurt to be used in proceeding with the Empathy Expansion Procedure (EEP).

   A. Is there a spectrum of hurtful incidents?
   B. Where does this incident lie in the spectrum of hurtful incidents?
   C. Would the couple be better served if a hurt of lesser or greater intensity were to be addressed? Or, must the most powerful hurt (e.g., an affair) be addressed because all other issues are dwarfed by this cataclysmic hurt?

3. Use your best clinical judgment and client input to select the most appropriate hurt to be examined. In your mind you should be thinking about what hurt mentioned seems critical to the injured party, and is regretted by the offending party.

4. Observe the offending person's attempt to apologize for the selected incident.

5. With no hint of sarcasm, ask the other member of the couple if the apology just offered satisfied her or him.

6. If the hurt individual states that she or he does believe the apology and they feel better, move on. However, in most cases, individuals will acknowledge that they know their mate is trying to apologize, it just simply does not remove the hurt.

7. Return now to the offending partner and ask, "Would you like to be able to apologize in such a way that you increase the likelihood that your mate is no longer as hurt and angry?" At this time, most clients will state that they would do almost anything to put this incident behind them. You can then proceed to explain that you would like to assist them with a procedure called the Empathy Expansion Procedure.

8. Tell them that you would like to concentrate on the selected incident, and you need to be sure that the details are clear. Sometimes the incident has been discussed so often that both people are quite clear on the details; in other cases, the actual moment-by-moment behaviors and thoughts are not clear to the offending party. In the case of needing further clarity, you need to ask the hurt party to describe the events and thoughts in a very clear, nonaccusatory manner. The offending party simply listens.

9. Explain the EEP to the couple. Inform them that they should only proceed if they really want to address this past hurt. Acknowledge to the offending party that he or she will feel as though all of the burden is resting on him or her. You can explain that for this particular incident, the procedure will ask him or her to see the world through the eyes of the other. It is not the time to look for excuses or rationalizations. This exercise demands that there is some tolerance and some innate empathic capacity. If the individuals do not possess these two abilities, the procedure is not as successful. It is necessary to assess if a client has at least a sufficient empathic capacity. Those clients who do appear to lack the necessary empathic capacity will not benefit from this exercise, and the mate is often only more frustrated by the deficiency when exhibited in therapy.

10. Begin the procedure.
   A. Eyes closed.
   B. "Be _____ on the day of the incident. See the world as he or she did. Try not to even place your thoughts and feelings into this description. This is your chance to understand why the hurt has been so deep. There are often circumstances that added to the hurt, and this is your chance to understand them fully."
   C. The images produced should be done largely by the individual, with his or her eyes closed; however, the other party may need to interject some relevant detail to keep the procedure accurate. It is your job as the therapist to be the primary guide. If the person who attempts the EEP is missing the details, then ask sensitive, probing questions. Be gentle, but firm.
   D. Make sure to have the client move though the incident step by step. If one tries to rush to the moment of hurt, it is very likely that too many details will be left out, thus not leading to an empathic breakthrough.
   E. Watch the client carefully, and listen for an indication that he or she has a sudden recognition of the pain. He or she might suddenly open their eyes, or else their voice will often slow down and the words become more choked. If this occurs, end the exercise and allow the couple to discuss their feelings.
   F. If no empathic insight seems to occur, talk about the importance of beginning to look at these issues and do not convey a sense of failure. The client may be achieving the best recognition of pain that he or she can.

Suggestions for Follow-Up

Whether or not the exercise results in an empathic breakthrough, the therapist must assure the couple that this is an important point of therapy. The importance of understanding the pain and frustrations experienced by each member of a couple has been established in a clear manner. Make sure that the next session involves balance. The client who had closed his or her eyes in order to understand the other needs to have his or her needs recognized. Do not jump into another EEP too quickly, however. Look for ways to support the client who may be feeling as if he or she has tried harder to help the couple than the other has. Assure the client who feels that he or she is doing more work that this process demands that each person be involved, and at times, one person does put more on the line than the other, but you, the therapist, will work to rebalance the issues.

Contraindications

This exercise is a powerful, positive experience for most couples. One must proceed with an awareness that the Empathy Expansion Procedure should not be attempted capriciously. A therapist who moves too quickly, or poorly prepares the couple, runs the risk of losing a critical therapeutic moment. The couple is unlikely to be badly damaged by the intervention if accomplished inadequately; however, it represents a lost opportunity. The couple may feel that you are unprepared and thus less professional, but even more important, it may be the couple's last chance to heal some traumatic incident.

In the case that the couple is not committed to trying a new experience to work out their issues, this exercise may not be effective. It is an exercise that demands serious effort on the parts of both parties. If one becomes silly, or if the anger is so great that any mention of the topic results in an argument, the procedure should be held off until a more preferable time.

In conclusion, it needs to be remembered that this exercise does not cause one to wish to apologize. Rather, the EEP is designed for those who wish to put some incident behind them, but have been unable to accomplish that task. The impasse may have been due to one member's anger or another's inability to see how deeply he or she may have hurt his or her mate. Therefore, be sure that the couple wants to do "whatever it takes" to heal a relational wound before proceeding with this exercise.

Readings and Resources for the Professional

Brock, G. W. and Barnard, C. P. (1992). *Procedures of marriage and family therapy*. Boston: Allyn and Bacon.

Chasin, R. and Roth, S. (1990). Future perfect, past perfect: A positive approach to opening couple therapy. In R. Chasin, H. Grunebaum, and M. Herzig (Eds.), *One couple: Four realities*. New York: Guilford Press.

Fisch, R., Weakland, J. H., and Segal, L. (1982). The tactics of change. San Francisco: Jossey-Bass.

Green, R. J., Bettinger, M., and Zacks, E. (1996). Are lesbian couples fused and gay couples disengaged? Questioning gender straightjackets. In J. Laird and R. J. Green (Eds.), *Lesbian and Gays in Couples and Families*. San Francisco: Jossey-Bass.

Katz, R. (1963). *Empathy: Its nature and uses*. New York: Free Press of Glencoe.

Paul, N. L. (1967). The use of empathy in the resolution of grief. *Perspectives in Biology and Medicine*, 11, 153-169.

Paul, N. L. and Paul, B. B. (1990). Enticing empathy in couples. In R. Chasin, H. Grunebaum, and M. Herzig (Eds.), *One couple: Four realities*. New York: The Guilford Press.

Bibliotherapy Sources for the Client

Bach, G. and Wyden, P. (1968). *The intimate enemy: How to fight fair in love and marriage.* New York: Avon Books.

Bolton, R. (1979). *People skills*. New York: Touchstone.

Fromm, E. (1956). *The art of loving*. New York: Harper & Row.

Lerner, H. (1989). *The dance of intimacy: A woman's guide to courageous acts of change in key relationships*. New York: Harper Perennial.

Scarf, M. (1986). *Intimate partners: Patterns in love and marriage*. New York: Randon House.

27

Primary Perceptual Modalities in Couples Therapy

Edward M. Markowski

Type of Contribution: *Activity/Homework/Handout*

Objectives

1. To determine the primary perceptual modalities of the partners.
2. To remediate communication difficulties attributed to modality issues.

Rationale for Use

People rely, to differing degrees, on their perceptual modalities in the way they perceive the world around them and in the way they communicate those perceptions. Individuals in their early development select either a visual, auditory, or kinesthetic modality. They learn to filter incoming stimuli in accordance with that modality, and to communicate messages to others in that modality. Therefore, it can be predicted that people with different perceptual modalities may have and may communicate a dramatically different experience when faced with the same real world experience. For example, a visual person experiences neatness in a room when everything is seen in its right place and the room is visually attractive. A kinesthetic person, on the other hand, experiences neatness in a room when objects are convenient and within easy reach, but may be unaware of visual attractiveness. Typically, kinesthetics complain that auditory and visual people are insensitive. Visuals complain that auditories do not pay attention to them, because they do not make eye contact during conversation. Auditory people complain that kinesthetics do not listen. It is apparent that such perceptual differences may lead to communication dysfunction in relationships, and that some of the frustration, stress, and conflict in an intimate, interpersonal relationship can be traced to these differences. When such difficulties are discovered, they may be remediated by training couples to communicate in their partner's primary modality.

In order to test the concepts discussed above, a Primary Perceptual Modality Inventory (PPMI) was developed and administered to a sample of forty couples in marital therapy and a control group of forty nontherapy couples. Individuals taking the PPMI rated the strength of their ability to cognitively recreate visual, auditory, and kinesthetic experiences. Three types of couples were identified by the PPMI testing: (1) couples in which one or both spouses had no identifiable primary modality, (2) couples in which both spouses had the same primary modality, and (3) couples in which both spouses had different primary modalities. The hypothesis that a significantly greater number of therapy couples would be composed of spouses with different primary perceptual modalities was supported. It was found that 47.5 percent of the therapy couples and only 20 percent of the nontherapy couples had different primary modalities. An analysis of the data resulted in a chi square statistic of 7.116 (df=2), which was significant beyond p =.05. The following table summarizes the data:

	Therapy Couples	Nontherapy Couples
No Primary Modalities	32.5%	50%
Same Primary Modalities	20%	30%
Different Primary Modalities	47.5%	20%

The above results suggest that the existence of different primary perceptual modalities between spouses may be an important factor related to the development of maladaptive communication and eventual marital maladjustment. Therefore, the identification of primary perceptual modalities between spouses can serve as a valuable assessment and intervention as couples attempt to understand and change their relationships.

Instructions

After the inventory is completed by each partner, three scores with possible totals of 100 are obtained by adding the following values for each item: Unable = 1, Vaguely = 2, Fairly Well = 3, Very Well = 4, Extremely Well = 5. A primary modality is identified when the highest score is more than three points greater than the next highest score.

Suggestions for Follow-Up

When different primary modalities are found, couples can be helped to overcome communication barriers by learning to use predicates and construct metaphors that do not fit naturally with their primary modalities. For example, a visually oriented person can be taught to use auditory and kinesthetic phrases such as: "I hear you; It sounds like . . . ; I grasp the point; It touches me when. . . . " Auditory and kinesthetic persons can be assisted to use visual phrases such as: "I see what you mean." and "It looks good to me." Likewise, individuals can be taught to construct metaphors in their partners' modalities. For example, a kinesthetic person in relationship with an auditory person can say: "When I have to walk over things left in the middle of the floor, I have the same reaction as you would have when listening to one of your favorite CDs and discovering that it has scratches on it." The auditory partner will relate to the sound metaphor and be more likely to understand the kinesthetic's reaction to things left in the middle of the floor. Practice in using the partner's predicates and in constructing metaphors in the partner's modality can be used as homework assignments as well as in session activities.

Contraindications: None

Readings and Resources for the Professional

Bandler, R. and Grinder, J. (1975). *The structure of magic I.* Palo Alto, CA: Science and Behavior Books.
Bandler, R. and Grinder, J. (1976). *The structure of magic II.* Palo Alto, CA: Science and Behavior Books.

Davis, D. I. and Davis, S. L. (1985). Integrating individual and marital therapy using neurolinguistic programming. *International Journal of Family Psychiatry, 6,* 3-17.

Davis, S. L. and Davis, D. I. (1983). Neurolinguistic programming and family therapy. *Journal of Marital and Family Therapy, 9,* 283-291.

Dilts, R. (1990). *Beliefs: Pathways to health and well-being.* Portland, OR: Metamorphous Press.

McMasters, M. and Grinder, J. (1994). *Precision: A new approach to communication.* Scotts Valley, CA: Grinder Delozier.

Bibliotherapy Sources for the Client

Bandler, R. and Grinder, J. (1979). *Frogs into princes.* Moab, UT: Real People Press.

Cameron-Bandler, L. (1978). *They lived happily ever after: A book about achieving happy endings in coupling.* Cupertino, CA: Meta Publications.

THE PRIMARY PERCEPTUAL MODALITY INVENTORY (PPMI)

Developed by

Edward M. Markowski and Joseph H. McVoy Jr.

Marriage and Family Therapy Program

East Carolina University*

Greenville, NC 27834

The following inventory offers individuals an opportunity to make an objective study of the patterns by which they receive and send data in their interpersonal relationships. The results will enable the persons taking the inventory to better understand aspects of their interpersonal relationships and improve their communications with others.

The inventory is divided into three sections. Read the directions for each section. Then, respond to each item in the section by circling the number under the label that is most appropriate. Be sure to respond to all items.

General Information

Age_____Sex_____

Education _____

Occupation _____

Marital Status _____

Years Married (if applicable) _____

Ages of Children (if applicable) _____

* Supported in part by a grant from the University Research Committee

Read the following items and relate them to specific experiences from your memory. Attempt to reexperience each item as a specific sight. In other words see how well you can visually recreate the exact color and physical details of the items. Then rate how well you were able to mentally recreate the item by circling the number under the response that is most appropriate.

	UNABLE	VAGUELY	FAIRLY WELL	VERY WELL	EXTREMELY WELL
1. See a red sunset.	1	2	3	4	5
2. See a decorated Christmas tree.	1	2	3	4	5
3. See a red rose.	1	2	3	4	5
4. See a McDonald's restaurant.	1	2	3	4	5
5. See a slice of watermelon.	1	2	3	4	5
6. See your bedroom.	1	2	3	4	5
7. See waves rolling onto a beach.	1	2	3	4	5
8. See writing on a chalkboard.	1	2	3	4	5
9. See a fire in a fireplace.	1	2	3	4	5
10. See a dollar bill.	1	2	3	4	5
11. See a toothbrush.	1	2	3	4	5
12. See a high school.	1	2	3	4	5
13. See a heavy rain falling.	1	2	3	4	5
14. See a famous person.	1	2	3	4	5
15. See your own face in a mirror.	1	2	3	4	5
16. See your best friend.	1	2	3	4	5
17. See the scene outside your front door.	1	2	3	4	5
18. See a black bird.	1	2	3	4	5
19. See your signature.	1	2	3	4	5
20. See the face of someone special looking at you.	1	2	3	4	5

To score: Add all circled numbers together.   Visual Total_____

Read the following items and relate them to specific experiences from your memory. Attempt to reexperience each item as a specific sound. In other words tune into your ability to recreate the exact tones, timbers and sound levels of the items. Then rate how well you were able to mentally recreate the item by circling the number under the response that is most appropriate.

	UNABLE	VAGUELY	FAIRLY WELL	VERY WELL	EXTREMELY WELL
1. Hear the voice of a famous person.	1	2	3	4	5
2. Hear a band playing the National Anthem.	1	2	3	4	5
3. Hear the wind whistle in the trees.	1	2	3	4	5
4. Hear a musical instrument playing.	1	2	3	4	5
5. Hear waves rolling onto the beach.	1	2	3	4	5
6. Hear birds singing.	1	2	3	4	5
7. Hear your favorite song.	1	2	3	4	5
8. Hear crickets chirping.	1	2	3	4	5
9. Hear the voice of someone special whispering in your ear.	1	2	3	4	5
10. Hear a doorbell ring.	1	2	3	4	5
11. Hear the door of a car slamming.	1	2	3	4	5
12. Hear a crackling fire.	1	2	3	4	5
13. Hear a heavy rain falling.	1	2	3	4	5
14. Hear a dog barking.	1	2	3	4	5
15. Hear someone writing on a chalkboard.	1	2	3	4	5
16. Hear a cat purring.	1	2	3	4	5
17. Hear a choir singing.	1	2	3	4	5
18. Hear a baby crying.	1	2	3	4	5
19. Hear a glass shattering into pieces.	1	2	3	4	5
20. Hear yourself talking.	1	2	3	4	5

To score: Add all circled numbers together.   Auditory Total_____

Read the following items and relate them to specific experiences from your memory. Attempt to reexperience each item as a specific physical feeling. In other words get in touch with your ability to recreate the exact textures and sensation of the items. Then rate how well you were able to mentally recreate the item by circling the number under the response that is most appropriate.

	UNABLE	VAGUELY	FAIRLY WELL	VERY WELL	EXTREMELY WELL
1. Feel your feet in warm sand.	1	2	3	4	5
2. Feel a throbbing headache.	1	2	3	4	5
3. Feel yourself in a swing.	1	2	3	4	5
4. Feel a splinter in your finger.	1	2	3	4	5
5. Feel someone's hand in yours.	1	2	3	4	5
6. Feel the warmth of someone special hugging you.	1	2	3	4	5
7. Feel the soft petal of a flower.	1	2	3	4	5
8. Feel a heavy rain falling.	1	2	3	4	5
9. Feel soap burning your eyes.	1	2	3	4	5
10. Feel someone tickling you.	1	2	3	4	5
11. Feel yourself biting a crisp apple.	1	2	3	4	5
12. Feel an animal's fur as you pet it.	1	2	3	4	5
13. Feel rocks under your bare feet.	1	2	3	4	5
14. Feel the nervousness in your stomach when you are anxious.	1	2	3	4	5
15. Feel your body sensation as someone runs fingernails across a chalkboard.	1	2	3	4	5
16. Feel the cut of a sharp object.	1	2	3	4	5
17. Feel your hands digging in mud.	1	2	3	4	5
18. Feel your chest pounding after exercising.	1	2	3	4	5
19. Feel a hot object.	1	2	3	4	5
20. Feel your skin itching.	1	2	3	4	5

To score: Add all circled numbers together.   Kinesthetic Total_____

Note: One's primary perceptual modality is identified when the highest score is more than three points greater than the next highest score.

28

Imagery Exercises for Couples

Carol Rose

Type of Contribution: *Activity*

Objective

The purpose of this activity is to increase partner empathy by enabling clients to "see through the eyes of the other."

Rationale for Use

Both of the following imagery exercises can be used as diagnostic tools to help the therapist assess the state of a couple's relationship. The exercises are also used to facilitate understanding, empathy, and compassion between partners.

Instructions

Imagery work begins with the individual stating his or her intention for the session. This can be done mentally, or the intention can be written on a piece of paper with the date in the upper righthand corner of the page. The couple then does a general "cleansing" exercise. An example of a cleansing exercise appears below.

(1) *Close your eyes and breathe out three times, slowly. First exhale, and then inhale; exhale, inhale.*
   The therapist instructs clients to first exhale, then inhale, reversing the habitual pattern of breathing and slowing the system down. This both relaxes the client and turns his/her attention inward.
(2) *Imagine every exhaled breath leaving the body on a thin film of grey smoke, removing anything that is old, stale, or toxic.*
   When this new breathing pattern has been established, the therapist continues:
(3) *See yourself walking in a forest. As you walk, notice a small leafy branch that has fallen to the ground. It seems to glow golden in the sunlight. Pick it up and begin brushing yourself*

Note: Exercises (1) and (3) are based on the work of Jerusalem therapist Colette Aboulker-Muscat. Madame Muscat has used her imagery techniques for more than sixty years, and she is currently training people from around the globe in this system. Exercise (2) is one that the author has designed, and uses regularly in conjunction with the others.

with it, from head to toe. Hear the dead cells fall away from your body with each stroke. Know that as you brush the dead cells from your body, you are also cleansing the inside as well. Brush yourself gently and briskly with this golden bough, until all that is no longer necessary has fallen away. Return the small branch to the ground, and continue walking along the forest path. Listen for the sound of water coming from the right side of the path. Follow the sound until you reach a river, a lake, a waterfall, or a brook. Go to the water and cup your hands in its clear, blue flow. Take some of the water and splash it on your face, your neck, on any body part that you feel needs it. If you wish, you may remove your clothes and enter the water. When you have finished washing yourself, cup your hands again and take a few sips of the crystal clear waters. Dry yourself in the sunlight and then return the same way that you came, passing the small golden bough as you leave the forest and return to this room. Sense how refreshed and renewed you feel as you breathe out, and open your eyes.

Suggestions for Follow-Up

Following the exercise, clients may wish to describe their experience. Allow a few moments for discussion and then proceed. Listen attentively to the clients' language and imagery. These may prove helpful in designing future exercises for them. If the individuals say that they have not "seen" anything, assure them that the work is being done anyway, with the change in breathing.

Provide a pad of unlined paper and oil pastels or crayons for the actual couple work. This allows clients to concretize an image and to reflect upon it later. Assure clients that artistic skill is not a prerequisite for this work. It is simply a technique for remembering.

EXERCISE 1: "REFLECTIONS"

For the purpose of this exercise, have the couple decide who will be partner A and who will be partner B.

Instructions to Clients

- Breathe out slowly three times.
- Imagine yourself looking into a mirror with your partner. Partner A is behind; partner B is in front.
- Notice how you are feeling when you see this image of yourselves.
- Breathe out one time.
- Still looking into the mirror, see partner A move to the left of partner B. What are you sensing, feeling, and knowing as you see yourselves in this position?
- Breathe out one time.
- See partner A move in front of partner B. What are you sensing, feeling, knowing as this position is assumed?
- Breathe out one time.
- See yourselves in the mirror as partner A moves to the right of partner B. What are you sensing, feeling, knowing, in this position?
- Breathe out slowly and open your eyes.

Suggestions for Follow-Up

After the exercise, give the clients a pad of paper to sketch the image that spoke to them most profoundly. When each has finished drawing, ask them to give it a title. Then, have them put it aside for a moment. Open the discussion by asking that each, in turn, report his or her experiences. The therapist may prefer to break this up, having each partner report on one position at a time, beginning with the image of partner A standing behind partner B. Encourage the couple to listen to the language and the imagery of the other. When the four positions have been described by each partner, have them take out their drawing and share what it is that prompted them to draw this particular image of their relationship. Positions may give the therapist and the couple a sense of where the relationship currently is. In the Aboulker-Muscat system, the right position always has to do with the future. Thus, it is how each one felt when standing to the right of their partner that can be a helpful diagnostic tool for the therapist. If the couple wishes, the exercise can be repeated at a later stage of therapy.

EXERCISE 2: "SEEDS"

1. Have each partner formulate an intention for today's session.
2. Give a general "cleansing" exercise. Remember to instruct the couple to breathe out slowly three times, seeing each exhaled breath as a thin film of grey smoke that is removing anything that is no longer necessary, healthy, or productive.

Instructions to Clients

- Imagine that your partner has given you a small seed.
- Breathe out and plant the seed in the moist earth.
- Standing in front of the seed, see what is growing.
- Breathe out and sense what the seed needs from you in order to continue growing. What must you do to keep it alive?
- Breathe out and move to the left of the newly growing seed. What is happening?
- Move behind it. What are you sensing in this position?
- Breathe out and move to the right of the seed. What are you feeling?
- Imagine that you are sitting in a tree and looking down at your seed. What do you see, sense, and feel as you look at your seed from this perspective?

Suggestions for Follow-Up

When the exercise is completed, have each partner draw what they have seen, and have them give their drawing a title. Put the drawing aside, and discuss what each position has shown them. Let them acknowledge what it is that they each received from the other, and what it is that they are required to do in order to keep it alive. Have them share their drawings and describe what they felt or sensed in each position. Remind them that seeds need to be watered regularly and that (for homework) they are to imagine themselves watering their seed daily. At the end of one week, have them report what it is that they have sensed. (The star position can provide the therapist and the couple with an overview of where each person is in the relationship.) Suggest that each partner record his or her dreams and that, for the next session, he or she should select one dream to work with.

EXERCISE 3: "DREAMS"

1. Have the couple formulate their individual intention for today.
2. Give a cleansing exercise, reminding them to breathe out slowly three times. Tell them to see each exhalation as a thin film of grey smoke that is clearing the body of anything that is too heavy, dark, or depressing.

Instructions to Clients

- Ask partner A to share his or her dream in detail.
- Invite partner B to breathe out slowly and to enter and continue A's dream, seeing, feeling, or sensing all that is happening.
- Give partner B a sheet of paper to draw all that he or she experienced in the dream.
- Reverse the procedure. Ask partner B to share her or his dream.
- Invite partner A to breathe out slowly and to enter and continue B's dream, seeing, feeling, or sensing all that is happening.
- Have partner A draw the experience.
- When both dreams have been shared and recorded (in a drawing), encourage the couple to speak about their experience. This exercise is a wonderful way of learning "to walk in the moccasins of another," to see as the other sees.

Because this experience can be intense, it is recommended that the couple "do something concrete" for each other. Before they leave, have them see (e.g., on a TV screen) what they would like their partner to do for them during the coming week.

Contraindications

Although some individuals may have difficulty "seeing" (at first), they can be invited into the process via another sense. Ask them to hear or smell or taste or "know" something; seeing will follow later. Women often tend to have more detailed and elaborate imagery, which may be intimidating for a male partner. Simply state this at the outset, removing the sense of "failure" that sometimes limits a client. If clients have difficulty closing their eyes, allow them to do the imaginal work with their eyes open. When clients feel more secure in the work, they will close their eyes more easily.

Readings and Resources for the Professional

Epstein, G. (1989) *Healing visualizations: Creating health through imagery.* New York: Bantam Books.
Epstein, G. (1992). *Waking dream therapy: Dream process as imagination.* New York: ACMI Press.

Although there are numerous books written on the use of imagery, those recommended above refer specifically to the techniques developed by Madame Colette Aboulker-Muscat.

Bibliotherapy Sources for the Client

Epstein, G. (1994). *Healing into immortality.* New York: Bantam Books.

29

Feelings Flash Cards

Sharon A. Deacon

Type of Contribution: *Activity/Handout*

Objective

The objective of this activity is to help couples learn to express their underlying feelings, instead of using surface-level, defensive emotions to protect themselves from being vulnerable. The activity is directed toward couples who desire to open up more to one another, build trust and intimacy, and become more emotionally expressive. This activity is a first step toward reaching such a goal.

Rationale for Use

Many couples complain that at least one of the partners does not express emotions, or hides behind defensive behaviors. Theoretically speaking, such a complaint usually indicates that both partners have difficulty trusting one another and taking risks. Couples often have problems expressing how they really feel to each other because they are afraid of being vulnerable, getting hurt, and/or being humiliated. This activity gives partners a chance to be vulnerable, without having to verbalize and discuss their feelings. Couples take the first step toward becoming more open and honest with each other by expressing their emotions.

Instructions

Before beginning this activity, couples should be able to identify their underlying emotions and the defensive behaviors and emotions that disguise these inner emotions. An activity such as "Feeling from the Inside-Out" (located elsewhere in this book) may be a good precursor.

Begin by giving each partner a copy of the handouts attached. Ask the clients to fill in the clouds, or bubbles, with various emotions that they have. Tell them to be sure to include their most difficult emotions and happy emotions as well. These clouds or bubbles become their feelings flash cards.

Then, ask the couple to imagine a comic strip, in which the cartoon character's thoughts are in a bubble over his or her head. The clients are to cut out these feelings or bubble/cloud cards, and use them as if they were bubbles over their heads, telling their partner the feeling behind their behavior. Tell the couple to use these feeling flash cards as messages, or communication, of their feelings. For instance, when they are arguing, they should each pass each other a feeling flash card that has their underlying emotion written on it ("insecurity," "sadness," "jealousy," etc.); when they are happy, the may pass their partner a "happy" card, and so on. In doing so, the couple learns to identify their feelings and connect it to their defensive behavior, while at the same time, becoming more vulnerable with their partner.

Rules may also need to be set up in regard to this activity. The couple needs to decide if it is okay to then talk about the feelings, or if it would be too threatening at that point. What happens after a card has been exchanged? Does the other person have to respond? In what way?

The partners should always return the feeling flash card to the giver, thus indicating who "owns" the feeling. Rules regarding when and where the cards can be used also need to be addressed.

Suggestions for Follow-Up

As the couple becomes more comfortable with identifying their emotions and symbolically expressing them to each other, it is time to take further steps. Teach the clients to verbalize their emotions, and feel "safe" with each other. The couple could then continue on in some other type of emotion-expressiveness training.

Some details may need to be ironed out as the couple learns to use the cards on a consistent basis. Some of the rules may need to be changed to fit with the couple's situation.

Contraindications

This activity is not recommended for couples who are stuck in blame patterns and are unable to take responsibility for their own actions and feelings. Partners must be able to "own" their own role in the problem and relationship.

Also, this activity may be contraindicated for couples in crisis, or who are violent and/or substance abusers. These other issues should be addressed first.

Readings and Resources for the Professional

Greenburg, L. S. and Johnson, S. M. (1988). *Emotionally focused therapy for couples.* New York: Guilford Press.

145

146

30

Gratitude Lists

Mary E. Dankoski

Type of Contribution: *Homework/Handout*

Objective

The objective of this homework activity is to counter the feelings associated with being taken for granted by one's partner, and to increase positive exchanges between the couple in general.

Rationale for Use

A common complaint of couples in therapy is the feeling of being taken for granted by one's partner. This often leads both to mutual blame and resentment. This homework assignment is designed to interrupt this pattern by assigning both partners to identify and share the qualities of their partner that they appreciate. Blame can be bypassed, because both partners have equal responsibility to participate. After completing the assignment, both partners may experience an increased positive feeling about their relationship and a renewed sense of being loved, appreciated, and special in their partner's eyes.

Instructions

The assignment may be introduced as follows:

Relationships are like muscles; you have to work at them to keep them strong. Taking your partner for granted is like taking your health for granted, and it sometimes keeps you from being grateful for what you have and working to maintain it and strengthen it. One of the ways to maintain and strengthen your relationship is by making a special date to share with each other how much you appreciate your partner and your relationship. This is the way this homework assignment works: Each of you makes what is called a "Gratitude List." This is a list of what you are grateful for and appreciate about your partner and your relationship. These lists often take a few days to develop. You may want to reflect on this through the next few days, and add to it as things come to mind. They can be small things such as "always replacing the toilet paper roll" to bigger or more emotional things such as "understanding how I feel about my parents." Another way to make this especially meaningful is to share your lists with each other at a place that has special meaning to you, for example, a special restaurant where you had your first date. Another couple that did this assignment used to sit and kiss under a certain tree when they were first dating. They had not been to this tree in a long time, and they chose to read their lists there. Some couples feel a little nervous doing this because it is not something you usually do, especially when you have had some problems in your relationship and have felt taken for granted by your partner. It is like when you work out and your muscles feel a little pain. Sometimes when you actively work on your relationship, it can be a bit uncomfortable at first. It takes a lot of trust and commitment to take this risk, but the results can really be worth it. After engaging the couple in the assignment, the therapist can use the "Gratitude List Take Home Sheet" that follows to facilitate the homework.

Suggestions for Follow-Up

If the couple decides to try this assignment, they should have a specific time and place in mind to share their lists before the session ends. If they leave the session without a specific plan in mind, the chances of them following through with the assignment are significantly reduced. The therapist should also discuss with the couple any fears or discomfort they may have with the assignment.

It is very important to follow-up on this assignment in the next session. If the couple completes the task, the process should be discussed in great detail. The trust and commitment that it takes to do this activity should be amplified as being very important to progress in their treatment. Both partners should be encouraged to expand upon what it was like to hear their partner's list, and how this activity affected them throughout the week, both while they were preparing the lists and after sharing them.

If the clients did not follow through with the assignment, the therapist must be sure to discuss this with the couple in detail. Perhaps the couple did not feel safe enough to share their lists outside of session. The task could be modified to be completed in session in the future.

Contraindications

This assignment is not recommended for couples just beginning therapy, nor for severely conflictual couples or those considering divorce. This activity is recommended for couples who have established a trusting relationship with the therapist and who may have already made some progress toward their goals. The couple should not be at such a conflictual or precarious place in therapy where this assignment would be an opportunity for sarcasm or negativity. Also, it is very important for both partners to commit to following through with the assignment. It should not be assigned if one of the partners cannot make a commitment to doing the assignment. If one partner does not complete a gratitude list, the potential is there to communicate to the other partner that he or she is not appreciated at all, which defeats the purpose of the activity.

Readings and Resources for the Professional

Jacobson, N. S. and Margolin, G. (1979) *Marital therapy: Strategies based on social learning and behavior exchange principles*. New York: Brunner/Mazel.

Bibliotherapy Sources for the Client

Louden, J. (1994). *The couples' comfort book: A creative guide for renewing passion, pleasure, and commitment*. San Francisco: Harper.

Gratitude Lists Take Home Sheet

This sheet is designed to stimulate your thinking, and to guide you through developing your gratitude list. Keep this form in a prominent place, since these lists often take a few days to complete. Fill in the blanks and use the back or another sheet of paper if you run out of room. Try to think both of the small things that are easy to take for granted, as well as some special qualities or things your partner does that are unique to him or her.

I appreciate it when you _____.

I appreciate it when you _____.

I am grateful for you because _____.

I am grateful for you because _____.

I like the way you _____.

I like the way you _____.

I feel special when you _____.

I feel special when you _____.

I appreciate our relationship when _____.

I appreciate our relationship when _____.

I am grateful for our relationship because _____.

I am grateful for our relationship because _____.

_____ makes our relationship special and unique.

_____ is one of your strengths.

_____ is one of the strengths of our relationship.

I feel closest to you when _____.

Thank you for _____.

31

Rewriting Marriage Vows: Consolidating Gains in Marital Therapy at Termination

Miriam R. Hill

Type of Contribution: *Homework/Handout*

Objectives

The objectives of giving spouses the homework assignment of writing personalized, relevant marriage vows as they near termination of therapy are:

- To provide a tangible way for the spouses to reflect on their therapeutic work and the relationship changes resulting from their engagement in marital therapy.
- To encourage the spouses to identify that which is most important for them to pursue if they are to have a lasting, fulfilling marriage.
- To enable the spouses to consolidate the gains they made in their relationship during therapy, and to do so in a way that reinforces personal responsibility and ownership.
- To prepare the spouses for termination of therapy by eliciting their version for ongoing positive relationship transformation, and by reinforcing their commitment to pursue that vision.

Rationale for Use

Marriage vows, or wedding vows, are a salient symbol of marriage in our country. Most couples in the United States are married in a religious or civil ceremony in which the partners exchange wedding vows with one another. Usually, these vows are standardized, general, and so familiar as to go unnoticed quite easily. Some couples write personalized vows for the wedding ceremony. In either case, many couples, when they present for marital therapy, have experienced some sense of failure in the marriage, and feelings of betrayal over broken marriage vows. This is particularly true in cases with one or more extramarital affairs.

The experience of marital therapy is in many ways a reworking of the marriage relationship. This reworking may involve change, acceptance, boundary clarification, inclusion, shifting of power structures, rebuilding, and healing. Often, spouses have to renegotiate expectations that

Note: The author gratefully acknowledges the helpful comments of Dr. Fred Piercy on earlier versions of this chapter.

they brought into marriage. As a result, they come to a clearer understanding of what they can realistically expect in their marriage, and what it will take on the part of each to have that type of marriage.

Giving spouses the homework assignment of writing personalized, relevant marriage vows as they near termination of therapy is an effective way to underscore this entire therapeutic process and to help bring closure to the therapeutic work.

The rationale for use of this homework assignment includes the following:

- In order to write the marriage vows, the spouses will have to clarify for themselves and for one another what they believe is most critical in making their particular marriage relationship work. This generally includes issues, cognitions, emotions, or behaviors that have been processed in marital therapy. The exercise, therefore, enhances the level of consciousness or intentionality spouses have toward their marriage, because the vows are written down.
- Rewriting their marriage vows pushes spouses to a decision point in terms of what they are willing to commit to once therapy is terminated. It is behaviorally appropriate because it encourages reciprocity and free gifts. This concretizing of commitment solidifies the therapeutic changes that have occurred through therapy.
- Marriage vows connote fresh beginnings, because they are most frequently used in association with weddings. Bridging the current state of the marital relationship with the connotation of a fresh beginning can help create an aura of hopefulness and anticipation for the future of the marriage.
- The act of rewriting marriage vows underscores the necessity of continually reshaping, reforming, and recreating the marriage in order to keep it healthy and thriving. It helps to normalize the evolving nature of relationships and commitment.
- Because the vows are written down, they both ground the meaning and provide a launching pad for creative living out of those meanings. Roberts (1994) writes that "the concreteness of words on paper can help hold intense emotions and let people see various ways to express them. Writers . . . can also read the words at different times and places and then integrate the ideas put forth into their lives in some new ways" (p. 98).
- Because the marriage vows are made by the two spouses, it helps to bring closure to the therapeutic relationship by de-emphasizing the role of the therapist and highlighting the roles of the spouses in taking responsibility for the marriage.

Instructions

1. Introduce the homework assignment by noting the significance of marriage vows as an expression of mutual understanding and mutual commitment in a marriage. Note also that having a common vision and a common commitment to that vision are necessary components for success.
2. Explore the wedding vows the couple made initially, as well as the meanings and contexts of those vows.
3. Review with the couple the subsequent changes in their marital relationship in various areas, especially those areas you have worked with in therapy. (Examples might be the areas of self-understanding, understanding and acceptance of the other, conflict resolution, fidelity, or communication skills.)
4. Discuss how their making marriage vows at this point in the relationship would be different contextually. Especially identify additional resources they have at this point that they did not have at their wedding.

5. Tell them that as a homework assignment to prepare for therapy termination, you would like them to write personalized, relevant marriage vows that fit who each of them is, and what they know is necessary and important in their marital relationship.

6. Suggest that each of them write personal vows individually, then set a time to share them with one another and to add, change, and edit the vows once they have seen both sets.

7. Give them issues or topics to consider addressing in their vows, based on your knowledge of them and your work with them. Suggested areas might include:
   - commitment and inclusion
   - faithfulness, fidelity, and accountability
   - dealing with conflict
   - differences between them
   - what to do when one hurts the other; forgiveness
   - personal expressions of love, appreciation, and respect
   - areas of their marriage (e.g., emotional intimacy, communication, sexuality) to intentionally nurture
   - areas of ambiguity and responses to that ongoing ambiguity

8. Give them phrases they might want to use in writing their vows. Phrases might include:
   - I commit/devote myself to . . .
   - I promise/pledge to . . .
   - I will work to/seek to/strive to . . .
   - I will nurture/cultivate . . .
   - I respect/appreciate/value . . . in you

9. Ask them to bring written copies of their vows to their next therapy session.

Suggestions for Follow-Up

1. Process with clients the experience of writing, sharing, and editing their vows.

2. Have clients read their vows out loud to one another in the session.

3. Suggest to clients that they have an additional private ritual that they plan and in which they incorporate another reading of the vows in a more intimate setting. They might integrate into this ritual event symbols of the rebuilding and healing in their marriage. (If you have not worked with them on the use of ritual, you will need to explain what you are suggesting.)

4. Suggest that the next time the couple encounter marital difficulties, or at each wedding anniversary, they do that same ritual, including the rewritten marriage vows.

5. Suggest that once per year (or per quarter year or per month) the couple review the vows and make any additions or changes that reflect the growth of their marriage relationship.

6. Suggest to clients that they make a copy of their vows and post it someplace in their house where they will frequently see it. They might want to frame the copy of the vows, put it in the center of a photo collage, or tape it by the kitchen sink.

7. Ask clients how they think they might utilize their rewritten marriage vows to nurture their marital relationship and then encourage them to carry through on their ideas.

Contraindications

This homework assignment is appropriate for married couples that are mutually committed and have settled inclusion issues, have reached basic agreement on a working model for their marriage, and have resolved any big issues in their marriage during your therapy with them.

It should not be used with couples that are still highly conflictual and that have volatile, unresolved issues or couples that do not have mutual commitment of comparable levels. It also should not be used with couples in which one or both spouses have limited literacy.

Readings and Resources for the Professional

Imber-Black, E., Roberts, J., and Whiting, R. (1988). *Rituals in families and family therapy.* New York: W. W. Norton & Company, Inc.
Roberts, J. (1994). *Tales and transformations: Stories in families and family therapy.* New York: W. W. Norton & Company, Inc.
White, M. and Epston, D. (1990). *Narrative means to therapeutic ends.* New York: W. W. Norton & Company, Inc.

Bibliotherapy Sources for the Client

Roberts, J. (1994). *Tales and transformations: Stories in families and family therapy.* New York: W. W. Norton & Company, Inc.

Rewriting Marriage Vows Handout

DIRECTIONS

Using the worksheet, write your own personalized marriage vows that currently fit you and your marriage relationship. After both you and your spouse have individually written your marriage vows, share them with one another, and make any additions and changes you want to. Then bring written copies of your revised vows to your next therapy session. These vows are free gifts you will give to your spouse. Be creative and have fun!

You might want to address some of the following issues in your vows:

- commitment
- faithfulness, fidelity, and accountability
- dealing with conflict
- dealing with differences between you
- what to do when one of you hurts the other; forgiveness
- personal expressions of love, appreciation, and respect
- areas of your marriage (e.g., emotional intimacy, communication, sexuality) you want to intentionally nurture

You might want to use some of the following phrases in writing your vows:

- I commit/devote myself to . . .
- I promise/pledge to . . .
- I will work to/seek to/strive to . . .
- I will nurture/cultivate . . . by . . .
- I respect/appreciate/value . . . in you

WORKSHEET

1. What do you do that helps your marriage to work well that you want to continue doing? What are the strengths you bring to the relationship?

2. What are the challenges you face in relating well with your partner?

3. What will you do more of that will strengthen your marriage?

4. What will you do less of that will improve your relationship?

5. What will you accept about your partner that will bring you and your partner closer together?

6. What special messages of love and appreciation do you want to send your partner?

7. Using the ideas you have jotted down, draft a set of marriage vows that you would like to make as a gift to your partner. (If you get stuck, refer to the directions handout for suggestions or look at the example handout for ideas to help you get started.)

EXAMPLE OF ONE PERSON'S MARRIAGE VOWS

I love you, and I joyfully choose you to be my wife/husband!

I commit myself to prioritizing our marriage relationship by taking time to tell you about my life and listening as you share your experiences with me.

I will not take you for granted. I will try to show you I care by nurturing you emotionally, romantically, and sexually.

I promise to be honest with you. I will also be faithful to you. You are my lover and best friend. My romance and passion are for you alone.

I know that you and I are very different in some ways. I value the ways that you are different from me—your practical view of the world, the direct way you tell me things, and your willingness to take risks. I will strive to understand you more and to help you understand me. When our differences clash, I will work with you to discover solutions that bring out the best in both of us.

When we have conflict, I will treat you with respect, listen to your perspective, and take time out if I'm about to say something hurtful or unfair. I will ask for your forgiveness when I hurt you, and I will forgive you when you hurt me. I am committed to making our marriage feel safe to you so that you can be free to be yourself.

When things get rough, I pledge to use those times to become a better partner. I promise to stick with you and our marriage as we seek to find our way together. If we cannot work things out on our own, I will go with you to get outside help.

I make these vows because I love you. I anticipate marriage with you and the good things ahead of us.

32

Recalling the Way We Were

J. Maria Bermúdez

Type of Contribution: *Activity/Handout*

Objective

This activity can be used as an assessment tool for the therapist to obtain demographic information from the couple, learn their reactions to experiences early in their relationship, assess what the couple is wanting in their relationship now, and to examine the current themes emerging from the couple's wedding experience.

Rationale for Use

These activities were designed in the spirit of Narrative Therapy. The style reflects the therapeutic form suggested by White and Epston (1990), that would: (a) "Encourage a perception of a changing world through the plotting or linking of lived experience through temporal dimension, (b) invoke a subjective mood in the triggering of presuppositions, establishment of implicit meaning, and generate a multiple perspective, (c) invite a reflexive posture, (d) encourage a sense of authorship and re-authorship of one's life and relationships in the telling of one's story" (p. 83).

The first activity, "When We First Met," enables a couple to think back to a time in their relationship which was not as problematic, and to rediscover what attracted them to each other. Through this experience, the couple is able to amplify an alternate, positive story, rather than the problem saturated story that brought them into therapy.

The second activity, "Our Wedding Day," is an opportunity for couples to describe their wedding day experience in detail. The wedding day can reflect endless dynamics of the couple's current relationship. For example, the therapist is able to see how the couple prepared for that day, who was responsible for certain tasks, what their priorities were, how their families of origin were involved, how they felt during that day, their families reactions to their marriage, and so on. Was it a big wedding or did they elope? Were there compromises? What were the major obstacles in preparing for that day? These are all important indicators of patterns that may still be present. The dynamics surrounding this event are numerous and can make for a unique assessment device.

These activities give the couple an opportunity to reminisce and feel a sense of togetherness that they may not be currently feeling. As Jacobson and Margolin (1979) suggest, the therapist can begin to rebuild a collaborative set that is helpful to serve as a base for improving the couple's marriage. This, combined with the narrative approach, enables the couple to amplify their subjugated story. The current subjugated or alternate story may have been the dominant story at one time (i.e., we married for love, we were so attracted to each other, I admired him/her, etc.); however, because of time and circumstances, the dominant story may have lost its significance in the relationship. This format serves as a template that enables the therapist to highlight predominant themes and amplify the couple's alternate, more favorable story about their relationship.

Instructions

The instructions are simple, and are at the top of each exercise. Remind the couple that they are to write the first thing that comes to mind, and that both of them will probably recall things differently. This exercise is most helpful when done at the onset of the therapeutic relationship and during a therapy session, so it can be discussed and processed.

Suggestions for Follow-Up

At the beginning of the next session, it is helpful to ask the couple if they have had any additional thoughts about the exercise during the course of the week which they would like to discusss.

Contraindications

This activity should not be given to couples who are currently violent, highly conflictual, or who have had a traumatic or less desirable wedding experience and wish not to discuss it.

Readings and Resources for the Professional

Jacobson, N. S. and Margolin, G. (1986). *Marital therapy: Strategies based on social learning and behavior exchange principles.* New York: Brunner/Mazel.
White, M. and Epston, D. (1990). *Narrative means to therapeutic ends.* New York: W. W. Norton & Co.

Bibliotherapy Sources for the Client

Gray, J. (1992). *Men are from Mars, women are from Venus: A practical guide for improving communication and getting what you want in your relationships.* New York: Harper Collins.
Matthews, A. (1988). *Why did I marry you anyway? Good sense and good humor in the first year . . . and after.* Boston: Houghton-Mifflin.
Weiner-Davis, M. (1992). *Divorce busting: A revolutionary and rapid program for staying together.* New York: Summit Books.

When We First Met

Please fill in the blanks. Write the first thing that comes to mind and do not erase or speak to your partner during the process.

The very first time that I saw him/her we were at_____. I was_____ years old and he/she was_____. The day that we actually met I felt_____ because _____. The time and day was approximately _____. The first thing I thought about him/her was_____ _____. The first thing we said to each other was _____. The thing that I remember most about that day was_____. I think what attracted me most to my partner was _____because _____.

On our first date we went to _____. What I remember the most about the way I felt that day/night was_____ _____. Looking back on the day when we first met or our first date makes me feel_____because _____ _____. If I could take one thing from that day and bring into our life now it would be _____. This would be special because _____. What I miss the most about the way we were when we first started to date is_____. This is important to me because _____. I realize that in order to make the changes that I would like to have in our relationship, I too will have to change. The thing that I could do to begin to obtain this again would be _____. This would show my partner that I still care, and would like to make our relationship better.

Our Wedding Day

Please fill in the blanks. Write the first thing that comes to mind and do not erase or speak to your partner during the process.

We were married on_____(date), at_____

_____(place), located in_____(city).

I was wearing_____and he/she was wearing_____.

It was a_____wedding. The thing that we thought would be the most

important that day was to have_____because_____

_____. As we prepared for the wedding I remember feeling

_____. The thing I found was the most difficult for me

to deal with was_____because_____.

The thing that I thought was the easiest to deal with was_____.

What I appreciated the most about my spouse was the way he/she_____

_____. The way that my friends reacted to us getting married

was_____. My parents and family felt_____

about us getting married. The way that my spouse's family felt about us getting married

was_____. This affected me in a_____

way because _____. If we could have changed

anything about that day it would be_____because_____.

The most memorable part of the whole day/evening for me was when_____.

It was special because_____.

33

Feeding the Relationship
by Feeding Each Other

Daniel J. Wiener

Type of Contribution: *Homework*

Objectives

1. To help couples experience the effect(s) of attentiveness and nurturance from their partners;
2. To help couples experience the trade-offs inherent in:
   a. being taken care of via loss of full autonomy, and
   b. being empowered by serving another;
3. To offer couples a cooperative experience of reciprocal partnership.

Rationale for Use

Although traditional marriage assigns unequal status and differing roles to husbands and wives, a majority of American couples today value personal autonomy and equality in marriage (Schwartz, 1994). Nonetheless, nearly all couples living together experience a degree of enduring inequality in their relationships. Inequalities result both from actual differences in (a) power, access, knowledge, skill, and ability; and (b) attitudes in assuming responsibility for the outcome of tasks and for the functioning of the relationship itself.

Couples in therapy regularly present with dissatisfactions over perceived inequalities in the contributions of each partner. Usually one partner is considerably more overt in complaining about the unfairness and/or burden imposed by such inequality, which may concern financial contributions or expenditures, time spent on behalf of the relationship, degree of attentiveness or caring (for children or for the complaining partner), and/or degree of thoroughness in accomplishing tasks. Typically, these complaints are accompanied by negative generalizations about the competence, benevolence, and intentions of the partner. At some point, the partner is provoked into counter-complaining or defending him- or herself, and a familiar quarrel ensues. Both parties then look to the therapist to overcome the inevitable deadlock or impasse.

What is less easily grasped by such conflictual partners is that inequality itself need not be experienced as a problem or a source of distress—provided that some reciprocity and a coordination of efforts are present in the relationship. The complexity of understanding the process of such mutual adjustment to one another has long been noted by social scientists (see Asch, 1952, pp. 173-174), although its desirability is assumed by virtually all clinicians who work with relationships. What is likely to be clinically helpful is a corrective experience for such clients that assigns them unequal yet reciprocal roles.

The technique described below is one of a class of experiential exercises that teaches through enactment rather than verbal-conceptual instruction (Wiener, 1994). Specifically, the

Feeding Homework is designed to give couples a temporary experience of reciprocal attention giving and getting, doing for and having things done for one that simulates tasks in everyday life, requiring coordination of effort under conditions of functional inequality. Through the transformation of a familiar, necessary, and frequent individual activity into an evocative, interpersonal task, it teaches partners to coordinate their unequal actions to produce a functionally unambiguous and, occasionally, an emotionally impactful outcome in the process.

Instructions

Clients are asked whether they are willing to try a fifteen-minute exercise that will teach them more about their difficulties concerning inequality. Explain that your are asking them to set aside time at home, free from other distractions, to take turns feeding each other (the Feeding Exercise). Each partner states his/her food choices in advance, and is responsible for making the food available. Finger-food such as grapes, small cubes of cheese, or nuts is recommended. Occasionally, couples prefer the messier option of spoon-feeding applesauce or pudding. (Bibs are recommended!)

In the Feeding Exercise, the task of the Feeder is to attend closely to the Eater, placing food in the Eater's mouth only when previous bites have been chewed and swallowed, and offering the next bites at appropriate intervals. Deliberately avoid giving advice on how much is to be fed/eaten; that is part of what the couple is to work out. During the exercise, Eaters may not use any part of their bodies except the mouth. As with homework assignments in couples therapy, it is generally advisable to reach agreement in-session on the arrangements for doing the homework (when it will be done, who will initiate doing it).

Divide the exercise into two phases. In Phase I, the Eater may speak to instruct the Feeder. Give the instructions for Phase I verbally during the session, along with a sealed envelope marked "Phase II." If the couple agrees that doing Phase I homework has not been distressing or tension provoking, and is willing to go further, they may open the envelope and proceed with Phase II. Otherwise, ask that the envelope be returned unopened at the next session. (Naturally, curiosity is aroused by the mystery of the sealed envelope, and the couple is therefore more likely to proceed to Phase II!) The Phase II instructions read: "Repeat the Phase I exercise, except that this time, no speaking is allowed by either the Eater or the Feeder."

In order for the couple to perform this homework assignment to their mutual satisfaction, the Feeder must attend closely to the Eater's readiness to accept more food; thus, the Feeder can be viewed more as *serving* the Eater, rather than *controlling* the presentation of food. Correspondingly, the Eater, though in a physically more passive role, has the responsibility to signal readiness (verbally or nonverbally) for the next bite of food. As the Feeding Exercise has both partners take turns in each role, empathy for the partner's performance is heightened.

Suggestions for Follow-Up

At the next session, inquire as to whether the couple attempted the homework and, if so, how it went. Follow up with general questions such as:

• Did this experience go as you expected? If not, in what ways?
• Did it change your experience of your partner?
• Did it change any of your beliefs about your relationship?
• What was different about Phase II from Phase I?

I find that couples who attempt the Feeding Exercise divide about equally in one of three broad response patterns: *Players*, who used the experience for enjoyment; *Fighters*, who replicated their conflict; and *Discoverers*, who found the exercise moving and/or enlightening.

How to proceed is contingent on the response pattern reported. With Players, first note if their recounting of the story is collaborative (each supporting both the mood and content of the other's telling of what happened, indicating that they are once again in a cooperative mind-set). If so, then congratulate them on having created a cooperative experience (of reciprocal partnership), and explore how they might transform their everyday conflicts using the same playful energy they generated during the homework activity. If not, first point out that during the exercise they had achieved a level of reciprocal partnership. Next, find out what intervened, causing them to lose their playful togetherness. Finally, explore choices and opportunities to reevoke it.

With Fighters, make it clear that theirs was not a failed experience, but an experiment permitting all to learn from what occurred. Then proceed with specific questions aimed at connections and patterns, linking performance on the homework to their presenting complaints.

With Discoverers, attend to what was experienced as significant and different, particularly in the domain of emotions. Either feeding or being fed by another may have evoked the nurturer-dependent roles of parent-infant or caretaker-invalid, leading to an exploration of the couple's associative past experiences with these roles. As the physical feeding/eating activity is a potentially messy, visceral event, that is not unilaterally controllable by either partner, each one, especially when in the Eater role, may have experienced anxiety over not controlling food intake, vulnerability to being force-fed, or embarrassment if food dribbled. (By contrast, Players often like messes, and sometimes create them intentionally.) Frequently, Discoverers report having had their prior expectations challenged by the experience. Far from being an expected chore, some clients report enjoying the opportunity to nurture their partners from the Feeder role. The experience of having (literally) nurtured one another can shift the mood of the therapy to a more generous and cooperative level. Conversely, clients who regard themselves as neglected or exploited by their partners are likely to experience having things done for them as unpleasantly limiting of autonomy and control (particularly in Phase II), despite their earlier stated wishes for attention and nurturance from their partners. For example, in sessions prior to the homework, one wife had complained of being overworked, and had repeatedly expressed her wish that her husband would, for once, wait upon her. Far from the anticipated enjoyment in the Eater role, she reported considerable tension and anxiety at being helpless to prevent her Feeder husband from "doing it wrong," and had taken the spoon out of her feeder/husband's hand in violation of the instructions!

When client answers and reactions indicate ambiguity or confusion regarding the impact of the entire experience, you may suggest that they repeat the exercises.

Contraindications

Do not offer the Feeding Exercise after the initial session. Clients first need to become acquainted with therapy and to get a sense of themselves within the present therapeutic context. Accordingly, it is more useful to time the introduction of this homework to a point when humor, boredom, or an obvious impasse in the therapy work exists—a point when both clients and therapist are optimally receptive to novelty. This point often lies between those times when things are tolerable in life (and when therapy is perceived as working), and a point when things are going badly, when the couple is in pain and wants immediate relief rather than gradual change. It is also inadvisable to offer the Feeding Exercise to clients who are highly insecure with their relationship (including those who are actively traumatized or when partner abuse is a factor).

Readings and Resources for the Professional

Asch, S. (1952). *Social psychology.* Englewood Cliffs, NJ: Prentice-Hall.

Schwartz, P. (1994). Peer marriage: What does it take to create a truly egalitarian marriage? *Family Therapy Networker,* September/October, 56-61, 92.

Wiener, D. J. (1994). *Rehearsals for growth: Theater improvisation for psychotherapists.* New York: Norton.

34

Keeping the Honeymoon in the Marriage

Tara R. Gootee

Type of Contribution: *Activity/Handout*

Objective

Couples often find themselves in a rut in their marriage. They are busy working and/or taking care of the children, and it is hard for them to find time for each other. However, it is very important for the adults to relax and allow themselves time to enjoy one another. It is important to "keep the honeymoon in the marriage" in order to build up a reserve of positives in the relationships, to weather the stresses of daily life. The purpose of this activity is to help couples make pleasure a priority in their marriage.

Rationale for Use

The cards you will find included in the activity are romance and intimacy cards, and they can be used to reach the activity's objective. They can be given to clients to use with their partner whenever they need some special time alone, just one on one. It is a unique way for couples to share intimate time with each other.

Instructions

Cut out the cards and place them in a deck. Fan the cards apart, face down, where all cards can be easily reached. Next, have each partner take turns choosing one card at a time. They may read the contents of their card aloud, or they may chose to keep it a surprise. However, there are some terms that the couple needs to agree to before starting the game. The instructions to the client are:

1. Cards may be redeemed whenever the bearer desires, provided both partners agree that they are willing to follow the card's instructions. If not, the reluctant spouse should agree to "make a date" to redeem the card.
2. The bearer has the choice as to whether they want to give or receive the activity. For example, he/she can either give his or her mate a gift of sexy clothing, or he/she can give the coupon to his/her partner, who will then buy the gift.
3. Each partner should agree to try the activity together, even if it is something they usually do not do. For instance, some partners might not like to spend an entire evening snuggling on the couch. However, it may mean a lot to the person receiving the affection.

4. The couple can add their own personal cards to the deck whenever they may need a little boost in their love life. If they do not know how to tell each other what they would like to do together, this may be a good way for them to share their desires.

Once all of the cards have been passed out, the couple is allowed to take them home and redeem them at agreeable times. When all of the cards have been redeemed, the couple can gather the cards together and start the game over. They may want to alter the cards' suggestions before resuming the activity. This will keep the element of surprise in the game.

Suggestions for Follow-Up

It is a good idea to ask the couple how the activity is going every few sessions. This will ensure that the couple is following the "rules," and it will also give you a chance to get some new ideas for future cards. Couples can be very creative in what they write on their personal cards.

Contraindications

This activity will not be beneficial for clients who are in conflict or in crisis. Instead of being an enjoyable activity, it could provide another source of conflict. People who are upset may not be able to share intimacy and warmth with each other.

Readings and Resources for the Professional

Baucom, D. H. and Epstein, N. (1990). *Cognitive behavioral marital therapy.* New York: Brunner/Mazel Publishers.
Jacobson, N. S. and Margolin, G. (1979). *Behavioral marital therapy.* New York: Brunner/Mazel Publishers.

Bibliotherapy Sources for the Client

Bolin, C. and Trent, C. (1995). *How to be your husband's best friend: 365 ways to express your love.* Colorado Springs, CO: Pinon Press.
Byrd, D. and Wolf, L. (1994). *Permission granted: Coupons for couples.* Marietta, GA: Longstreet Press.
Corn, L. (1995). *101 Nights of grrreat sex.* Oklahoma City, OK: Park Avenue Publishers.
DeAngelis, B. (1995). *Real moments for lovers.* New York: Bantam Doubleday Dell Publishing Group, Inc.
Gray, J. (1995). *Mars and Venus in the bedroom: A guide to lasting romance and passion.* New York: HarperCollins.
Haynes, C. and Edwards, D. (1995). *2002 ways to say "I love you."* Holbrook, MA: Adams Media Corporation.
Sanna, L. (1996). *How to romance the man you love—the way he wants you to!* Rockland, CA: Prima Publishing.
Sanna, L. and Miller, K. (1995). *How to romance the woman you love—the way she wants you to!* Rockland, CA: Prima Publishing.

COUPON GOOD FOR:	COUPON GOOD FOR:	COUPON GOOD FOR:
A gift of sexy clothing.	Draw a picture of each other.	An intimate activity of . . . sitting back to back on the floor; each partner is allowed 15 minutes to talk without interruption.
COUPON GOOD FOR:	COUPON GOOD FOR:	COUPON GOOD FOR:
Revelation: If you were back in high school, and could choose your career all over again, what would you pursue?	Tell your partner the most embarrassing thing that has ever happened to you.	Tell your partner the thing you like best about him/her.
COUPON GOOD FOR:	COUPON GOOD FOR:	COUPON GOOD FOR:
Ask your partner to dress in an outfit you particularly like, and go out to lunch or dinner.	A description of your very first kiss with each other.	If you had to rename your partner, what would you name him or her?
COUPON GOOD FOR:	COUPON GOOD FOR:	COUPON GOOD FOR:
Agree to do an activity of your partner's choice—no complaining allowed.	Your choice!	Spend dinner together feeding one another.
COUPON GOOD FOR:	COUPON GOOD FOR:	COUPON GOOD FOR:
Seduce your partner without saying a word.	A private revelation . . . If money were no object, what would your lifelong dream accomplishment be?	A description of your ideal vacation.
COUPON GOOD FOR:	COUPON GOOD FOR:	COUPON GOOD FOR:
Reveal your idea of the perfect spouse. How is your relationship better? How could it be more "perfect?"	Fulfillment of one of your partner's needs or wishes.	A revelation . . . If your partner was someone famous, who would it be?

COUPON GOOD FOR:	COUPON GOOD FOR:	COUPON GOOD FOR:
Two hours of talking, with the exception of stressful topics (e.g., kids, money, work, etc.).	Tell your partner something about yourself that he or she does not already know.	Switch daily roles with your partner for one day.
COUPON GOOD FOR:	COUPON GOOD FOR:	COUPON GOOD FOR:
A description of your favorite childhood memory.	A description . . . If your partner was a flavor, what flavor would he or she be? Why?	Washing each other's hair.
COUPON GOOD FOR:	COUPON GOOD FOR:	COUPON GOOD FOR:
Breakfast in bed.	Hot coffee made for you in the morning.	A foot massage.
COUPON GOOD FOR:	COUPON GOOD FOR:	COUPON GOOD FOR:
Two hours on your own while I watch the children.	I will listen to you carefully, without interrupting, for twenty minutes.	A date of your choice (I will arrange the sitter).
COUPON GOOD FOR:	COUPON GOOD FOR:	COUPON GOOD FOR:
An evening of dining and dancing.	An entire afternoon together—no phones allowed.	A bottle of massage oil or lotion and 30 minutes alone together.
COUPON GOOD FOR:	COUPON GOOD FOR:	COUPON GOOD FOR:
Breakfast in bed—no clothes allowed.	A three-minute kiss!	20 minutes of cuddling.

35

First Date Recollections
and Fantasies with Couples

Edward M. Markowski

Type of Contribution: *Activity/Homework/Handout*

Objectives

1. To discover metaphors, myths, or beliefs in couple relationships.
2. To create possibilities for new patterns of functioning.

Rationale for Use

In recent years, constructivist, narrative, brief, and metaphor models have ascended to prominence in marriage and family therapy. Unique to each of these models is the principle that clients create solutions and new realities by using resources found within themselves. Early recollections are memories of events from one's life that have special meaning for the individual. These constructions of the client's own past have been recognized as valuable sources of information about lifestyle for many decades. Alfred Adler (1937) wrote about the purposiveness of early memory. He believed that no recollections were indifferent or nonsensical; events are remembered according to their importance for a specific psychic tendency or attitude which dominates the personality as a whole. Ansbacher and Ansbacher (1965) drew implications from Adler's work, and suggested that recollections will be positive and encouraging when an individual's tendency is to move toward objects, situations, or people. Similarly, recollections will be negative if the underlying attitude is to flee. Thus, pleasant or unpleasant, positively or negatively toned memories will be connected to meaningful life events.

Willhite (1981) also recognized early recollections as containing important lifestyle clues, and developed a procedure for using them in clinical settings. He used the content of the recollections as indicators of important issues and goals in people's current life situations, and developed a protocol to include feelings associated with the content. Together, the content and feelings give the therapist ideas about persons' views and experiences of present predicaments. Willhite further expanded the procedure by adding a fantasy to be created by the client. Individuals are asked to change their early recollections in any way they want, on the premise that fantasy gives clues to ideals or goals toward which clients are striving, thus providing helpful clinical information. The therapist, then, will be better positioned to enable movement from the present to the ideal, or, at least minimally, to a more satisfying future for the client.

In as much as early recollections indicate current lifestyles, likewise, first date recollections can provide information on a couple's marital style. Since fantasies have been accepted as indicators of ideal expectations for an individual, fantasies of a first date with a spouse can indicate an individual's ideal for an intimate relationship.

The techniques described in this chapter have been used successfully with couples. They are enjoyable and nonthreatening means for obtaining useful information while building rapport. First date recollection content can point to the private logic that guides an individual's current relationship behavior, while first date fantasies will contain indications of how individuals would construct their relationship if they believed they had the power to change it. As a further bonus to both the client and therapist, first date recollections and fantasies usually contain metaphors that can expedite the search for manageable solutions.

Instructions

First Date Recollections

1. The therapist takes a verbatim record of the individual's recollection of his/her first date with the partner. If the first date cannot be remembered, accept a date that the individual can remember. The recollection should be eight to ten sentences in length, and include how the date began, what happened during the date, and how the date ended. It is helpful for the therapist to keep the client informed of the number of each sentence as it is recorded.
2. The therapist obtains an overall feeling associated with the recollection by reading the complete recollection, and asking: "What is the overall feeling you have about the date?" or "As I read your recollection, what feelings started to be present for you?"
3. The therapist obtains a headline for the recollection by asking: "Suppose this recollection was going to be printed in a newspaper. What would the headline over it say in three or four words?"
4. The therapist obtains a feeling associated with each sentence of the recollection by reading each sentence and asking: "What were you feeling while this was happening?" If a client struggles to come up with feelings, reread the sentence and ask: "What would someone be feeling while this was going on?" The feelings are recorded beside the sentence on the recollection form.

First Date Fantasies

1. The therapist asks the individual to create a fantasy first date by responding to directives such as: "Pretend the date did not happen as you described it, and you could create a whole new date without having to worry about money, time, obligations, or other constraints. Be creative and let your imagination take you wherever it wants to go." Some individuals will be hesitant to create a new date. A tactic that generally works when spouses say they cannot think of anything is to have them pretend they are writing a romance novel, and need to include a date in the first chapter that would entice a reader to finish the rest of the book. If the person continues to resist, ask the person to describe a fantasy date for a brother, sister, or friend. Then continue with: "How would the date begin? What would happen during the date? How would the date end?" Indicate that you want the same number of sentences that were given for the first date recollection. Indicate the number of the sentence as it is recorded, and how many more sentences are left.
2. The therapist obtains an overall feeling associated with the fantasy by reading the complete fantasy, and asking: "What is the overall feeling you have about the date?" or "As I read your fantasy, what feelings started to be present for you?"

3. The therapist obtains a headline for the fantasy by asking: "Suppose this fantasy was going to be printed in a newspaper. What would the headline over it say in three or four words?"
4. The therapist obtains a feeling associated with each sentence of the fantasy by reading each sentence and asking: "What would you be feeling while this was happening?" If a client struggles to come up with feelings, reread the sentence and ask: "What would someone be feeling while this was going on?" The feelings are recorded beside the sentence on the fantasy form.

Suggestions for Follow-Up

First date recollections are completed in a session with one partner present, while the other partner completes work in an adjoining room. Subsequently, the second partner completes a recollection, while the other partner is completing tasks in another room. Partners are asked to share their recollections and examine their content for differences and similarities immediately after the session. They are directed to continue discussing them until the next appointment. This procedure provides content for conversation other than the present problems, and often results in shared insights and creative solutions before the next session. First date fantasies are obtained at the next meeting, and couples are again directed to share, examine, and discuss them.

First date recollections allow the couple to revisit the roots of their relationship, which generally were filled with more positive emotions than their present state. First date fantasies allow the couple to construct an imagined future which outlines in concrete terms those things each partner wants in the relationship. In effect, the couple will have set goals for their therapy. For instance, a client who projects an overall feeling of "rushed" for the first date and "contented" for the fantasy, gives a clue to what is going on in the relationship now and what the relationship should be. The content of the recollection will reflect relationship issues that lead to feeling rushed. Likewise, the fantasy is constructed of things that create the feeling of contentment for the client. Both the client and partner will have a clearer understanding of the issues and concrete ideas for change. Similarly, the headline, the events, and the way they are remembered, as well as the feeling connected to each sentence provide a wealth of client generated content in which possible solutions are embedded.

Contraindications

This activity should not be used with intensely hostile couples.

Readings and Resources for the Professional

Adler, A. (1937). Significance of early recollections. *International Journal of Individual Psychology, 3,* 283-287.

Ansbacher, H. L. and Ansbacher, R. R. (Eds.). (1965). *The individual psychology of Alfred Adler: A systematic presentation in selections from his writings.* New York: Harper Torch Books.

Bagarozzi, D. A. and Anderson, S. A. (1989). *Personal, marital, and family myths: Theoretical formulations and clinical strategies.* New York: Norton.

Combs, G. and Freedman, J. (1990). *Symbol, story, and ceremony: Using metaphor in individual and family therapy.* New York: Norton.

Crandall, J. W. (1971). The early spouse memory as a diagnostic aid in marriage counseling. *Journal of Contemporary Psychotherapy, 3*(2), 82-88.

Kopp, R. R. (1995). *Metaphor therapy: Using client-generated metaphors in psychotherapy.* New York: Brunner/Mazel.

White, M. and Epston, D. (1990). *Narrative means to therapeutic ends.* New York: Norton.

Willhite, R. (1981). "The Willhite": A creative extension of the early recollection process. In L. G. Baruth and D. G. Eckstein (Eds.), *Life style: Theory, practice, and research* (pp. 84-94). Dubuque, IA: Kendall/Hunt.

Bibliotherapy Sources for the Client

Gray, J. (1992). *Men are from Mars, women are from Venus.* New York: HarperCollins.

Hendrix, H. (1988). *Getting the love you want: A guide for couples.* New York: HarperCollins.

Hendrix, H. (1992). *Keeping the love you find.* New York: Simon & Schuster.

First Date Recollection Form

Date:_____Client Name:_____

Headline:_____

Recollection	**Feelings**
1.	1.
2.	2.
3.	3.
4.	4.
5.	5.
6.	6.
7.	7.
8.	8.
9.	9.
10.	10.

Overall feeling(s):_____

First Date Fantasy Form

Date:_____**Client Name:**_____

Headline:_____

Recollection	Feelings
1.	1.
2.	2.
3.	3.
4.	4.
5.	5.
6.	6.
7.	7.
8.	8.
9.	9.
10.	10.

Overall feeling(s):_____

36

Structured Trial Separation

Liberty Kovacs

Type of Contribution: *Activity/Handout*

Objectives

The Structured Trial Separation is designed to give the couple space and time apart from each other in order to:

1. prevent further deterioration of the marriage;
2. gain a more realistic perspective of self, the other partner, and the relationship;
3. determine what his/her individual needs are, as well as the relationship needs;
4. determine how each wants the relationship to be different;
5. help each partner decide what s/he is willing to contribute to make the relationship work more effectively.

Rationale for Use

When a marital relationship becomes overwhelmed by distress, disillusionment, and painful emotionality, discussions of separation and/or divorce increase between couples. The threat of divorce may be an attempt to control the other and, at times, some couples even try separating for a few days, or weeks, and return to find that the situation has not improved. By the time a couple seeks professional help, the relationship may be well on the way toward disintegration. This is a critical time for the couple and the marriage. There are several marital situations that have benefitted from structured trial separations:

1. The couple who want to save their marriage. (If one has decided that a permanent separation is necessary and divorce is inevitable, then it goes without saying that a trial separation is not a consideration. Divorce therapy is more appropriate.)
2. When the levels of anger and conflict between a couple have escalated to a degree that neither partner can reach a more objective position;
3. When couples have grown so distant and disengaged that they cannot reconnect without assistance;
4. When an affair has been discovered or revealed;
5. When one partner leaves the marriage repeatedly, and both have difficulty reaching an understanding of differing needs.

This chapter was previously published in *Journal of Couples Therapy*, 1994, 4(3/4), 83-94.

Instructions

Initially, a thorough assessment of the present relationship, including observed interactions and reports of marital history, will provide the necessary information for determining the appropriate intervention for each couple. When a structured trial separation is decided to be the intervention of choice, both spouses are seen together to review the purpose of the separation and to establish "rules" that both agree to follow. Guidelines or rules must be flexible enough to meet the needs of each couple.

The following subjects are discussed thoroughly with each couple: therapy, family finances, length of time apart, child care, dating (others/each other), and contacts with each other.

The therapeutic environment offers the couple a safe place where each may express him- or herself and to "practice" their communication skills. The therapist's role is that of guide and facilitator for both individuals and for the relationship. Individual therapy is usually recommended for each spouse on alternate weeks, and couple therapy on the third week. This arrangement gives each person time to focus on individual issues, learn new ways of communicating, and develop interpersonal skills. The couple sessions frequently become a laboratory to test their newly found insights and skills with each other.

Deciding who will move from the couple's residence is one of the first decisions that must be made. Sometimes this is easily arranged, because one has been insistent on leaving. However, if this is not the case, a decision on this issue must be made before continuing with the others. Once a decision is made of who will depart, the following issues are then explored in depth. This process may take several weeks to complete.

Discussions of *family finances* are important because the maintenance of two households is an expensive proposition. Some couples attempt to divide their present household into two living arrangements. This approach is met with limited success. Moving in with parents, friends, or working associates is also not an optimal solution as these living arrangements have the propensity for distracting the individual from the purpose of the separation. A separation should be used as time alone to explore and discover one's self and to gain perspective on the relationship. Each will share with the therapist their experiences with seclusion and being apart from spouse (and children). This may be the time for each partner to rediscover hobbies, start an exercise program, do some reading, or develop whatever interest has been put aside due to lack of time.

Women usually discover that they have not allowed themselves the time to develop interests or have time alone in the family. Many women are troubled with feeling selfish if they take time for themselves. Usually, with therapy, women will come to realize that time alone to recharge one's energy, to relax and recreate one's self is not selfishness; rather, this time alone is a necessity. Otherwise, couples find themselves "burned out," depleted, depressed, or susceptible to infections and illnesses.

The length of time for the separation is initially set for three months. This is the minimum amount of time that allows the couple to make the transition to "single life" and "single parenthood." The trial separation also allows the couple to miss each other and to begin seeing the work that needs to be done on the relationship.

Some couples choose to extend the period of separation to six and twelve months. The longer period of separation can allow the couple time to work through the pain associated with the relationship (particularly when an affair has taken place), to deal with dysfunctional patterns of interaction, and even to deal with past "unfinished business."

Child care is another crucial element that must be considered and dealt with together. The children must be informed that "mom and dad have decided to live apart for the time being." The big fear of children is that parents will get divorced, and it is difficult for children to understand that the separation is an important way to avert divorce. One couple agreed to take turns living in a rented apartment so the children's lives would not be disrupted. Interestingly, most couples find that the time they spend with their children (after the separation) is often more focused on the children and is a more enjoyable time for parents and children.

As with divorce, the more conflicted the relationship between the parents, the more disruptive the separation is for the children. Family therapy is helpful at these time, and gives the children an opportunity to express their own feelings and concerns.

Personal contact between the two spouses requires careful negotiation. The issue of dating others is discussed thoroughly. Affairs are considered counterproductive, and are distractions that take the focus off the individual's and couple's developmental processes. One couple agreed that they could see friends of the opposite sex for dinner or a movie, but sexual contact was not acceptable.

Frequent telephone calls are discouraged, as is "dropping in" on each other. The couple must decide on the frequency and the type of contacts they need to make. Outside of therapy, seeing each other for the first month is also discouraged. When they do see each other again, they agree to meet in a neutral place—a restaurant, a park, etc.—not in the rented apartment or their home.

Gradually, as time passes, "dating" experiences are explored with the couple. Both are encouraged to call the other and arrange a "date." Now, dating becomes a more conscious process than it was originally. Both are making conscious efforts to plan activities together that are pleasurable and satisfying. Reestablishing their sexual relationship is usually discussed in the therapy sessions, particularly, in dealing with problems they may have had previously and learning to ask for the kind of sexual activity that each wants to experience.

If an affair has occurred in the past, fidelity and rebuilding trust are discussed throughout the therapy sessions until both feel satisfied that the issue is resolved. This process is long and difficult: the one having had the affair decides to give up the other relationship, grieves for the loss (usually in individual therapy) and makes a renewed commitment to work on rebuilding the marital relationship with the partner. The other partner will spend much time dealing with the hurt, anger, sense of betrayal, and letting go of the pain in order to go forward in the rebuilding process.

An important transition occurs when (if) each partner makes the decision to return to the relationship. This, too, is discussed thoroughly before the move is made. By this time, the couple is more confident about themselves as individuals, and they know how they want to relate to each other as a couple. They have put considerable time and energy into redesigning the relationship, developing communication skills (including conflict resolution and problem solving), and negotiating their wants and desires. They have achieved a renewed sense of empathy, love, and respect for each other's individuality, and they are enjoying their newfound abilities to be open in talking with each other about any issue that comes up between them. They feel safe in having interests and activities separately from each other, and they can enjoy each other when they are together.

For the therapist, guiding and facilitating the trial separation process with the intent of helping two people to redesign their marriage and making it flexible enough to include two whole individuals and the relationship, is a fulfilling and gratifying experience.

Suggestions for Follow-Up

It is important for couples to understand that, under stress, there may be some backsliding into old patterns. However, with immediate crisis intervention, long-term problems can be avoided. A periodic checkup with the therapist is recommended.

Contraindications

The structured trial separation is contraindicated in relationships in which one or both partners exhibit signs of personality disorder and/or are suffering with severe abandonment issues, early childhood sexual/physical abuse, or adults who are in abusive relationships.

Readings and Resources for the Professional

Granvold, D. K. (1983). Structured separation for marital treatment and decision making. *Journal of Marital and Family Therapy, 9*(4), 403-412.

Kovacs, L. (1982). A conceptualization of marital development. *Family Therapy, 10*(3), 183-210.

Kovacs, L. (1988). Couple therapy: An integrated developmental and family systems model. *Family Therapy, 15*(2), 132-155.

Kovacs, L. (1990). Today's marriage: The six stages. (videotape). Author.

Kovacs, L. (1994). Separateness/togetherness: A paradox in relationships. *Journal of Couples Therapy, 4*(3/4), 83-94.

Bibliotherapy Sources for the Client

Campbell, S. M. (1984). *The couple's journey. Intimacy as a path to wholeness.* San Luis Obispo, CA: Impact Publishers.

Gottman, J. (1994). *Why marriages succeed or fail.* New York: Simon & Schuster.

Gray, J. (1992). *Men are from Mars women are from Venus.* New York: HarperCollins.

Hendrix, H. (1988). *Getting the love you want: A guide for couples.* New York: Henry Holt & Co.

Lerner, H. G. (1986). *Dance of anger.* New York: Harper & Row.

Lerner, H. G. (1990). *Dance of intimacy.* New York: Harper & Row.

Markman, H., Stanley, S., and Blumberg, S. L. (1994). *Fighting for your marriage.* San Francisco: Jossey-Bass.

Preparation for a Structured Trial Separation

Couples who attempt a marital separation without the guidance and support of a professional therapist usually find themselves floundering, feeling isolated, frightened, and hurt. Frequently, the couple will reconcile and "get back together" without having worked on the significant issues and, more important, without any significant changes taking place.

In order to assist you in making the separation a purposeful and productive undertaking, the following items are suggested as "things to consider" in preparing for the separation. When you are ready to write your separation agreement, these areas will be included in the agreement.

1. What is the *purpose of the separation* for you? State specific needs, wants, and goals that you want to examine and address with your spouse and therapist.

2. *Who will move out* becomes one of the first issues to be decided. Usually, the one who wants to leave will move out. However, this is not always the case, especially when there are small children in the family. This decision may take several weeks to decide, and there are various options to be explored. Consider as many options as possible before making a final decision.

3. *Financial Support.* In addition to your regular expenses and monthly payments, other living arrangements will need to be made for the one who will move out of the home. This will include money for renting an apartment, food, transportation, etc. Review your budget with your spouse and decide what adjustments will have to be made in order to provide the necessary funds for the change in living arrangements.

4. *Child Care.* When you and your spouse are convinced that a separation is inevitable, your child/children will need to be informed. Children need assurance that they are not responsible for the separation, and that both parents will be available to care for them. A family meeting is one way of discussing the separation, as long as both adults can present the separation in an objective manner without blaming or faulting each other. If the children become anxious and distressed over the impending separation, a family therapy session may be necessary. It is very important for both parents to spend time with the children; therefore, a consistent schedule for parenting by both adults must be designed.

5. *Length of time for the separation* is usually set for three months. Although some couples may prefer six weeks or less, three months permits the couple to experience "single life," and to develop a perspective of the relationship that they never had before. At the end of this time, an evaluation of the separation will occur with your spouse and your therapist. If more time is desired by one spouse, this will be renegotiated.

6. *Contact with spouse.* A period of time with no contact between the spouses is a way to ease into the separation, and to begin the transition into singlehood. A month is preferable, but this is negotiable, as long as both respect the privacy of the other.

Frequent phone calls are discouraged, as is "dropping in" on each other or overseeing your spouse's activities. After a few weeks have passed, you may want to discuss in the conjoint therapy sessions the matters of dating and initiating sex with your spouse.

7. *Dating others* is a topic of concern to one or both spouses, and this must be explored thoroughly in conjoint therapy and with your spouse. An agreement should be made in regard to what type of contact with others is acceptable to both spouses.

8. *Sexual contact* with others is also a topic to be examined and discussed openly so you and your spouse will know what rules are established regarding sexual contact between yourselves or with others.

9. *Homework* will be initiated in the therapy sessions, and will require a commitment of time and energy to bring about the desired changes in self and in the relationship, and will indicate that your marital relationship has priority during the separation. Also important in this area is the use of positive methods of encouragement to support your spouse in his/her efforts to grow and make changes.

10. *Contact with attorney.* The question of whether or not to retain an attorney arises frequently. In the last decade, some attorneys have trained as mediators and will see the couple together to discuss the legal aspects of separation. This approach can be useful in answering questions about finances, child support, and other matters of legal liability. Clients are encouraged to read books as well as attend classes that may be offered in the community on the subject of separation and divorce.

After a thorough and thoughtful examination and discussion of each of the items suggested to prepare for the separation, you may be ready to write your own marital separation agreement. The following is a sample marital agreement to use as a guide in writing your own agreement. This is only a guide, and the terms of your separation may be much different. Your therapist can be helpful in aiding you in these negotiations.

MARITAL SEPARATION AGREEMENT

I, _____ , agree to marital separation from my spouse for

_____ (weeks/months), during which time I will not make a decision to remain

married or divorce. I agree to the following stipulations:

Therapy. I will attend conjoint and alternate individual therapy sessions during the

separation period as I prefer and in consideration of _____ (therapist's)

recommendations.

Financial Support. It is agreed that the following payments will be made on a monthly

basis: (list specific accounts and dates that are due):_____

_____

Child Care. I agree to spend individual time with my child on alternate weekends

unless work or travel prevent me from doing so.

Contact with Spouse. I agree to have no direct contact for_____(weeks) or as

recommended by_____(therapist), except in case of emergency. After this

period of time, I will have telephone contact with my spouse only to arrange our

"dates." If a meeting with my spouse is necessary, I agree to meet him/her in a

neutral place (e.g., restaurant or park) for no more than one hour; otherwise, I will

make no effort to see my spouse more frequently than the designated times permit.

Sexual Contact with Spouse. I understand that my spouse and I may have sexual

contact, following the initial hiatus, and that either of us may initiate sexual activity. If

one spouse is not ready to resume sexual activity, this matter will be discussed in the

next conjoint therapy session.

Dating Others. I understand that each of us is eligible to date others. My prefer-

ence for myself is_____.

Sexual Contact with Others. I understand that sexual contact with others is an

option. My preference for myself is_____.

Privacy. I will make no effort to "drop in," oversee my spouse's activities, or make

telephone calls, except those specified above.

Homework. I will make every effort to carry out the homework assignments to which I agreed during the therapy sessions. I understand that my marital relationship is to have priority during this separation period. I will use only positive methods to encourage my spouse to participate in doing the homework.

Renegotiation. Should my spouse and I, in collaboration with our therapist, prefer to sustain the separation period, I will participate in renegotiating the separation agreement at the end of the separation period. Furthermore, should either my spouse or I wish to alter any part of this agreement at any time, it is to be discussed and renegotiated during a conjoint therapy sessions with _____ (therapist).

Signed_____

Date_____ .

(Three copies are required. Each spouse signs a copy and provides it to his/her spouse. The third copy is for the therapist's file.)

37

Mate Selection Criteria for Compatibility

Sid Levine

Type of Contribution: *Handout/Homework*

Objective

This is a guide to help people think about what they want in a mate. When asked why a couple married, they usually say, "We were in love." When pressed further with "Why?," they might say, "We liked being together" or "We had fun together," and so on. This guide is to help a person pursue the answers to "why?" in as many conceivable aspects, qualities, characteristics, traits, activities, wants, interests, attitudes, values, and goals as possible. This is a subjective survey meant to give the couple and therapist new information about the relationship.

Rationale for Use

Using Paul Hauck's definition of love being the strong feelings one has toward a person who meets another's needs and wants, it is assumed the greater the compatibility of need satisfaction a couple has, the more successful and satisfying a mate will be. The mate selection criteria can help the therapist find areas in which to work therapeutically, to enable couples to increase their need satisfaction. It can also be used with single individuals to heighten their awareness to what they are looking for in a relationship.

Instructions

The following handout and inventory can be given to the couple to complete (separately) as a homework assignment. The therapist can then process the activity in session, by asking questions such as: "What was most surprising to you about this assignment?" and "What types of things did you find you appreciated more about your relationship after completing this survey?"

Suggestions for Follow-Up

Assignments may be given to a couple after discussing the criteria to increase need satisfaction. For example, if they agree that the theater is a priority for each of them, a play may be in order.

Contraindications

With highly acrimonious couples, this instrument would best be processed individually first, and as a couple if the therapist believes it could be used therapeutically, rather than as something which further divides the couple.

Readings and Resources for the Professional

Hauck, Paul A. (1977) *Marriage is a loving business*. Philadelphia, PA: The Westminster Press.

Mate Selection Criteria for Compatibility

Instructions: Humans have been using the same courtship rituals for thousands of years. You will not find a perfect mate. The following questions are a *guide* to help you think about your desires for a mate, as well as things you do not want in a mate.

Fill in the following mate selection criteria as thoroughly as possible. Remember to choose your answers to the following questions according to your own thinking, *not* what you think your partner wants to hear.

Write comments or questions in the blanks provided that you may want to discuss with your prospective mate.

Instructions: Check any and all of the boxes that apply. Decide which of the following issues are important to you individually, which are important to your marriage and you would like to have as part of your marriage, or which you do not want in your marriage. Make comments you would like to discuss with your partner.

Topic: Common Interests	Important to me individually	Important to me in marriage	Do not want in marriage	Neutral regarding this topic	Comments
Interests or Hobbies					
MUSIC					
singing					
playing an instrument					
listening to (type(s): (_____)					
THEATRE					
viewing plays					
viewing movies					
participating in theater (acting)					
ART					
creating art					
viewing art					
collecting art					
CRAFTS/HOBBIES					
creating crafts					
performing a hobby: (_____)					
LEISURE TIME					
reading					
movies					
photography					
gardening					
SPORTS					
baseball					
basketball					

188

Topic: Common Interests	Important to me individually	Important to me in marriage	Do not want in marriage	Neutral regarding this topic	Comments
SPORTS (continued)					
football					
volleyball					
tennis					
fishing					
skating					
swimming					
bicycling					
jogging					
boating					
hiking					
hunting					
camping					
other: (_____)					
POLITICS					
voting					
Republican party					
Democratic party					
other party					
RELIGION					
attendance of worship					
belief in a particular religion: (_____)					
importance of similar beliefs					
following doctrine of: (_____)					

Topic: Common Interests	Important to me individually	Important to me in marriage	Do not want in marriage	Neutral regarding this topic	Comments
SOCIALIZING					
entertaining					
going to parties					
going to bars					
dancing					
visiting friends					
visiting family					
knowing neighbors					
PETS					
having pets					

B. Assessing Common Attitudes, Values, and Goals. Please answer the following questions and check whether they are important to you, important to your marriage, or whether you do not want this attitude, value, or goal in your marriage.

	Important to me individually	Important to me in marriage	Do not want in marriage	Neutral regarding this topic	Comments
CHILDREN					
Do you want children?					
If so, how many?					
Why do or don't you want to have children?					
How should children be disciplined?					
Who should make decisions about child rearing?					
RELIGION					
What basic beliefs, doctrine, tenets do you follow? Why?					
How religious are you?					
What religious rituals do you observe?					
Do you pray?					
What holiday customs do you observe?					
If you are religious, where do you want to worship?					
MONEY					
Who will handle bill paying?					
Who will handle planning of finances?					
What are your financial goals?					
If you both work, will incomes be pooled?					
How do you plan to save?					
What yearly income do you want?					
in 10 years?					
in 20 years?					
in 30 years?					

191

	Important to me individually	Important to me in marriage	Do not want in marriage	Neutral regarding this topic	Comments
MONEY (continued)					
What type of luxuries do you want that you must plan for financially?					
If you have children, will you establish a college fund? How?					
LIFESTYLE					
Where do you want to live now?					
Where would you like to live in the future?					
Do you want to live near family?					
What kind of dwelling do you want to live in (house, apartment, etc.)?					
What type of environment do you want to live in (rural, urban, etc.)?					
Are you willing to move for a better job? For you? For your spouse?					
How will you divide household work?					
Cooking?					
Laundry?					
Lawn care?					
Cleaning?					
How will you divide child care should you have children?					
What are your views on your own job/career?					
What are your views on your spouse's job/career?					
Do you have any traits or habits that you are unwilling to give up? What are they?					
Does your partner have any traits or habits that you think he/she should give up? What are they?					

Instructions: Check if you want the following personality/socialization traits in yourself, and in your mate. Make any comments you think are relevant to your discussion with your partner.

PERSONALITY TRAITS AND SOCIALIZATION SKILLS	Want this in myself	Want this in my mate	Comments
COMMUNICATION:			
Talking about experiences, ideas, interests?			
Be frank and open about feelings?			
Constructive criticism?			
Clear (nonviolent) expression of anger?			
Intelligent?			
Positive outlook/attitude?			
Friendly to others?			
Outgoing?			
Affectionate?			
Complimentary?			
Good listener?			
Sensitive?			
Caring?			
Tolerant of others?			
Able to express anger constructively?			
Willing to compromise?			
Flexible?			
Share decisions?			
Kiss and make up after an argument?			
Spend time together?			
Willing to develop new interests?			

PERSONALITY TRAITS AND SOCIALIZATION SKILLS	Want this in myself	Want this in my mate	Comments
COMMUNICATION (continued):			
Want to go out without spouse?			
Willing to apologize for hurting another?			
Jealous?			
Other: _____			

Instructions: Check if you want the following behavior(s) in your marriage. Make any comments you think are relevant to your discussion with your partner.

SEXUAL PREFERENCES	COMMENTS FOR DISCUSSION WITH MATE
Want to communicate openly about sexual needs and wants ☐ YES ☐ NO	
Want partner to communicate openly about sexual needs and wants ☐ YES ☐ NO	
Would like to have sexual intercourse _____ times per week (ideally)	
Prefer the following sexual position: _____	
I am open to exploring other sexual positions ☐ YES ☐ NO	
I want my spouse to be open to exploring other sexual positions ☐ YES ☐ NO	
I am open to the following marital aids:	
use of erotic films ☐ YES ☐ NO	
use of pornography ☐ YES ☐ NO	
sexual toys ☐ YES ☐ NO	
cybersex ☐ YES ☐ NO	
It is important for me to connect emotionally before I can be physically turned on ☐ YES ☐ NO	
I expect monogamy from my spouse ☐ YES ☐ NO	
I am into sexually unusual behavior (please describe): _____	
I expect my spouse to participate in or be tolerant of the above behavior ☐ YES ☐ NO	
It is important to me to be caressed without it necessarily leading to sex ☐ YES ☐ NO	
I have a sexual handicap (list): _____	
I have the following sexual preference	
☐ heterosexual ☐ homosexual ☐ bisexual ☐ other	
Specifically, during foreplay, I enjoy: _____	
I particularly like doing _____ to my partner during foreplay.	
Specifically, during sex, I enjoy: _____	
I particularly like doing _____ to my partner during sex.	
After sex, I like to: _____	
If my partner is sexually responsive to me, he/she acts in the following way: _____	
The most important part of intimacy to me is: _____	

195

Instructions: Check if you want the following behavior(s) in your marriage. Make any comments you think are relevant to your discussion with your partner.

FAMILY EXPERIENCES	COMMENTS FOR DISCUSSION WITH MATE
I want my spouse to participate with me in extended family activities. ☐ YES ☐ NO	
I want to participate in my spouse's extended family activities. ☐ YES ☐ NO	
It is important to me to be financially independent from my family of origin. ☐ YES ☐ NO	
It is important to me to be financially independent from my spouse's family of origin. ☐ YES ☐ NO	
I enjoy children. ☐ YES ☐ NO	
I am willing to not have children in my marriage. ☐ YES ☐ NO	
If we cannot biologically have children, I am willing to adopt. ☐ YES ☐ NO	
I am willing to accept and love children from my spouse's previous marriage. ☐ YES ☐ NO ☐ N/A	
I want my spouse to accept and love children from my previous marriage. ☐ YES ☐ NO ☐ N/A	
It is important to me that we nurture our marriage and work to keep it healthy. ☐ YES ☐ NO	
Ideas to keep marriage healthy: _____	
PHYSICAL CHARACTERISTICS AND HEALTH OF MATE/SELF	
I enjoy my spouse's body. ☐ YES ☐ NO	
I expect my spouse to accept me as I am. ☐ YES ☐ NO	
I am comfortable with my own body. ☐ YES ☐ NO	
I am pleased by my mate's physical characteristics. ☐ YES ☐ NO	
I am pleased by the way my mate takes care of his/her body/health. ☐ YES ☐ NO	
I would tolerate my mate smoking. ☐ YES ☐ NO	
I would tolerate my mate using drugs. ☐ YES ☐ NO	
I would tolerate my mate drinking. ☐ YES ☐ NO	
I would expect my mate to tolerate my smoking. ☐ YES ☐ NO	
I would expect my mate to tolerate me using drugs. ☐ YES ☐ NO	
I would expect my mate to tolerate my drinking. ☐ YES ☐ NO	
I am a spiritual person. ☐ YES ☐ NO	
I expect my mate to be a spiritual person. ☐ YES ☐ NO	
I understand the mental and physical health strengths and limitations of my spouse's family of origin. ☐ YES ☐ NO	

38

Couple Intimacy and Sexuality Questionnaire

Thomas W. Blume

Type of Contribution: *Homework/Activity/Handout*

Objective

This activity is designed to help couples move away from indirect, unproductive discussions. Conversely, it is also designed to help therapists lead clients into an open, focused, specific discussion of attitudes, preferences, interests, and beliefs about their sexual relationship.

Rationale for Use

Even in the early weeks and months of their relationships, many couples experience difficulty in their sexual relationships. Some do not directly acknowledge the sexual problem when they seek therapy. Others refer to the sexual problem, but the description sounds as if the specialized skills of a sex therapist are not needed; the problems result from ignorance, misunderstanding, fear, miscommunication, and misattribution about their experiences. Therapists frequently face client reluctance to talk openly about sexual matters, and many therapists are uncomfortable "pushing" the discussion.

This brief questionnaire provides a safe, structured way to lead sexual discussions into productive arenas where aid in problem solving, information giving, and communication can help move the couple toward their intimacy goals. Several common problem areas are addressed as the couple answers the structured questions:

1. Individual variations in sexual response are normalized. The emphasis on helping each partner to understand the other's preferences reassures both partners that there is not a standard way of being sexual.
2. Sexual pleasure is separated into giving and receiving modes. Both modes are valued, and the partners are asked to identify their favorite activities for each mode of sexual pleasure.
3. Sexual pleasure is also subdivided according to the differing goals partners may have: seeking a sense of comfort through sex, and/or seeking a sense of excitement. Partners are invited to recognize that they may respond both ways at different times.
4. Genital sexuality is placed in context as only one kind of sexually pleasurable stimulation, and partners are asked to share their awareness of, and their feelings about their bodies.

5. The interplay of self-concept, moods, settings, and responses is acknowledged, and partners are encouraged to describe their turn-ons and their turn-offs.
6. Orgasm is presented as an option—one of the possible goals of sexual intimacy. This redefinition of orgasm as an optional activity reduces partners' anxiety about reaching their own orgasms or "making" their partners reach orgasm, and allows discussions of options.
7. The concept of unwanted sexual activity is introduced, allowing the partners and/or the therapist to discuss coercion, assertiveness, and personal rights.
8. Change—the inclusion of new activities and the modification of current practice—is suggested as a desired goal for both partners.

Instructions

The questionnaire is used two ways:

1. Partners are given the questionnaires in session, and asked to read them over, then pick one or two items they would be most interested in discussing in the session. This instruction generally accesses one or two of the more easily discussed issues, and provides the therapist with the opportunity to help the partners to be more open and specific in their discussions.
2. Partners are asked to take the questionnaires home and write out their answers separately, then attempt a discussion of some answers they did not cover in the session. They are told that they will most likely find some issues hard to discuss in a productive way, and they should bring the questionnaires to the next session to continue the discussion.

Suggestions for Follow-Up

Once the door is opened for factual, open discussion of sexual activity, the partners will generally continue to pursue their goals if the necessary problem-solving and conflict management skills are present. If sexual discussions are unproductive, it is suggested that the conflict management process be addressed directly.

Contraindications

This kind of sexual discussion is likely to create additional anxiety if a sexual dysfunction is part of the distress. Sexual dysfunctions should be ruled out before proceeding with this activity/homework.

Readings and Resources for the Professional

Apt, C. and Hurlbert, D. F. (1992). The female sensation seeker and martial sexuality. *Journal of sex and marital therapy, 18,* 315-324.
Atwood, J. D. and Dershowitz, S. (1992). Constructing a sex and marital therapy frame: Ways to help couples deconstruct sexual problems. *Journal of sex and marital therapy, 18,* 196-218.
Carroll, J. L., Volk, K. D., and Hyde, J. S. (1985). Differences between males and females in motives for engaging in sexual intercourse. *Archives of sexual behavior, 14,* 131-139.
DeLamater, J. (1987). Gender differences in sexual scenarios. In K. Kelley (Ed.), *Females, males, and sexuality.* Albany, NY: SUNY Press.

Fisher, R. and Ury, W. (1981). *Getting to yes*. New York: Penguin.

Gagnon, J. H. and Simon, W. (1973). *Sexual conduct: The social sources of human sexuality*. Chicago: Aldine.

Keesling, B. (1993). *Sexual pleasure: Reaching new heights of sexual arousal and intimacy*. New York: Hunter House.

Milkman, H. and Sunderwirth, S. (1987). *Craving for ecstasy: The consciousness and chemistry of escape*. Lexington, MA: Lexington Books.

Bibliotherapy Sources for the Client

Keesling, B. (1993). *Sexual pleasure: Reaching new heights of sexual arousal and intimacy*. New York: Hunter House.

Louden, S. (1994). *The couple's comfort book*. San Francisco: Harper San Francisco.

Love, P. and Robinson, S. (1994). *Hot monogamy: Essential steps to more passionate intimate lovemaking*. New York: Dutton.

COUPLE INTIMACY AND SEXUALITY QUESTIONNAIRE

This questionnaire is designed to help you and your partner to explore your beliefs, attitudes, preferences, and interests related to sex and intimacy. There are no right or wrong answers. For each of the following questions, please answer how you think or feel TODAY. You should complete your questionnaires separately before discussing your answers.

The most sexually sensitive part of my body, APART FROM MY GENITALS, is:_____

_____

The sexual activity I would find most COMFORTING is:_____

_____

The sexual activity I would find most EXCITING is:_____

_____

I am MOST INTERESTED in sexual activity when:_____

_____

I am LEAST INTERESTED in sexual activity when:_____

_____

I am most likely to engage in UNWANTED sexual activity when:_____

_____

My favorite activity for PLEASING MY PARTNER would be:_____

_____

My favorite activity for RECEIVING PLEASURE would be:_____

_____

My partner's orgasm is: (choose one)
_____the goal of every sexual experience.
_____expected most of the time we have a sexual experience.
_____not expected, but a welcome part of a sexual experience.
_____a disruptive event that can spoil a sexual experience.

My own orgasm is: (choose one)
_____the goal of every sexual experience.
_____expected most of the time we have a sexual experience.
_____not expected, but a welcome part of a sexual experience.
_____a disruptive event that can spoil a sexual experience.

Of all the sexual behaviors I know of, the one I am LEAST interested in trying is:_____

_____

The part of my body I am most PROUD of is:_____

The part of my body I am most DISAPPOINTED by is:_____

39

Sexual Response and Interaction Inventory

Fred E. Stickle

Type of Contribution: *Handout*

Objective

The handout's objective is to identify frequency, desired frequency, and level of enjoyment one thinks his or her partner has with various lovemaking activities.

Rationale for Use

The majority of couples have never discussed personal questions of this nature. The Sexual Response Inventory opens up couple communication.

Instructions

The therapist gives each partner the Inventory to complete as honestly and accurately as possible. The couple is instructed to answer the questions in reference to the past six to twelve months. After the Inventory is given back to the therapist, each question is gone over with the couple. Areas of agreement are discussed, and the couple is reinforced by the therapist for their agreement. Discrepancies between the two will provide an opportunity for discussion and compromise. The process will take several sessions. Pushing through the Inventory too quickly could be a negative experience. The process will take time. If a disagreement item is discussed and a compromise is reached, the couple is given an appropriate assignment, the results of which are discussed at the next therapy session.

Suggestions for Follow-Up

Following the discussion of the disagreed items, the couple is encouraged to compromise. During the following session, the couple reports on the compromise, and the therapist continually evaluates their progress.

Readings and Resources for the Professional

Hawton, K. (1985). *Sex therapy: A practical guide.* New York: Oxford University Press.
Herman, J. and LoPiccolo, J. (1988). *Becoming orgasmic: A sexual and personal growth program for women.* New York, London: Simon & Schuster.

Leiblum, S. and Rosen, R. (1989). *Principles and practice of sex therapy.* New York, London: The Guilford Press.

Maters, W., Johnson, V., and Kolodny, W. (1995). *Human sexuality.* New York: HarperCollins College Publishers.

Penner, J. and Penner, C. (1990). *Counseling for sexual disorders.* Dallas: Word Publishing.

Weinstein, E. and Rosen, E. (1988). *Sexuality counseling: Issues and implications.* Pacific Grove, CA: Brooks/Cole Publishing Company.

Wincze, J. and Carey, M. (1991). *Sexual dysfunction: A guide for assessment and treatment.* New York, London: The Guilford Press.

Woody, J. (1992). *Treating sexual distress: Integrative systems therapy.* Newbury Park, CA: Sage Publications.

Bibliotherapy Sources for the Client

Barbach, L. (1984). *For each other: Sharing sensual intimacy.* New York: Penguin Group.

Kreidman, E. (1989). *Light his fire: How to keep your man passionately and hopelessly in love with you.* New York: Villard Books.

Kreidman, E. (1991). *Light her fire: How to ignite passion and excitement in the woman you love.* New York: Villard Books.

Renshaw, D. (1995). *Seven weeks to better sex.* New York: Random House.

Rosenau, D. (1994). *A celebration of sex.* Nashville, TN: Thomas Nelson Publishers.

Stoppard, M. (1992). *The magic of sex.* New York: Dorling Kindersley.

Womack, W. and Strauss, F. (1991). *The marriage bed.* Oakland, CA: New Harbinger Publications.

Yaffe, M. and Fenwick, E. (1988). *Sexual happiness: A practical approach.* New York: Henry Holt and Company.

Sexual Response and Interaction Inventory

1. Short sexual lovemaking—from start to finish 15 minutes or less
2. Medium sexual lovemaking—from start to finish 15 minutes to 30 minutes
3. Longer sexual lovemaking—from start to finish 30 minutes to 45 minutes
4. Talking during sexual lovemaking
5. Seeing your partner naked
6. Being seen naked
7. French kissing (tongue in each other's mouth)
8. Giving your partner a body massage, not touching the breasts or genitals
9. Receiving a body massage, not touching the breasts or genitals
10. Exploring and stroking your partner's genitals
11. Having your partner explore and stroke your genitals
12. Giving your partner an orgasm by manual stimulation
13. Being manually stimulated to orgasm by your partner
14. Having intercourse in a man-on-top position
15. Having intercourse in a woman-on-top position
16. Having intercourse in a rear-entry position
17. Using oral stimulation to bring your partner to orgasm
18. Being brought to orgasm by oral stimulation
19. Talking after climax
20. Cuddling after climax

ANSWER SHEET

(Circle the number that corresponds with your response)

How often does this activity occur during lovemaking?

5 = Regularly
4 = Often
3 = Sometimes
2 = Seldom
1 = Never

How often would you like this activity to occur during lovemaking?

5 = Regularly
4 = Often
3 = Sometimes
2 = Seldom
1 = Never

#	How often does	How often would you like
1.	5 4 3 2 1	5 4 3 2 1
2.	5 4 3 2 1	5 4 3 2 1
3.	5 4 3 2 1	5 4 3 2 1
4.	5 4 3 2 1	5 4 3 2 1
5.	5 4 3 2 1	5 4 3 2 1
6.	5 4 3 2 1	5 4 3 2 1
7.	5 4 3 2 1	5 4 3 2 1
8.	5 4 3 2 1	5 4 3 2 1
9.	5 4 3 2 1	5 4 3 2 1
10.	5 4 3 2 1	5 4 3 2 1
11.	5 4 3 2 1	5 4 3 2 1
12.	5 4 3 2 1	5 4 3 2 1
13.	5 4 3 2 1	5 4 3 2 1
14.	5 4 3 2 1	5 4 3 2 1
15.	5 4 3 2 1	5 4 3 2 1
16.	5 4 3 2 1	5 4 3 2 1
17.	5 4 3 2 1	5 4 3 2 1
18.	5 4 3 2 1	5 4 3 2 1
19.	5 4 3 2 1	5 4 3 2 1
20.	5 4 3 2 1	5 4 3 2 1

How pleasant do you want
this activity to be?

5 = Extremely Pleasant
4 = Pleasant
3 = Neither Pleasant
    nor Unpleasant
2 = Unpleasant
1 = Extremely Unpleasant

How pleasant do you think your
partner finds this activity to be?

5 = Extremely Pleasant
4 = Pleasant
3 = Neither Pleasant
    nor Unpleasant
2 = Unpleasant
1 = Extremely Unpleasant

1. 5 4 3 2 1   5 4 3 2 1
2. 5 4 3 2 1   5 4 3 2 1
3. 5 4 3 2 1   5 4 3 2 1
4. 5 4 3 2 1   5 4 3 2 1
5. 5 4 3 2 1   5 4 3 2 1
6. 5 4 3 2 1   5 4 3 2 1
7. 5 4 3 2 1   5 4 3 2 1
8. 5 4 3 2 1   5 4 3 2 1
9. 5 4 3 2 1   5 4 3 2 1
10. 5 4 3 2 1   5 4 3 2 1
11. 5 4 3 2 1   5 4 3 2 1
12. 5 4 3 2 1   5 4 3 2 1
13. 5 4 3 2 1   5 4 3 2 1
14. 5 4 3 2 1   5 4 3 2 1
15. 5 4 3 2 1   5 4 3 2 1
16. 5 4 3 2 1   5 4 3 2 1
17. 5 4 3 2 1   5 4 3 2 1
18. 5 4 3 2 1   5 4 3 2 1
19. 5 4 3 2 1   5 4 3 2 1
20. 5 4 3 2 1   5 4 3 2 1

40

Using Gender as a Therapeutic Technique: The Gender Assessment Device (GAD)

Jan Nealer
William F. Northey Jr.

Type of Contribution: *Handout/Homework/Activity*

Objective

Everyone's development and personality are shaped by innumerable circumstances and influences such as race, age, ethnicity, and religion. One influence that is currently under examination by various scientists and professionals is gender. There are gender differences in the ways of talking, listening, and interpretation which need to be identified and understood. Without such understanding, we are destined to blame others, ourselves, or even the relationship for the bewildering and destructive effects of differing communication styles and intentions (Tannen, 1990). In the therapeutic process, gender awareness is vital in all aspects of treatment. Thus, the crucial question for therapists is how awareness of gender behavior gets translated into effective clinical practice (Walters et al., 1988). The Gender Awareness Device (GAD) has been developed to assist to this end.

The GAD was not developed to define, measure, or point out deficiencies in client or therapist gender awareness; rather, this instrument was designed to be an interactive tool to help elucidate, for supervisors, therapists, and clients, their own personal gender expressions and experiences. Typically, men and women are unaware of their belief systems, since they are deeply ingrained (Walters et al., 1988). Recognizing belief systems and gender differences frees individuals from the burden of individual pathology (Tannen, 1990). In this way, supervisors, therapists, and/or clients may begin to explore and examine issues, problematic communication expressions, and examine covert and overt gender assumptions, biases, and understandings.

Rationale for Use

Men and women have very different ways of expressing and discussing problems, issues, and life experiences. Assuming that women and men are the same hurts both men and women. The way women are treated is based on the norms for men. Men speak to women as they would to men, and are perplexed when their words do not work as they wanted or expected (Tannen, 1990). In the therapeutic setting, these varied ways of experiencing life and communicating are amplified, because of the very nature of therapy. It is inevitable that there are various combinations and mixtures of gender sets in the therapeutic setting. Therapists of one gender, with a client or clients of the same or opposite gender, communicate their issues and problems through their genderized perspective. This can often lead to misunderstandings for client(s), between client(s) and therapist, and furthermore, between therapist and supervisor.

Frequently, meaning in conversation does not involve the words spoken, but is composed by the person listening (Tannen, 1990). In addition to the manner in which people listen, the covert nature of communication style and nuance adds complexity and controversy to the layers of relational interaction. With this considerable potential for misinterpretation, unfounded assumptions, and unchecked biases, miscommunication also increases exponentially, depending upon the number of different people involved. Defining and recognizing these differing views can help detoxify the situation, and all participants (e.g., supervisors, therapists, clients) can learn to identify discrepancies and make adjustments.

Instructions

Based on the aforementioned, the Gender Awareness Device provides a context for supervisors, therapists, and clients to openly discuss gender assumptions, viewpoints, and implications. This checklist has several uses, each with a slightly different set of instructions. For clarity and brevity, each use will be explained separately. It should be noted that the examples provided are just that. The GAD may be used with heterosexual individuals and couples, as well as with gay and lesbian individuals and couples. The utility of this instrument is only limited to the imaginations of the supervisors, therapists, and clients using the device.

The goal of the GAD requires that when a client uses the device, he/she should begin by thinking about comparisons between oneself and a specific individual (e.g., partner, spouse, parent) or group (e.g., males, females). The participant then checks the side of the form indicating whether they are "more" or "less" on a particular descriptor relative to that individual or group. For example, the therapist may want a couple to consider their personal gender differences. Therefore, each member of the couple would complete the GAD, considering whether they are "more" or "less" like the descriptor than their partner or gender group. Furthermore, the clients could complete the GAD twice, once thinking of their gendered group, and once thinking of their partner. These variations are dependent on what the therapist is trying to elicit and/or what the client(s) is working on in therapy. As always, every case is unique, so adjustments should be made accordingly.

Using the Gender Awareness Device as a Therapist Checklist

It is time to deconstruct the idea of the gender neutral position, the clinical myth that therapists do not introject their own values in therapy (Walters et al., 1988). Often, feelings of being "stuck" during the therapeutic process may be related to covert gender inferences and/or misinterpreted value assumptions. Implicit or explicit gender expectations of the client by the therapist may preclude effective treatment. Furthermore, behaviors expressed by clients often illicit responses from the therapist which may not be easily reconciled with the role of "helper." That is, clients at times will evoke anger, frustration, fear, and the like, when behaving in ways that do not fit the therapist's expectations, particularly gender-based expectations. When this occurs, the checklist can be used to explore some of these issues. By using the GAD, the therapist can explore and identify personal aspects of the client's behavior that elicit these responses.

To do so, the therapist completes the GAD by first thinking of how the client behaves or expresses him/herself. The therapist can then go back through the GAD and think of the therapist expectations of the client and/or what behaviors, expressions, or positions illicit the feeling of irritation or discomfort. By exploring the "person of the therapist" (Watson, 1993), the therapist allows for exploration and examination of his or her feelings and thoughts about the client and the direction of the therapy.

Using the Gender Assessment Device as a Therapeutic Tool with a Client

In addition to using the GAD as a way to explore therapist assumptions, the checklist can also be used to create a context in which to discuss gender issues directly between client and therapist. This is especially helpful if gender issues are part of the client's treatment concerns. By keeping the context of therapy in the here and now, the therapist can actively engage the client in working through these issues. In addition, the therapist needs to question "normal" behavior and attitudes that are fostered by tradition, and must become responsive to the manifestations of gender conditioning in daily interactions (Walters et al., 1988). Consequently, this device may be used by having the client fill it out and then discuss his/her responses during the session. The goal here is similar to the therapist's use of the GAD, and would enable the client to become more overt about his or her gender assumptions in a psychologically safe situation.

A variation on this exercise would be to have the therapist and client each fill out a GAD, and then compare their responses during the session. This would give the therapist and client an opportunity to discuss how they view each others' expressions, assumptions, and/or behaviors, specifically in terms of genderized behavior. It is likely that a discussion of disagreements or concordance, understanding or misinterpretation, surprises or lack thereof, could then be placed in how these behaviors and/or expressions may be interpreted characteristically by men, women, mothers, fathers, sons, daughters, or other important relationship partners.

Using the Gender Assessment Device as a Relationship Tool

The inequitable acknowledgment of the contributions of male and female roles in the larger society is a fundamental influence in marital relationships; therapists should be aware of this, as it is interwoven into daily interactions, expectations, and assumptions (Walters et al., 1988). Thus, the GAD may be used to facilitate exploration of these gender assumptions between couples and in families. The therapist has the couple and/or all family members complete the GAD, and then discuss the checklist during the session. To facilitate discussion of the expectations and assumptions that partners make about each other, the therapist might ask the clients to complete the GAD once in terms of themselves, and once in terms of how they think their partner might fill it out. Or, just have each person "guess" how his or her partner may differ in response.

Men and women assess relationships from contrasting vantage points; the same behaviors and expressions can appear very different to each, while they often have opposite interpretations of the same action (Tannen, 1990). Comparing and contrasting couple responses on the GAD offers a format that can be used for effective exploration of the needs/wants of each member of the couple. Additionally, by using an objective format, the couple can view the process as less threatening and more equitable. To increase efficacy, the therapist can add comments on the couple's processes, needs, wants, and differences, to help clarify and facilitate positive adjustments and outcomes.

Using the Gender Assessment Device as a Supervision Tool

The clinical supervision of therapists is a primary component in the education and development of therapists (Stoltenberg and Delworth, 1987). Supervision allows the supervisor and the person he/she supervises to reciprocally learn from one another. The supervisory relationship is considered a intricate and complex process, devised to expedite change and foster professional development (Robyak, Goodyear, and Prange, 1987). Difficulties in the supervisory relationship may transpire from varying degrees of understanding of how gender works. Although most supervisors possess a general sense of the impact of gender on the quality of the supervisory relationship, they may not explore these issues in an overt manner. This may be especially true of male supervisors who fail to recognize the covert and overt power of their position. Females who have male supervisors may be intimidated by the power imbalance, and may not know how to work within the hierarchical structure of the supervisory relationship. While same-gender supervisory relationships may be more comfortable and provide opportunities to learn from similar viewpoints, the result may be the support of existing gender biases and power differentials. This may mean that supervisors need to extend themselves and provide opportunities to talk about and explore possible problems of the power differential. Once again, the GAD may be used as a tool to open lines of communication. Supervisors and therapists may use the GAD as described above, as well as exploring it as an isomorphic process. The GAD can assist in exploring how the therapist and supervisor are working together, in addition to how the therapist and client are doing likewise.

Suggestions for Follow-Up

Follow-up uses of the GAD are at the discretion of the supervisor, therapist, and client. It is advised that gender issues not remain implicit and that further discussions ensue. Checking in with the participants later, after the use of the GAD, is always recommended.

Contraindications

There are no considerable contraindications for the use of the GAD. It is suggested that the GAD not be used with clients or couples that are in the midst of highly emotional states of conflict. For example, to use the GAD with a couple that is not communicating well would seem to be putting the cart before the horse. The GAD should be used to stimulate discussion and to increase the likelihood of making the covert more overt. Therefore, the use of the GAD should be well placed in the overall therapeutic plan.

Additionally, cultural, ethnic, religious, and other circumstances, influences, and issues that are part of the client's distress, must also be part of the therapeutic strategy. The GAD must be used as a planned intervention, and ethically handled throughout the therapeutic process.

Readings and Resources for the Professional

Betcher, R. and Pollack, W. (1993). *In a time of fallen heroes: The re-creation of masculinity.* New York: The Guilford Press.

Blaisure, K. R. and Allen, K. R. (1995). Feminists and the ideology and practice of marital equality. *Journal of Marriage and the Family, 57,* 5-19.

Brown, L. (1994). *Subversive dialogues: Theory in feminist therapy.* New York: Basic Books.

Cook, E. (1993). *Women, relationships, and power: Implications for counseling.* Alexandria, VA: American Counseling Association.

Erickson, R. J. (1993). Reconceptualizing family work: The effect of emotion work on perceptions of marital quality. *Journal of Marriage and the Family, 55,* 888-900.

Goodrich, T., Rampage, C., Ellman, B., and Halstead, K. (1988). *Feminist family therapy: A casebook.* New York: W.W. Norton & Company, Inc.

Hare-Mustin, R. (1981). Sexism in family therapy. In A. Gurman (Ed.), *Questions and answers in the practice of family therapy* (pp. 204-207). New York: Bruner/Mazel.

Hare-Mustin, R. T. (1988). Family change and gender differences: Implications for theory and practice. *Family Relations, 37,* 36-41.

Hess, B. B. and Ferree, M. M. (Eds.). (1987). *Analyzing gender: A handbook of social science research.* Newbury Park, CA: Sage.

Hartmann, H. (1981). The family as the locus of gender, class, and political struggle: The example of housework. *Signs: Journal of Women in Culture and Society, 6,* 366-394.

Jagger, A. and Rothenberg, P. (1978). *Feminist frameworks: Alternative theoretical accounts of the relations between women and men.* New York: McGraw-Hill.

Larsen, R. and Richards, M. (1994). *Divergent realities: The emotional lives of mothers, fathers, and adolescents.* New York: BasicBooks.

McGoldrick, M., Anderson, C., and Walsh, F. (1989). *Women in families: A framework for family therapy.* New York: W.W. Norton & Company, Inc.

Meth, R. (1990). *Men in therapy.* New York: Guilford Press.

Mirkin, M. (1994). *Women in context: Toward a feminist reconstruction of psychotherapy.* New York: The Guilford Press.

Okin, S. (1989). *Justice, gender, and the family.* New York: Basic Books.

Osmond, M. and Thorne, B. (1993). Feminist theories: The social construction of gender in families and society. In P. G. Boss, W. J. Doherty, R. LaRossa, W. Schumm, and S. Steinmetz (Eds.), *Sourcebook of family theories and methods: A contextual approach* (pp. 591-623). New York: Plenum Press.

Rave, E. and Larsen, C. (1995). *Ethical decision making in therapy: Feminist perspectives.* New York: The Guilford Press.

Robyak, J., Goodyear, R. and Prange, M. (1987). Effects of supervisors' sex, focus, and experience on preferences for interpersonal power bases. *Counselor Education and Supervision, 26,* 299-309.

Sollie, D. and Leslie, L. (1994). *Gender, families, and close relationships: Feminist research journeys.* Newbury Park, CA: Sage Publications.

Stoltenberg, C. and Delworth, U. (1987). *Supervising counselors and therapists.* San Francisco: Jossey-Bass Inc.

Thompson, L. (1993). Conceptualizing gender in marriage: The case of marital care. *Journal of Marriage and the Family, 55,* 557-569.

Thompson, L. and Walker, A. (1989). Gender in families: Women and men in marriage, work, and parenthood. *Journal of Marriage and the Family, 51,* 845-871.

Thorne, B. and Yalom, M. (Eds.). (1992). *Rethinking the family: Some feminist questions.* Boston: Northeastern University Press.

Vannoy-Hiller, D. and Philliber, W. (1989). *Equal partners: Successful women in marriage.* Newbury Park, CA: Sage Publications.

Walters, M., Carter, B., Papp, P., and Silverstein, O. (1988). *The invisible web: Gender patterns in family relationships.* New York: Guilford Press.

Watson, M. (1993). Supervising the person of the therapist: Issues, challenges, and dilemmas. *Contemporary Family Therapy, 15,* 21-31.

Bibliotherapy Sources for the Client

Schaef, A. (1981). *Women's reality*. Minneapolis, MN: Winston Press, Inc.

Silverstein, O. and Rashbaum, B. (1994). *The courage to raise good men*. New York: Penguin.

Tannen, D. (1986). *That's not what I meant: How conversational style makes or breaks relationships*. New York: Ballentine Books.

Tannen, D. (1990). *You just don't understand*. New York: Ballentine Books.

Tannen, D. (1994). *Talking from 9 to 5*. New York: William Morrow & Company, Inc.

Instructions: Think about yourself in comparison to a specific individual (e.g., partner, spouse, parent) or group (males or females). Check whether you have more or less of the following descriptors than this person or group.

The Gender Checklist		
Name:		Date:
More	**Behavior**	**Less**
	Abusive	
	Adaptable	
	Aggressive	
	Amenable	
	Analytical	
	Argumentative	
	Autonomous	
	Avoids conflict	
	Caring	
	Chivalrous	
	Competent	
	Consistent	
	Consoling	
	Conventional	
	Cooperative	
	Dependent	
	Detached	
	Distant	
	Docile	
	Emotional	
	Expressive	
	Forceful	
	Friendly	
	Illogical	
	Independent	
	Interdependent	
	Logical	
	Monogamous	
	Moody	
	Needy	

More	Behavior	Less
	Nontraditional	
	Nurturing	
	Open	
	Oppressed	
	Passive	
	Patient	
	Powerful	
	Predictable	
	Privileged	
	Progressive	
	Protected	
	Protective	
	Protector	
	Rational	
	Reliable	
	Resistant	
	Responsible	
	Rigid	
	Rude	
	Scared	
	Scary	
	Self-aware	
	Self-reliant	
	Sensitive	
	Strong	
	Submissive	
	Subordinate	
	Sympathetic	
	Tactful	
	Tender	
	Traditional	
	Warm	
	Weak	

41

The Intimate Justice Question

Brian Jory

Type of Contribution: *Handout/Activity*

Objective

A study of family therapy clients indicates that possibly two-thirds have experienced a physical assault by their intimate partner in the last year (O'Leary, Vivian, and Malone, 1992). Another study found that the rate of psychological abuse in therapy clients may be even higher and more damaging (Tolman and Bhosely, 1991). The foremost difficulty in clinical work with those who physically or psychologically abuse their partners is their propensity to deny, minimize, and rationalize their abusive behavior (O'Leary and Murphy, 1992). There are two reasons for this. The first is that a large number of those who abuse their partners were childhood victims of abuse themselves (Langhinrichsen-Rohling, Neidig, and Thorn, 1995). These childhood victims are often unaware of what constitutes abusive behavior and the negative impact which it has on those around them. A second reason is that abusive individuals—abusive men in particular—typically feel entitled to treat their partners maliciously. These individuals are resistant to questions or challenges by therapists about how they treat their partners. This often leaves the therapist focused on helping the victimized partner make changes, while the abuser goes unchallenged and unaccountable for change.

The primary objective of the intimate justice question is to facilitate a dialogue between the therapist and abusive individuals about what abuse is, why it is destructive, and how the abuser can accept responsibility for changing. A second objective is to help those abusive individuals who were childhood victims of abuse hold their own abuser(s) accountable, and to understand their own behavior within the intergenerational context of the cycle of violence. A third objective, which is encouraged only after there has been considerable therapeutic progress toward a complete cessation of physical violence and psychological abuse, is to facilitate couple dialogue about how the couple can improve their partnership by exploring issues of justice.

Rationale for Use

Intimate justice theory was developed by the author for clinical treatment of abuse and violence in intimate partnerships. The theory originated in a three-year study of ethical theory, moral development theory, feminist theory, and contextual family therapy, and then evolved as concepts were integrated into clinical work with abusive couples (Jory, Greer, and Anderson, in press). The theory is based on the premise that systemic thinking should lead clients toward a greater sensitivity to personal ethical responsibility as they come to recognize their own potential for either a constructive or destructive impact on their own emotional system. Intimate justice is comprised of three interrelated domains that encompass the psychological and ethical dimensions of intimate partnerships: equality, fairness, and care (see handout). Equality incorporates the concepts of accountability, respect, and freedom, which establish the *structure* of equal rights and responsibilities in the partnership. Fairness incorporates the concepts of mutuality, reciprocity, and accommodation which ensure justice in the ongoing *interpersonal processes* of the partnership. Care incorporates concepts which promote justice in the *affective* and *biological* aspects of intimacy—empathy, nurturance, and attachment.

The increased awareness of self/other responsibility infused into therapy by intimate justice theory can be used by the therapist to *confront* disempowerment and abuses of power within the partnership, to *challenge* internalized beliefs about how one should treat others—particularly one's intimate partner—to *explore* experiences with justice in the family-of-origin, and to *develop an awareness* about social contexts which impinge on justice in intimate partnerships (see Figure 41.1).

Instructions

The activity starts in an individual therapy session with the abusive individual. The therapist begins by asking, "What if something strange happened, and you were suddenly transformed into your partner. Knowing how you treat her (or him), how would you feel? What would it be like, being in an intimate partnership with you?" Since those who abuse others typically avoid self-reflection, the initial reaction is usually resistance to a serious consideration of the question. Some will act as though they do not understand the question, and will need it repeated. Others will extol their own virtues as they villify their partner. Many clients will acknowledge their own abusive behavior, but will instantly turn the blame on their partner for making them act this way. The effective therapist will be supportive, but will firmly and repeatedly challenge the client to use this as an opportunity to learn about himself or herself. It is essential that the therapist introduce the intimate justice question to the client as a learning activity. Therapists who create a judgmental environment, or who engage in a power struggle with the client are likely to foster further defensiveness.

After a brief discussion, the therapist should give the intimate justice question handout to the client. The handout is designed to stimulate clients to become reflective about how they treat their partner by asking twenty-seven questions—three for each of the nine concepts of intimate justice theory. Some of the questions overlap because every concept is interrelated with the others, and injustice in one area will lead to problems in others. Another stimulating aspect is that many of the words will be foreign to the vocabulary of the client (e.g., reciprocity, accountability, mutuality). Therapists should assure the client that this is not to make him/her feel inferior, but is by design to help the client consider new ideas through engaging new words. Some clients may go home and look up the words in a dictionary to gain further insight into their own behavior. The therapist should review the handout thoroughly at this point, clarifying what the words mean, and encouraging the client to write notes on the handout, if necessary.

Suggestions for Follow-Up

Clients should take the handout home and reflect on the questions as they observe their own behavior until the next appointment. Clients should be encouraged to begin their self-reflection

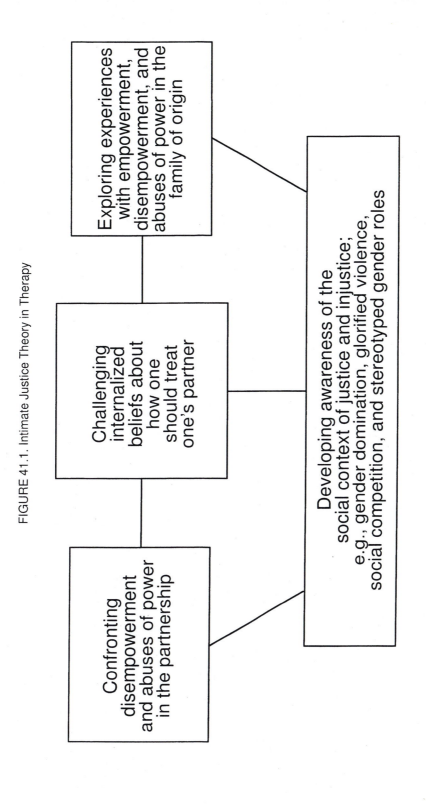

FIGURE 41.1. Intimate Justice Theory in Therapy

on the left side of the handout, with questions related to equality and the concepts of accountability, respect, and freedom. Equality is viewed as fundamental to fairness, and equality and fairness are the foundation for genuine intimacy and caring. Although the therapist cannot absolutely control this, the client should be discouraged from discussing the handout with the partner. A discussion may lead to arguments that increase the risk for further abuse to the victim. The client should bring the handout to the next session where dialogue about the intimate justice question will usually continue over a period of two to four weeks of sessions.

Contraindications

Therapists should be aware that the safety of victims and potential victims should be the primary considerations in structuring treatment for physical violence and psychological abuse. The intimate justice question should be conducted in individual therapy with the abuser, and should not be utilized in conjoint therapy until there has been a complete cessation of violence and psychological abuse. Otherwise, some abusive individuals will use the handout and the therapy sessions as a weapon to blame and denigrate their partner. Conjoint therapy has the potential to result in further abuse if the victim speaks freely about the abuse, or if the abusive individual becomes agitated. A risk assessment should consider the motivation of the abuser for being in therapy, the intensity and frequency of the abuse, and the impact on the victim.

Problems of the victimized partner should be addressed in separate, individual sessions, sometimes with another therapist. As a result of the abuse, victims often appear uncooperative with therapy, appear to lack self-esteem, and easily accept blame for the relationship problems. They are often clinically depressed, and will need treatment. A safety plan should be designed with the victim, should the abuse escalate. This may involve networking with local domestic violence shelters and crisis services. Victims of abuse who are confronted with the intimate justice question are likely to blame themselves for the relationship problems, and may begin changing themselves while the abusive individual remains unaccountable. Victims should not be encouraged to stay in a dangerous relationship to work on relationship problems if they elect to leave.

Readings and Resources for the Professional

Balcom, D. and Healey, D. (1990). The context for couples treatment of wife abuse. In M. P. Mirkin (Ed.), *The social and political contexts of family therapy* (pp. 121-137). Needham Heights, MA: Allyn and Bacon.

Hamberger, L. K. and Lohr, J. (1989). Cognitive and behavioral interventions with men who batter: Application and outcome. In P. L. Caeser and L. K. Hamberger (Eds.), *Treating men who batter: Theory, practice, and programs* (pp. 77-99). New York: Springer.

Jory, B., Anderson, D., and Greer, C. (1997). Intimate justice: Confronting issues of accountability, respect, and freedom in treatment for abuse and violence. *Journal of Marital and Family Therapy, 23*(4), 399-419.

Langhinrichsen-Rohling, J., Neidig, P., and Thorn, G. (1995). Violent marriages: Gender differences in levels of current violence and past abuse. *Journal of Family Violence, 10,* 159-175.

O'Leary, K. D. and Murphy, C. (1992). Clinical issues in the assessment of spouse abuse. In R. Ammerman and M. Hersen (Eds.), *Assessment of family violence: A clinical and legal sourcebook* (pp. 26-46). New York: John Wiley & Sons.

O'Leary, K. D., Vivian, D., and Malone, J. (1992). Assessment of physical aggression against women in marriage: The need for multimodal assessment. *Behavioral Assessment, 14,* 5-14.

Pence, E. and Paymar, M. (1993). *Education groups for men who batter: The Duluth model.* New York: Springer.

Tolman, R. and Bhosely, G. (1991). The outcome of participation in a shelter sponsored program for men who batter. In D. Knudsen and J. Miller (Eds.), *Abused and battered: Social and legal responses to family violence* (pp. 113-122). Hawthorne, NY: Aldine, DeGruyter.

Bibliotherapy Sources for Clients

Kivel, P. (1992). *Men's work: How to stop the violence that tears our lives apart.* New York: Ballantine Books.

The author draws on his personal experience, thoughtful analysis, and years of therapeutic experience to explore the centrality of violence, deep in the cultural structure of men's lives. The paperback is full of insights which challenge deeply held beliefs of men about gender, race, class, and age which contribute to violence.

Paymar, M. (1993). *Violent no more: Helping men end domestic abuse.* Alameda, CA: Hunter House.

This paperback was written by the training coordinator for the Duluth Domestic Abuse Intervention Project. The book outlines positive, straightforward steps that men can take to recognize and change their own abusive behavior such as rejecting sexist beliefs, recognizing cues for violence, using time-outs, findings healthy ways to deal with conflict, and handling jealousy.

The Intimate Justice Question: What if you were suddenly transformed into your partner? Knowing how you treat her or him, what would it be like to be your partner?

Freedom
Would you control your partner by threats or bodily harm?
Would you treat your partner as an object?
Would you encourage your partner to seek fulfillment?

Reciprocity
Would you be fair in terms of give and take?
Would you value your partner's contributions?
Would you practice compromise and negotiation?

Empathy
Would you listen to your partner nonjudgmentally?
Would you be supportive during loss and distress?
Would you care about your partner's feelings?

Attachment
Would you make others aware of your partnership?
Would you be committed to your partner as a person, not just a role?
Would you communicate with your partner about your weaknesses?

Nurturance
Would you promote your partner's emotional and physical health?
Would you practice responsible sexual expression and behavior?
Would you help your partner access medical care and comfort?

Accommodation
Would you adapt to your partner's different ways of doing things?
Would you apply rules fairly and stick to your agreements?
Would you accept the limits and limitations of your partner?

Mutuality
Would you collaborate on decision making and problem solving?
Would you be deceptive in your communication?
Would you be committed to share and share alike?

Accountability
Would you cause your partner psychological or physical harm?
Would you consider social rules and authority?
Would you rectify your mistakes and accidents?

Respect
Would you respect your partner's needs and ideas?
Would you respect your partner's individual differences?
Would you respect your partner's gender and heritage?

Freedom · Reciprocity · Empathy · Attachment · Nurturance · Accommodation · Mutuality · Accountability · Respect · Equality · Fairness · Care

©1996 by Brian Jory

220

42

The Diversity Dilemma

Brian Jory
Cassandra V. Greer

Type of Contribution: *Handout/Activity*

Objective

The diversity dilemma is designed to facilitate a therapeutic dialogue between therapists and clients about personal freedom and the need to respect the diverse needs and preferences of others in their emotional system, particularly those of the client's intimate partner. The diversity dilemma focuses on helping individuals understand how they feel about the restrictions on their freedom in their partnership, particularly how restrictions are decided and enacted. A study conducted of psychological abuse and violence discovered several types of unfair restrictions that may come to light in this dialogue (Jory, Anderson, and Greer, 1997). Some individuals deny their partners self-fulfillment by demanding that their own needs and preferences come first. This is often done through the use of manipulation, abusive power tactics, or even violence. Other individuals restrict their partners because of their insensitivity to the diverse needs and preferences of the partner, including failing to acknowledge the partner's contributions or accomplishments. Another type of abusive restriction is motivated by punitiveness toward the partner when he/she fails to live up to expectations; this can involve shunning, making disparaging remarks, or other power tactics. The most damaging and severe type of restriction to personal freedom and self-fulfillment results from treating the partner as an object or as property (Tolman, 1992; Schneider, 1994).

Rationale for Use

The diversity dilemma is based on intimate justice theory, which was developed for the treatment of abusive, violent relationships (Jory, Anderson, and Greer, 1997). While all partnerships impose some restrictions on individual freedom, self-esteem and self-fulfillment are optimized in an environment where human diversity is valued, where personal preferences are respected, where variations in psychological and physical development are appreciated, and where personal accomplishment is rewarded. In a perfectly just partnership, restrictions are freely negotiated to fit the values, needs, and desires of the individuals. If restrictions are too limiting, individuals feel enmeshed and constrained by rigid conformity to the requirements of the partner. If restrictions are too lax, individuals may feel disconnected and unattached. If restrictions are not uniformly applied, individuals will feel manipulated or exploited. The roots of psychological abuse and physical violence can be understood in terms of both the severe levels of restrictions and the tactics used to impose the restrictions. This refers to the "power and control" problems, well known in the domestic violence community.

Instructions

The diversity dilemma is designed to be used in a number of therapeutic situations. It works well in individual sessions to challenge abuse and violence based on rigid conformity to unrealistic and unfair restrictions. With some couples' situations where abuse and violence are not part of the presenting scenario or have ceased, the diversity dilemma can be used to stimulate couple dialogue. The activity can be assigned either as a take-home assignment or as an in-session activity. It is also effective in educational seminars to stimulate discussion about diversity within families. In session, the therapist asks the client to consider, "What would it be like if everyone were forced to do everything alike?" We have found that the best way to stimulate the client is to then give him or her the handout, and ask the direct question, "What is wrong with this picture?" Of course, there are many things wrong with the picture. The clothes do not fit the wife or child (and barely fit the man!). The food is evenly portioned, despite different nutritional needs of the three individuals. Most clients focus first on the plight of the infant, who is drinking from an adult glass, eating adult foods, and wearing adult clothing. They usually ask something such as, "Babies can't drink or eat this kind of food, can they?" To be effective, the therapist may need to play devil's advocate by asking follow-up questions such as, "So what is wrong with that?" The point of the dialogue is to permit clients to arrive at their own realization of what is wrong with the picture *for them*. The underlying ethical and psychological message, that people's diverse needs and preferences are rooted in size, shape, age, developmental level, gender, and untold other psychological, social, and emotional needs and whims is reinforced, allowing clients to arrive at their own conclusions. The cartoon contains and will carry its own message if therapists are willing to stimulate and guide the client into a thoughtful consideration of it.

The cartoon is slanted slightly to challenge men with power and control issues. For example, the man is noticeably larger than the woman in order to call attention to the physical advantages of men in physical confrontations. This emphasizes that a threat, a push, or a shove—which are typically minimized by men—has far greater impact on the smaller partner. Another slant is that the woman and the infant are both wearing men's clothing. With some clients, the therapist might ask if they can tell from the cartoon who made the decision about what everyone would wear.

Therapists should be cautious to treat this as a learning activity, rather than a confrontation. The cartoon deals with a serious topic in many, perhaps most, intimate partnerships, yet it is designed to be only a little humorous so as not to cause defensiveness or to lock anyone into a power struggle. The goal is to address the roots of power struggles, not to engender one with the activity. If the therapist has succeeded in creating a nonthreatening environment for the activity, clients will often feel safe enough to identify and discuss their own emotional reactions to the cartoon. For example, some men honestly reveal that they reacted favorably, precisely because the man appears to have imposed his own will on the others. This should be firmly challenged by the therapist, "But how would you feel if the picture were reversed, and the man were forced to wear a dress?" Many women who are involved with controlling, dominating men will experience considerable anger discussing the cartoon. The source of the anger should be therapeutically identified and addressed by the therapist.

Suggestions for Follow-Up

Therapists who use the diversity dilemma as a therapeutic intervention will need to assess the relationship issues and dynamics which arise from the activity, and proceed with appropriate clinical interventions. For example, some clients identify with the infant in the picture as family-of-origin issues of parental dominance and rigidity flood into their awareness. Other clients identify with the woman in the cartoon, and raise issues about restricted freedom and their lack of life fulfillment. For some, this issue can be addressed within the context of relationship therapy. For others, issues about domination and lack of freedom are embedded in psychological or physical abuse, and would be better addressed in individual sessions where the abusive individual can be appropriately challenged and where the victimized partner can feel safe discussing these concerns. Those who identify their own domination and abuse issues can be treated with other interventions from intimate justice theory.

Contraindications

As with all therapeutic activities, the diversity dilemma should be utilized within the context of a planned course of intervention. The diversity dilemma should not be used in relationship therapy where it may be incorporated by abusive individuals as another weapon to exploit or cause harm to the victimized partner. This would occur with severely abusive men who refuse to be accountable for their violent tactics; these men tend to view themselves as victims, and would use the cartoon to blame their partner for restricting their freedom. As with all projective activities, the diversity dilemma is contraindicated for clients with thought disorders who might get "secret" messages from it. It is also contraindicated for those with major affective disorders such as clinical depression. These individuals may be forced deeper into their mood problems by struggling with the issues raised by the cartoon.

Readings and Resources for the Professional

Jory, B., Anderson, D., and Greer, C. (1997). Intimate justice: Confronting issues of accountability, respect, and freedom in treatment for abuse and violence. *Journal of Marital and Family Therapy*, 23(4), 399-419.
Schneider, E. M. (1994). The violence of privacy. In M. A. Fineman and R. Mykitiuk (Eds.), *The public nature of private violence*, (pp. 36-58). New York: Routledge.
Tolman, R. (1992). Psychological abuse of women. In R. Ammerman and M. Hersen (Eds.), *Assessment of family violence*, (pp. 291-312). New York: John Wiley and Sons.

Bibliotherapy Sources for Clients

Satir, V. (1972). *Peoplemaking*. Palo Alto, CA: Science and Behavior Books.
In our search for therapists who have directly addressed respect and freedom in intimate relationships, we were drawn to Virginia Satir's eloquent description of the nurturing family:

> I feel that if I lived in a nurturing family, I would be listened to and would be interested in listening to others; I would be considered and would wish to consider others; I could openly show my affection as well as my pain and disapproval; I wouldn't be afraid to take risks because everyone in my family would realize that some mistakes are bound to come with my risk taking—that my mistakes are a sign that I am growing. I would feel like a person in my own right—noticed, valued, loved, and clearly asked to notice, value, and love others. (Satir, 1972, p. 13)

While the book does not directly deal with many of the issues we have raised, it is an insightful and inspiring look at well-functioning family relationships and is easily applicable to other kinds of intimate partnerships.

The Diversity Dilemma: What would it be like if everyone was forced to do everything alike? What is wrong with this picture?

43

Negotiating Drug-Free Activities:
An Activity for Couples
in Substance Abuse Treatment

Joseph L. Wetchler

Type of Contribution: Activity

Negotiating drug-free activities is a specific acitivity within a larger treatment model, Systemic Couples Therapy for Substance Abusers (SCT) (McCollum et al., 1993; Wetchler et al., 1994; Wetchler et al., 1993). It was the experimental treatment in a five-year research project, testing the effectiveness of adding couples therapy to standard drug treatment for substance-abusing women (Nelson et al., 1996). Results showed that adding SCT to standard drug treatment significantly improved the treatment outcome for substance-abusing women (Lewis et al., 1996).

SCT views substance abuse within a relationship context. It incorporates aspects of structural (Minuchin, 1974), strategic (Haley, 1987; Watzlawick, Weakland, and Fisch, 1974), and transgenerational (Kerr and Bowen, 1988) family therapies. The primary tenet of this approach is that couple relationships maintain an individual's substance abuse.

Objective

Several reasons exist for having couples (in which at least one member is a substance abuser) negotiate drug-free activities. First, there appears to be a high rate of marital conflict in couples where one spouse is a substance abuser (Leonard, 1990). Unsatisfactory conflict resolution can lead to men abusing substances to feel powerful, and to women abusing substance to squelch angry feelings (Bepko, 1989). Furthermore, the way a couple attempts to resolve a member's substance abuse can maintain the problem (Haley, 1987; Watzlawick, et al., 1974). Also, couples experiencing substance abuse problems often find that discussions about substance use are one of the few things they have in common to talk about (McCrady, 1990). Finally, substance abuse may rest at the heart of all activities the couple does together.

Rationale for Use

Negotiating drug-free activities addresses the problems listed above in several ways. First, by having a couple negotiate in the presence of their therapists, clinicians are able to monitor the couple's interactional pattern and relational structure, and help them to negotiate in a different way. This enables therapists to control the couple's emotional reactivity and block their attempts to get off track. Second, discussing how to resolve the problem serves as a metaphor for resolving other underlying problems in a couple's relationship (Haley, 1987). Rather than focusing on specific marital problems that a couple is unwilling to discuss, having them resolve their presenting problem (i.e., substance abuse) forces them to use the same techniques they would use in solving other marital problems.

This activity also deals with the role of substances within a couple's relationship. Taking away a substance without adding something to replace it can leave a large void for both an individual and a couple to fill. What can they possibly do with their lives if substance is removed? In negotiating drug-free activities, the couple discovers things to replace the void that a given substance initially filled. Further, as they engage in these activities, they have new things to discuss that are not drug related.

Instructions

This activity is designed to be an in-session task. Therapists first tell their couples about the importance of developing drug-free activities to maintain their drug-free lifestyle. They explain how the couples' lives have revolved around drugs, and that in stopping their substance use, they will need to fill the void left behind. Therapists then structure an enactment (Minuchin and Fishman, 1981) in which the couple discusses specific activities they would like to engage in, and to develop a list that they both agree on. Activities that only one partner wants are to be omitted. A more immediate version of this task is for the couple to negotiate a drug-free date to be completed before the next session.

Therapists need to be aware that most of the couples will have difficulty with this task. As the tension mounts they may return to their old pattern of discussion which often includes arguments and frustration. Therapists need to work on altering the interaction as they negotiate. For example, they may support a spouse who usually gives in to stress his/her point while supporting the other one to listen. Therapists will need to block symmetrical escalations, and help clients to discuss the underlying emotions behind an angry response (Greenberg and Johnson, 1988). This activity may take several sessions for those couples who have a particularly hard time negotiating. This is not a problem, as altering the process of their negotiation is more important than a quick completion of the task.

Suggestions for Follow-Up

Following the completion of the task, the couple is then assigned to follow through with their plan. For couples who plan a date, they are to follow through with their outing prior to the next session. For those who create a list of activities, they are to choose one to start doing before the next session. The therapist then actively tracks how the homework went during the next session. Those couples who had a successful activity are to discuss why it went so well and how they can continue to be successful. Those couples who had problems are told to discuss why the task did not work and to create a new plan to ensure success. This creates a situation in which the couple continues to negotiate and provides the therapist with the opportunity to again block destructive patterns of communication, and to enhance new behaviors.

Contraindications

Negotiating drug free activities is best avoided with violent or highly conflictual couples. Conducting an enactment in which a couple has to openly discuss disagreements can escalate their conflictual behavior if they do not have some semblance of control (McCollum, Trepper, Nelson, Wetchler, and Lewis, 1993). The concern with violent couples is that this might lead to aggressive behavior following the session. With these couples, it might be better for therapists to lessen the anxiety by discussing present-centered and transgenerational sequences that lead to substance abuse. Lessening the anxiety in session can be a more efficient means of altering patterns in low differentiated couples (Bowen, 1978).

Therapists are reminded that the primary goal of "negotiating drug-free activities" is to develop new patterns for couple negotiations, and secondarily to aid the couple in initially developing drug-free activities. While beginning therapists might be concerned with a couple developing a complete list, they are advised that a negotiation process that takes several sessions may be more helpful. Through keeping a couple on track and encouraging them to share their ideas, a therapist does more to help them develop a solid relationship and to maintain a drug-free lifestyle than having them quickly develop a drug-free activities list.

Readings and Resources for the Professional

Suggested Readings and Videos on Systemic Couples Therapy for Substance Abusers

McCollum, E. E., Trepper, T. S., Nelson, T. S., Wetchler, J. L., and Lewis, R. A. (1993). *Systemic couples therapy for substance-abusing women: A treatment manual.* West Lafayette, IN: Purdue Research Foundation.

Nelson, T. S., McCollum, E. E., Wetchler, J. L., Trepper, T. S., and Lewis, R. A. (1996). Therapy with women substance abusers: A systemic couples perspective. *Journal of Feminist Family Therapy, 8*(1), 5-27.

Wetchler, J. L. and DelVecchio, D. L. (1995). Systemic couples therapy for a female heroin addict. *Journal of Family Psychotherapy, 6*(4), 1-13.

Wetchler, J. L. and DelVecchio, D. L. (in press). The relapse is your friend. In T. S. Nelson & T. S. Trepper (Eds.), *101 Family therapy interventions* (second ed.). Binghamton, NY: The Haworth Press.

Wetchler, J. L., McCollum, E. E., Nelson, T. S., Trepper, T. S., and Lewis, R. A. (1993). Systemic couples therapy for alcohol-abusing women. In T. J. O'Farrell (Ed.), *Treating alcohol problems: Marital and family therapy in alcoholism treatment* (pp. 236-260). New York: Guilford.

Wetchler, J. L., McCollum, E. E., Trepper, T. S., Nelson, T. S., and Lewis, R. A. (Executive Producers), Kamalipour, Y. R. (Producer), and Wolfe, D. (Director). (1993). *Systemic couples therapy for substance-abusing women* [Videotape]. West Lafayette, IN: Purdue Research Foundation.

Wetchler, J. L., Nelson, T. S., McCollum, E. E., Trepper, T. S., and Lewis, R. A. (1994). Couple-focused therapy for substance-abusing women. In J. Lewis (Ed.), *Addictions: Concepts and strategies for treatment* (pp.253-262). Rockville, MD: Aspen.

Suggested Readings on Marital and Family Treatment for Substance Abuse

Berg, I. K. and Miller, S. D. (1992). *Working with the problem drinker: A solution-focused approach.* New York: Norton.

Elkin, M. (1984). *Families under the influence: Changing alcoholic patterns.* New York: Norton.

Greenberg, L. and Johnson, S. (1988). *Emotionally focused therapy for couples.* New York: Guilford.

O'Farrell, T. J. (Ed.). (1993). *Treating alcohol problems: Marital and family therapy in alcoholism treatment.* New York: Guilford.

Stanton, M. D., Todd, T. C., and Associates (1982). *The family therapy of drug abuse and addiction.* New York: Guilford.

Steinglass, P., Bennett, L. A., Wolin, S. J., and Reiss, D. (1987). *The alcoholic family.* New York: Basic Books.

Todd, T. S. and Selekman, M. D. (Eds.). (1991). *Family therapy approaches with adolescent substance abusers.* Needham Heights, MA: Allyn & Bacon.

Wakefield, P. J., Williams, R. E., Yost, E. B., and Patterson, K.M. (1996). *Couple therapy for alcoholism: A cognitive-behavioral treatment manual.* New York: Guilford.

REFERENCES

Bepko, C. (1989). Disorders of Power: Women and addiction in the family. In M. McGoldrick, C. M. Anderson, and F. Walsh (Eds.), *Women in families: A framework for family therapy* (pp. 406-426). New York: Norton.

Bowen, M. (1978). *Family therapy in clinical practice.* Northvale, NJ. Jason Aronson.

Greenberg, L. S. and Johnson, S. M. (1988). *Emotionally focused therapy for couples.* New York: Guilford.

Haley, J. (1987). *Problem-solving therapy* (second ed.). San Francisco: Jossey-Bass.

Kerr, M. E. and Bowen, M. (1988). *Family evaluation.* New York: Norton.

Leonard, K. E. (1990). Marital functioning among episodic and steady alcoholics. In R. L. Collins, K. E. Leonard, and J. S. Searles (Eds.), *Alcohol and the family: Research and clinical perspectives* (pp. 220-243). New York: Guilford.

Lewis, R., McCollum, E., Nelson, T., Trepper, T., and Wetchler, J. (1996). Outcome results: Couples therapy for drug-abusing women. Paper presented at the American Association for Marriage and Family Therapy 54th Annual Conference. Toronto, Ontario: Canada.

McCollum, E. E., Trepper, T. S., Nelson, T. S., Wetchler, J. L., and Lewis, R. A. (1993). *Systemic couples therapy for substance-abusing women: A treatment manual.* West Lafayette, IN: Purdue Research Foundation.

McCrady, B. S. (1990). The marital relationship and alcohol. In R. L. Collins, K. E. Leonard, and J. S. Searles (Eds.), *Alcohol and the family: Research and clinical perspectives* (pp. 338-355). New York: Guilford.

Minuchin, S. (1974). *Families and family therapy.* Cambridge, MA: Harvard.

Minuchin, S. and Fishman, H. C. (1981). *Family therapy techniques.* Cambridge, MA: Harvard.

Nelson, T. S., McCollum, E. E., Wetchler, J. L., Trepper, T. S., and Lewis, R. A. (1996). Therapy with women substance abusers: A systemic couples perspective. *Journal of Feminist Family Therapy, 8*(1), 5-27.

Watzlawick, P., Weakland, J. H., and Fisch, R. (1974). *Change: Principles of problem formation and problem resolution.* New York: Norton.

Wetchler, J. L., McCollum, E. E., Nelson, T. S., Trepper, T. S., and Lewis, R. A. (1993). Systemic couples therapy for alcohol-abusing women. In T.J. O'Farrell (Ed.), *Treating alcohol problems: Marital and family therapy in alcoholism treatment* (pp. 236-260). New York: Guilford.

Wetchler, J. L., Nelson, T. S., McCollum, E. E., Trepper, T. S., and Lewis, R. A. (1994). Coule-focused therapy for substance-abusing women. In J. Lewis (Ed.), *Addictions: Concepts and strategies for treatment* (pp. 236-260). New York: Guilford.

44

The "Mrs. *K'negdo*/Mrs. Opposite" Assignment: A Biblical Injunction for Orthodox Jewish Couples and Christian Couples

Debby Schwarz-Hirschhorn

Type of Contribution: Homework

Objective

The objective of the homework is to help orthodox Jewish couples, as well as Christian couples, understand their conflicts in a different way.

Rationale for Use

To systemic family therapists with a social constructionist (McNamee and Gergen, 1992) orientation, an arguing couple's problem is not in any identified individual. Thus, it is not necessary for the therapist to assess who might be right or wrong. The clients most likely do not see it this way. Part of their problem may be the lack of flexibility which has dictated that one person must be right and the other, wrong (Hudson and O'Hanlon, 1991). Their limited number of choices—either I am right or you are right—boxes them into this corner. The notion that a shift in their perspective (O'Hanlon and Wilk, 1987) can allow both members of the couple to be correct is an incredible idea for a warring couple new to social constructionist models of therapy. A social constructionist framework therefore seems to be a vital basis for marital therapy.

Because social constructionist models of therapy also underscore the importance of speaking to clients in language that makes sense to them (Fisch, Weakland, and Segal, 1982), such models lend themselves to utilizing the Bible as an authoritative resource when working with religious couples (Hirschhorn and Rambo, 1996). Christian counselors have discovered this powerful tool and have applied it using rational-emotive therapy (Johnson, 1993; Young, 1984), cognitive-behavioral therapy (Tan, 1987), Gestalt therapy (Cowart, 1980), specially created biblical models (Carter, 1980), and family therapy (Salinger, 1979). Within the latter, Christian counselors have discussed the ethics of paradoxical interventions (Deschenes and Shepperson, 1983), and analyzed the healing properties of the language of the Psalms (Meyer, 1974).

Jewish counselors working with an orthodox population primarily have a psychodynamic orientation (Strean, 1994). Exceptions are systemic family therapists who may (Bilu and

The author would like to thank Dr. Anne Rambo, Nova Southeastern University, for her helpful comments.

Witzum, 1994; Shulem, 1988; Wieselberg, 1992) or may not be orthodox (Friedman, 1985; Nichols, 1995; Nichols, 1996), but who have not drawn on the influence of the Bible as an interventive resource. Orthodox therapists who do rely heavily on religious doctrine for authority, such as Radcliffe (1988), often use a tone of gentle coaxing to obtain improved behavior. For example, she cajoles: "A woman must try not to resent the fact that her husband does not always live up to her expectations and standards in his personal conduct. (She herself no doubt disappoints him on occasion as well!)" (p. 16). Radcliffe's premise, that the husband somehow fails his wife, is no different than that of her clients. She does not promote a meaningful difference in their outlook (Watzlawick, Weakland, and Fisch, 1974). It appears that therapists working with orthodox clients have not taken advantage of the power and flexibility of a social constructionist approach in combination with the authority of the Bible as resource.

A social constructionist application of systemic family therapy has the potential to find the systemic wisdom in the couple's behavior such that neither has to be wrong and neither has to view the spouse as wrong. A biblical injunction bolsters the shift in position. The intervention thus gains its power from: (1) the fact that nobody is wrong and that nobody has to change because the clients are doing exactly what G-d expects, (2) the potency of the Bible as authority, and (3) speaking the client's language (Fisch, Weakland, and Segal, 1982). The intervention to follow has worked well with orthodox Jewish clients, as well as other Jewish people with traditional views of the Bible. With only the slightest changes in language, as suggested below, the intervention can be also adapted to Christian clients.

Instructions

The intervention occurs in two steps. The first is a statement meant to produce an immediate context shift (O'Hanlon and Wilk, 1987). It not only allows, but encourages, opposing views. To my orthodox Jewish clients, I make all biblical references in Hebrew as follows:

> You know where it says in *Bereshis* [Genesis] that G-d needed to create for Adam an *aizer k'negdo*; a lot of English translations are happy to call this creation "a helpmate," but of course we know that "*k'negdo*" means "as if against him" (Zlotowitz, 1977, pp. 104-105). Why would G-d want that?—Obviously, the wife is supposed to complement her husband (Hirsch, 1867/1973, pp. 65-66); her job is to bring some perspective into the discussion. So, of course you (as I face the wife) are *supposed* to think differently! That's what G-d wants! Two opposing views bring depth to the discussion and produce balance in the relationship.

Christian counselors can make the following statement to clients:

> You know where it says in Genesis that G-d needed to create for Adam a wife, the real translation is not "a helpmate," but "a help-opposite!" Why would G-d want that? Obviously, the wife is supposed to complement her husband. Her job is to bring some perspective into the discussion. So, of course you (as I face the wife) are *supposed* to think differently! That's really *helpful*; two opposing views bring depth to the discussion and produce balance in the relationship.

The partners generally stop short of their arguments with the most surprised expressions on their faces. Often they break out into giggles. They always listen attentively at this point to what comes next.

This generally leads to further discussion about the couple's complementarity. Very often, one of them realizes that at least one of the unwelcome characteristics in the other was precisely what was attractive about the other in the first place. This conversation lays the groundwork for a homework assignment based on de Shazer's first session formula task, in which he asks clients to "observe what happens in your . . . relationship that you want to continue to happen" (1985, p. 137). By having clients notice what they like about their situation, the therapist produces a hopeful mindset and positive focus.

Here is the "Mrs. *K'negdo*/Mrs. Opposite" assignment:

> Between now and next week, I would like you to notice [your husband's] behaviors that have been really annoying to you until now. I would like you to ask yourself whether they might not just be opposite characteristics from yours, characteristics you were once attracted to for that very reason and which make you "Mrs. *K'negdo*" ("Mrs. Opposite").

In this version of the noticing task, clients are directed to focus on their previous positive assessment of what now appear to be annoying viewpoints or characteristics. This desirability constitutes a further context shift (O'Hanlon and Wilk, 1987): not only is this annoying behavior okay, but it was precisely because of it that a client was attracted to his/her spouse.

Suggestions for Follow-Up

The first moment after the intervention is given initiates follow-up. de Shazer (1985) points out that the client's body language indicates whether the intervention was well received. Given the probability that it fits for this person or couple, the following week the therapist must be careful in wording the information-seeking question. It should be something such as, "Tell me in what ways you realize how you originally saw yourself as, and always have been, Mrs. *K'negdo*? (or, Mrs. Opposite)." A question focusing on the spouse's negative behaviors would not be within the spirit of this homework.

Contraindications

Complaints of abuse must be taken very seriously. If the wife's objections to her husband's behavior center around verbal put-downs or worse, this activity is not indicated. This intervention is solely meant for couples whose quarrels are over differing points of view. For the same reason, if the objectionable behavior is addiction, philandering, illegal activity, or psychosis, other approaches would be more appropriate.

A second category of client for whom this homework is not suitable are people who may state that they believe in G-d, yet not believe that the Bible is His work. Thus, the presence of Jewish people who consider themselves spiritual or religious may not discriminate the believer from the nonbeliever. It is easy enough to ask a client directly; otherwise, clients who call themselves *frum*, or orthodox, believe that the Bible is G-d's Word. (Many non-*frum* people also share this belief, so be careful not to eliminate prospective clients.) In the Christian world, those who have become accustomed to the concept of "helpmate" may resist this intervention. The client's body language during the revised translation will indicate whether or not to proceed with the intervention.

You will notice that the Bible directs the attention to the woman: she is opposite to the man. If a woman gives the impression that she does not want to do an assignment or she objects to the assignment directed toward her, the intervention could easily be directed toward the husband. The therapist asks him to notice the characteristics in her that he was attracted to because they are different, making her his Mrs. *K'negdo* (Mrs. Opposite).

Bibliotherapy Sources for the Client

Feldman, A. (1987). *The river, the kettle, and the bird: A Torah guide to successful marriage.* Jerusalem: CSB Publication.

Hirsch, S. R. (1973). *The Pentateuch.* (Vol. 1 Genesis). (Isaac Levy, Trans.). (Rev. ed.). Gateshead, England: Judaica Press. (Original work published 1867.)

Hudson, P. O. and O'Hanlon, W. H. (1991). *Rewriting love stories: Brief marital therapy.* New York: Norton.

Schwartz, P. (1994). *Love between equals: How peer marriage really works.* New York: Free Press.

BIBLIOGRAPHY

Bilu, Y. and Witzum, E. (1994). Culturally sensitive therapy with ultraorthodox patients: The strategic employment of religious idioms of distress. *Israel Journal of Psychiatry and Related Sciences, 31*(3), 170-182.

Carter, J. D. (1980). Towards a biblical model of counseling. *Journal of Psychology and Theology, 8*(1), 45-52.

Cowart, H. M. (1980). Towards a theology of preaching and counseling: An exploration of the epistemology common to gestalt therapy and Jesus' proclamation of the kingdom of God. *Dissertation Abstracts International, 41*(3-A), 1099.

de Shazer, S. (1985). *Keys to solution in brief therapy.* New York: Norton.

Deschenes, P. and Shepperson, L. (1983). The ethics of paradox. *Journal of Psychology and Theology, 11*(2), 92-98.

Fisch, R., Weakland, J. H., and Segal (1982). *The tactics of change: Doing therapy briefly.* San Francisco: Jossey-Bass.

Friedman, E. H. (1985). *Generation to generation: Family process in church and synagogue.* New York: Guilford.

Hirsch, S. R. (1973). *The Pentateuch.* (Vol. 1 Genesis). (Isaac Levy, Trans.). (Rev. ed.). Gateshead, England: Judaica Press. (Original work published 1867.)

Hirschhorn, D. and Rambo, A. H. (May 19, 1996). CHABAD Family Counseling Services: A synagogue-based therapy program. Paper presented at the meeting of the Florida Association for Marriage and Family Therapy, Miami, Florida.

Hudson, P. O. and O'Hanlon, W. H. (1991). *Rewriting love stories: Brief marital therapy.* New York: Norton.

Johnson, W. B. (1993). Christian rational-emotive therapy: A treatment protocol. *Journal of Psychology and Christianity, 12*(3), 254-261.

McNamee, S. and Gergen, K. J. (Eds.). (1992). *Therapy as social construction.* London: Sage.

Meyer, S. G. (1974). The Psalms and personal counseling. *Journal of Psychology and Theology, 2*(1), 26-30.

Nichols, W. C. (Ed.). (1995). *Contemporary family therapy: An international journal. Special issue: Family Therapy in Israel, Part I, 17*(4).

Nichols, W. C. (Ed.). (1996). *Contemporary family therapy: An international journal. Special issue: Family Therapy in Israel, Part II, 18*(1).

O'Hanlon, B. and Wilk, J. (1987). *Shifting contexts: The generation of effective psychotherapy.* New York: Guilford.

Radcliffe, S. C. (1988). *Aizer k'negdo: The Jewish woman's guide to happiness in marriage.* Southfield, Michigan: Targum.

Rambo, A. H., Heath, A., and Chenail, R. (1993). *Practicing therapy.* New York: Norton.

Salinger, R. J. (1979). Towards a biblical framework for family therapy. *Journal of Psychology and Theology, 7*(4), 241-250.

Shulem, B. (1988). The introduction of humor in supervision and therapy—work is depressive enough without being too serious. *Journal of Strategic and Systemic Therapies, 7*(2), 49-58.

Strean, H. S. (1994). *Psychotherapy with the orthodox Jew.* Northvale, NJ: Jason Aronson.

Tan, S. (1987). Cognitive-behavior therapy: A biblical approach and critique. *Journal of Psychology and Theology, 15*(2), 103-112.

Watzlawick, P., Weakland, J., and Fisch, R. (1974). *Change: Principles of problem formation and problem resolution.* New York: Norton.

Wieselberg, H. (1992). Family therapy and ultraorthodox Jewish families: A structural approach. *Journal of Family Therapy, 14,* 305-329.

Young, H. S. (1984). Practicing RET with Bible Belt Christians. *British Journal of Cognitive Psychotherapy, Special issue: The work of Howard S. Young, 2*(2), 60-76.

Zlotowitz, N. (Trans.). (1977). *Bereishis/Genesis: A new translation with a commentary anthologized from Talmudic, Midrashic, and Rabbinic sources.* New York: Mesorah.

SECTION III:
HOMEWORK, HANDOUTS, AND ACTIVITIES FOR FAMILIES

45

Strategies for Building Stronger Families

Mary L. Franken
Patricia E. Gross

Type of Contribution: *Activities/Homework/Handouts*

1. Family Wellness Inventory
2. Commitment: Family Logo
3. Appreciation: Admiring My Family Members
4. Communication: Family Meeting
5. Time Together: Making Family Time a Priority
6. Coping with Stress, Conflict, and Crisis: Temperature's Rising
7. Family Wellness: Celebrating Our Family
8. Commitment: Family Shield
9. Appreciation: Intrafamily Memorandum
10. Communication: Feedback
11. Time Together:"Timely" Coupons
12. Coping with Stress, Conflict, and Crisis: Peace in the Family
13. Family Wellness: Wellness Wheel

Objectives

1. To involve family members in activities that build on six characteristics found in strong families.
2. To encourage positive family interactions.
3. To provide therapists with strategies to use with clients in therapy sessions or as homework assignments.

Rationale for Use

What are family strengths? "Family strengths are those relationship patterns, interpersonal skills and competencies, and social and psychological characteristics which create a sense of positive family identity, promote satisfying and fulfilling interaction among family members, encourage the development of the potential of the family group and individual family members, and contribute to the family's ability to deal effectively with stress and crisis" (Stinnett and DeFrain, 1985).

Building Family Strengths (BFS)* is a blueprint for developing a family's potential. It is a program to help individuals and families identify and build on their strengths. Based on research with healthy families, this proactive approach assumes that all families have strengths. Despite many stresses and pressures, the family has continued to nurture, socialize, and support its members.

The BFS materials can be used and/or adapted for use with intact, single parent, or stepfamilies. The program may help parents by having them look back at family-of-origin strengths and issues, to better understand their present family(ies). Children may be involved in homework activities and strategies—all designed to build more positive relationships. While the strengths can be addressed separately, there are many interrelationships between the six strengths. Additional activities for each family strength are recommended to enhance the outcomes of the BFS program.

Individuals in therapy may also benefit from the positive approach in identifying and building on family strengths. The concepts also apply to other important groups in one's life. For example, a work group or team could use the model to analyze the same characteristics as its members seek to develop rapport and trust.

Suggestions for Follow-Up

The activities developed for use by individuals and families include directions. Some are designed to be completed alone and later discussed as a family, while others could be completed as a family group. Therapists will find it helpful to discuss lessons and outcomes from completing the activities and homework assignments. Therapists can assist with processing the strategies.

Readings and Resources for the Professional

Achord, B., Berry, M., Harding, G., Kerber, K., Scott, S., and Schwab, L. (1986). *Building family strengths—A manual for families, building family strengths—Facilitator manual,* and *Building family strengths—A collection of exercises.* U.S. Department of Health and Human Services, Grant Number 90-CW-0749. University of Nebraska-Lincoln: Department of Human Development and Family and Conferences and Institutes.

Olson, D. H. and McCubbin, H. I. (1983). *Families: What makes them work.* Thousand Oaks, CA: Sage.

Schvaneveldt, J. D. and Young, M. H. (1992). Strengthening families: New horizons in family life education. *Family Relations,* 41, 385-389.

Stinnett, N. and DeFrain, J. (1985). *Secrets of strong families.* New York: Berkley Books.

Bibliotherapy Sources for the Client

Crary, E. (1984). *Kids can cooperate.* Seattle, WA: Parenting Press.

Faber, A. and Mazlish, E. (1987). *Siblings without rivalry.* New York: W.W. Norton.

---

*BFS program materials were developed at the University of Nebraska-Lincoln under a federal grant. Dr. Franken was one of the leaders trained under the grant in 1986 to prepare facilitators to offer six- to eight-session programs to community and church groups in all the states. Since that time, the BFS office at the University of Nebraska has closed, and materials are no longer printed. The materials in this unit are from the original materials (credited when used) and from materials developed for workshops by the authors.

Schmidt, F. and Friedman, A. (1989). *Fighting fair for families*. Miami Beach, FL: Peace Education.

Wiehe, V. (1991). *Perilous rivalry: When siblings become abusive*. Lexington, MA: Lexington Books.

REFERENCES

Lingren, H. (1982). *Family life inventory*, cited in Achord, B., Berry, M., Harding, G., Kerber, K., Scott, S., and Schwab, L. (1986). *Building family strengths facilitator manual*. Lincoln, NE: The Center for Family Strengths, University of Nebraska–Lincoln.

Stinnet, N. and DeFrain, J. (1985). *Secrets of strong families*. New York: Berkeley Books.

Family Wellness Inventory

The Family Wellness Inventory is designed to help you decide how satisfied you are with your family's strengths and wellness. It will help you assess your family's well-being, and suggests ways to improve it.

In each of the six areas in the inventory, consider your family relationships in terms of how satisfied you are with them right now. Using a scale from 1 to 10, evaluate where you believe your family is now in realizing its full potential.

| 1 | 2 | 3 | 4 | 5 | 6 | 7 | 8 | 9 | 10 |

Place your rating under the column marked **"Actual."** Now go back and decide where you would like your family to be in each of the areas. Place this under **"Desired."** (For example, you might have a 3 under **Actual** in the category "Spending Time Together," but a 9 under **Desired**.)

Now, after you have filled in all of the categories, figure the difference between each of the scores in **Actual** and **Desired**, and write those figures in the **Potential** column. The total score in the **Potential** column suggests how much more wellness your family could have.

	Actual	Desired	Potential
1. Commitment: A promise of time and energy to seeing each family member develop his/her potential			
2. Communication: Clear and direct channels of verbal and nonverbal communication			
3. Appreciation: Recognizing the positive aspects of others, and letting them know you value these qualities; begins with appreciating self			
4. Time Together: Quality and quantity time which gives a family a sense of identity			
5. Ability to Deal with Stress, Conflict, Crisis: Power drawn from other strengths to survive and grow through crisis			
6. Wellness: Collective health of mind, body, and spirit			

Have each family member rate and score your family on the Family Wellness Inventory. Then compare your individual inventories, and discuss the differences. Look closely at the potential for wellness your family has.

Let each member help determine where your family trouble spots are, and what has caused them (such as not spending time together, lack of appreciation, poor communication, etc.). Reach agreement on the important areas for work and improvement in your family, and get a firm commitment from each family member to work as a team to realize your family's potential. This is a place where every improvement is a win.

Adapted from Lindgren, H. (1982).

COMMITMENT: FAMILY LOGO

Have each individual design a logo that represents something all family members value or enjoy. Discuss these with one another. An alternative would be to work together in designing the logo. Consider having your "family" shirts printed.

Appreciation: Admiring My Family Members

List the people in your family.	Write down two things you admire or appreciate about each.	Write down two things others can admire about you.
1.	1.	1.
	2.	
2.	1.	
	2.	
3.	1.	2.
	2.	
4.	1.	
	2.	

For each person listed above, describe the ways in which you could express your appreciation:

1. _____

2. _____

3. _____

4. _____

Communication: Family Meeting

What is a family meeting?
- [ ] a gathering of everyone in the family at a designated time and place; 15-30 minutes
- [ ] a meeting that has a chairperson and recorder
- [ ] a meeting with fixed rules and procedures
- [ ] a cooperative way to making decisions that affect all family members

What a family meeting is *not!*
- [ ] a discussion around the dinner table or in the car
- [ ] a meeting called only when there is a problem
- [ ] a place for kids to gripe and whine
- [ ] a time for parents to discipline

How a family meeting works and establishes ground rules:
- [ ] Meeting is called
- [ ] Start with a round of compliments
- [ ] All members have a chance to say what they think or feel
- [ ] All possible solutions are considered, and one solution is decided upon
- [ ] Compromise is expected
- [ ] The decisions are recorded
- [ ] Checking back is part of the process
- [ ] End with something fun and which affirms everyone—such as a family hug, a short game, watching a favorite television program, or anything that leaves a positive experience

How a family meeting works:
A meeting is called, the issues are faced, and all the members have a chance to say what they think and/or feel (no put-downs). All possible solutions are considered, and the discussion continues until a solution emerges that is acceptable to each family member. This does not mean they each like it, but each is willing to live with it for a period of time to see if it works. Each person is expected to support the decision, and work for its success.

Now practice—hold a family meeting!
Establish the ground rules (see above). Choose a chairperson and a recorder. Now select an issue and get started. Possible ideas: planning a family outing, making a family decision that affects everyone, working out a scheduling conflict, or whatever is happening in your family! Family meetings may seem clumsy at first—keep working on it on a regular basis, and report back to the group.

An issue I would like to bring up in a family meeting is _____

Time Together:
Making Family Time
a Priority

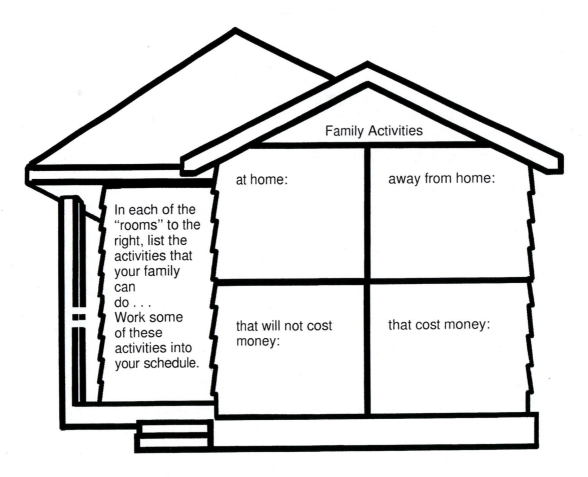

Family Activities

In each of the "rooms" to the right, list the activities that your family can do . . .
Work some of these activities into your schedule.

at home:

away from home:

that will not cost money:

that cost money:

Coping with Stress and Conflict:
Temperature's Rising

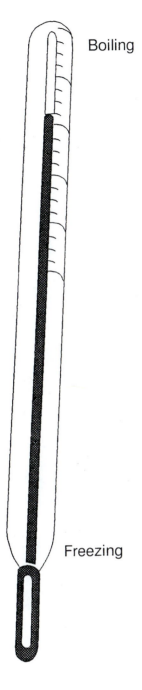

Boiling

Freezing

1. Cut three, three-inch square pieces of paper for each family member (or use Post-It notes).

2. On each piece of paper, each family member describes one thing that makes her/him angry or frustrated (temperature's rising).

3. Each person should put the papers on the thermometer at the level that represents her/his feelings about each particular issue.

4. Set a ten-minute time limit for each person. Have each person discuss her/his feelings and the ways in which the family can help this person cope with his/her feelings more appropriately.

Wellness:
Celebrating Our Families

Using pictures and words cut from magazines (or original drawings), have each individual family member make a collage on "What my family means to me." Glue the pictures and words on 8½" × 11" paper. After all are finished, have each member tell about her/his collage.

Commitment: Family Shield

Draw symbols to represent the following in the spaces below. Discuss these with family members.

1. A value or goal our family would agree is important; something we stand for.
2. A memory or a happy time we spent together as a family.
3. Something I wish my family would do or do more often.
4. Something that keeps our family from showing commitment to each other.

Appreciation: Intrafamily Memorandum

Each family member needs large doses of appreciation. It is important to feel valued just because you are who you are—as well as for the specific things you do. Appreciation is often easier to accept when a person describes a specific behavior. Copy the following memorandum so that family members can write appreciation messages to other family members. Remember that accepting a compliment is also important—just say, "Thank you."

Intrafamily memorandum

Date:

To:

cc:

Subject: Appreciation

I appreciate . . .

_____

_____

_____

_____

_____

_____

_____

_____

_____

_____

Communication: Feedback

Effective communication includes sending clear messages, listening, and receiving feedback. Feedback is the process whereby the listener checks out what he/she has heard and understood from the sender.

Without naming the object in the picture, have one person describe the first picture to another person in the family. Have the listener draw the object that is being described. You may not respond to any questions.

Repeat the above using the second picture, but this time the listener may ask questions and you may give feedback. How did this improve communication? Practice giving clear messages to each other.

Time Together: "Timely" Coupons

Redeem the following coupons with members of your family. Create your own coupons for spending special time with someone in your family.

GOOD FOR One evening of "hanging out" together	GOOD FOR Helping with an outdoor task	GOOD FOR Helping with an indoor task
GOOD FOR Helping with homework	GOOD FOR Playing a game	GOOD FOR Going on a walk together
GOOD FOR Going to a special event	GOOD FOR Helping with housework	GOOD FOR An afternoon of bowling
GOOD FOR	GOOD FOR	GOOD FOR
GOOD FOR	GOOD FOR	GOOD FOR
GOOD FOR	GOOD FOR	GOOD FOR

Coping with Conflict: Peace in the Family

A family is where each person should feel valued and safe. Yet it may be hard to feel secure and important when conflicts occur. Conflicts are a normal part of everyday life, but hurtfulness and violence should not be considered okay. To make your family stronger, work on making yours a more peaceful place. Learn how to handle conflicts so that each family member feels respected and cared for.

I. Where to Begin. (It may be helpful for the therapist to model this process or give some guidance.)

Hold a *family meeting* to talk about the importance of having peace in the family.

1. Have each member talk about a conflict he/she has had with a family member that was hurtful. Listen to each without disagreeing or defending.

2. Add to the following list of rules, and seek agreement:
   a. It is never okay to physically hurt each other. Each person is important and deserves caring and respect.
   b. No name calling or put-downs should be used.
   c. Parents should avoid taking sides and comparing their children. Cooperation should be encouraged.
   d. Be kind to each other—avoid cruel behavior. When anger flares, cool down.
   e. Work for "win/win" solutions to a problem, rather than one person winning over another.
   f. Problem solving should replace fighting.

3. Use the steps in *problem solving*:
   a. Stop the action (fighting).
   b. Listen to each other (really hear how each feels).
   c. Name the problem.
   d. Think of solutions.
   e. Choose a win/win solution.
   f. Carry out the plan.
   g. Look back and see how well the plan worked. If you need to, find a different solution.

II. Time to Practice!

Choose a conflict that has occurred between two family members. The therapist or adult family member can show how the mediation/problem-solving process works. All should listen to learn how to use the process, even when a mediator is not present. Focus on finding ways to have peace in the family:

Mediator: "Do both of you want to solve the problem, and agree to follow our rules from above (no put-downs, listen without interrupting, etc.)?"
If yes, continue.
"I would like each of you to state what you see the problem to be, and then describe how you feel about it." (Help each use "I" statements to tell his/her view of the problem.)

Person #1: "I think the problem is . . . . . . and I am feeling . . . . . .

Mediator: "Person # 2, can you repeat back what you heard Person #1 say?" (After this is done to #1's satisfaction, go on.)

Now repeat the process with person #2 describing, and #1 repeating back.

Mediator: "Now I would like each of you, in turn, to tell three possible solutions to the problem." Write down all solutions from each participant.
After hearing solutions from each participant, ask each, in turn, which solutions he/she is willing to try. See if there seems to be agreement on one to try. Ask, "Person #1, are you willing to try this solution?" If yes, ask Person #2, "Are you willing to try this solution?" If yes, "How will you know if it is working? What will you do if does not work?" (Help make a plan.)

Later, ask the two if the solution worked.

III. Apply the process to other conflict situations, seeking win/win, nonhurtful solutions.

Family Wellness: Wellness Wheel

Wellness involves several important components. Balance is also an important part of a healthy lifestyle. Make copies of the "wellness wheel," and have all family members assess the following aspects of their lives.

How balanced is your "wellness wheel"? On a 1 to 10 scale (10 being "I feel great about it"), rate each component of your current lifestyle. Write your score in the center of the wheel.

1. Is your wheel balanced? Which aspects of your life do you feel best about?
   Where would you like to improve?
2. Make a plan for addressing your needs.
   I would like to . . .
   I will start by doing . . .
   I will know I am making progress by . . .
3. Discuss as a family. How can family members help accomplish my goals?

46

Family Assessment Tool

Sharon A. Deacon

Type of Contribution: _Activity/Handouts_

Objective

The Family Assessment Tool can be used at an inital meeting with a client family as a guide for gathering information that is needed in therapy. It provides the therapist with a structure to follow; it also prompts the therapist to gather information that might otherwise be overlooked.

Rationale for Use

Every therapist has his/her own method and style for conducting an initial assessment of a family. However, in the midst of conversation, it is often easy to forget details or ask all of the pertinent questions. This assessment tool is a guide to follow for an initial interview. Once completed, it contains valuable information from which hypotheses can be generated.

Instructions

Ask the questions or fill out the information as it appears on the form.

Suggestions for Follow-Up

Once the basic information has been gathered, the therapist can decide which issues to probe deeper, and what other information may be necessary. This guide can be used as a reference throughout therapy, to apprise the therapist of important contextual data.

Contraindications

The therapist should avoid becoming so absorbed with filling out the assessment that he/she is not listening or paying attention to nonverbal cues. It is best for the therapist to be flexible, and to fill out the assessment while joining with the family. Strict adherence to the form may make the family feel "on the spot" and ignored.

Date: _____   Case #: _____

Family Information

Client Name: _____   D.O.B.: _____

Race: _____   Sex: _____   Marital Status: _____

Personal Information: (Career, education, interests, etc.)

Spouse: _____   D.O.B.: _____

Race: _____   Sex: _____   Marital Status: _____

Personal Information: (Career, education, interests, etc.)

Children	**Age**	**Grade**	**Personal Information**
_____	____	____	_____
_____	____	____	_____
_____	____	____	_____
_____	____	____	_____
_____	____	____	_____

Others involved with family:

Previous experiences with therapy? Yes   No
Comments:
_____
_____
_____

Previous psychiatric hospitalizations? Yes   No
Comments:
_____
_____
_____

Past or current involvement with alcohol or drugs? Yes   No
Comments:

_____

_____

_____

Medical History of Family Members:

_____

_____

_____

Family Stresses

Death

_____

_____

Divorce

_____

_____

Trouble with Law

_____

_____

Financial Strain

_____

_____

Job/Career

_____

_____

School

_____

_____

Illness/Operation

_____

_____

Mental Illness

_____

_____

Physical Abuse

_____

_____

Sexual Abuse

_____

_____

Family Life Cycle Stage:

Relationships with Outside Systems

Genogram:

Extended family/family of origin information:

Are other therapists involved?

Is the family involved with any social services?

Outside resources for support: (e.g., friends, religious organization, support groups, clubs)

258

Presenting Problem and Problem History

When did the problem begin?

_____
_____
_____
_____

Possible causes?

_____
_____
_____
_____

Why therapy now?

_____
_____
_____
_____

Past attempts at solving problem?

_____
_____
_____
_____

Therapist Observations

Tracking behavioral sequences:

_____

_____

_____

_____

Family structure and parenting style:

_____

_____

_____

_____

Communication and interaction style:

_____

_____

_____

_____

Overall Impressions

Further comments:

_____

_____

_____

_____

Mood of session:

_____

_____

_____

_____

Therapist's hypotheses:

_____

_____

_____

_____

_____

_____

Treatment goals: (F= family goal, T= therapist goal, LT= long-term, ST= short-term)

47

The Therapeutic Journey

Sharon A. Deacon

Type of Contribution: *Activity*

Objective

This activity is designed to help both the therapist and client(s) to set specific, behavioral goals for therapy. The activity involves defining a goal, specifying the steps that need to be taken to reach that goal, and how things will look different once the goal has been achieved.

Rationale for Use

When clients come into therapy, they are often very vague about what it is they want to accomplish or resolve in therapy; they have a problem, but do not have any ideas about how to resolve it. Most clients come in with the purpose of making a problem "go away." This activity helps clients to concretely break down the problem, and to focus on finding a solution that is achievable in the confines of therapy. Clients are able to track their progress toward reaching the resolution, and the steps they need to take to achieve their goal state. In doing so, both the therapist and clients have a frame to work from and a direction for therapy.

Instructions

This activity should begin after the therapist has established some rapport with the family, and the clients' problems are verbalized and somewhat defined.

The activity begins with the therapist reframing the therapy experience as a journey. The therapist is to tell the clients that they are on a road to the resolution of their problem(s). Ask the clients to draw this road that they will travel on.

The first task is to ask the clients to write down their problem (or somehow symbolize it) at the beginning of the road. Each person in the room can contribute to defining the problem. The therapist can help to clarify the problem and to add behavioral terms. Then, the therapist asks the clients what will be different when the problem no longer exists. The clients are instructed to write down, in behavioral terms, what things will look like when the problem is resolved, at the end of the road.

The clients should "own" the journey. Therefore, encourage the clients to add scenery to their journey. They may want to add some tools that can help then go faster, such as a skateboard or trampoline. They may also want to define some of the roadblocks they may encounter along the way, such as financial difficulties or fear.

Once the starting point and end point are described, the clients are asked what steps need to be taken in order to go from start to finish. During this time, the therapist can help the clients to be specific and to use concrete, behavioral steps. The clients can make the divisions in the road, such as bricks, after each step (just like the cracks on the sidewalk). The steps toward solving the problem should follow chronologically, and build upon one another.

For example, clients may have a starting point of "children are not completing their homework." The ending point may be described with comments such as "better grades," "less than one note, per month, sent home from the teacher," "only have to ask children once to sit down and do their homework," and "less family fights about homework." The steps, systematically, might be:

1. Arrange with the teachers at school to send home a list with the homework written on it
2. Create a time and place in the home where homework is to be completed
3. Set up a behavioral checklist and reward system for doing homework, with consequences for not doing homework
4. Check child's homework, every day, before any playtime, telephone, friends, or television is allowed

After the assignment is complete, the therapy can progress each session by focusing on completing the steps necessary to reach the goal. When a step has been taken, and the results are successful, the clients can draw a footprint over that step, to show that part of the journey has been completed. Clients may also want to add some more scenery that brightens up the picture, or encourages them to continue (e.g., the sun, a rainbow, an audience cheering them on). Once all the bricks have been stepped on, the goal is reached, and the changes can be seen.

Suggestions for Follow-Up

Follow-up involves constantly monitoring so that the clients complete the steps that are being worked on. Designing interventions for each step, to help the clients take that step, is also a necessity.

Each time the clients return to therapy, it is important to take a look at the journey, and discuss the progress that has been made, the next step that needs to be taken, and the direction in which therapy is progressing. The therapist must also do some troubleshooting along the way, when some steps are too big to be taken all at once, and need to be broken down into smaller steps which the clients can achieve more successfully.

At times, the journey may be altered, and a new road may be taken. In those cases, simply add a detour to the map.

Contraindications

This activity can be helpful for almost any client, any case, and any problem. Even in crisis situations, externalizing the steps necessary to end the crisis can be helpful.

48

Good Cops and Bad Cops in Parenting

Lorna L. Hecker

Type of Contribution: *Activity/Handouts*

Objective

This activity is designed to teach parents how to enforce rules and distribute punishment, while at the same time encouraging children to take responsibility for their actions. This activity will help parents gain control of rewards and punishments within the home.

Rationale for Use

This activity is for families in which parents are having difficulty controlling their children, and need help with parent education and enforcement of discipline. It is also a very appropriate activity for parents who become overwhelmed with anger when extolling punishment to children. In addition, single parents may find this activity useful, as it makes punishing less of a personal affront against the parent, and requires less thought when under stress.

Instructions

The therapist asks parents if they feel as though they have been "spinning their wheels" when it comes to parenting their children. If they answer "Yes," this may be an appropriate activity. With the children in the room, the therapist engages the family in the following conversation.

Step 1: Telling the Good Cop/Bad Cop Story

To the parents: "Have you ever been pulled over for speeding by the police?" (Most people usually have, but if they have not, ask them to think about how they have seen police pull over people in television or movies.) "When you were pulled over, how was the policeman or policewoman to you? Was he/she nice, or did he/she make you feel as though you did not deserve to have a driver's license?"

Continue by explaining that there are basically two types of cops: good cops and bad cops. State that: "Bad cops are the ones who pull you over, berate you, and ask you demeaning questions or insult you. Bad cops ask you if you got your driver's license at Kmart! Good

The author gratefully acknowledges P.C. Moisan-Thomas as the originator of this intervention.

cops, on the other hand, pull you over, are polite, and simply ask for your driver's license and say 'you were going 50 mph in a 30 mph zone.' Good cops hand you your ticket, and simply say, 'Have a nice day.' If you had to be pulled over again, which cop would you prefer to be pulled over by?" At that point, discuss with parents how they feel about themselves with a good cop versus a bad cop. Ask the children with which cop they would want to interact.

Explain to the parents that it is the same with punishment for children. There are good parents and bad parents. Ruminate out loud that you suspect they would like to be seen as good parents by their children; people agree to this statement without fail. Discuss how parenting is like giving out a ticket, and parents need to be able to give out the punishment in the same manner that the good cop gives out his/her ticket (politely, matter of factly, and firmly).

Step 2: Engaging the Children in Constructing Tickets

Ask the children if they are willing to help their parents out by coming up with their tickets. Give them six of the following "punishment tickets" and one "reward ticket" (see handout). Reward tickets are to be used if no punishment tickets are given all week long. Children will often be much harder on themselves for punishments than parents usually are. They also know the perfect punishments. Engagement of the intervention occurs in the spirit of a game, and children have always been willing to comply. Parents have the final say in accepting a punishment or reinforcer ticket. Reinforcer tickets can be things such as "Mom and Dad take Carrie out for ice cream."

Step 3: Parents Issue Tickets as Needed

After tickets are drawn up for each child, ask the parents to collect them and keep them in a place where they can easily use them as needed (on the refrigerator is a common place). Ask parents if they think they will have any problems giving out tickets when needed. If they cite reservations, discuss them. Often, parents will ask what happens if the child is resistant to the punishment. In turn, ask, "What happens if you are belligerent to the cop who gives you a traffic ticket?" They generally respond that the cop gives them another ticket or may even throw them in jail; the therapist can respond, saying, "Exactly." The children then get another ticket. This activity reinforces the parental hierarchy in a fun and concrete manner. The therapist should also discuss the nature of the rewards and ask the children to redeem their reward tickets with parents at the end of the week if they have been able to go without punishment tickets all week.

Suggestions for Follow-Up

Follow-up includes checking in to see that the following components were followed:

- tickets were given out when needed;
- rewards were utilized if no punisher tickets were needed;
- parents played good cops and did not engage in yelling or other negative behaviors, by simply extolling tickets as needed;
- tickets were appropriate for age of children and the type of infraction.

Troubleshooting is done with parents for difficult situations. Additional tickets may be made up by parents as needed.

Contraindications

This activity is contraindicated for children below school age. Younger children can be helped by older children as needed, but if there are too many younger children, this activity will not be appropriate. This activity is also contraindicated if the parents are consistently "bad cops." The issue of parental ill will toward children must be dealt with in therapy before using this activity; these cases generally involve parents who believe that their children are willfully being disrespectful and nonloving when they break rules or act out. Therapists should explore these irrational beliefs and educate parents on the nature of children who are simply testing limits.

Readings and Resources for the Professional

Dinkmeyer, D. and McKay, G. D. (1989). *The parent's handbook: Systematic training for effective parenting*. Circle Pines, MN: American Guidance Service.

Bibliotherapy Sources for Clients

Phelan, T. (1994). *1-2-3 Magic*. New York: Guilford Press.

TICKET ISSUED TO:

_____

FOR THE CHILD-MOVING
VIOLATION OF:

_____

_____

ONCE THIS TICKET IS ISSUED,
I PROMISE TO DO THE
FOLLOWING:

_____

_____

_____

_____

Signature of Child:

_____

REWARD
TICKET ISSUED TO:

_____

FOR EXEMPLARY
FAMILY SERVICE OF:

_____

_____

ONCE THIS TICKET IS ISSUED,
I, AS A PARENT, PROMISE TO
DO THE FOLLOWING FOR/WITH
MY CHILD:

_____

_____

_____

_____

Signature of Parent(s):

_____

49

The "Talk About" Game

Sharon A. Deacon

Type of Contribution: *Activity*

Objective

This activity can be used as a joining and assessment tool with children and families. The objective is to get to know many things about family members in a short amount of time, and in a friendly, gamelike atmosphere.

Rationale for Use

In the beginning of therapy, children are often hesitant about what kinds of information to share with the therapist. It is often awkward for families to decide who should speak, who should say what, and who can participate in the discussion with the therapist at the same time. Children are often left out of the conversation, or their parents are constantly editing their remarks. This activity gives every family member a chance to tell the therapist about themselves. It is also a strategic way for the therapist to acquire much information about all of the family members, how they interact, and where the alignments may be. At the same time, the therapist is joining with the family and creating a comfortable atmosphere for the children and their parents.

Instructions

The therapist is to introduce the family to the "talking ball" (or any object that can be thrown). The person with the ball is the "talker." The therapist is to throw the ball to someone and say "Talk about . . . ," filling in the subject that the talker is to talk about. The talker must say five (5) things, as quickly as possible, about the subject the therapist has given him/her (a sort of free association). When the talker has mentioned five things, he/she can throw the ball to someone else and give that person a topic to talk about. The goal is to see how fast the family members can talk about various subjects, and for the therapist to define which subjects are the most difficult and easy for the family to talk about.

For example, the therapist could throw the ball to a child and say, "Talk about summer." The child responds, "Hot, no school, swimming, Grandma's house, and camping." The child then throws the ball to someone else and says, "Talk about the zoo" (for example). The therapist can play too, while at the same time learning about the family.

The therapist can then strategically ask people to talk about some more serious issues. Some good "talk about" topics include: other family members, feeling words, school, marriage, parents, holidays, rules, punishment, conflict, privacy, sickness, vacations, bosses, the house, my bedroom, etc. It is best to use these more difficult topics sporadically in the game and after the game already has momentum, thus preventing the family from becoming too afraid to share their ideas.

The therapist ends the game when people run out of topics or become tired of it. The game could also be timed, with the family trying to talk about as many topics as possible in a certain amount of time. Five rounds is usually sufficient for gathering information and joining.

Suggestions for Follow-Up

While playing the game, the therapist should take note of the various associations that are made with the different topics. After the game, the therapist may choose to go back and ask questions about the associations, or ask for further clarification. Clients are usually more open to discussing issues once they have initially voiced them in a nonthreatening way.

Contraindications

This activity is not recommended with families that are extremely withdrawn and/or guarded. If this is the case, it may be helpful to alter the game and use "safe and easy topics" that do not seem invasive.

This activity is also not recommended for use with clients who have poor cognitive abilities. If the activity singles a person out with low cognitive abilities, it may destroy joining efforts with that individual and make therapy uncomfortable.

50

A Box of Tenderness

Tara R. Gootee

Type of Contribution: *Activity*

Objective

This activity is designed to help establish personal boundaries within one's family (or other important relationships), while also facilitating positive feedback between family members.

Rationale for Use

This activity is designed to be used with families that interact and communicate in a negative manner, including speaking for each other and giving negative comments about the other members.

Instructions

In this intervention, small, plain cardboard boxes (or other containers) are presented to each family member. During the session, the members are asked to decorate their box with markers, crayons, colored paper, glue, buttons, or personal mementos that they have brought from home. They can use whatever they want to make their box unique and special to them. This activity also allows the family time to spend together on an enjoyable project. This part of the activity may also be given as a homework assignment.

During the next session, the family returns with their "boxes of tenderness." Each family member is given small pieces of paper. One member is asked to volunteer to start the activity. All other members are asked to write down at least one thing about that person that they like or admire. They can also write down one thing that they appreciated that the person did for them during that week or month. The papers are then folded and put into the first volunteer's box of tenderness. The next family member is then chosen and the process continues until each person has had a turn.

When everyone has had a turn, the members read the comments they have received aloud, one comment at a time. This provides a situation whereby positive comments can be exchanged among the family members. The members are allowed to take their boxes of tenderness home where they can reread the comments they have received when they feel the need for some tenderness. For families where boundaries are an issue, rules are established which state that each person's box is private, and that no one else may take or use another's box.

An alternative way to use this activity is to allow the family to create a common solution-focused "problem" box. This intervention is useful for families that deal with their problems in an ineffective or destructive way. A different box or container is used for this purpose. In between sessions, the members take the box home. Every time they have a problem or issue that they would like to address in the next session, they write down the problem and insert it into the box. This activity gives them time to cool down while also serving as a "release." When the clients write down their issues and put them inside the box, it symbolizes "putting the problem away" for awhile. The clients bring the box to their next session, where their problems can be addressed in a more calm and effective manner.

Suggestions for Follow-Up

This activity can be used as needed to help maintain boundaries and continue positive interactions among the family. The problem box can be used each session for further assessment of the issues the family is dealing with. It is also a good way to introduce problem-solving skills into the family's repertoire. As therapy progresses, it is important to note if clients are bringing fewer of their problems to sessions and solving them on their own instead.

Contraindications

This activity could be detrimental if the family members are unable, due to severity of a crisis or pending situation, to verbalize positive comments about others.

Readings and Resources for the Professional

Baucom, D. H. and Epstein, N. (1990). *Cognitive-behavioral marital therapy.* New York: Brunner/Mazel.

Jacobson, N. S. and Margolin, G. (1979). *Marital therapy: Strategies based on social learning and behavior exchange principles.* New York: Brunner/Mazel.

Minuchin, S. (1974). *Families and family therapy.* Cambridge, MA: Harvard University Press.

Bibliotherapy Sources for the Client

Branden, N. (1983). *Honoring the self.* New York: Bantam Books.

Buscaglia, L. F. (1984). *Loving each other: The challenge of human relationships.* New York: Fawcett Columbine.

Carlson, R. and Shield, B. (1995). *Handbook for the soul.* Boston: Little, Brown, and Company.

Caron, A. F. (1992). *Don't stop loving me: A reassuring guide for mothers of adolescent girls.* New York: Harper Perennial.

51

Out of the Middle with a Toss of the Coin

Sharon A. Deacon

Type of Contribution: *Homework/Handouts*

Objective

The objective of this homework assignment is to help children detriangle themselves when they are caught in the middle of two adults in a loyalty struggle. Instead of having to choose who to side with, children rely on a coin toss to make the decision for them. Thus, neither of the two adults can claim the child actively chose his/her side, and the child is relieved of the loyalty conflict.

Rationale for Use

When two adults are in conflict, it is common for them to bring in a third party to handle the dispute or take the attention off of the dispute. Children often become caught in the middle between adults or parents, and end up feeling as though they need to decide which adult to side with. At this point, it is not uncommon for children to exhibit behavioral symptoms, from the stress of loyalty conflicts and being triangled. This activity randomizes the child's decision, and relieves the child from having to make a decision. At the same time, since the child's decision is not his/her own, but the random act of a coin toss, the two adults can no longer use the child to settle the dispute or legitimately claim that the child is on his/her side.

Instructions

Before this homework assignment is given, the therapist must first determine that the child is being triangled, or caught in the middle, of two adults. The therapist, based on the situation and the child's cognitive abilities, may even choose to have a discussion with the child about what it is like to be "caught in the middle." Ask the child to verbalize how he/she knows when he/she is caught in the middle. For example, the child might recognize that his/her parents are not speaking or that one adult keeps complaining about the other to the child. Perhaps the child can even state instances when each adult gave him/her different instructions for behavior.

In front of the two adults, the therapist is then to give the child a "magic coin" and this homework assignment. Whenever the child feels trapped or "caught in the middle," he/she is to flip the coin. If the coin ends up "heads" the child is to side with "X" adult. If the coins ends up "tails," the child is to side with "Y" adult. The child is instructed to always follow the coin and not to attempt to make such decisions him/herself.

Suggestions for Follow-Up

Once the child has implemented this plan, it is important for the therapist to monitor that the coin is being used correctly. Some troubleshooting may be needed if the two conflicting adults somehow sabotage the plan and retriangle the child.

A discussion with the adults should take place about how they triangle the child and how they need alternate ways of dealing with their conflicts. Beware of other people taking the place of the child in the triangle.

Contraindications

This homework assignment will not be effective unless the adults are aware of the use of the coin in the child's decision making. This activity may not be helpful with children who have severe behavioral problems, or when adults are unwilling to admit that their conflicts exist. In such instances, this assignment may invalidate the child's efforts at helping the family to survive. This activity should not be used when child abuse is present, when the coin toss could bring harm to the child.

Alternate Use

The use of a coin toss may also be helpful when children have a problem with lying, or parents suspect that their child is lying. Give the child the "magic coin." Ask the child a series of easy questions (e.g., "How old are you?") and then tell the child to flip the coin. "Heads" means "tell the truth," and "tails" means "tell a lie." Instruct the child to answer the questions based on the results of the coin toss. Whatever the child's answer, it is obvious whether the child is lying or telling the truth. The child's lying becomes systematic, instead of a random, personal act. The child's behavior is externalized from him/her.

Tell the child to continue this activity at home with his/her parents. Instruct the parents to formulate ten or more questions (easy and self-incriminating) every day and have the child use the coin toss to answer the questions accordingly. It is also important for the parents to decide how to handle self-incriminating truthfulness. Parents can no longer accuse the child of lying, as the coin is responsible for the child's responses. Trust begins to be reestablished.

Readings and Resources for the Professional

deShazer, S. (1988). *Clues: Investigating solutions in brief therapy.* New York: W.W. Norton and Co.

Kerr, M. E. and Bowen, M. (1988). *Family evaluation.* New York: W.W. Norton and Co.

52

The "Oprah" Approach

Mudita Rastogi

Type of Contribution: *Activity*

Objective

The objective of this activity is to lay the groundwork for effective family-oriented treatment for individuals, families, and groups. If used with groups, the activity enables new entrants and seasoned group members to become acquainted with each other. With families, it helps bring important issues to the forefront that may not have been previously identified as presenting problems. Individual or family issues that surface can then be processed in the group as well as in future family therapy sessions.

Rationale for Use

- People entering open groups may have a difficult time initially with assimilation. This activity allows members entering the group to be incorporated without some of the awkwardness that accompanies initial self-disclosure.
- It is an enjoyable activity that the participants grasp easily.
- The activity builds teamwork.
- The activity allows the clients to share in-depth, family-related information in an atmosphere of openness.
- The activity promotes empathy and group facilitation skills among the members.
- The activity generates a tremendous amount of content that can be processed in therapy with the group or family.
- The activity is an excellent way to involve silent or less active family members, especially adolescents, or to redirect energies of the more active family members.
- For both groups and families, this activity can sometimes help circumvent clients' feelings of self-consciousness about being videotaped.

Instructions

Seat the participants in a semicircle. Explain that the exercise will be similar to being on a television talk show. Distribute the handout to participants (see below) and a pencil to each person. Encourage people to think of at least one topic they would like as the theme of the day's "talk show." Explain to the group at the beginning that the therapist reserves the final decision on the choice of topic for safety reasons. The group as a whole can then vote on the topic they wish to discuss. Other methods to pick a topic include the lottery system, or giving the choice to the person who had a birthday most recently. Suggested talk show themes include parent-child relationships, dealing with difficult family situations, peer relationships, substance abuse, etc. Give yourself ten to fifteen minutes for this "pre-show" activity.

Ask for a volunteer to be a "co-host" along with the therapist. Give the group five minutes to reflect on the topic and write down feelings that arise, possible material they might wish to share, or questions they want to ask of other family or group members, or the "expert" on the show. The therapist and the co-host can use this time to write down questions they want to ask guests and issues they feel will be important to raise in the show. (Use the therapist/host handout.) The therapist may want to make a note of possible difficulties likely to be encountered by individuals or the group regarding the topic. Areas that may be too sensitive to go into at this point should also be noted.

Arrange a video camera so that the entire group can be taped. Go over the ground rules with the group before starting. It may be important to stress that the videotape will be treated as confidential material. Newer members of the group will need reassurance that they will not be pressured to answer the host's follow-up questions. Any further questions the participants have regarding format can be answered at this time.

The therapist and co-host begin by introducing the topic. The "audience" shares their experiences or opinions. Follow-up questions may be asked of the person talking. The follow-up questions are framed in such a way so as to facilitate the family interaction or group process, and to work through some of the issues presented. Occasionally, the therapist can also switch gears and play the role of an "expert" on the topic being discussed. This allows the presentation of psychoeducational materials to take place smoothly. Notes made on the therapist/host handout can be used to keep the activity on track. This activity can run for about fifty to ninety minutes, depending on the size of the family or group. On rare occasions, the therapist may need to schedule time at the end to talk individually to a client in order to process difficult feelings that may have emerged for him/her during the course of the talk show.

Suggestions for Follow-Up

Parts of the tape can be replayed and viewed by the clients over the next couple of sessions. This will allow the therapist to do more in-depth processing and facilitate further family treatment. At times, material that emerges from the content of the talk show may be used to develop new goals for therapy.

Contraindications

Individuals who have experienced trauma may feel deeply uncomfortable with a topic or another group member's narration that serves as a reminder of their own unresolved experiences. Occasionally, there may be individuals who are uncomfortable with being taped. The therapist then needs to use clinical judgment to decide whether or not to continue the activity. There may be times when a family or group member challenges the usefulness of the talk show format itself. This needs to be discussed and processed as would any other instance of client reluctance and challenging.

Readings and Resources for the Professional

Krueger, M. A. (1983). *Intervention techniques for the child/youth care workers.* Dousman, Wisconsin: Tall Publishing.

Lamb, D. (1986). *Psychotherapy with adolescent girls.* New York: Plenum.

White, J. L. (1989). *The troubled adolescent.* New York: Pergamon.

Handout for Participants

My Name:

Today's Date:

Topic of Talk Show:

Things I Want to Share About This Topic:

    1.

    2.

    3.

My Feelings About This Topic:

    1.

    2.

    3.

Questions I Want to Ask Other People:

    1.

    2.

    3.

Handout for the Therapist and Co-Host

My Name:

Today's Date:

Topic of Talk Show:

Questions to Ask the Audience About This Topic:

1.

2.

3.

Follow-up Questions to Ask:

1.

2.

My Own Feelings and Thoughts About This Topic:

1.

2.

3.

Things to be Careful About:

1.

2.

3.

Things to Follow-up on at a Later Time:

1.

2.

3.

53

Teamwork

Sharon A. Deacon

Type of Contribution: *Activity*

Objective

This activity can be used both as an assessment device and an intervention in therapy. The purpose of this activity is to provide therapists with in vivo observations of how a client family operates and interacts, as well as to help families cooperate and build teamwork. This is also a helpful activity to use with resistant and uncooperative family members in therapy, in order to discuss the need for cooperation and participation to make therapy successful.

Rationale for Use

In families, it is not uncommon for one or two members to rebel against the family or refuse to cooperate or participate in family activities. The family often becomes frustrated when one of its members breaks family cohesion. This pattern is likely to repeat in therapy, with the same member(s) refusing to participate or cooperate. Therapists may use this activity to assess family cohesion and cooperation, family roles, and problem-solving skills. As an intervention, this activity can be used to illustrate such family patterns to clients and elicit discussion of how families operate smoothly and with cooperative efforts. Covert patterns of interaction are made overt, and uncooperative family members can be confronted in a less threatening manner.

Instructions

The first step is to gather all family members together in the therapy room. The therapist is to give each family member a piece of paper, tape, scissors, glue, and writing utensils. Then, read these instructions to the family:

> Together, as a family, I want you to create a family drawing. First, you need to decide what you will draw. Each one of you must draw a piece of the final product on the paper that I have given you. In the end, you are to put everyone's papers or creations together with tape or glue, to form a complete picture.

Sit back, do not interfere, and observe what the family does. For assessment purposes, notice the following:

- Who takes the lead role?
- How is the decision of what to draw made?

- How are tasks divided?
- Who contributes most? Least?
- What problem-solving strategies are used?
- What kind of communication takes place?
- How are differences of opinion handled?

Once the project is completed, ask the family to answer the same questions listed above. Emphasize family roles, decision-making abilities, problem-solving skills, and communication. Facilitate a discussion with the family about how this project relates to how they operate as a family system. Discuss the meaning of leadership and teamwork within the family and in the therapy room. What does it mean to have teamwork? How does it feel to cooperate? It may also be helpful to discuss what happens when teamwork fails, who suffers, and how uncooperative team members should be dealt with.

Suggestions for Follow-Up

Ask the family to think about how teamwork could be improved at home and in therapy. It is often helpful for families to take their completed project home, with all their names signed on it, as a reminder of the need for teamwork. As therapy progresses, use this project as a metaphor for the family's interactions and their problem-solving abilities. Refer back to this activity to discuss what types of changes need to take place in the family for teamwork to prevail. In the end of therapy, it may be useful to repeat this activity and to discuss what is different and the changes the family has made as a result of therapy.

Contraindications

This activity would not be beneficial with highly conflictual families who could not even decide what to draw. The family needs to have some cooperation skills in order to complete this project and be successful at it. If a family is unsuccessful, a discussion about why they were unsuccessful may provide some insight to the family about their patterns of interaction.

54

Involving Children in Family Therapy: Making Family Movies

Catherine E. Ford Sori

Type of Contribution: *Activity*

Objective

Family therapists sometimes find it difficult to include young children in family therapy. Children may seem reluctant to talk, or they may become noisy and disrupt family sessions. "Making Family Movies" is an activity that offers therapists a unique and playful way to involve family members in different stages of development in family therapy. This method uses drama and role-playing to encourage everyone in the family to participate in therapy, and to promote change.

Rationale for Use

Many of the "founding fathers" of family therapy were strong advocates for including young children in family sessions (Keith and Whitaker, 1981; Montalvo and Haley, 1973; Ackerman, 1970). Children can provide therapists with a wealth of information about the structure, interactions, and relationships within the family. However, family therapists may find it difficult to actively involve young children in family therapy. Young children may have a difficult time expressing their feelings, and are often limited by their ability to understand and use language (Gondor, 1957).

Play is the language of childhood, and it helps children express their feelings. Making a family movie helps family members of different stages of the life cycle develop a common "language." Ariel, Carel, and Tyano (1985) state:

> Young children have neither the ability nor patience to *verbally express* their own feelings, relate to other people's feelings, discuss problems, etc., in the manner grown-ups do. However, they do have both the patience and the ability to *perform* all these complex social activities by means of *their own natural medium of expression and communication: make-believe play.* (p. 48, italics added)

This activity appeals to children's (and adults') imagination and creativity, and uses the language of childhood: play.

Instructions

The therapist first videotapes the family enacting their latest argument, and then has them reverse roles. This accomplishes several goals. First, the therapist is able to assess the family's structure, patterns of interaction, and roles, and attempts to solve the problem. Second, the "Family Movie" activity helps the therapist intervene by changing the family structure, altering sequences of interaction, and helping the family explore alternative solutions to their problems. Third, creating a family movie promotes understanding and empathy among family members. Finally, in the latter stages of therapy, the therapist uses the video to assess the family's progress, and to punctuate change.

To begin, the therapist assigns roles and summarizes the scene(s). In the first video, each person plays him/herself. Have families enact their last argument, exactly as it happened. This helps the therapist see how fights begin, who does what and says what as they progress, and how the arguments end. As the family "fights" in front of the camera, you can literally "see" individual roles, alliances, coalitions, boundaries, and hierarchy. In this way, the invisible becomes visible.

Next, family members are asked to replay the same argument, but to switch roles. For instance, the acting-out child becomes the mother, and Mom plays the part of the angry child. This increases each member's understanding of the other's point of view, and promotes empathy. It also lessens the possibility of the fight being repeated in the same way, since the emotions associated with the argument have changed. The next time the same argument begins, the family will interact differently.

The therapist needs to decide his/her own role in the production. Ariel, Carel, and Tyano (1985) suggest several possible roles for the therapist, including reporter, involved audience, and actor-director. The combined role of actor-director helps cast the entire family in the movie, and allows therapists to guide the direction of the production. When therapists encourage the family to overact, clients often seem to forget they are acting! As the production continues, you will begin to get a sharper "picture" of the family's problems. This is an entirely different experience from merely listening to the family's description.

After shooting the film, the family is typically excited about being "movie stars," and are eager to watch themselves on TV. The therapist and family should view the family movie together and discuss both their reactions to the film and the following specific questions:

- How did they feel when they played themselves?
- How was it different when their roles were reversed, and they played another family member?
- What was the "moral of the story?"

Be prepared for some surprising and moving answers, especially from the children! Parents and children begin to understand and empathize with one another. It is exciting to hear voices soften with tenderness as family members gain new awareness of each other's experience.

Suggestions for Follow-Up

In follow-up sessions, the therapist may use the family movie for several purposes. First, the film often helps parents clarify specific goals for improving their relationship with their child, and for modifying their child's behavior. The movie may also be shown again in a session just for parents. The therapist may point out specific sequences of behavior, and ask parents if the movie shows events as they usually occur. Questions to explore with parents include:

- What do you think your child is feeling?
- What are you feeling?
- What could you do differently at this point?
- What do you think your child might do differently as a result of your change?
- How would you like it to end differently?
- What could you do to increase the likelihood of this happening?
- What have you learned from this?

In this manner, the therapist begins to help the family explore possibilities for changing their patterns of interaction.

In fact, the mere process of filming enactments of family arguments and then reversing family roles helps alter the family's patterns of interaction. This happens because the emotions that were associated with the old pattern have been changed. Ariel, Carel, and Tyano (1985) point out that:

> Playfulness enables the players to treat aspects of their own immediate reality *as if* they are not real here and now. For example, if a child has a temper tantrum . . . and then he plays a make-believe temper tantrum, the tantrum is disowned by him and becomes "alien" to him because, *by the definition of make-believe play, it is not true of him in the here and now.* (p. 53, italics added)

The next time the family starts to have the same argument, their emotional reactions will be different because of their experiences in making the family movie.

Another interesting phenomenon frequently occurs when parents watch the family movie. As they see themselves reduced to yelling or wrestling with their children, they often become eager to try something different. This offers the therapist a chance to explore alternate solutions to the problem. After watching the video, many parents literally "see" the need to take charge of their children—without losing control. They are now more motivated to change. The therapist can now begin making structural changes in the family, such as strengthening hierarchy or altering crossgenerational coalitions.

The "Family Movie" activity is also useful in assessing the family's progress in therapy. By occasionally reviewing the video, the family (and the therapist) can literally "see" the progress they have made. This is especially useful at termination, to punctuate change and clarify exactly what the family is doing differently. In fact, the therapist can ask the family to reenact the original "fight," and then discuss what they are now doing differently. This helps the family realize how much they have changed, and empowers them to handle future problems logically.

Contraindications

While this experience is especially useful with chaotic families or families with active children, it may be less effective with very reserved families or families with a depressed child. However, the therapist's enthusiasm and excitement about making a movie may motivate even the most reluctant "stars."

Therapists should be cautious if they suspect that the child might be punished should a family secret be revealed while making the family movie. Before beginning this activity, the therapist should know and assess the family well, and the children and family should feel comfortable and safe with the therapist.

Readings and Resources for the Professional

Ackerman, N. (1970). Child participation in family therapy. *Family Process, 9,* 403-410.

Ariel, S., Carel, C., and Tyano, S. (1985). Uses of children's make-believe play in family therapy: Theory and clinical examples. *Journal of Marital and Family Therapy, 11*(1), 47-60.

Combrinck-Graham, L. (1989). *Children in family contexts: Perspectives on treatment.* New York: Guilford.

Dowling, E. and Jones, H. (1978). Small children seen and heard in family therapy. *Journal of Child Psychotherapy, 4,* 87-96.

Gil, E. (1994). *Play in family therapy.* New York: Guilford Press.

Gondor, L. H. (1957). Use of fantasy communications in child psychotherapy. *American Journal of Psychotherapy, 5,* 323-335.

Guttman, H. A. (1975). The child's participation in conjoint family therapy. *Journal of American Academy of Child Psychiatry, 14,* 480-499.

Keith, D. V. and Whitaker, C. A. (1981). Play therapy: A paradigm for work with families. *Journal of Marital and Family Therapy, 7,* 243-254.

Montalvo, B. and Haley, J. (1973). In defense of child therapy. *Family Process, 12*(3), 227-244.

Safer, D. (1965). Conjoint play therapy for the young child and his parent. *Archives of General Psychiatry, 13,* 320-326.

Villeneuve, C. (1979). The specific participation of the child in family therapy. *American Academy of Child Psychiatry, 18*(1), 44-53.

Wachtel, E. F. (1991). How to listen to kids. *Family Therapy Networker, 4,* 46-47.

Zilbach, J. J. (1986). *Young children in family therapy.* New York: Brunner/Mazel.

Zilbach, J. J. (1989). *Children in family therapy: Treatment and training.* Binghamton, New York: The Haworth Press.

Zilbach, J. J., Bergel, E., and Gass, C. (1972). Role of the young child in family therapy. In C. J. Sager and H. S. Kaplan (Eds.), *Progress in group and family therapy* (pp. 385-399). New York: Brunner/Mazel.

Bibliotherapy Sources for Clients

Brown, L. K. and Brown, M. (1988). *Dinosaurs divorce: A guide for changing families.* Boston: Little, Brown & Co.

Cain, B. S. (1990). *Double-dip feelings: Stories to help children understand emotions.* New York: Magination Press.

Chaplan, R. (1991). *Tell me a story, paint me the sun: When a girl feels ignored by her father.* New York: Magination Press.

Girard, L. W. (1987). *At daddy's on Saturdays.* Morton Grove, IL: Albert Whitman & Co.

Ives, S. B., Fasler, D., and Lash, M. (1994). *Divorce workbook: A guide for kids and families.* New York: Talman Co.

Munsch, R. (1986). *Love you forever.* Willowdale, Ontario: Firefly Books.

Payne, L. M. (1994). *Just because I am: A child's book of affirmation.* Minneapolis, MN: Free Spirit Publishing.

55

Videotaped Coaching

Tracy Todd
Steve Gilbertson

Type of Contribution: *Activity/Homework*

Objective

From fly fishing to country line dancing, instructional videotapes are being used to teach new skills. The objective of this intervention is to create an instructional videotape in which the clients are the "stars," teaching themselves how to use a particular skill for their specific problem. Decreasing crisis calls, helping clients prepare for stressful situations, or assisting clients in maintaining clarity of homework are some examples of when this technique is useful. Videotaped coaching is useful with many clinical presentations and diagnostic populations, including individuals, families, couples, and disabled clients, as well as those considered to be in the "chronic" population.

Rationale for Use

No matter how many times we discuss or practice a particular skill in session, clients still have difficulty following through at "crunch time." Videotaped coaching is a useful tool to help clients remember how to do the intervention discussed in session. There are two general uses of this technique. First, it can be used by clients in a role-playing format. By rehearsing how to respond to certain situations, clients can watch the videotape as a reminder of how to cope with the problem area. Second, the videotape can be used as a step-by-step instructional guide. Clients can create these steps to recall what they should be considering when distressed.

This technique adds energy to a session, as clients can have fun rehearsing their tasks or response patterns. Clients typically have a good time practicing healthy skills, and are entertained by creating a videotape. Also, when clients get home, they can review the videotape as often as necessary. This dynamic adds a feeling of empowerment and hope during problematic periods.

Instructions

1. It is important to discuss this technique with the clients before starting the videotape. Make sure that clients have a VCR to play it on and that they can maintain privacy when watching the tape.

2. Get signed permission forms to videotape the session.
3. Spend twenty to thirty minutes rehearsing and/or scripting what is needed on videotape. If you are trying to alter responses, you may need to spend a great deal of time role-playing the response pattern so that clients are comfortable and confident when they make the videotape. If you are trying to set up a step-by-step teaching aid, be sure you have as many steps outlined and scripted as needed. It is especially important that you write a script that will remind the clients of what to say when on videotape.
4. Make the videotape. This step is easier said than done. Clients can become very self-conscious when they know they are making a videotape for themselves. You need to help them feel comfortable about doing so. For this reason, it is very important to have a script of what they will be saying on the videotape, or to have them practice a particular role-play.
5. Give the clients the videotape; with instructions of when to use it. It is critical that clients understand cues, prompts, and triggers of when they should use the videotape.

Clinical Examples

Depression. A useful fifteen-minute videotape might include discussing daily plans and structure. The videotape may be of the client outlining such daily living skills as showering, making phone calls, going to work, and exercising. The specificity depends on the clinical situation, and a therapist may need to have the client create a daily schedule, per hour, on the videotape. Following the step-by-step instruction, until the next appointment, gives the client strategies and skills to use.

Parenting skills. With the use of a videotape, parents can create an instructional video explaining and demonstrating how they should interact with their children regarding a parenting issue. For example, parents who realize the curfew has been broken can view the videotape for role-played responses on how to cope with the situation in a nonescalating manner. This technique is useful with strategic interventions in which the intervention may be difficult for a parent to complete or follow through with (paradox, positive connotations). Any new parenting skill can be created with the videotape, and parents can watch the videotape for the demonstration of the skill.

Crisis management. Clients who routinely access services in a crisis can manage these situations by constructing a videotape. Through role-playing and rehearsal, steps can be practiced which will solve the crisis. Although these steps could be outlined in writing, a videotape giving instructions and walking through the situation is more powerful, as the expert consulted in crisis is the client. The result is increased self-efficacy, as clients view a videotaped reminder of themselves on how to handle the crisis. When a call comes into an agency (provided the crisis is not life threatening), the clinical staff can intervene by asking clients if they have watched their videotape. If clients have not watched the videotape, they are told to watch it as an early crisis intervention step.

While some clients routinely call in crisis, and each situation can vary, a videotape can be constructed which will outline a theme of management. If relationships are an ongoing problem, clients can de-escalate the situation by taping themselves talking out the problem. Through self-reminding of previous successes in similar situations, clients can calm and correct their course of action. A videotape of past successes makes a very nice trophy to admire when things do not seem to be going well.

Relapse prevention. The maintenance phase of behavior change can be challenging for anyone. When dealing with issues of substance abuse or dependence, relapse can occur for clients not having the opportunity to be successful with new coping skills. Situations which pose risk of "using" are identified, a specific course of action is developed, and then a videotape is created. When clients recognize such a situation exists, whether arguments and anger, pressure from old friends, responsibilities, or unpleasant emotions are present, they can intervene by watching their videotape. Just by stopping their present course to insert the videotape into a VCR, the intervention process has begun. This videotape reminder serves to further anchor their success.

Suggestions for Follow-Up

1. Find out if clients have used the videotape. It is important to discuss how the videotape worked or did not work. If they used the videotape, did it help?
2. If the videotape could have been more helpful to them, discuss what modifications are needed on it, and create another tape.
3. It is common for clients to say, "It would have helped, but we forgot to use it." Remember, this is a new step for them and you should help set up prompts that will remind them to use the coaching videotape.

Contraindications

1. If the clients feel insecure, or unsure that the videotape can be kept private, this activity may be countertherapeutic. If clients are particularly worried that someone may discover this videotape, do not use this intervention. It is far too great a risk to have clients' confidentiality breached. Be absolutely sure that clients are confident they can keep the tape secure and private. Important situations to assess for confidentiality concerns are marital affair situations, when one person in a family is seeking counseling without the remainder of the family, and in threatening situations when violence is present and the discovery of the videotape could lead to a violent altercation.
2. Do not assign this activity if the clients are not willing to use tape after it is made. The videotape is only good if people are willing to watch themselves on tape. If the clients are stressed while watching the tape, then consider a different intervention. It should be used to help our clients, not to add more distress to their lives.

Bibliotherapy Sources for the Clients

O'Hanlon, W. H. and Hudson, P. (1995). *Love is a verb*. New York: W.W. Norton.
Weiner-Davis, M. (1992). *Divorce busting: A revolutionary and rapid program for "staying together."* New York: Summit Books.

56

The Family Constitution Activity

Thomas D. Carlson

Type of Contribution: *Activity/Handouts*

Objective

This activity is intended to help client families solidify the new family identity that they have chosen in the process of Narrative Therapy. While the idea of creating a family constitution is not an entirely new one, it is a new contribution to the ideas of Narrative Therapy. Throughout the process of Narrative Therapy, the therapist and clients are involved in discovering preferred identities: alternate stories and experiences that have been lost due to the influence of a dominant story (White, 1995). The final step of Narrative Therapy is performing the new identity before an audience (White and Epston, 1990). This performance is designed to help the clients' new identity be seen and solidified in their important relationships with others. Having client families write a constitution is designed to help clients solidify their new identities.

Rationale for Use

The main goal of Narrative Therapy is to help families re-author their lives (White, 1995). This is accomplished as both the client and the therapist (1) assess the dominant story; (2) externalize the problem; (3) discover alternate stories; and (4) perform the new story before an audience (White and Epston, 1990). The therapist and clients explore the influence that the dominant story has on their lives, and how to resist its destructive role.

This focus on resistance can be seen by the use of the Declaration of Independence in helping clients separate themselves from the problem. Michael White and David Epston (1990) have clients write their own Declaration of Independence from the problem. The original Declaration of Independence has a tremendous amount of language that is consistent with Narrative Therapy's ideas of freeing ourselves from oppression and subjugating powers. While this activity may have a powerful impact on clients, for a new identity to be created there is another step that needs to be taken. Resistance from the old story is important, but even more important is the creation of a new identity. This is the purpose of the family constitution.

Similar to the Declaration of Independence, the Constitution of the United States also uses language that is consistent with Narrative Therapy. The Constitution was originally created as a means to protect the freedoms that were presented in the Declaration of Independence. It was created under the assumption that no governing power should ever have the ability to oppress its people, and guidelines were placed therein to provide a way for the U.S. Constitution itself to be rewritten and amended if it no longer served to protect the freedom of the people. These guidelines are helpful to include in a therapeutic constitution, as clients attempt to solidify their new identities.

Instructions

This activity is designed to be used at, or near, the end of therapy. Therefore, before presenting the guidelines for creating a family constitution, certain things should have already occurred in therapy. Due to the focus that the family constitution has of solidifying a new identity, the therapist and clients should be very clear as to what the clients' preferred story is. The dominant story should have been identified, and its influence on all the family members explored. This exploration should include the main techniques that the dominant story has used to recruit the family into particular behaviors. As these techniques are revealed, and alternate stories of resistance are brought forth, a separation of the family from the problem should have taken place. This could be accomplished through a Declaration of Independence that was mentioned above. As this separation takes hold and the family has identified their preferred way of life, the process of performing before an audience should begin. It is at this point where the family constitution can be used.

The following is an outline for how a family constitution can be approached. It should be noted that this activity will most likely take place over the period of a few sessions. Therefore, it is both an in-session activity and a homework assignment.

1. The therapist should provide each family member with a copy of the first few pages of the U.S. Constitution. (The entire Constitution is several hundred pages. Since the family will determine the content of their own constitution, a short example such as provided below will suffice.)
2. The therapist and family should look through the Preamble and decide what their own preamble will say. This may be done in the session or as a homework assignment.
3. Once the language of their preamble is determined, the family should decide which topics they are going to include in their constitution (e.g., roles, how decisions will be made, how the family will prevent the dominant story from taking over again).
4. These topics should then be integrated into different articles of the clients' constitution, with specific examples of how the articles will be carried out. Clients can work on this section as homework, to be presented to the therapist in subsequent sessions. This serves a dual purpose. First, it helps clients to focus on their new identities together. Second, it provides a forum for the family to present their ideas before an audience.
5. The different articles are then reviewed by each family member, and changes are made accordingly.
6. When the family has agreed on the items and contents in their constitution, a formal copy is made, and plans are made for a ratification ceremony. On the final draft, a section should be included that provides guidelines for amendments and changes that may take place over the years.
7. At the ratification ceremony, the family's constitution should be read out loud to all present. The family members should then sign their names to the constitution as an agreement to their new identity together. The ratification ceremony is a good place for therapy to be terminated. It is a celebration of a new life together.

An example of a family constitution is provided at the end of this chapter.

Suggestions for Follow-Up

The family constitution itself provides a good base for follow-up sessions. Since the family agreed to the new identity outlined in the constitution, the principles that they outlined can be reviewed in a follow-up session. However, the therapist should not assume that the principles outlined are one hundred percent right for the family. The follow-up session should include an exploration of the impact that those principles have on each person. It may be that some of the principles are oppressive to certain individuals. If this is the case, amendments can be made to address these issues.

Contraindications

As a social constructionist theory, Narrative Therapy does not espouse an objective reality. There is some danger in presenting this constitution creation as a rigid new reality for the family. This may present difficulties down the road, as powers may be used in inappropriate ways. Therefore, it is important that the family be instructed to review their family constitution from time to time. This review should be an exploration of the impact of the family constitution on the thinking, feeling, and actions of each family member.

While a guideline for life may be helpful, there is always the danger that a family constitution will become a new dominant story in the lives of families. This activity appears to be best suited for those families, couples, etc., who are experiencing difficulty defining their new identities. For those people who do not experience this problem, a family constitution may not be helpful.

Readings and Resources for the Professional

Epston, D., White, M., and Murray, K. (1992). A proposal for a re-authoring therapy: Rose's revisioning of her life and a commentary. In McNamee, S. and Gergan, K. (Eds.), *Therapy as a social construction*. Newbury Park, CA: Sage Publications.

Phelan, T. (1995). *1-2-3 magic: Effective discipline for children*. Glen Ellyn, IL: Child Management Inc.

White, M. (1995). *Re-authoring lives: Interviews and essays*. Adelaide, South Australia: Dulwich Center Publications.

White, M. and Epston, D. (1991). *Narrative means to therapeutic ends*. New York: Norton.

Constitution of the Agent Family

We the people of this household, in order to form a more perfect union, ensure domestic tranquility, promote the general welfare to ourselves and our posterity, establish justice and spiritual harmony, do ordain and establish this Constitution for the Agent Family.

Article I ::: Legislative Powers

Section 1
All legislative powers herein granted shall be vested in a council comprised of all family members.

Section 2
The council shall be presided over by the Patriarch and Matriarch of the family, namely Papa and Mama. These two bodies comprise the Executive Committees, who also oversee the orderliness of each council meeting.

Section 3
All major issues of family concern, that is, concerning the family as a whole, physically or spiritually, shall be decided upon in a family council, whereby each member of the council shall be entitled to one vote, with a majority rule.

Section 4
The Executive Committee has the right to veto any and all rulings made by the council, but only where the rulings affect the best well-being of the family, as determined in all righteousness.

Section 5
Where issues cannot be decided in council, whether by tie in vote or otherwise, the issue will be decided in a private executive subcommittee.

Article II ::: Executive Powers

Section 1
Executive powers shall mainly be concerned with the financial matters of the family.

Section 2
These financial matters shall be decided by the Financial Committee, which consists of the Executive Committee and any other family members contributing to the financial upkeep of the family.

Section 3
Each member of the Financial Committee shall have one vote for each issue, with the Executive Committee reserving the right to veto any rulings not considered conducive to the overall well-being of the family. In such a case where a veto is issued, the matter will be decided upon in a private executive subcommittee.

Section 4
Aspects of the highest concern in all Financial Committee meetings (in this order) will be (1) the elimination of major debts incurred by the family; and (2) the well-being and happiness of the family in general by providing funding toward family activities that are conducive to a spiritual and righteous way of life.

Clause 1

There shall be a main family account from which all bills and debts are paid. This account shall also be maintained by the Executive Committee. It shall be comprised of a checking account, from which the debts are paid, and a savings account, from which general family expenses, such as family vacations, are paid. This account shall receive any and all income from each member of the Financial Committee and, immediately, ten percent is to be removed from any increases for tithing purposes.

Clause 2

Each member of the Financial Committee shall have his or her own private account from which he or she may do as he or she wishes. This account receives its funding from the main family account by the following guidelines:

(A) Ten percent of the income they add to the main family account goes to this individual account, and

(B) additional amounts may be added to the individuals' accounts, as determined by the Financial Committee, when the family account is at a point of little or no major debt.

Article III ::: Judicial Powers

Section 1

Judicial and disciplinary powers are the exclusive right of the Executive Committee, but to be carried out in all righteousness, and not done so in anger or retribution.

Section 2

These powers are also guided by the 'ONE-TWO-THREE MAGIC' guidelines [behavior modification program], but not when they override spiritual matters.

Article IV ::: Special Powers to the Executive Committee

Section 1

The Executive Committee reserves the right (and has a duty) to establish time periods where it may gather together for not only its subcommittee meetings, but also for extracurricular activities deemed necessary for the well-being of itself, as in the case of weekly dates.

Section 2

Of primary concern to the Executive Committee is the commitment of the Patriarch to the Matriarch, and conversely the Matriarch to the Patriarch. This commitment shall be maintained in righteousness, love, and overall well-being for one to the other.

Article V ::: Church Issues

Section 1

Members of the Agent family household Executive Committee have agreed that church is an important facet of their lives and will be so for their children, until they are old enough to make this decision for themselves. Included in a proper perspective of a righteous lifestyle is:

(A) Church attendance
(B) Daily family prayer

(C) Nightly Executive Committee prayer
(D) Daily individual prayer
(E) Weekly family home evening

Article VI ::: Family Council

Section 1

Family council shall be held once per month to discuss issues of importance to the family as a whole. These issues include such subject as:
(A) Family Planning
(B) Addressing problems (real or potential)
(C) Establishing family goals
(D) Determining of member's responsibilities

Article VII ::: Executive Committee

Section 1

The Executive Committee shall meet once per week to discuss any and all issues of importance regarding the family or the committee itself. These may include:
(A) Committee planning
(B) Family planning
(C) Committee goals
(D) Family goals
(E) Personal goals

Article VIII ::: Amendment Creation

Section 1

This constitution is to be considered by no means perfect, and subject to the flaws of its makers. It is thereby only obvious that there should be procedures set up for creating amendments. These procedures will follow these guidelines, with the Executive Committee determining the exact methodology:
(A) Executive Committee discussion/vote
(B) Family Council discussion/voting
(C) Revisions and final draft

THE UNITED STATES CONSTITUTION

We the People of the United States, in Order to form a more perfect Union, establish Justice, insure domestic Tranquility, provide for the common defence, promote the general Welfare, and secure the Blessings of Liberty to ourselves and our Posterity, do ordain and establish this Constitution for the United States of America.

Article. I.

Section. 1.

All legislative Powers herein granted shall be vested in a Congress of the United States, which shall consist of a Senate and House of Representatives.

Section. 2.

Clause 1: The House of Representatives shall be composed of Members chosen every second Year by the People of the several States, and the Electors in each State shall have the Qualifications requisite for Electors of the most numerous Branch of the State Legislature.

Clause 2: No Person shall be a Representative who shall not have attained to the Age of twenty-five Years, and been seven Years a Citizen of the United States, and who shall not, when elected, be an Inhabitant of that State in which he shall be chosen.

Clause 3: Representatives and direct Taxes shall be apportioned among the several States which may be included within this Union, according to their respective Numbers, which shall be determined by adding to the whole Number of free Persons, including those bound to Service for a Term of Years, and excluding Indians not taxed, three fifths of all other Persons. The actual Enumeration shall be made within three Years after the first Meeting of the Congress of the United States, and within every subsequent Term of ten Years, in such Manner as they shall by Law direct. The Number of Representatives shall not exceed one for every thirty Thousand, but each State shall have at Least one Representative; and until such enumeration shall be made, the State of New Hampshire shall be entitled to chuse three, Massachusetts eight, Rhode-Island and Providence Plantations one, Connecticut five, New-York six, New Jersey four, Pennsylvania eight, Delaware one, Maryland six, Virginia ten, North Carolina five, South Carolina five, and Georgia three.

Clause 4: When vacancies happen in the Representation from any State, the Executive Authority thereof shall issue Writs of Election to fill such Vacancies.

Clause 5: The House of Representatives shall chuse their Speaker and other Officers; and shall have the sole Power of Impeachment.

Section. 3.

Clause 1: The Senate of the United States shall be composed of two Senators from each State, chosen by the Legislature thereof, for six Years; and each Senator shall have one Vote.

Clause 2: Immediately after they shall be assembled in Consequence of the first Election, they shall be divided as equally as may be into three Classes. The Seats of the Senators of the first Class shall be vacated at the Expiration of the second Year, of the second Class at the Expiration of the fourth Year, and of the third Class at the Expiration of the sixth Year, so that one third may be chosen every second Year; and if Vacancies happen by Resignation, or otherwise, during the Recess of the Legislature of any State, the Executive thereof may make temporary Appointments until the next Meeting of the Legislature, which shall then fill such Vacancies.

Clause 3: No Person shall be a Senator who shall not have attained to the Age of thirty Years, and been nine Years a Citizen of the United States, and who shall not, when elected, be an Inhabitant of that State for which he shall be chosen.

Clause 4: The Vice President of the United States shall be President of the Senate, but shall have no Vote, unless they be equally divided.

Clause 5: The Senate shall choose their other Officers, and also a President pro tempore, in the Absence of the Vice President, or when he shall exercise the Office of President of the United States.

57

The Systemic Wave

Sharon A. Deacon

Type of Contribution: *Activity*

Objective

The purpose of this activity is to teach families how they operate as systems, and to demonstrate the concept of circular causality. This activity can be used for psychoeducational purposes with groups or families. This activity can also be used as a metaphor for the problematic interactions that occur within the family. The optimal outcome of this activity is not that the family learn vocabulary, but that discussions are generated about how the family operates as a system and affects each member.

Rationale for Use

Families operate as systems. Each person's behavior affects everyone else's and vice versa. If one person changes, the rest of the family will be affected. Oftentimes, families do not realize how much their actions influence one another, or how patterns of interaction are created. This activity experientially demonstrates the workings of a family system. At the same time, family members can begin to think about what changes need to take place in their family.

Instructions

Have all family members stand up and join hands, therapist included. Start "the wave" by lifting your right hand up, which raises the next person's left hand, and tell that person to "pass it on." That person is then to raise his/her right hand, raising the next person's left hand and so on. "Do the wave" a few times around the circle. This is circular causality. Explain and discuss how one person's actions affected everyone else in the circle. Have the family think of examples of how circular patterns occur in their family.

Now, have everyone rejoin hands. Ask someone else to start the wave. Notice the pattern—it is the same. Explain to the family the concept of equifinality—different starting points can lead to the same end. Discuss how change can occur in many ways, in many people, and the same outcome can still occur. Ask the family to think of the many different ways they could use to solve the same problem.

Rejoin hands. Restart the wave, but this time go from left to right. A similar pattern occurs but in a different direction. Explain that this is equipotentiality—the same start can lead to different ends. Ask the family to think of how one change in their family could lead to many different outcomes. Discuss how difficult it is to predict what one little change can do.

Next, ask one set of adjacent family members to disconnect their hands. (You may choose this set of people strategically by choosing the family members most likely to make changes in the family and disrupt enduring patterns.) Start the wave again. Notice what happens when the wave gets to the disconnected family members—it stops. Discuss with the family how one little change can interrupt a pattern. How was everyone affected by the disconnection or change? Have the family think of examples of how one family member's little change caused many changes throughout the family.

What is important in this activity is not that everyone learn the jargon and memorize the vocabulary. Instead, this activity is meant to propel the family into thinking about how they operate as a system and how each person affects the others.

Suggestions for Follow-Up

Use this activity as a metaphor for some problematic pattern that is occurring within the family. Discuss how the pattern starts, how everyone is affected, and what the outcome is. Is the outcome always the same, or does the same person always start the pattern (equifinality/equipotentiality)? Where could the pattern break, stopping it from progressing? What could each person do differently to prevent the pattern, or "wave" from continuing?

Contraindications

In order for this activity to be fun and demonstrative, you need at least five people to participate.

Readings and Resources for the Professional

Nichols, M. P. and Schwartz, R. C. (1991). *Family therapy: Concepts and methods.* Boston, MA: Allyn and Bacon.

Bibliotherapy Sources for the Client

Blevins, W. (1993). *Your family, your self: How to analyze your family system to understand yourself, and achieve more satisfying relationships with your loved ones.* Oakland, CA: New Harbinger Publications, Inc.

58

Letter from the Grave

Eugene Schlossberger

Type of Contribution: *Homework/Handout*

Objective

This assignment is designed to help clients process the loss of a loved one.

Rationale for Use

Assuming the role of the deceased helps clients deal with issues concerning the deceased, including unresolved feelings of guilt, unresolved conflict, and an overwhelming sense of loss. Writing a letter helps focus thought, allows family members to share their feelings, and creates a permanent record that can be read again and again when feelings about the deceased resurface.

Instructions

Set up for activity: The therapist explains that it is sometimes easier to live with the loss of a family member when you see things from his or her perspective instead of your own.

Step 1

Therapist: I am going to ask each of you to write a letter from Dad [the deceased] to you. Imagine that you are Dad looking down from heaven, and you have a chance to write a letter to your wife/son/daughter. What would you say? Do not worry about sounding like him, just write what you feel. And do not worry about grammar or spelling—this is not an English class. Just ask yourself "What would Dad say to me? What does he want me to know about his life, about how he sees me? What does he want me to feel?" If you are hurt or angry about something, what might Dad say to you about it? You might cry as you write, or you might not: both responses are perfectly natural. Pick a time when you will not be interrupted. Try to write as much of the letter as you can in a single session, but it is fine to put it aside for a while or add to the letter later if you think of something else. The letter can be very long or very short—it does not matter.

Step 2

The therapist provides clients with sample letters. Sample letters sometimes help clients who have trouble getting started or who are not sure what to put in the letter. Therapists may wish to devise their own samples or use the two samples given below.

Step 3

Family members bring their letters to therapy. Each family member, from youngest to oldest, reads his or her letter aloud. When all letters have been read, the family talks about the letters. What did they feel when the heard the other letters? The therapist helps the clients work through their feelings.

Suggestions for Follow-Up

Outside of therapy, the clients can share the letter with friends, wider family, and others who knew the deceased well. Clients may reread their letter when feelings about the deceased resurface.

Contraindications

The assignment is contraindicated when clients' language skills are poor and attemping to write generates frustration rather than fulfillment or understanding. Families with severely deficient writing skills might be asked to share verbally with each other what Dad would want to say to them.

Readings and Resources for the Professional

Shapiro, E. R. (1994). *Grief as a family process: A developmental approach to clinical practice*. New York: Guilford Press.

Bibliotherapy Sources for the Client

James, J. W. and Cherry, F. (1988). *The grief recovery handbook: A step-by-step program for moving beyond loss*. New York: Harper & Row.

HANDOUT

Sample Letter 1

Dear Son,

    There is so much I want to say to you. I told you before I died that I want to live forever, but that you shouldn't feel sad for me when I die because I had a good life. We had some hard times. During the depression we were so poor, we didn't know when we'd eat again. But I had your mother, and you can get through anything as long as you have each other. I'm so proud of my sons. I never finished school, I was just a tailor, but you, you're a doctor. You can't know how proud I was when I said "my son the doctor." I want you to remember how much I loved life. Remember when we went to Florida and it rained the whole time? We got out our boots and splashed in the puddles and had a good time. I had a good life. What more can anyone ask?

    I never got to see my grandson, but Dave is so sweet, you couldn't give me a better gift. When you were a little boy, I came home from work at eleven o'clock and read you stories and made you laugh. Your mother yelled at me for keeping you up so late. I always dreamed that one day you would read stories to your son and make him laugh. When I see you playing with Dave, I know I did something right. I miss you and I know you miss me. But I'll always be there with you. As long as you remember me, I won't be far away.

                                                      Love,

Sample Letter 2

Dear Sis,

    You're still mad that I married Jack. You think, "You're my sister, how could you steal my boyfriend?" I didn't want to, Sis. I wanted to love someone else. I tried not to love him, but I just couldn't help it. I felt real bad that I hurt you. You thought I didn't care, but I did. For a long time, I was confused and I didn't know what to do. I wanted to tell you, but I didn't want to hurt you. I hoped maybe it would all go away, like when I lost your Raggedy Ann and hoped you didn't notice she was gone. You felt I was selfish, Sis, and maybe I was. I want you to understand that Jack and I were happy, and that you couldn't be happy with Jack because he loved me. You think I should have told him to get lost, but I couldn't do that, Sis, because he was the one for me. Maybe I said mean things to you because I felt guilty. We fought so bad, I wish I could come back and tell you I love you. I know now you're sorry you didn't come to my wedding. I know you didn't mean what you said the last time we fought. We had some good times together. Let's never forget them. Remember when we put on Mom's clothes and danced on her bed? You ripped her blue dress and we hid it in the shed. She never did find it, did she? I bet it's still there somewhere. I want to tell you that things went wrong between us, but I never stopped loving you. I know you loved me, even when you were mad at me.

                                                      Love,

59

Dealing with a Fire Setter

Sharon A. Deacon

Type of Contribution: *Handout*

Objective

This handout can be used as a guide for families in which one of the members is a fire setter. The handout lists various precautions that can be taken to prevent a fire and protect everyone in the house in the event of a fire.

Rationale for Use

The precautionary measures on this handout can be used to help the family feel safer in their house when a fire setter is present. These steps to safety also illustrate to the fire setter the seriousness of the problem, and the disruption it has caused for all involved. This is a crisis intervention strategy; it also serves to enforce a functional hierarchy within the fire setter's family.

Instructions

Give a copy of the handout to each family member. Go over the handout step by step, with the whole family present, and get commitment from the family members to complete each task.

Step 1

Instruct the family to remove or lock up all fire starting devices in the house. This includes lighters, matches, spare electrical wires, and pilot lighters. Also have them lock up all flammable liquids, such as kerosene and gasoline.

Step 2

Instruct the family to install additional fire detectors throughout the house, in every room (especially the fire setter's bedroom) if necessary. The fire setter may be held responsible for paying for these devices.

Step 3

Create a safety plan with the family for what to do in case of fire. List the phone numbers of the police, fire department, and other emergency services by every phone in the house. Have the parents instruct the children how to call for help, how to detect smoke/fire, how to alert others, and how to get out of the house safely. (The local fire department may be able to help instruct the family.) Then, practice with fire drills, using various escape routes and alternate plans.

Step 4

Make a plan with the family. For a period of time (e.g., eight weeks), the fire setter is not to be left alone or unescorted anywhere, twenty-four hours a day. The fire setter is not allowed to be in a room alone, including the bedroom and bathroom (someone may be standing outside the door). The fire setter may have to sleep on the floor in someone else's bedroom or in the hallway. (Alternatively, a door alarm could be attached to the fire setter's bedroom door.) The fire setter is to be escorted to school, and the school should be notified of the plan. The fire setter should be checked for any fire starting devices each time he/she enters the house. If no fires are set in the allotted time period, restrictions can begin to be reduced.

Step 5

Help the family find ways to involve the fire setter in some fire-related activity, such as a class for fire setters, volunteer work with families who were victims of a fire, or volunteering at the local fire station.

Step 6

Instruct the parents to teach the child about fires, how they are controlled, and the consequences that could result.

Step 7

Set up rewards for the fire setter for good behavior. Keep monitoring the family's implementation of the plan, rewarding everyone for compliance and reframing their efforts as concern for one another.

Suggestions for Follow-Up

After the crisis has been handled, the therapist should begin to probe for reasons the person is setting fires, and the function of the fire setting in the family. A psychological assessment may also be recommended.

If the plan fails, and another fire is set, outside placement for the fire setter may be necessary. Additionally, if the family refuses to comply with the plan, outside agencies may need to be involved (e.g., child welfare).

Contraindications

If the fire setting is too severe and/or uncontrollable, an in-house crisis plan may not be enough, and outside agencies should be involved. If the fire setter is psychologically unstable, hospitalization may be necessary. If the fire setter is an adult who may outsmart the plan, it may be necessary to remove him/her, or the others, from the house for safety reasons.

Readings and Resources for the Professional

Auerbach, S. and Stolberg, A. (1986). *Crisis intervention with children and families.* Washington, DC: Hemisphere Publishing Corporation.

Everstine, D. S. and Everstine, L. (1983). *People in crisis: Strategic therapeutic interventions.* New York: Brunner/Mazel.

Gilliland, B. E. and James, R. K. (1988). *Crisis intervention strategies.* Pacific Grove, CA: Brooks/Cole Publishing Company.

Dealing with the Threat of Fire

1. Remove or lock up all fire setting devices

2. Install fire detectors throughout the house

3. Create a Safety Plan

    — escape route (check with fire department)
    — emergency phone numbers
    — fire drills

4. 24-Hour Supervision

    — escort in all rooms
    — sleeping arrangements
    — notify school
    — search fire setter upon entering house

5. Fire-Related Activity

    — volunteer at fire department
    — fire setters class
    — work with fire victims

6. Lessons About Fire

    — how to control fires
    — dangers and consequences

7. Reward System

    — recognize good behavior and compliance

60

Involving Larger Systems:
An Often Forgotten Therapeutic Technique

Jan Nealer
Stephanie Mueller

Type of Contribution: *Activity/Handouts*

Objective

Individuals, couples, and families experiencing difficulties often turn to more than one source for comfort and assistance. As clients become involved with various individuals and systems, they may become pulled in many directions. Typically, individuals, family members, friends, and professionals involved develop plans and goals designed to alleviate the problems or issues. Subsequently, plans and goals made by one or several people may be in direct opposition to the agenda of others. As a result, difficulties may become more complex or exacerbated, while the client remains stuck, despite all efforts aimed at correcting identified problems.

When clients become engaged with several individuals or systems as a means of solving problems, the likelihood of increased confusion and fragmentation of services is predictable. The most recently acquired therapist or human service professional may employ techniques and interventions that have already proven futile, or may not be privy to information that would guide therapy to a successful resolution. Clients may be hesitant to share information about past experiences due to anger and/or embarrassment over failed attempts at change. Clients may also be fearful that the current therapist may not be willing to tackle their issues and problems. Thus, clients do not authorize professionals to share vital information for successful problem resolution and therefore remain stuck in a never-ending cycle.

Additionally, professionals utilize various types of treatment regimens, educational plans, and therapeutic approaches, and may get caught up in defending their particular theoretical frameworks. Even worse, various professionals involved with the client may dispute the "correct" way to work through the issues presented. For many clients, especially disorganized and resistant families, this equates to more professional involvement and less control for the client. The professionals may end up taking responsibility for the client's problems instead of assisting in finding solutions.

Solutions to this dilemma involve bringing together the various individuals, agencies, and systems to discuss the issues, and make expansive, collaborative plans for problem resolution. While this makes sense in theory, many professionals are reticent to engage larger systems for the benefit of clients. New therapists, as well as seasoned professionals, are hesitant to push professional boundaries, and risk offending colleagues and other professionals in the community. Fear of the unknown, trepidation of insulting other professionals, concern about intimidating the client, or apprehension about conducting such a meeting can make the task of organizing and implementing such a meeting overwhelming. In reality, no matter how well trained or confident the initiating therapist, the value of larger system knowledge and experience with the client cannot be disputed.

Rationale for Use

The fragmented larger system involved with the client must be enlisted to develop a comprehensive treatment plan that will maximize the family's level of functioning. To adequately address the multiple needs of these clients, counselors, family therapists, social workers, and psychologists alike must look to and rely upon the use of organizing the larger system for information, support, and intervention. Other components of the larger systems may include extended family, school officials, social service workers, lawyers, probation officers, employers, and human service agencies, just to name a few. Because this process may seem overwhelming, a strategy has been developed to make this type of collaborative process as painless as possible for all participants. What follows is an outline of the procedural steps for engaging larger systems as an intervention with individuals, couples, and families.

Larger System as an Indicator of Smaller System Processes

A comprehensive examination of the larger system allows for an appraisal of the underlying interactional processes within and between the client and other systems. This expanded view may be therapeutic in and of itself. Not only does this meta-analysis allow covert communication to become overt, but it also offers a clear perspective regarding patterns enacted in the family system.

Often the larger system will assemble itself into a constellation similar to the pattern the family system employs, but on a larger scale. Therefore, observing the larger system will identify and demonstrate patterns manifested in the family. This allows the larger system to become active in the reorganization of the system, and relieves some of the blame felt by family members, and perhaps in the system as well. Indeed, coalitions, hierarchies, and alliances may form between certain family members and professionals, with some parties maintaining polarized positions. As these dynamics begin to emerge in the larger system, it becomes clear as to how these processes are formulated and impact the family system. With this information, the team becomes better informed and more proactive. This is invaluable information to share with team members, and sanctions professional cooperation and collaboration.

The Challenge

This technique of involving larger systems is offered as a tool to be used regularly in the treatment of clients, especially families with multiple problems. Although this method is initially time consuming and tedious, it is an efficient and effective way to manage clients who are involved with several other professionals or agencies. By acknowledging the difficulties up front in working with so many outside systems, the clients' hidden agendas and professionals' miscommunications and varied approaches will become streamlined and more serviceable to the clients and professionals. This technique should not be the last ditch effort; instead, it should often be used as a proactive method for working with individual clients, families, and various professionals.

Instructions

Who to Invite

The first step in organizing a meeting of the larger system is to determine which individuals, agencies, and systems are involved with the client, and the significance of their role(s). As is often the case, clients may have been involved with several mental health professionals, physicians, legal authorities, human service agencies, etc. It is important to obtain a detailed list of whom the client has worked with in the past, who is currently working with the client, the issues presented and currently being addressed, duration of involvement, and how the relationships between the client (microsystem) and the macrosystems are viewed by both parties. This helps determine which individuals, family members, agencies, and systems are key components of the larger system.

The most instrumental participant in the larger system meeting is the client/family. The client has the most to lose or gain in this process, and must be given some control over the decisions being made regarding his/her welfare. Enlisting the client as a partner in this process enhances the potential for success. If the client is not involved in the meeting, suspicion, resistance, and/or disagreement is inevitable. This type of isolation or exclusion is detrimental, not only to the organization of the treatment plan, but to the therapeutic process as well. By participating in this meeting, the clients learn to proficiently utilize the resources being devised and offered to them.

To assist in organizing the larger system meeting, a checklist is presented at the end of this chapter to facilitate information gathering regarding the client's treatment history. (See the Organizing a Larger Systems Meeting form.)

How to Organize and Invite Participants

The next step is contacting identified professionals and requesting their attendance at the larger system meeting. The key component in organizing the larger system is to make it clear to all parties that this is going to be a team approach, a collaborative event, and that all perspectives and experiences are pertinent in order to effectively treat the client. It is essential to begin the process in a positive manner, maintain utmost professional behavior, and avoid conveying blame or disrespect when interacting with the client or other professionals. The objective of this meeting is to form a collaborative network, not to debate the effectiveness or ineffectiveness of any style or approach.

Involved parties generally possess a variety of backgrounds, experiences, and knowledge that contribute to the larger system and the collaborative effort. It is impossible for one individual to be cognizant of all of the potential constraints (e.g., legal, structural, medical) that will impact treatment (Imber-Black, 1988). An open dialogue for sharing information and experience is beneficial so that all parties can contribute to the comprehensive treatment approach. This also decreases the probability of unforeseen barriers emerging and stalling progress in the future.

To set a tone of mutuality and cooperation for the meeting, a sample letter addressed to participating professionals and agencies is included (see Sample Letter). It is also prudent to follow this letter with a personal phone call to reiterate the purpose and necessity of the meeting.

How to Organize and Conduct the Meeting

The primary objective of this meeting is to pull together those systems which clients have indicated as being significant and influential in their lives. The intent is not to merely exchange information and report on individual progress with the client; rather, the purpose is to focus all efforts toward finding resolution for the client. This is a shift in perspective from each professional picking specific issues and working on those, while others tackle separate concerns. Instead, all professionals pool resources and collectively make decisions, with the help of the client, about how to proceed, and who will be most effective in actualizing the designated changes.

This requires a recognition of what each professional or agency has to offer. Individual and agency strengths, as well as available resources, should be discussed openly among members of the team. Weaknesses or services which are lacking need to be discussed without ascribing blame or failure. This allows the team to delegate responsibility for various interventions throughout the professional group, as well as with the client/family. With this type of team effort, everyone benefits: efficient, effective, and supportive reformation occurs.

One member of the treatment team must be commissioned to keep the group focused and moving. It is logical that the group will look to the initial organizer of the meeting as the leader. Yet, it is more circumspect and accommodating to discuss who might be the best person or agency to act as the leader, director, or manager. This does not mean that one person dictates treatment development and/or doles out duties to the other members. In fact, a discussion about the process and how collaboration will be viewed is a good place to begin this stratagem. This is a collaborative effort, and all parts of the system contribute different perspectives, resulting in a holistic view of the issues and treatment agenda. Therefore, the person/agency acting as director faces the task of organizing meetings, checking with the family to ensure their participation and support, and to arrange, coordinate, confirm and validate the completion of all tasks agreed upon during the meetings.

Prioritizing issues will allow treatment team members to emphasize areas that require immediate attention, and help clients focus efforts on making changes. Generating hypotheses about the problem, possible solutions, and constraints are components that should be covered in the meeting. Also, expectations regarding outcome and prognosis should be solicited from the client and all involved parties. To help with the organization, management, and outcome of the larger systems meeting, a sample agenda is provided to assist in conducting the meeting (see Larger Systems Meeting Agenda). This will help to establish, prioritize, and recruit assistance from the larger system participants.

Suggestions for Follow-Up

One of the most crucial considerations in this process is continuity of treatment. Even when the meeting goes well, if follow-up does not occur, the positive nature of the intervention ends and the plan disintegrates. Furthermore, the group may become discouraged, and blame may fall upon individual professionals, or worse, the client. Therefore, subsequent meetings must be a part of the initial plan, including the appointment of a lead agency to ensure follow through and coordination. A schedule for future meetings should be developed at the original meeting so all participants know the format and pace of the intervention.

Contraindications

There are several contraindications for larger systems meetings. First, meetings with families that are experiencing violence (e.g., spousal or child abuse) or are in the midst of legal proceedings (e.g., divorce, abuse charges) should be managed with care. Depending upon the issues and/or the stage of treatment, a larger systems meeting may still be beneficial; however, it may be advisable for all professionals to meet first to discuss any extenuating circumstances. After the legal and ethical issues are defined and understood, the group can then proceed with a logical and pragmatic strategy.

Additionally, cultural, ethnic, gender, and religious issues must be addressed in larger systems meetings. Clients and families of various backgrounds and development must be allowed their civil and human rights. Therefore, inquiring about these particular issues with the client is a necessary component in organizing the larger system and in developing treatment objectives and tactics. If the multiple systems meeting is designed to assist the client from a minority culture, then professionals with expertise in that culture must be part of the larger systems meeting. Furthermore, all identifying demographic information that may contribute to misunderstandings and/or discrimination (e.g., single mothers, low socioeconomic or educational status) must be considered when the meeting is organized and convened.

Finally, professionals attending the meeting must agree that professional and ethical behavior is essential, and that the purpose of the meeting is to assist and advocate for the client. If this cannot be agreed upon at the onset, a larger systems meeting may be contraindicated.

Readings and Resources for the Professional

Falicov, C. (Ed.) (1988). *Family transitions: Continuity and change over the life cycle.* New York: Guilford Press.

Imber-Black, E. (1988). *Families and larger systems: A family therapist's guide through the labyrinth.* New York: Guilford Press.

Liddle, H., Breunlin, D., and Schwartz, R. (1988). *Handbook of family therapy training and supervision.* New York: Guilford Press.

Karpel, M. (Ed.) (1986). *Family resources: The hidden partner in family therapy.* New York: Guilford Press.

McCown, W., Johnson, J., and Associates (1993). *Therapy with treatment resistant families: A consultation-crisis intervention model.* Binghamton, NY: The Haworth Press.

Rave, E. and Larsen, C. (Eds.) (1995). *Ethical decision making in therapy: Feminist perspectives.* New York: Guilford Press.

Schartzman, J. (1984). *Family and other systems: The macrosystemic context of family therapy.* New York: Guilford Press.

Walsh, F. (1982). *Normal family processes.* New York: Guilford Press.

Wynn, L., McDaniel, S., and Weber, T. (1986). *Systems consultation: A new perspective for family therapy.* New York: Guilford.

Organizing a Larger Systems Meeting

1. Gather information from whom the family sought mental health services:

With whom: Reason/duration of treatment: Outcome: Relationship with the professional:	With whom: Reason/duration of treatment: Outcome: Relationship with the professional:

2. Who they are currently seeing as mental health professionals:

With whom: Reason/duration of treatment: Outcome: Relationship with the professional:	With whom: Reason/duration of treatment: Outcome: Relationship with the professional:

3. Who they have ever sought guidance or counseling from (e.g., extended family, clergy):

With whom: Reason /duration of treatment: Outcome: Relationship with the professional:	With whom: Reason/duration of treatment: Outcome: Relationship with the professional:

4. Have they ever been involved with the child welfare system?

Caseworker: Reason/Duration: Outcome: Relationship with the professional(s):

5. Have they ever received home-based services?

Describe: (e.g., child care, homemaker services, therapy, wraparound services)

6. Are they currently receiving medical assistance, or been under a physician's care in the past year?

Describe:

7. Have they been involved in the legal system in any way?

Describe: (e.g., incarceration, probation, parole, divorces, child support, felonies, misdemeanors)

8. Have they been involved with any services offered at their place of employment or educational institution?

Describe:

9. Are they receiving any financial assistance at this time?

Describe:

10. Have they received any services through the school system for themselves or a family member?

Describe:

11. Have them describe any other services they think would be beneficial to them at this time:

Larger Systems Meeting Agenda

Introductions:

It is extremely important to introduce everyone at the table, and allow time for individuals to discuss their experiences and ideas. If nothing else is accomplished at the meeting, it is imperative to complete this task. The family and professionals must feel personally connected and comfortable with one another.

Explanation of the Purpose of the Meeting:

All professionals need to be aware of the purpose of the meeting and the intended outcome. Again, discussion should be encouraged so that everyone feels included and understood.

Identification of the Problem(s)/Issue(s):

This is an interactive process that occurs among the family, professionals who are new to the case, and professionals who have worked on the case for any length of time. Concrete identification of the problem is essential in developing objectives and outcomes.

Discussion of Previous Attempts at Solution:

Now that the problem(s) have been identified and everyone is acquainted with the history of the family, previous attempts at rectifying the problem should be discussed. This is not to prolong any discomfort, but to clarify what has been done so failed attempts are not repeated. Professionals and family members should be supported through this process so that they do not feel attacked, ridiculed, or unsuccessful. It is a time for group members to come together and support further development of solutions.

Establishment of Objectives:

Objectives must be developed and documented in concrete terms for the establishment of a comprehensive treatment plan. Remember to write it all down in the form of a contract.

Establishment of Roles and Expectations for All Involved:

Everyone must commit to his/her role in the treatment plan, explain goals, and identify means of supporting other components of the treatment plan.

Expectations for the Future:

All group members must express thought, ideas, and expectations for the family, as well as expectations regarding their level of involvement with this family in the future. Additionally, all members must discuss their level of commitment to the larger system, willingness to attend meetings, and expectations of others participating in the treatment team.

Scheduling of Upcoming Meetings

Meetings should be scheduled in advance so that all members know when and where they will be. Everyone should be in agreement with these dates and times.

EVERYONE, INCLUDING ALL PROFESSIONALS AND FAMILY MEMBERS INVOLVED, MUST SIGN OFF ON THE PLAN AND EXPRESS A COMMITMENT TO WORKING TOWARD SUCCESSFUL RESOLUTION.

Sample Letter

Use a letterhead for an official look to your letter/request.

August 10, 1998

Jane Doe, PhD
Director, Child Protective Services
12345 Main Street
Averageville, Nebraska 12345

Dear Dr. Doe:

Recently I have begun work with a new client, Joe Smith. Mr. Smith has reported spending time with you/your agency in the past. Currently, we are working on a treatment plan, and would like to hold a meeting with all prior service providers in order to facilitate a comprehensive, effective approach to working with Mr. Smith and his family. Therefore, you are invited to a meeting to be held on Monday, August 31, 1998, at the Family Resource Center.

Your attendance at this meeting would be greatly appreciated, along with your expertise on the issues at hand. Your experience and understanding of this family are valuable to the formulation of a successful treatment plan. So that there will be no problems regarding confidentiality, a copy of the release of information signed by Mr. Smith is attached. If you have any concerns or questions about this meeting, please do not hesitate to contact us directly.

Thank you in advance for your time and consideration in this matter.

Sincerely,

Stephanie Mueller, MS
Marriage and Family Therapist

Jan Nealer, PhD
Director, UNL Marriage & Family Therapy Program

314

SECTION IV:
HOMEWORK, HANDOUTS, AND ACTIVITIES FOR CHILDREN

61

"The Many Sides of Me":
A Storytelling Intervention for Children

Jill Woodward

Type of Contribution: *Activity*

Objective

1. To increase and facilitate children's self-disclosure of memories, feelings, and events, thereby decreasing the need for interpretation.
2. To help children separate reality from fantasy.
3. To encourage children to expand their self-image, and generate new possiblities for living.
4. To create opportunitities for planning further individual and/or family interventions.

Rationale for Use

This intervention combines methods of art therapy and narrative therapy, and is based on the theory of social constructionism. Art therapy provides a means for the child to express and release feelings by creating illustrations for the book. Children are helped to confront and reconstruct personal narratives, self-statements, and beliefs as they tell the stories that correspond to their artwork. Children are encouraged to author new stories that change old, stereotypical ideas about themselves. The underlying rationale for this intervention is the social constructionist belief that personality and personality problems are a socially generated phenomenon that occurs in language, and that personalities are created by internalized conversations.

"The Many Sides of Me" activity is suitable for use with children ages eight to twelve. It is especially effective with (1) children who have a constricted self-image or limited view of their personalities, roles, and expectations; (2) children who have been labeled as "being the problem" in a family; or (3) children who are convinced that the problem is all that they are about. It is a counseling technique that can be used across cultures.

Instructions

"The Many Sides of Me" is a picture/story book comprised of autobiographical stories based on real events, feelings, or fantasy stories related to a child's wishes and dreams. The stories are narrated and illustrated by a child during counseling.

The counselor introduces the intervention by asking the child if he/she would be interested in drawing a book about him/herself. It is explained that the book will help the counselor get to know the child, and therefore be better able to help him/her. The counselor explains that there will be several chapters to the book. For each chapter, the child will draw two pictues, one that tells a true story about the child's life and one that is an imaginary story about the child's dreams or fantasies.

Together, child and counselor begin the process of developing a list of chapter titles. The counselor suggests some positive topics such as "The Day I Felt Most Loved," "When I Made a Good Decision," "A Time I Was Proud," "A Time I Was Happy," or "A Fun Time I Had." After discussing some positive chapters, the counselor explains that in every person's life good and bad things happen, and therefore some "not so happy" chapters should be included too. These "no so happy" chapters have three purposes. The first is to provide an opportunity for the counselor to gain a variety of information. Second, the child is encouraged to do negative reminiscing and discuss a variety of feelings in an accepting and supportive environment. Third, the chapters can serve as keys to uncovering emotional, physical, and/or sexual trauma. The counselor should encourage the child to draw an equal number of positive and negative pictures. This will help the child to balance his/her perspective of life events. "Not so happy" chapter titles might include: "Something Scary That Happened to Me," "A Sad Day," or "A Bad Dream I Had."

Once a list of chapters is started, the child makes a drawing of the day, event, or situation described in the title. The conversation or dialogue that develops regarding the drawing is an intervention in itself. The counselor encourages the narrative by asking the child to describe the drawing and by asking process questions based on the drawing. Every detail of the story is explored. For example: What did you say? How did you look? How did you feel? What did your mom (dad, brother, etc.) say (do, look like)? What happened right before? What happened right after? How did you get the courage to act this way? How did you know you could do this? etc. This process increases the child's awareness of the event. The conversation that results from these questions creates the narrative for the story which the counselor writes for the child.

As the child narrates the stories' common themes, patterns and roles become apparent. The counselor can discover these themes by identifying the stories' characters, plots, settings, moods, climaxes, and conclusions or resolutions. The counselor can use the following questions as a guide to uncover themes: How does the child see himself/herself in this story? How does the child view the environment? How do others treat the child? Who else shares the child's view? What are the dominant/marginal stories? These are valuable keys for understanding a child's world view. The counselor can use this information to help the child expand on chapter titles to include stories that contradict the view of the problem or negative themes. These contradictory or alternative stories provide a foundation for growth and change by expanding a child's horizons, increasing possibilities, and broadening self-concept.

The following are three brief examples of contradictory stories. One child wanted to include a chapter titled, "A Time I Used My Brain." She was seen by her family as a forgetful, silly "airhead." Her story was about her level-headed and well-thought-out plan for locating and then rescuing her lost kitten. Another story involves one boy who was frequently compared unfavorably to his brother, titled, "Something I Do Better Than My Brother." It was a story about the awards and recognition he had received for his artistic talents. Another boy diagnosed with ADHD included a chapter called, "When I Concentrated." It was a story about all the planning and hard work he had put into building a tree house with "running water."

Perhaps a theme of "victim" appears in a child's narratives. A chapter might be added titled, "A Time I Protected Myself" or "A Time I Stuck Up For Myself." "A Time I

Controlled My Temper" could be included for a child with anger problems. The idea of the activity is to help children identify situations that are exceptions to their problems or their view of themselves. If a child cannot recall a time he/she acted at odds with a negative view, the child can create a fantasy about acting differently. Once a fantasy story is drawn and written, a plan can be made for the child to act in accordance with the fantasy. The counselor asks for ideas on how it might be done in real life, and then helps the client make a simple plan that can be followed through outside the counseling session.

When fantasy stories are discussed, it is important for the counselor to explain how he/she knows the story is a fantasy (e.g., saying, "I can tell that this is not a true story because I do not believe your dad could pick up a pop machine."). Also, the counselor can tell about personal reactions to a fantasy story being told as if it were true, and talk about how others might feel in a similar situation.

Depending on the child and the story being told, each chapter can take up to one session. Sometimes as many as three chapters can be completed in a session.

Suggestions for Follow-Up

Prior to disclosing any information to the family, it should be discussed with the child. It can be explained in simple terms why the counselor believes it is necessary to share the story. The counselor can model how the information will be shared by role-playing word for word what will be said.

Stories can also be used to make parents and siblings more aware of the roles they play in maintaining a child's negative self-perception. Sometimes it may be necessary for the counselor to meet alone with the parents to reinforce, support, or elaborate on the theme expressed in a child's story.

Stories can be reviewed periodically to maximize their impact. Also, stories can be sent home to be read and looked at by the child between sessions as a form of reinforcement and encouragement for change.

Contraindications

At times, it may become necessary to discuss information from a child's book with parents for safety reasons or because the information could involve the family in the child's treatment. For example, when telling the story for a chapter titled "Something Dangerous I Did," a child told how he and a friend had started a fire in the park. The counselor used a positioning paradoxical intervention, taking a "one down" position, and letting the client convince her about the dangers and consequences of fire starting. With the child's permission, the story was shared with his mother, who then made plans for improved supervision, and made a greater effort to keep matches and lighters in a safe place. Additionally, if a child tells a story of abuse or neglect, proper steps may need to be taken to assure safety of the child, and to follow state legal mandates concerning abuse.

Readings and Resources for the Professional

Gardner, R. A. (1971). *Therapeutic communication with children: The mutual storytelling technique.* New York: Science House.

Levick, M. F. (1983). *They could not talk and so they drew: Children's styles of coping and thinking.* Springfield, IL: Charles C Thomas.

Rubin, J. A. (1984). *Child art therapy: Understanding and helping children grow through art* (Second Edition). New York: Van Nostrand Reinhold.

Rubin, J. A. (1984). *The art of art therapy.* New York: Brunner/Mazel, Inc.

White, M. (1989). *The externalizing of the problem and the re-authoring of lives and relationships.* Dulwich Centre Newsletter, Summer.

White, M. and Epston, D. (1989). *Challenging stereotyping and opening space for alternatives.* Institute presented at the meeting of the American Association for Marriage and Family Therapy. San Francisco, CA.

White, M. and Epston, D. (1990). *Narrative means to therapeutic ends.* New York: Norton.

62

My Uniqueness

Sharon A. Deacon

Type of Contribution: *Activity*

Objective

The purpose of this activity is to raise a child's self-esteem and highlight the child's uniqueness and talents.

Rationale for Use

Many children often feel that they are not special. They compare themselves to their peers, and tend to notice all the things about their peers that are better than their own traits. Sometimes children have a difficult time seeing what is unique about themselves, instead only focusing on the negative aspects of themselves.

This activity serves to help children recognize their own special qualities and traits. This activity is very effective with children who have many siblings, or middle children, who feel left out of the family or feel unrecognized.

Instructions

Using an ink pad and paper, make a fingerprint of the child's thumb. On a copy machine, blow up this fingerprint to the size of a standard sheet of paper. (If you do not have these materials available, you can also ask the child to draw a fingerprint.)

On each of the fingerprint lines, have the child write something that is special about him/herself. The child can include special personality traits, talents, physical traits, events, etc. Keep the comments positive. The rest of the family may also be included, helping the child to think of all his/her uniquenesses. (Including other family members can reinforce the child, and change other people's perceptions of the child.)

Talk with the child about how every person's fingerprint is one of a kind, and no one in the world has the same exact fingerprint as he/she does. Build upon how the child is special and different from everyone else.

Suggestions for Follow-Up

This activity can be part of therapy focused on raising a child's self-esteem. Continue with other activities that highlight the child's special traits and abilities.

If you work with children often, you may want to have each child you see complete this project. Hang all of the fingerprints on a wall, nameless. This way, the children can literally "see" how different and special they are from everyone else.

Contraindications

This activity may not be very effective with severely behaviorally disturbed children. It is important for the therapist and parents to be able to think of many positive things about the child. Thus, if the behavioral problems are outstanding at this point, this activity may not be very easy to do. Once behavioral problems have been more subdued, this activity can be a helpful reinforcement strategy.

Readings and Resources for the Professional or Parents

Eyre, L. and Eyre, R. (1984). *Teaching your child joy.* New York: Fireside.

63

My Family in the News

Stacy Hernandez
Sharon A. Deacon

Type of Contribution: *Activity/Handout*

Objective

This activity has many uses, depending on which section of the handout is used. It can be used as an assessment tool, to gather information about the child's perception of his/her family, major family events going on, or the child's most important concern. It can also be used for joining and building the child's self-esteem.

Rationale for Use

In the beginning of therapy, children are often hesitant about what kinds of information to share with the therapist. Children often have a lot to say, but are not sure what they are supposed to say or how to say things. Their verbal skills may be limited, as they are often better at expressing themselves more honestly through nonverbal means. This activity allows children to use art to show the therapist how they feel about their families, their life/world, and themselves.

Instructions

The therapist can begin by asking the child if he/she ever watches the news or reads the newspaper. A discussion may take place about what kinds of things can be found in the news: stories about people, scary things that happen, special events, sports teams, etc. The therapist then gives the child the handout, and asks the child to create his/her own newspaper.

The first section of the handout is a depiction of the top news story of the day. Here, the child is asked to draw the most important thing that will happen that day. This drawing can depict something the child will do that day, something that already happened that stands out in the child's mind, what the child is thinking about most during that day, or what the child wants to remember about that day. The therapist can ask the child questions about the drawing, and acquire information about the child's concerns, successes, likes, dislikes, etc. The therapist may also ask the child what the top news was the day before, or weeks before, or the last holiday, etc.

The second section of the handout is used to get information about how the child perceives his/her family and the events that are going on within the family. In the "My Family in the

News" box, the child is to write or draw a story about something that happened or will happen that would put his/her family in the news. The child may write about the biggest event that ever took place in the family, what he/she is most proud of his/her family for, the scariest event, etc. The therapist may brainstorm with the child first, before the child decides what event to write/draw about. This way, the therapist obtains information about many events in the family, instead of just the one the child chooses to depict.

The third section of the handout provides space for the child to write about him/herself and the qualities that make him/her special. Ask the child to draw a picture of him/herself and write or tell a story about why he/she is a star.

Suggestions for Follow-Up

If this activity is being used with a group of children, it can be fun to have a newscast after, in which each child tells his/her news to the others. It can also be helpful to have the children "read" their news to their parent(s), and explain their perceptions to their parents. Throughout therapy, each time the child comes in, the therapist can ask for the "news of the day."

Contraindications

There are no contraindications in using this activity. Younger children can draw the news, while older children may choose to write the stories.

Readings and Resources for the Professional

Combrinck-Graham, L. (1989). *Children in family contexts*. New York: Guilford Press.

Kottman, T. and Schaefer, C. (1993). *Play therapy in action*. Northvale, NJ: Jason Aronson Inc.

Schaefer, C. and Carey, L. (1994). *Family play therapy*. Northvale, NJ: Jason Aronson Inc.

The Daily News

1 section, 1 page

50 cents

Nation/World

TODAY'S TOP STORY

MY FAMILY IN THE NEWS

STAR OF THE DAY

The "Key" to Anger Control

Ronn Tyrrell
Linda Wark

Type of Contribution: *Homework*

Objective

The purpose of this homework assignment is to help children learn to control their anger. The assignment was born out of the first author's need to reach a ten-year-old male client who had an increasing history of physical fighting with other children, particularly at school; this intervention has been used subsequently with a number of children. The assignment occurs in stages and integrates several techniques from family therapy models including: Solution-Focused therapy (Walter and Peller, 1992), externalization (White and Epston, 1990), the Internal Family Systems Model (Schwartz, 1995), and Strategic Therapy (Haley, 1976).

Rationale for Use

A consistent concern presented for therapy by parents with school-age children is uncontrollable anger. These outbursts of anger range in their expression from nastiness, demandingness, and screaming, to dangerous physical aggression. Children who are labeled with anger management problems are very aware of the feelings toward them by adults and by other children. They experience embarrassment and shame, as well as a loss of friends or status within their peer group. In addition, extreme anger is frightening to the children themselves.

There are a number of effective techniques to assist children with anger management, including negative consequences for angry outbursts, rewarding children for times of self-control, or addressing unconscious conflicts and anxieties in a psychodynamic orientation (Wachtel, 1994). The intervention presented here makes greater use of the child's strengths and resources, and also promotes self-control.

Jean Piaget's cognitive developmental stage model includes concrete operational thinking (Nielsen, 1991), which develops between the age of seven and eleven, and figures well with this homework activity. Skills acquired during this stage include: equivalence, reversibility, class inclusion, associativity, and expansion of thinking skills to include repositional and perspective thinking (Nielsen, 1991). During this stage, children become capable of seeing the relationship between objects and ideas, physical symbolism, (Simons, Irvin, and Drinnin, 1987) or in Piaget's terms, develop "concrete operational thinking." This homework assignment is designed for children at the level of concrete operational thinking.

Instructions

To implement the intervention, the therapist explores the circumstances presented when the client is out of control with his/her anger. Exception questions (Walter and Peller, 1992) are used to determine the times a client has successfully controlled his/her anger, and how the control was accomplished. Tenacious questioning typically unearths proof that there are certain people with whom the child does control his/her anger. Time should be spent exhausting all of these exceptions. After discovering that the client is not completely out of control, the therapist should move on to step two (in session two).

The second session is spent using a modification of the Internal Family Systems approach (Schwartz, 1995), with the bulk of time spent explaining and exploring the many emotional parts that make up the whole of the client. Children at this age generally have the cognitive ability to categorize, allowing them to understand that part of them can become angry, and at the same time be hurt; children usually warm up to the idea that they have various "parts." The child should then be encouraged to describe his/her different emotional parts by assigning faces, shapes, objects, or colors to them.

For example, when working with an eight-year-old boy, his anger became "Red Squirt." He gave his anger this name because "this is what happens when either you get hit, or hit someone else." He was referring to a blood splatter. His sad part looked like a "Blue Pillow" which was the color of his pillow case. He used to cry at night when his mother left him alone to go out on dates. His happy part looked like "Gray Hair." He was referring to his gray-haired grandmother, who represented a safe and happy place to be.

During the third session, after establishing that the client has many different parts and has designated names and labels to those parts, externalization (White and Epston, 1990) is elaborated further. The therapist suggests that the client's anger be externalized to a closet (or room) that has a door on it. Discuss at length how the anger does not like being locked up, and will, on occasion, push the door open and get out. Sometimes the anger will bang on the door and yell before coming out; at other times, it comes out fast and quietly. Explain that it is the fast and quiet times that probably get the child in trouble. These are the times when the child loses control of his/her anger and lashes out.

At this point, the therapist can begin mentioning how the anger might be kept confined. Some clients think that something heavy should be put against the door so that the anger cannot push it open; or that a guard should stand by the door and keep the anger where it belongs. Give clients the opportunity to present ideas of their own. Later, the therapist offers to present an idea and also a "tool" to keep the anger locked up until the child can talk to an adult about his/her feelings. However, using a devil's pact (Haley, 1976), explain that you do not want to tell the client yet because he/she might think it was silly, and maybe he/she is not ready to hear the idea, but you *might* tell the plan during the next session.

The next session usually finds the client ready and anxious to hear the idea about keeping the anger locked up. The therapist should say that he/she has a very special "key" that will lock the door so the anger cannot get out. Then (very dramatically) give them an old-fashioned skeleton key (which can be picked up easily at low cost). Inform the child that only he/she has the power to lock up the anger, and that he/she alone has the key to unlock the door and let the anger out. No one else can make the anger come out because they do not have the key. Then encourage the child to practice locking and unlocking the door that keeps the anger confined.

Proceed with the intervention by asking if the child is left- or right-handed. Children usually strike out with their dominant hand when they are angry. Placing their hands to grasp a key in a pocket (or reaching for a key hung around their neck) instead of hitting provides an extra measure of change. Request that the child carry the special key in the same pocket of his/her dominant hand. For example, if he/she is right-handed he/she should carry the key in his/her right pocket or hang the key on a string around his/her neck inside or outside of clothing. Then tell the child to carry the key everywhere for the next week. The client is instructed that whenever he/she feels the anger trying to get out of the closet, he/she should reach into the pocket, or around his/her neck, and hold the key. This way, he/she would know the door is still locked, and the anger cannot get out when he/she does not want it to.

Talk to the parents, with the child present, about reminding their son/daughter to take the key everywhere, especially to school. Also inform parents that the child has been instructed to discuss with them any angry feelings which were controlled earlier. The parents thus become active partners in the intervention and with the therapist in and out-of-session (Haley, 1976). In addition, instruct parents that if their child should become angry at home, they should ask him/her if he/she has the key, and if the anger is locked up. This structure serves the purpose of reinforcing both the task itself, and the parts language the child and therapist have established.

The therapist can spend the fifth session exploring the various times that the child has used the key to be sure that the anger stayed behind the locked door. Enthusiastically congratulate the child on his/her behavior, and give him/her the same task for the next week. At this point, the location of the key can be switched to keep children thinking about the key's location and not take it for granted.

Suggestions for Follow-Up

Follow-up sessions should center on maintaining whatever progress the child is making in controlling anger with the key. If the success in anger control is minimal, revert back to the earlier steps of externalization and parts language. Be sure the child knows what his/her anger looks like, and reiterate that the anger is only *one* part of him/her. If children have a setback, it can be due to thinking of themselves as "all bad." At this point, it pays to amplify clients' strengths, and concentrate on the times they have controlled their anger using the key, rather than concentrating on their setback.

Contraindications

Parents' involvement in the intervention is crucial for effective results. If parents carry out the between-session reminders, the intervention is more effective. When the parents do not actively participate, the intervention usually fails.

The authors do not recommend using the "key" intervention without an exploration of the context for expression of uncontrolled anger. Supplemental techniques may be necessary.

Target concerns for which this intervention can be used are the management of various emotions which trouble children such as anxiety, jealousy, sadness, and embarrassment. Metaphorically locking up a difficult emotion might be best used with children. However, adult clients who are playful and imaginative might also be good candidates. The "key" intervention should only be used in the attempt to control feelings that lead to problem behavior.

Caution against the key's use in cases of sexual or physical abuse should be exercised. The visualization process required by this intervention could lead to unwanted recall on the part of the child victim. Furthermore, any attempt to control appropriate anger over abuse is not desirable. Externalization and symbolization in such cases could be threatening, and possibly damaging, to the child.

Readings and Resources for the Professional

Combrinck-Graham, L. (1989). *Children in family contexts*. New York: The Guilford Press.
Wachtel, E. (1994). *Treating troubled children and their families*. New York: Guilford Press.

Bibliotherapy Sources for the Client

Cain, B. S. (1990). *Double-dip feelings: A book to help children understand emotions*. New York: Magination Press.
Crary, E. (1994). *I'm furious*. Seattle: Parenting Press.
Shapiro, L. E. (1994). *The very angry day that Amy didn't have*. King of Prussia, PA: Childswork/Childsplay.

REFERENCES

Haley, J. (1976). *Problem-solving therapy*. San Francisco: Jossey-Bass.
Nielsen, L. (1991). *Adolescence: A contemporary view*. New York: Harcourt-Brace-Jovanovich.
Schwartz, R. C. (1995). *Internal family systems therapy*. New York: Guilford.
Simons, J. A., Irwin, D. B., and Drinnin, B. A. (1987). *Psychology: The search for understanding*. St. Paul, MN: West Publishers.
Wachtel, E. (1994). *Treating troubled children and their families*. New York: Guilford Press.
Walter, J. L. and Peller, J. E. (1992). *Becoming solution-focused in brief therapy*. New York: Brunner-Mazel.
White, M. and Epston, D. (1990). *Narrative means to therapeutic ends*. New York: Norton.

65

It's Okay to Cry

Sharon A. Deacon
Stacy Hernandez

Type of Contribution: *Activity*

Objective

The purpose of this activity is to generate a discussion about sadness with children, and how to handle difficult emotions such as loneliness, fear, anger, and grief. The main objective is to give children permission to let their feelings out in therapy, and send the message to them that it is okay to cry.

Rationale for Use

Children often do not know how to verbalize what they are feeling; thus, their feelings come out in their behavior. Children may act out, withdraw, or say inappropriate things when they have feelings that they do not understand or do not know how to express. A therapist can help children to define their feelings as well as help them find more acceptable ways to show their feelings and deal with them.

Children are often told not to cry, or are made fun of for crying. Thus, they will avoid crying in front of other people, and feel embarrassed to even let the tears out in front of the therapist. However, a release of emotions through tears can be very cleansing for children. This activity serves as a foundation for a discussion about feelings and things that make us cry.

This activity is best used with children who come from stressful environments, where their behavior is a concern. These children often have "stuffed their emotions" or bottled them all inside; they do not know how to let their feelings out.

Instructions

Begin by talking to the child about what tissues are useful for. In most cases, children will come up with many uses for tissues (blow one's nose, make flowers, wipe the counter, make as parachutes), except for wiping tears. The therapist can start a conversation about times when people cry. Brainstorm with the child about all the various things that people cry about, slowly narrowing down to situations that have made the child cry or want to cry. This provides the therapist with much information about what the child has experienced in life, and what issues are most pressing for the child.

Next, give the child some kind of container which can be drawn on and personalized (small, empty jewelry boxes or envelopes work quite well). Tell the child that this container will hold his/her tissues, in case he/she "ever needs to cry." This "emergency packet" can fit in the child's pocket and be carried everywhere as a reminder that it is "okay to cry."

Spend time with the child decorating the container. Children may want to list things that make them sad on one side, and list happy things on the other side. Children may write "open in case of an emergency" or "handle with care" on the packet. In this way, children have personalized their own packet of tissues and given themselves permission to cry when needed.

Next, it is time to fold some tissues to put in the packet. There are a few different ways to integrate this task in the activity. For every tissue put into the packet, the child can talk about a time in the past when he/she cried or wanted to cry. The child may choose to label the tissues for various situations that make him/her cry (e.g., the "got yelled at" tissue, the "hurt feelings" tissue, the "scared and lonely" tissue, etc.). When parents are involved, it can also be useful to have each person in the room put a tissue into the child's packet, symbolically giving the child permission to cry.

Suggestions for Follow-Up

Each time the child comes to therapy, the therapist can check that the child is carrying his/her emergency packet, and ask questions about if the packet was used or needed during the past week. The therapist can also refill the packet for the child and/or ask the child's parents to make regular "deposits" (of tissues) into the packet. Ironically, once the child has permission to "let go," parents often feel more comfortable letting their own tears out. The whole family can participate in a discussion about their feelings regarding the events going on at home.

Contraindications

Many children have built-up defenses against showing emotions, and may not be ready to even admit they have any feelings about what is going on at home. In such cases, it is helpful to preface this activity with many joining sessions and trust-building activities.

If the child's parents send the message that "it is not okay to cry," the therapist may need to spend time with them discussing how children express their feelings, and their child's need for some sort of outlet for his/her feelings.

The therapist must also be careful to watch for signs that the child is using crying to manipulate people, or get his/her way. It is important to clarify the difference between crying and tantrums. Sometimes, crying has a closeness or distancing function. In these cases, it is helpful to discuss with the child ways that he/she can ask for space or security without crying.

Readings and Resources for the Professional

Combrinck-Graham, L. (1989). *Children in family contexts*. New York: Guilford Press.

Kottman, T. and Schaefer, C. (1993). *Play therapy in action*. Northvale, NJ: Jason Aronson Inc.

Schaefer, C. and Carey, L. (1994). *Family play therapy*. Northvale, NJ: Jason Aronson Inc.

66

Greeting Card Messages:
Reading Between the Lines

Sharon A. Deacon

Type of Contribution: *Activity*

Objective

The purpose of this activity is to create a fun project for children in therapy, while learning about children's perceptions of their family and friends at the same time. Children will have an opportunity to share events going on in their lives without feeling "on the spot" or bombarded with questions.

Rationale for Use

Children often express themselves more fully through nonverbal means, rather than simply talking about how they feel. This activity combines a child's need for action and nonverbal expression with a therapist's need for information about how the child perceives those people that are close to him/her.

Through art therapy, children are able to "show" the therapist how they feel. By making greeting cards, children can indirectly express their feelings about the people they are close to, while having fun at the same time. Therapy becomes less threatening for the child, and more "game-like."

Instructions

Begin by having a conversation with the child about times when people receive greeting cards. Give the child examples, if necessary, about holiday cards, birthday cards, anniversary cards, and so on. It may also be helpful to have a stack of cards available for the child to look at and read, so that the child has some idea about what messages greeting cards give, and how they look.

Together, with the child, come up with a whole list of occasions on which people might give each other cards. Be sure to include the following occasions on your list: birthday, illness, anniversary, wedding, "I'm sorry," good-bye, thinking of you, "I love you," sympathy, encouragement, congratulations, thank-you, friendship, and "I miss you."

Next, turn the office into a "greeting card factory," where the child has a job as a "greeting card maker." Supply the child with plenty of paper, scissors, glue, crayons, markers, and other materials that the child might use (doilies, yarn, glitter, felt). Give the child an "order"—the list of greeting cards you made earlier. Ask the child to make one of each type of greeting card listed for someone he/she knows. (This may take a few sessions.) The therapist can help the child with creating the cards; however, leave the message and recipient portion of the card blank—it is up to the child to decide upon those.

As the child creates each card, discuss with the child how he/she chose the recipient of the card. The child will have many stories to tell about why each person deserves the card he/she is getting. Pay attention to what cards are most fun, and those which are the most difficult to make. What cards is the child anxious about? What cards is the child eager to make?

Helpful Tips

- Birthday cards can be given to most anyone. Thus, save that topic for the end, to give to anyone that did not fit the other categories.
- Get well cards work great for sick relatives, family members with substance abuse problems, depressed parents, and symptomatic/psychosomatic siblings. Discuss why that person is "sick," and how stress is handled in the family.
- Anniversary cards can be given for special dates, yearly events, or as a reminder of a day that sticks out in the child's mind, from his/her past.
- Good-bye, sympathy, and "I miss you" cards work well for loss issues, deaths, and grieving difficulties.
- Encouragement and friendship cards can be used for people the child feels a need to "cheer up." Watch for care-taking tendencies on the child's part.
- Wedding cards are a great way to get the child to talk about how he/she perceives his/her parent's marriage.

Once all the greeting cards are made, the child should distribute them to the various people as homework. One person may receive many cards, and that is okay. These cards serve as a means for the child to communicate his/her feelings to the therapist and his/her family and friends.

Suggestions for Follow-Up

Once cards have been distributed, ask the child about the recipients' reactions. If possible, talk to the recipients about how they felt receiving the card, and what the card means to them.

Contraindications

While making the cards has no contraindications, distributing the cards needs to be done with caution. If someone may take offense to the card, be in denial about problems, or react negatively to the child, the cards should not be distributed immediately. In such cases, the child may save the cards to give at a later time.

If the child is too young to write, the therapist can write the message for the child, using the child's words. The child can still decorate the card.

67

Helpful Homemade Props
for Children in Therapy

Dawn Viers

Type of Contribution: *Activities/Handouts*

Objective

These activities are designed for the therapist to use everyday household items to make inexpensive props for children in therapy. These props can be used in a variety of ways, from activities in session, to homework outside of session. The handout format also allows parents to utilize these activities at home, as a therapeutic measure and as a fun learning activity.

Rationale for Use

These activities are designed to provide developmentally and age-appropriate activities for young children in therapy. Each of these activities can be used in different ways, and fit different therapy modalities. Creating the masks can be used to facilitate the sharing of emotions. Making the stress balls can serve to help children (and adults) come up with different anger management techniques. Using the finger paint can help children make symbolic representations of objects. Finally, making children's crayons can help promote manual dexterity in young children.

Instructions

Making Masks

This activity can be used to visually access and facilitate the sharing of emotions in order to promote therapeutic change. With this activity, the therapist encourages a child to describe feelings, and through pictures or facial expressions, has the child visually express his or her feelings. The therapist then helps the child to make a mask representing a particular feeling. Together, they make the mask following the attached directives. The mask is then painted with facial expressions that show the desired feelings. The child can wear the mask as an outward symbol of his/her internal emotions. The child can later repeat this activity to symbolize other emotions.

Stress Balls

This activity can help children learn to use acceptable anger management skills. The therapist and child can make the stress balls in therapy according to the attached directives. The stress ball is designed to be kneaded with the fingers to help alleviate stress. The therapist can then contract with the child regarding alternative, acceptable anger management techniques. Kneading the stress ball can be part of this contract, or perhaps be the first step in effectively managing anger. When the child feels angry or upset, he or she could knead the stress ball for a contracted amount of time or until the anger and stress start to dissipate. This is also a good activity for parents and children to do at home. The parents can help model effective anger management techniques for their children by using the stress ball themselves. The therapist may want to encourage children (and parents) to make several stress balls and keep them in different places, such as at home, in the car, or at work.

Fun and Tasty Finger Paint

This activity encourages children (even as young as one year old) to be artistic and creative. In therapy, this activity can be used for children to symbolically illustrate their families or themselves. The therapist alone or with children can make the finger paint and add colors according to the children's taste. At home, this activity can provide hours of fun for a child. Since this "paint" is nontoxic, parents will not need to worry if children stick their fingers into their mouths. This activity could even combine playtime with snack time, as the child can eat his or her creation! Be careful—while the finger paint may be nontoxic, the food colors may stain skin and clothes. Plastic aprons are recommended.

Kid-Friendly Crayons

Children, especially younger children, may not have the manual dexterity to grip regular crayons. As such, they might not be able to use crayons, either in the therapy room or at home. By transforming the shape of the crayon into a shape that is easier to grip, the therapist helps create an instrument that even a one-year-old child can use. This crayon can then be used as a toy or as a therapeutic prop for drawing certain objects or people. This activity and its handout may be helpful, as it teaches parents to make drawing and coloring easier for young children without having to resort to expensive props.

Suggestions for Follow-Up

As stated, these activities can be used in therapy or at home. For use at home, the therapist can copy the handouts for the parents. The therapist should then track the utility and usefulness of these activities at home, both from the child's and the parents' point of view.

Contraindications

These activities work best with children, especially with younger children. However, the stress balls and masks are also suitable for older clients, with modifications. These modifications include devising other anger management techniques, such as time-outs, in conjunction with the stress balls. The therapist may encourage older clients to use the masks as reflections of transformations of feelings and emotions.

Readings and Resources for the Professional

Harvey, S. (1994). *Dramatic play therapy: Expressive play interventions with families.* New York: John Wiley & Sons

Lane, P. S. (1995). *Conflict resolution for kids: A group facilitator's guide.* Bristol, PA: Accelerated Development, Inc.

Santrock, J. W. (1995). *Children*. Dubuque, IA: Brown & Benchmark

Santrock, J. W. and Yussen, S. R. (1992). *Child Development*. (Fifth Edition). Dubuque, IA: William C. Brown Publishers

Smith, S. C. and Pennells, M. (Eds.) (1995). *Interventions with bereaved children*. London: Jessica Kingsley Publishers, Ltd.

Zilbach, J. J. (1986). *Young children in family therapy*. New York: Brunner/Mazel, Inc.

Bibliotherapy Sources for the Client

Schwartz, S. and Miller, J. E. (1996). *The new language of toys: Teaching communication skills to children with special needs: A guide for parents and teachers*. Bethesda, MD: Woodbine House, Inc.

Making Masks

Papier-mâché can be used to make many different things—including realistic masks

You will need:

flour
water
round balloons
strips of newspaper
acrylic paints

- Mix equal parts of flour and water. If the mixture is runny, add more flour until the mixture becomes firm.

- Blow up a balloon. Dip the newspaper strips in the papier-mâché mixture and wipe off excess mixture with your fingers.

- Layer the newspaper strips on the balloon, covering the entire front of the balloon in the shape of a face.

- When the papier-mâché dries, pop the balloon, and paint the mask with acrylic paints.

Stress Balls

This easy recipe shows you how to make inexpensive stress reliev-
ers. Just knead the balls with your fingers, and let stress flow away.
Take out your frustrations on the stress balls—they never complain!

You will need:

flour
small, round balloons
uncooked rice (optional)

- Put one balloon inside of the other, and partially blow up the balloons.

- Fill the balloons close to the top with flour and tie balloons in a
  knot. You can also add rice to the mixture.

- Knead the balls to relieve stress and anger.

- Keep some stress balls in your house, at work, or in your car—
  wherever you may feel stressed out!

Fun and Tasty Finger Paint

Here is an easy way to take household goods and make nontoxic finger paints for young children.

You will need:

Vanilla pudding
food coloring
wax paper
small paper cups

- Mix pudding according to its directions.
- Put equal amounts of pudding into different cups.
- Add food colors to each of the cups, and mix.
- Put down wax paper for children to paint on.

Kid-Friendly Crayons

Young children often have a hard time using regular crayons because they are hard to grip. Here is an easy way to take those crayons and make them "kid friendly" for the little tikes.

❑ Put different color crayons into individual cups in a cupcake pan.

❑ Heat in the oven on low heat until crayons melt.

❑ Take out of oven and let crayons set.

❑ Let children use as they would regular crayons.

68

The Puzzling Problem-Solving Activity

Marilyn M. Steinberg

Type of Contribution: *Activity*

Objective

The objective of the Puzzling Problem-Solving Activity for children is to assist the client who is having difficulty problem solving or decision making to see that other, sometimes unexplored, options are available.

Rationale for Use

Children, and adults, often become stuck seeing things only one way. Broadening their perspective can open up solutions for their problems.

Instructions

Materials Needed

You will need one ten- or twenty-piece puzzle, and two different colors of paint.

Assembly

Disassemble the puzzle, and paint one side of the puzzle one color (blue, for example), except for two pieces. Paint these remaining two puzzle pieces a different color (yellow, for example). On the back of the puzzle pieces, paint the opposite color that you painted on the front side. The border of the puzzle can be painted either color. For example, if you are working with a ten-piece puzzle, you will paint eight puzzle pieces blue, and two puzzle pieces yellow on the front side. The back of the puzzle will have eight yellow puzzle pieces and two blue puzzle pieces.

Present the puzzle to the client with *all the blue puzzle pieces face up*. Explain to the client that the puzzle border represents the problem or situation they are having trouble solving, and the puzzle pieces are the solutions. Ask the client to put the puzzle together. Some clients will assume that since the puzzle or problem was presented with only the blue pieces or solutions face up, those are their only available options. As clients begin to work with the puzzle, they will soon find that two puzzle pieces do not fit, like some of the solutions they have already tried, and they will feel stuck. As children begin to explore alternatives to making the puzzle pieces fit back together, they will eventually flip over the two remaining puzzle pieces (the two pieces that were painted the opposite color), and solve the puzzle. Once the puzzle is back together, retrace the steps the client took to solve the puzzle, and explain to the client that sometimes unexplored solutions are available.

For example, if the child is experiencing trouble at school with a bully beating him or her up for lunch money, you can represent the border to the puzzle as the problem itself. The puzzle pieces are the solutions. The two yellow puzzle pieces can represent solutions the client has tried before (such as swearing at the bully or turning over the lunch money) and been unsuccessful with, thus not fitting into the border. The eight blue pieces can represent new alternatives to solving the problem such as telling the parents, teacher, lunchroom monitor, or principal. These blue puzzle pieces will fit into the border just as the new solutions fit the problem.

Suggestions for Follow-Up

As the child terminates therapy, present him/her with the puzzle again and this time, label the pieces of the puzzle with the solutions he/she tried, those that worked and those that did not. Explain to the child that this path to problem solving can be used with any difficulty he/she may experience in the future, not just the one that was presented in therapy.

Contraindications

The age range for this activity will be the same as the age range on the puzzle you choose to use. For children, use a smaller puzzle with fewer puzzle pieces; for adolescents, you may use a larger puzzle with more pieces. However, this activity was not designed for use with a severely cognitively limited population.

Readings and Resources for the Professional

Berg, C. A. and Calderone, K. S. (1994). *Mind in context: Interactionist perspectives on human intelligence.* New York: Cambridge University Press.

Butterfield, W. H. and Cobb, N. H. (1994). Cognitive-behavioral treatment of children and adolescents. In D. K. Granvold (Ed.), *Cognitive and behavioral treatment: Methods and applications* (pp. 65-89). Pacific Grove, CA: Brooks/Cole Publishing Company.

Compas, B. E. (1989). Coping with stress during childhood and adolescence. In S. Chess, A. Thomas, and M. E. Hertzig (Eds.), *Annual progress in child psychiatry and child development, 1988* (pp. 211-237). New York: Brunner/Mazel, Inc.

Donovan, D. M. and McIntyre, D. (1990). Child psychotherapy. In J. G. Simeon and H. B. Ferguson (Eds.), *Treatment strategies in child and adolescent psychiatry* (pp. 177-197). New York: Plenum Press.

Feindler, E. L. (1991). Cognitive strategies in anger control interventions for children and adolescents. In P. C. Kendall (Ed.), *Child and adolescent therapy: Cognitive-behavioral procedures* (pp. 66-97). New York: Guilford Press.

Goldstein, A. P. (1988). *The prepare curriculum: Teaching prosocial competencies.* Champaign, IL: Research Press.

Herbert, M. (1991). *Clinical child psychology: Social learning, development and behavior.* Chichester, England: John Wiley & Sons.

Ronan, K. R. and Kendall, P. C. (1990). Non-self-controlled adolescents: Applications of cognitive-behavioral therapy. In S. C. Feinstein, A. H. Esman, J. G. Looney, G. H. Orvin, J. L. Schimel, A. Z. Schwartzberg, A. D. Sorosky, and M. Sugar (Eds.), *Adolescent psychiatry: Developmental and clinical studies: Volume 17. Annals of the American Society for Adolescent Psychiatry* (pp. 479-505). Chicago: University of Chicago Press.

Treffinger, D. J. (1995). Creative problem solving: Overview and educational implications. Special issue: Toward an educational psychology of creativity: II. *Educational Psychology Review, 7,* 301-312.

Urbain, E. S. and Savage, P. (1989). Interpersonal cognitive problem-solving training with children in the schools. In J. N. Hughes and R. J. Hall (Eds.), *Cognitive-behavioral psychology in the schools: A comprehensive handbook* (pp. 466-497). New York: Guilford Press.

69

Prescribing Fluctuations in Developmental Time

Stephen A. Anderson

Type of Contribution: *Homework/Activity*

Objective

The objective of this activity is to provide a rationale and specific homework activities to help families address child- and adolescent-centered problems that appear related to unre-solved family life-cycle issues. Such difficulties may manifest as externalized behavior prob-lems (e.g., conduct or oppositional disorders, truancy, learning problems in school, problems with peers, unwanted pregnancy, substance abuse), internalizing disorders (anxiety, depres-sion, suicidal tendencies, physical complaints), or problems in parent-child relationships (communication difficulties, ineffective discipline, lack of parental emotional support).

Rationale for Use

Families often come to therapy describing a child as having the presenting problem. Many such problems can be traced to unresolved issues from previous life-cycle stages or other past events. A common therapeutic assumption, and one consistent with family developmental theories, is that these earlier events must be reworked before the present impasse or conflict can be successfully resolved. In this instance, resolution is not addressed in the intrapsychic sense of requiring internal reflection, catharsis, and enhanced self-awareness. Rather, the emphasis is transactional. The focus is upon altering interactional patterns in the present by changing the context and drawing attention to these formative experiences in the past. The key dimension addressed by the homework assignment is time. It is assumed that changing the family's time orientation is an effective way to alter its relational context.

Instructions

The facts surrounding the *present* complaint are reviewed and connected to *past* events that are viewed as having led to the present impasse. Clients are then informed that their present-ing complaint is related to the "incomplete resolution" of an earlier period in their family's development. Clients are further informed that the best way to improve functioning in the *future* is to go back in time to reexperience the earlier time period, but this time with a fresh perspective. Several examples are provided to illustrate the assignment.

Example 1

A couple presented for therapy with their young adolescent son who performed poorly in school, related to his parents in a whining, demanding manner, and preferred playmates who were younger in age. A pattern was observed in which mother covertly encouraged her son's behavior, while blaming father for not being more concerned and involved with the boy.

The parents were informed that even though their son was fourteen in real years, he was actually developmentally at about the age of eight. They could continue to treat their son as a fourteen-year-old, but that had not led to much success. Their son's behavior was perhaps an indication that he was not yet ready to handle being fourteen years old. He was asking by his behavior to be treated as an eight-year-old. Of course, this meant that he needed more supervision, attention, and education about socially appropriate behaviors than would a young adolescent. This education task would have to be undertaken by both parents. Their son needed their cooperation to help him learn what other eight-year-old boys know. Once the parents accepted the rationale for their son's behavior, the specific homework assignment was discussed in terms of the particular expectations the parents should have for an eight-year-old boy, and what he needed to learn from his parents.

The assignment challenged the son to behave in an age-appropriate manner, the father to become more involved, and the parents to work together to "reparent" their son. Subsequent therapy sessions addressed the differences that emerged in the parents' expectations for the boy.

Example 2

A mother, father, and sixteen-year-old daughter appeared for therapy, with the parents' chief complaint being that the daughter was "uncontrollable." She was associating with an older crowd which included the daughter's nineteen-year-old brother, who no longer lived in the parental home. The daughter was consistently disregarding her curfew. Several nights a week, she would stay out all night with her twenty-year-old boyfriend. Her parents were unable to follow through on "grounding" her because she would simply leave after school before her parents returned home from work. The parents were frightened for her well-being because they "never knew where she was or who she was with." She "never called to let [them] know that she was safe." Her sexual activity also worried them greatly. Both parents reported feeling powerless at being able to control their daughter. All of their efforts had failed, and they were at their wits' end as to what else to do.

The daughter, for her part, felt that her parents were making "too big a deal out of everything." She reported that she was usually either at her boyfriend's apartment or at a local corner where her friends congregated. She noted that she frequently saw her older brother, as they both shared many friends in common and that he was there to look after her if she needed it. Her assessment of what was needed for the problems in the family to resolve themselves was for her parents to "get off her back."

The parents were asked to recall an earlier point in which they were able to effectively manage their daughter's behavior. They recalled a time several years earlier when their daughter was fourteen years old, and her brother was still living at home. They described their daughter as generally well behaved. However, they recalled that it was the brother who was "wild" and "hard to manage" at that time. Their efforts to discipline him resulted in intense conflicts to which he responded by eventually moving out on his own.

It was suggested to the parents that history seemed to be repeating itself, and that this might be because the transition of the son's leaving home had not been successfully completed. That is, his abrupt departure had not allowed him to work through the inevitable tensions that developed during this period between becoming an independent young adult and his lingering dependency upon his parents for guidance and support. His departure had left the parents and son (and parents and daughter) angry and bitter toward one another. The son had not been able to renegotiate his relationship with his parents from parent-child to parent-young adult, and the daughter had no older sibling to emulate in her effort to do the same.

The parents were encouraged to bring both their son and daughter to future therapy sessions, where they could revisit the time when both children were living at home. The goal of the therapy was to provide all family members with the opportunity to make the son's launching from the family one that respected his need for both connection and individuation, and to help the parents establish a sense of reconnection with both of their children. A further goal was to assist the parents in being able to reassert some control over their daughter's behavior, while allowing her the degree of autonomy that was appropriate for her developmental age.

Example 3

Divorce and remarriage exemplify two developmental transitions that can evoke child-focused presenting problems if they are not fully resolved at the time of their occurrence. The case of an eleven-year-old boy who presented for therapy with his mother and younger sister is illustrative. The mother described the boy as angry and disrespectful at home, and as having trouble at school. His grades had declined, and he had been involved in several fights with other boys.

The boy's parents had divorced about two years earlier. The mother had just recently begun dating another man on a regular basis, although she expressed ambivalence over whether she should make a greater level of commitment to this relationship. The period directly following the divorce had been uneventful for the family. Initially, the children saw their father several times a week, but over time, this had declined to once or twice a month. The relationship between the parents was described by the mother as "superficially cordial." In the initial sessions, she described feelings of resentment toward her former husband for having "abandoned" her and her children. The children expressed generally positive feelings toward their father, and were angry at their mother for not trying "hard enough" to work things out with him. The addition of a "new man" in their mother's life had apparently intensified these previously subdued feelings, and directly challenged the children's hopes of their parents reuniting.

It was suggested to the mother that her divorce from her former husband, although legally completed, was perhaps not emotionally closed. The family was asked to go back in their minds to a time when the family was still together. Each family member was asked to share the memories that came to them as they reflected in this manner. The children acknowledged how they liked having their dad around more often, but the son also acknowledged that his dad was often too busy to play with him. Both children also reflected upon the fights that mom and dad used to have, and how uncomfortable these made them feel. The mother was able to share with her children how much she tried to make the marriage work. She recalled her own feelings "of walking on eggshells" all the time, trying to keep the peace in the family. They remembered together how much they hated it when the father drank. The mother also shared her own sense of relief that their family life, until recently, had been in less turmoil. As the family recalled these various memories, the affect in the family changed from one of anger and tension to one of sadness.

The goal for subsequent sessions was to allow each family member to sort out his/her feelings of anger, resentment, sadness, loss, relief, and caring for one another. The mother was encouraged to reestablish a connection with her former husband so that she could reach a sense of closure for that period of her life, and to facilitate the reconnection of the children with their father on as regular a basis as possible.

There is a danger of oversimplification when reducing what are typically complex interpersonal issues to brief anecdotes. The examples provided above are only intended to illustrate the utility of sending family members back in time to an earlier period of their developmental history to provide them with a fresh perspective and an opportunity to introduce new alternatives into what have typically becomes redundant, inflexible patterns of interaction.

Suggestions for Follow-Up

The homework assignment and related tasks become an integral (seamless) part of the therapy. Regardless of how successful or unsuccessful clients are in implementing the task, important feedback is provided to the therapist about family members' beliefs, motivations, and underlying feelings, and the degree of rigidity or flexibility in the family system. This information then informs the therapeutic process, sometimes requiring revisions or alterations in the present therapeutic goals and objectives. The goals and objectives for therapy are a product of ongoing negotiation and renegotiation between the therapist and clients over the course of therapy. They must take into account the clients' changing constructions, perceptions, interpretations, needs, and goals as the therapy unfolds. In any case, it is the mutually constructed goals for therapy that drive the choice of a homework assignment and its use in the therapy, not the other way around. When clients describe their current relational problems as "time bound," or linked to events in their past, this assignment may help to introduce sufficient cognitive, affective, and interactional variation to disrupt the current stasis.

Contraindications

This homework activity is contraindicated when the presenting problem appears unrelated to a life-cycle issue or when clients do not accept the basic premise that earlier, unresolved life-cycle events affect present and future functioning. It is also contraindicated when clients are unable to recall their pasts due to the repression of traumatic memories or because of serious past deprivations. Finally, this assignment is not recommended when the level of conflict between family members is so great that they cannot disengage from escalating cycles of blaming or attacking, when violence is present, or in other circumstances when the primary therapeutic task is to insure the safety and well-being of all family members.

Readings and Resources for Professionals

Anderson, S. A. and Russell, C. S. (1982). Utilizing process and content in designing paradoxical interventions. *American Journal of Family Therapy, 10*(2), 48-60.

Anderson, S. A. and Sabatelli, R. M. (1995). *Family interaction: A multigenerational, developmental perspective.* Needham Heights, MA: Allyn & Bacon.

Boscolo, L. and Bertrando, P. (1992). The reflexive loop of past, present, and future in systemic therapy and consultation. *Family Process, 31*(2), 119-130.

Erickson, M. (1954). Pseudo-orientation in time as a hypnotherapeutic procedure. *Journal of Clinical and Experimental Hypnosis, 2,* 261-283.

Penn, P. (1985). Feet-forward: Future questions, future maps. *Family Process, 24*(3), 299-310.

70

HELP! My Child Won't Do Homework!

Laura Reinke

Type of Contribution: *Handouts*

Objective

These handouts are designed for parents who are burnt out on how to get their child to complete schoolwork and other tasks at home.

Rationale for Use

Oftentimes, children become bored with schoolwork or they are simply not motivated. With the "Homework Guidelines for Parents" handout, parents can introduce new reasons for their children to become interested in schoolwork. Parents and children become bored with the same rewards and punishments associated with completing schoolwork. The following handout is designed to offer suggestions that may accommodate many different families in helping children complete schoolwork and in helping parents reduce frustration.

The "Children's Schedule" handout is a visual way to encourage children to work toward rewards. The schedule is designed as a tool for parents and children to keep track of the completion of (the child's) chores or schoolwork. Consecutive happy faces can earn rewards for children, while sporadic happy faces help parents stay consistent with enforcing rules and withholding reinforcers.

The "Parent-Child Contract" handout is a democratic way to structure rules, consequences, and rewards at home. Children often feel that parents invoke unfair rules and punishments. The purpose of a contract is to encourage family discussion about what is "fair and reasonable" and have the child(ren) and parents agree in contract form.

Instructions

When the therapist gives the "Homework Guidelines for Parents" handout to parents, it is important to go over several instructions with them. First, review some general guidelines that parents should be aware of in order to effectively monitor their child's schoolwork. These are listed at the top of the handout. Next, discuss the various techniques parents can use to ensure that their child is completing his/her homework. It is necessary to talk to parents about the various techniques, and find out what they have done in the past. Ask them what has worked and what has not. Then, ask why their various strategies did or did not work. Explain to parents that without being aware of the aforementioned details, parents may choose something that is bound to fail. Ask parents what strategy they would most like to utilize. Then discuss if they have a plan in case their initial strategy is not successful.

The "Children's Schedule" handout may be given to parents with instructions to write down those chores or homework tasks they want their child to complete on a daily basis. Examples of daily tasks may include: making their own bed, completing homework, picking up their toys before bed, or setting the table before dinner. The chart works like a token economy. Parents fill these tasks in on the numbered lines. Then, at home, they show the schedule to their child and explain what the child is expected to do daily. When he/she completes the tasks, either the child or the parent will then mark the appropriate happy face. If the child receives a predetermined number of marked happy faces in a row, a reward then may be distributed. For example, if the child brushes his/her teeth four days in a row, the child may be allowed a snack after dinner on the fifth day. When establishing the reward schedule, it is important for parents to keep in mind what is reasonable to expect from a child at a particular age and which reinforcers will motivate their child.

The "Parent-Child Contract" handout may be an effective way to agree to chores, rewards, and punishments. Parents and children should discuss which tasks are reasonable to expect from the child. Those can then be written in the contract. Next, parents and children are instructed to talk about rewards and consequences that correspond to the successful completion or failure to complete the contracted task.

Suggestions for Follow-Up

When utilizing the "Homework Guidelines for Parents" handout, make sure to discuss consequences of the various strategies parents have employed with their children. Ask parents and children alike what was different about how the parents reacted when homework was not done. If parents' attempts were successful, ask the child what he/she thought of the consequences. If a particular strategy is working, it may be possible to add some rewards (if not already utilized) for the child so that not all consequences associated with failure to do homework are not negative. The goal of these interventions is to help the child become self-motivated to complete homework. However, this may be a slow process. Therefore, encourage parents to use what is working for them and their children, keeping in mind the goals of these strategies.

For the "Children's Schedule" and the "Parent-Child Contract" handouts, ask parents and children to describe their schedules or contracts. Obtain feedback from the parents about the effectiveness of the handout, if distributing the reinforcement was more of a hassle than punishment, and their opinions about the activity. If the children come to session, ask them about the reinforcement they received, and how fond they were of it. Likewise, ask the children about the punishments that were given, and their perception of how fair it was (if using the "Parent-Child Contract"). Finally, ask the children about the tasks, and whether or not they had difficulty completing them regularly. Keep in mind that children may complain about rules, regardless of their input in establishing them.

Contraindications

The problem with these activities is that parents may become carried away with experimentation and not properly evaluate why each strategy worked or did not work. Too much experimentation will leave a child more confused about homework expectations, and does not provide the consistency a child needs. Furthermore, if a child continues to not complete homework even after various attempts by the parents, it is necessary to consider the possibility of a learning disorder. Specifically regarding the "Children's Schedule" and the "Parent-Child Contract" handouts, parents may expect something that is not developmentally appropriate for a child. For example, an eight-year-old cannot be expected to care for an infant every day from 3 to 6 p.m. If this is a rule, the child will most likely fail, as the expectation is unreasonable. Setting a child up for failure defeats the entire purpose of these handouts. Therefore, follow-up is important to guard against unreasonable expectations. If a child does not respond to the contract or daily schedule, parents may need to find more appropriate reinforcers for the child.

Readings and Resources for the Professional

Doyle, M. A. (1990). *Homework as a learning experience.* Washington, DC: National Education Association.

Bibliotherapy Sources for Clients

England, D. A. (1985). *Homework, and why.* Bloomington, IN: Phi Delta Kappa Foundation.
Lee, C. (1987). *Homework without tears.* New York: Perennial Library.

HOMEWORK GUIDELINES FOR PARENTS

IT'S IMPORTANT TO...

1. BE INVOLVED IN YOUR CHILD'S SCHOOLWORK. ASK FOR ASSIGNMENTS, HELP THEM READ DIRECTIONS, AND CHECK TO MAKE SURE HOMEWORK IS COMPLETE.
2. MAKE SURE YOUR CHILD HAS A REGULAR PLACE TO STUDY AND THAT YOU HAVE EXPRESSED YOUR EXPECTATIONS ABOUT HOMEWORK.

SUGGESTIONS FOR PARENTS

1. CREATE A DAILY SCHEDULE FOR YOUR CHILD INCLUDING MEALS, EXTRACURRICULAR ACTIVITIES, AND HOMEWORK TIME.
2. RESPOND TO YOUR CHILD AS A BROKEN RECORD WOULD, "I WANT YOU TO DO YOUR HOMEWORK NOW...I WANT YOU TO DO YOUR HOMEWORK NOW...ETC."
3. HAVE YOUR CHILD CONTRACT FOR REWARDS. IF HOMEWORK IS DONE "X" NUMBER OF DAYS, A REWARD MAY BE CONTRACTED FOR.
4. PARTNER UP WITH YOUR CHILD'S TEACHER AND SEND AN ASSIGNMENT NOTEBOOK TO SCHOOL. ASK TEACHERS TO INITIAL YOUR CHILD'S ASSIGNMENTS.
5. IF ASSIGNMENTS ARE NOT BROUGHT HOME, MAKE IT CLEAR THAT CHORES WILL BE DONE DURING THE TIME USUALLY SCHEDULED FOR HOMEWORK. SUGGESTIONS INCLUDE WASHING THE CLEAN DISHES FROM THE CUPBOARD.
6. GO TO YOUR CHILD'S CLASSROOM TO COLLECT ASSIGNMENTS WEARING 2 DIFFERENT SHOES, WITH YOUR PANTS PULLED ABOVE YOUR WAIST, ROLLERS IN YOUR HAIR, ETC.
7. TELL YOUR CHILD YOU ARE GLAD HE/SHE FORGOT HIS/HER HOMEWORK SO YOU CAN SPEND QUALITY FAMILY TIME. SUGGESTIONS FOR "FAMILY TIME" INCLUDE RENTING A NATURE MOVIE ABOUT PLANTS, BIRDWATCHING, COLLECTING WORMS, ETC.
8. PRAISE YOUR CHILD WHEN HOMEWORK IS DONE.

354

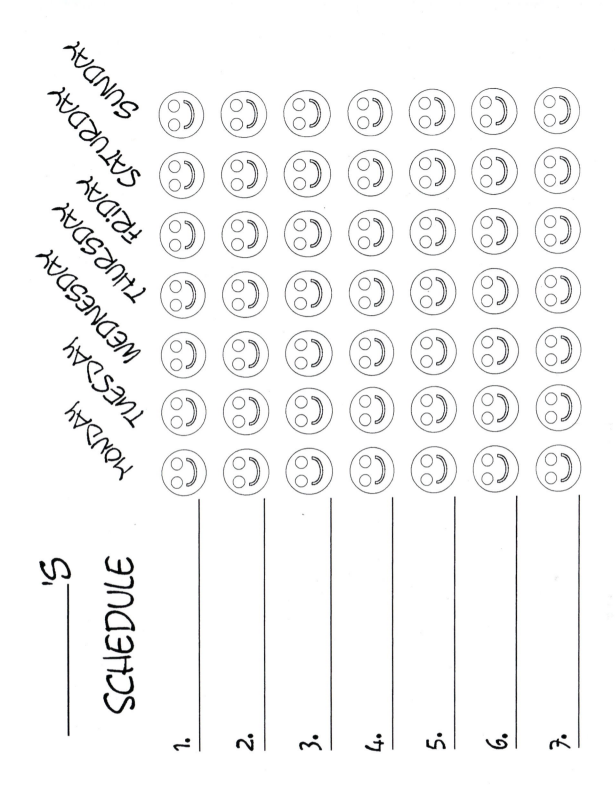

SUNDAY

SATURDAY

FRIDAY

THURSDAY

WEDNESDAY

TUESDAY

MONDAY

_____'S

SCHEDULE

1.

2.

3.

4.

5.

6.

7.

I, _____ promise to:

1. _____   5. _____

2. _____   6. _____

3. _____   7. _____

4. _____

according to the schedule my parent(s) decide(s) on.

If I complete my tasks, I can look forward to:

1. _____

2. _____

3. _____

4. _____   or

5. _____

If I do not complete those tasks, the

consequences will be:

1. _____

2. _____

3. _____

4. _____   and/or

5. _____

_____   _____
(Parent)   (Parent)

_____
(Child)

356

71

Divorce and Children:
Guidelines for Parents

Mary Anne Armour

Type of Contribution: *Handout*

Objective

The handout's purpose is to give divorcing parents suggestions to handle the emotions and behaviors of children during the divorce process and during the adjustment following divorce.

Rationale for Use

Divorce, at best, is distressing for all family members involved. Emotions of fear regarding separation and abandonment are especially prominent. Other emotions which are frightening for all of the family are anger, jealousy, confusion, and hate. Parents are usually concerned and sometimes at a loss to understand their children's emotions regarding separation and divorce. The children are often the last to know about the pending divorce. Parents assume that their relationship is for them to decide, and indeed it is. Yet not only is the marriage dissolving, family life and structure as the child has experienced it from birth changes drastically. This is especially so with the decreased presence of a parent who has been actively involved in the child's life. Even when the child is told about the divorce, and given adequate time to adjust prior to the breakup, each child will have concerns about safety issues, loyalty, and generally how life will be for him/her after the separation. In addition, a child who appears to be self-sufficient and not affected by upsetting family events can be overlooked for help during the divorce process. The child who is very emotional but unable to directly express his or her feelings can be assessed as being upset by something else, such as school problems or the loss of a pet. Thus, divorce can too easily be overlooked as a major distressing event in the life of a child. The focus of this handout is to help parents understand the reactions of their children to divorce, and aid them in dealing with their children's feelings and behaviors.

Instructions

Therapists usually have their own timetable regarding when to direct the divorcing couple toward the needs and distress of their children. Use of this handout is most helpful after parents have made the final decision to divorce, and find themselves asking the question, "How should we tell the children?" While it is useful to deal with parental concerns as part of divorce therapy, parents are usually so involved in divorce issues, it is difficult to focus on children's concerns. If parents do not query the therapist about the effects of divorce on children, it is important that the therapist outline the effects for them. This should be done with reassurance that children are resilient and will survive, but need attention to their loss as well. Especially important is emphasis on the grief process that a child may go through without ever showing outward grieving emotions or talking about it. Articles on divorce and children (see Reading and Resources for the Professional and Bibliotherapy Sources for the Client) can be useful to parents. Often, after the decision to divorce is reached, couples will stop therapy. It is helpful instead to ask for a session with the children and both parents to help parents learn how to constructively address their children's concerns. Providing the parents with the handout that follows will be both informative and therapeutic.

Suggestions for Follow-Up

The custodial parent is usually the one who notices the child who is struggling with the decreased presence of the other parent, the loss of a two-parent structure, or anger at the change in lifestyle. A telephone call at regular intervals (one month, three months, and six months) to check the progress of the children can be useful to both parents. If signs of grieving are not lessened, additional therapy should be recommended. Issues which may need to be covered are: family triangles, parental enmeshment, the ability of parents to agree on child visitation, parental violation of the child's need for privacy with the other parent, and the child's acting as message carrier between parents.

Contraindications

If emotional behaviors (such as crying excessively, severe acting-out, not sleeping, or not eating) do not subside within two to three weeks, it is recommended that a physician evaluate the child.

Readings and Resources for the Professional

Ahrons, C. (1994). *The good divorce*. New York: HarperCollins.
Beal, E. W. and Hochman, G. (1991). *Adult children of divorce*. New York: Dell Publishing.
Hodges, W. F. (1986). *Intervention for children of divorce*. New York: Wiley.
Miller, A. (1986). *Drama of the gifted child*. New York: Basic Books.

Bibliotherapy Sources for the Client

Brown, L. K. (1986). *Dinosaurs divorce*. Boston: Atlantic Monthly Press.
Turow, R. (1977). *Daddy doesn't live here anymore*. Matteson, IL: Great Lakes Living Press.

Divorce and the Children:
Guidelines for Parents

Divorces are a real problem for children. Adults can sometimes romanticize divorce or make it into a creative adventure. Children feel much more sharply the interpersonal failure and the way in which it is a psychological amputation. The children need to know as much about the divorce as possible, and it is best that they find out in the total family situation therapy provides. The dreams and fantasies are way ahead of the horror that they permit.

—David Keith, MD

Divorcing parents need to have as one of their primary concerns the growth and development of their children. This will include how divorce affects their children's future lives, as well as how their children accept and cope during the year following divorce.

Children of divorcing parents face long-range adjustment. Their successful management of this life event is directly related to what happens within the family following divorce.

The distress of divorce for a child represents many fears which may or may not be expressed, and often lie just beneath the surface. Fear of decreased presence of the child's parent while he or she is still dependent brings up many questions. "What will happen to me?" "Where will I live?" "Will I get to see Mommy or Daddy as much as I want to?" "What will happen to Mommy or Daddy at Christmas?" "Other holidays?" "When can I go to live with the other parent?" "Will I get to see my grandparents again?" "Is the divorce my fault?" "Was I a good enough child?" "If I had been different, would it not have happened?"

Divorce can be compared to other major losses, such as the death of a grandparent or perhaps losing one's community after a natural disaster. It disrupts close family relationships, weakens support systems and the protection the child has known, and leaves a diminished family structure.

What does the child experience? The trauma begins with a time-limited crisis, followed by an extended period of disruption which may last from one year to several years past the actual event. Divorce introduces a chain of long-lasting events which are unpredictable and reach into every area of the child's family life. He or she must grieve the loss each time he or she confronts a situation where the noncustodial parent ordinarily would have been present.

For the very young child, grief will stretch over childhood and adolescence, and may have some effect on his/her own marriage. When reorganization and adjustment to divorce take place, the child has added challenges and burdens to face. Examples are: more help and responsibility are required of older children with younger children when only one parent is present; reduced income is usually necessary in both new families, causing lifestyle changes due to financial necessity; the oldest child is often called on to act in place of the noncustodial parent and thus, misses out on some of the freedom of being a child or an adolescent.

Some children remain conflict-ridden and have trouble addressing the task of resolving the divorce. Others try various ways to cope, and never seem to find the right one. One finding is clear from research—five to ten years after marital breakup, the divorce remains the central event of growing up for many children and adolescents.

After the first pain subsides, effects often remain: depression, confusion, disorganization, gradual decline in grades, withdrawal from friends, anger, acting out at school, or becoming physically ill. The following may occur: a child may have fear of separation, and/or get anxious and regress to a previous developmental stage (e.g. bedwetting, disturbed sleep patterns, experiences of acute mourning, or expressions of anger at one or both parents). A child may experience pervasive sorrow and a keen sense of vulnerability. He or she may have concerns of being unloved or unlovable; may yearn for the missing parent; or a loyalty conflict may exist, including thoughts such as: "Will I make Mommy mad if I visit Daddy?" Feelings may include an overwhelming sense of neediness and being very burdened. Even small children will be nostalgic for the intact family.

Specific tasks follow, which help children to mourn and adjust to their new lifestyle.

Task #1: Acknowledge the Reality of the Marital Breakup.

The child has frightening fantasies of abandonment and disaster triggered by parental conflict followed by one parent leaving. The child experiences intense feelings of sorrow, anger, and rejection. He or she has a powerful need to deny and block the thoughts and feelings which are terrifying.

What to Do:

> (a) explain the family events; discuss the "who," "what," "where," and "how" of the divorce.
> (b) provide continued support and reassurance that the child is not at fault;
> (c) explain repeatedly to the child that he or she is still loved by *both* parents;
> (d) allow frequent contact with the noncustodial parent and visits with grandparents when convenient.

Task #2: Disengage from Parental Conflict and Distress and Resume Customary Pursuits.

The child is often unable to concentrate, has daydreams, and gets bored, restless, or irritable when exposed to parental conflict.

What to Do:

> (a) return to customary activities and relationships at school and at play as quickly as possible;
> (b) help the child to avoid the anger and distress of the parents;
> (c) speak directly to each other and avoid sending messages through the child.

By the end of the first year, he or she is usually able to resume normal activities.

Task #3: Resolve the Losses in the Child's Life.

The losses for a child are many: continuity of two parents in the home; partial loss of familiar routines, symbols, and traditions; the intact family, home, neighborhood, school, and economic support. While not every child will experience all these losses, even small loss looms large in the midst of a child's fears regarding divorce. Feelings include humiliation, powerlessness, feeling unlovable, and rejection even when parents and grandparents are reassuring.

What to Do:

   (a) talk about and acknowledge feelings of loss for specific parts of the child's life; give the child permission to cry about them; avoid promising solutions which cannot be delivered;
   (b) provide ways to see the missing parent;
   (c) try to maintain as much of the familiar living and school conditions as possible for one year.

Task #4: Resolve Anger and Self-Blame.

To forgive is a difficult concept for adults. For children to forgive parents and develop a capacity to recognize differences between them may be a long time in coming, but helps resolve the anger and self-blame. Another step is to help the child realize that adults make their choices based on their own thoughts and feelings. Children are not responsible for their parent's choices regarding divorce.

What to Do:

   (a) talk about the child's anger even though he or she may deny it; young children (elementary school age and younger) can more easily talk about the feelings of animals or other people;
   (b) encourage the child to forgive him- or herself for having wished the divorce to happen or for being unable to restore the broken marriage.

Task #5: Accept the Permanence of Divorce.

Children usually live with the hope of getting their parents back together. They fantasize and dream about life as being perfect when their family was intact. That is part of the adjustment, and allows them not to have to feel the pain all the time. Children gradually adjust to the reality of the divorce.

What to Do:

   (a) reassure the child that he or she is loved by both parents—that even though Mom and Dad cannot live together, their love for the child is forever. Even when one parent makes little effort at contact, reminding the child of fun times and looking at pictures of the child and parent can be helpful. Letter writing can also be therapeutic for an older child.
   (b) make clear that the divorce is a reality, that there will not be a reconciliation. Children need clear messages which are gentle, but also straightforward and honest.

Task #6: Achieve Realistic Hopes Regarding Relationships.

Both parents and children live with the fact that life offers good times as well as adversity. Divorce is one of the adversities that his or her family can withstand. Learning to live with it is a challenge, and presents an opportunity for growth. Yes, it hurts, but we must cry (give ourselves permission to grieve often) and know that we will survive. Our dreams are important, and we make new dreams when the old ones are broken.

What to Do:

   (a) instill hope that the pain will not always be there; that the child can love and be loved by others; and that life can be healthy and whole in a single-parent family or a stepfamily;
   (b) as the parent, believe that you and the children will not only survive, but that you will live happy and healthy lives again; remember, the children draw strength from you;
   (c) successfully negotiate the five previous tasks; if you get stuck along the way, find help from someone who has negotiating and communication skills—a pastor, therapist, or a neutral friend, perhaps one who has been through your experience.

Remember that children usually need both parents in order to feel safe in their world; therefore, it is very important when divorcing that the children stay connected to both parents.

72

Red Light/Green Light:
An Intervention for Families
with Children Who Have Molested

Julie A. Reinlasoder Patten
Linda Wark

Type of Contribution: *Activity*

Objective

Our society has always had great difficulty acknowledging the presence and scope of the sexual abuse of children by adults (Johnson, 1988). It should come as no surprise then, that the recognition of the sexual abuse of children by children has been slow to occur (Johnson, 1990a). The small amount of research which has been conducted has shown that many children who molest have been sexually abused themselves—in most cases by a family member (Johnson, 1989). In addition, virtually all children who molest live in homes with a covert sexualized atmosphere, where physical, sexual, and emotional boundaries are virtually nonexistent (Gil and Johnson, 1993). Since the families of children who molest are characterized by a distinct lack of appropriate boundaries, the primary goal of the present intervention is to aid these children and their families in establishing healthy boundaries between family members.

Rationale for Use

Children who molest are often between four and thirteen years of age (Johnson and Berry, 1989). Approximately 15 to 20 percent of these children are females (Gil and Johnson, 1993). The types of sexual behaviors typically perpetrated by these children include oral copulation, vaginal intercourse, anal intercourse, penetration of another child's anus or vagina with fingers or other objects, genital contact without penetration, and fondling (Gil and Johnson, 1993).

The victims of children who molest are generally verbally coerced or physically forced into participating with the sexual behavior, or they are too young to realize that abuse is occurring (Johnson, 1988). There is usually an age difference of at least two years between the offender and the victim (Gil and Johnson, 1993). The victim is almost always known to the child who molests, and is often a relative or sibling (Friedrich and Luecke, 1988; Johnson, 1988, 1989).

In a study of forty-seven boys who had molested children younger than themselves, Johnson (1988) found that 49 percent of the boys had themselves been sexually abused, and

66 percent had been physically and/or sexually abused. This percentage is considered to be low, as it includes only those victimization experiences acknowledged by the children. A similar study of thirteen girls who had molested other children found that 100 percent of the sample had previously been sexually abused (with 85 percent abused by a family member), and 31 percent had been physically abused (Johnson, 1989). Friedrich and Luecke (1988) studied a sample of fourteen boys and four girls who had molested other children, and found that 75 percent of the boys and 100 percent of the girls had been sexually abused.

As previously mentioned, virtually all children who molest live in homes with a covert sexualized atmosphere (Gil and Johnson, 1993). The behaviors of the parents of these children can range from having pornographic materials readily accessible to the children in the home to sharing intimate details of their own sexual activities with their children. In many cases, it appears that these parents cross the lines of appropriateness not because they are overtly attempting to sexually abuse their children, but because they are unaware of what constitutes appropriate emotional, physical, and generational boundaries (as many of these parents have also had a history of sexual abuse) (Gil and Johnson, 1993).

The issue of boundaries is obviously very important therapeutically for these children and their families. Since the behaviors of children who molest are so closely tied to their family dynamics, family therapy is essential in the treatment of children who molest (Johnson, 1990a). Family therapy must include a focus on the victimization and perpetration issues of the child, as well as on the establishment of appropriate boundaries between the family members.

The "Red Light/Green Light" intervention, based on the childhood game of the same name, is designed primarily for children between the ages of six and thirteen (middle childhood). According to Piaget (as interpreted by Papalia and Olds, 1993), children in middle childhood generally are in the cognitive developmental stage of concrete operations. Children in this stage should be able to apply the concept of boundaries if it is presented in a concrete situation. Therefore, these children will be able to apply the distances and boundaries learned during the game to other concrete, interpersonal situations in their daily life.

Johnson (1990b) suggests that interventions such as the one described below would be beneficial for children who molest because they not only work on boundary issues, but also serve the purpose of teaching children impulse control. Children who molest have problems with impulse control, and interventions and games such as this provide a fun way for children to learn to control their impulses and body movements.

Instructions

"Red Light/Green Light" is based on the children's game in which one child plays the traffic cop and the others become the traffic. The traffic cop stands with his/her back to the other players, and those playing traffic begin the game standing in a line some distance away from the traffic cop player. When the traffic cop yells "green light," the traffic is free to move forward, but when the traffic cop yells "red light," traffic must freeze and remain frozen until "green light" is heard once more. Those playing traffic must remain perfectly still until the traffic cop player says "green light" again. If they even flinch, the traffic players must go back to the starting point and try again. Whoever gets to the traffic cop first is the winner. A large room or an outdoor area is best for this game.

In preparation for this intervention, it is vital that the therapist educate family members about appropriate physical space boundaries, including a discussion of "safe touch" and "unsafe touch," as well as comfortable distances for people in various social situations. The family must understand the characteristics of their current boundaries and their relation to the child's molestation behavior. It is helpful if they also understand the characteristics of healthy boundaries and the necessary presence of these boundaries for reducing the potential for further molestation behavior.

The "Red Light/Green Light" intervention parallels the traditional game in that one person serves as the traffic cop. However, only two people play the game at a time (one is the traffic cop, the other is the traffic, and the other family members look on). In addition, rather than reaching the traffic cop, reaching the "edge" of the traffic cop's boundary is the goal. It is explained to the traffic cop that he/she can yell "red light" and "green light" an unlimited number of times, but when the traffic reaches the traffic cop's physical space boundary, the traffic cop should yell "red light, red light" to signal that the game is over. At this time, the therapist uses a measuring tape to measure the distance between the two people and writes it down. The therapist also encourages the two persons to find a way to remember and measure the distance between them (i.e., by using the length of their arm). Gil and Johnson (1993) recommend using a measuring tape to solidify the issue of boundaries and distance. The observing family members are invited to critique how well the "traffic" respected the boundaries of the "traffic cop."

The therapist should always be vigilant during family therapy sessions for individuals who may be encroaching upon another's physical boundary. In line with the metaphor of traffic cop, if physical boundaries are violated, the family member in the role of cop can yell "traffic ticket!" Gil and Johnson (1993) have developed a useful metaphor that can be used by both the therapist and family members whenever a person's boundaries are being crossed. Anyone who crosses another individual's physical space (or emotional) boundary is a "space invader." Gil and Johnson (1993) suggest that metaphors can be a light, humorous way to let someone know that he/she is not respecting another's boundaries. The therapist encourages the use of such a metaphor at home, so that the idea of healthy boundaries is generalized outside of the therapist's office.

Suggestions for Follow-Up

This intervention can be repeated as many times as necessary so that each family member has a chance to establish boundaries with each other family member. The therapist will keep a record of the distance measurements and can use these (as well as the "space invader" metaphor previously described) to remind family members when boundaries are being crossed. The game can be played again at various times throughout the therapy process to reinforce previously established boundaries.

Success can be determined through observation of the family members' ability to respect each others' boundaries during family therapy sessions and through frank discussions with the family regarding the number of "traffic tickets" or "space invasions" committed outside of the therapy sessions (Gil and Johnson, 1993). Consistent reports of interactions at home should be obtained. While it is necessary to point out times when boundaries are violated, it is even more vital to reward family members for times when boundaries are being respected, especially if these times represent a significant change for family members.

Contraindications

"Red Light/Green Light" is not recommended for use with families in which the perpetrator of the child who molests and the victim are both present prior to both children dealing with their own victimization issues. Likewise, the perpetrator needs to successfully work on the perpetration issues before his/her presence in family therapy would be therapeutic.

Readings and Resources for the Professional

Cunningham, C. and MacFarlane, K. (1991). *When children molest children: Group treatment strategies for young sexual abusers*. Orwell, VT: Safer Society Press.

Gil, E. (1991). *The healing power of play: Working with abused children*. New York: The Guilford Press.

Gil, E. (1994). *Play in family therapy*. New York: The Guilford Press.

MacFarlane, K. and Cunningham, C. (1990). *Steps to healthy touching*. Charlotte, NC: Kidsrights.

Ryan, G. D. and Lane, S. L. (Eds.) (1991). *Juvenile sexual offending: Causes, consequences, and correction*. Lexington, MA: Lexington.

Bibliotherapy Sources for the Client

Gil, E. (1986). *I told my secret*. Rockville, MD: Launch Press.

Gil, E. (1995). *A guide for parents of children who molest* (Second Edition). Rockville, MD: Launch Press.

Gordon, S. (1992). *A better safe than sorry book*. New York: Prometheus.

Hillman, D. and Solek-Tefft, J. (1980). *Spiders and flies*. Lexington, MA: Lexington Press.

McGovern, J. (1985). *Alice doesn't babysit anymore*. Portland, OR: Mcgovern & Mulbacker Publishers.

Satullo, J. A. W., Russell, R., and Bradway, P. A. (1987). *It happens to boys too*. Pittsfield, MA: Rape Crisis Center of the Berkshires Press.

BIBLIOGRAPHY

Becvar, D. S. and Becvar, R. J. (1993). *Family therapy: A systemic integration* (Second Edition). Boston: Allyn and Bacon.

Friedrich, W. and Luecke, W. (1988). Young school age sexually aggressive children. *Professional Psychology: Research and Practice, 19*(2), 155-164.

Gil, E. and Johnson, T. C. (1993). *Sexualized children: Assessment and treatment of sexualized children and children who molest*. Rockville, MD: Launch Press.

Johnson, T. C. (1988). Child perpetrators—Children who molest other children: Preliminary findings. *Child Abuse & Neglect, 12*, 219-229.

Johnson, T. C. (1989). Female child perpetrators: Children who molest other children. *Child Abuse & Neglect, 13*, 571-585.

Johnson, T. C. (1990a). Children who act out sexually. In J. McNamara and B. H. McNamara (Eds.), *Adoption and the sexually abused child* (pp. 63-73). Portland, ME: University of Southern Maine: Human Services Development Institute.

Johnson, T. C. (1990b). Important tools for adoptive parents of children with touching problems. In J. McNamara and B. H. McNamara (Eds.), *Adoption and the sexually abused child* (pp. 75-88). Portland, ME: University of Southern Maine, Human Services Development Institute.

Johnson, T. C. and Berry, C. (1989). Children who molest: A treatment program. *Journal of Interpersonal Violence, 4*, 185-203.

Nichols, M. P. and Schwartz, R. C. (1991). *Family therapy: Concepts and methods* (Second Edition). Boston: Allyn and Bacon.

Papalia, D. E. and Olds, S. W. (1993). *A child's world: Infancy through adolescence* (Sixth Edition). New York: McGraw-Hill, Inc.

73

Awards

Sharon A. Deacon

Type of Contribution: *Handout*

Objective

These handouts can be used at the termination of therapy or when a child has completed a goal in therapy. It is an award given to the child for a job well done, and a reinforcement of praise to continue the good work.

Rationale for Use

When children make changes, they need to be reinforced to know that they are doing a good job. Giving a child an award is a way to show the child that the therapist recognizes the change he/she is making, and that the child should be proud of his/her accomplishment. At termination, the award can be given as a sign of completion and accomplishment.

Instructions

Fill out the award with the child's name and accomplishment. Present the award to the child in a play "ceremony" that highlights the improvements the child has made, and shows the child that he/she is special.

Contraindications

Be careful how the accomplishment is worded. Do not be too specific, as the child may want to display the award without revealing what the therapy was for. More generic wording may be appropriate to order to protect the child's confidentiality.

This Award is presented to

_____

in recognition of

_____

_____

_____

on this day

_____

CONGRATULATIONS!!

_____
Presenter

_____
Director

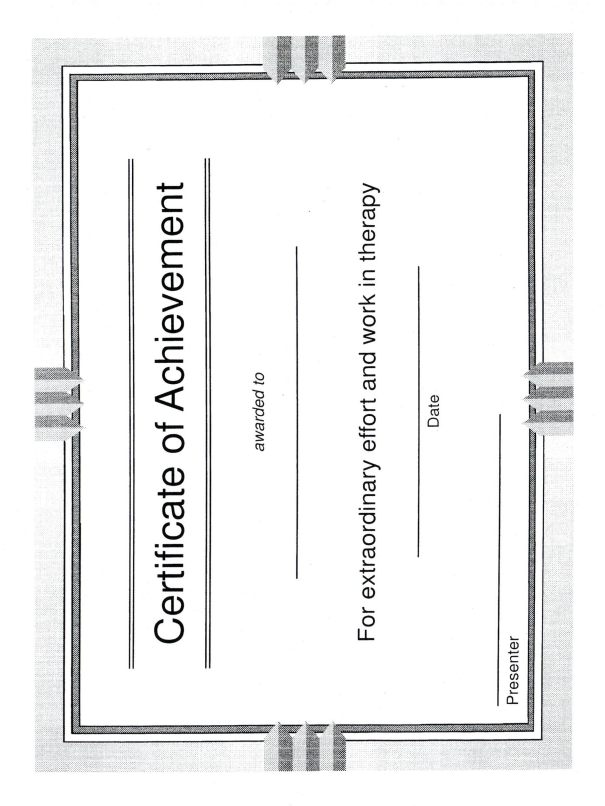

Certificate of Achievement

awarded to

_____

For extraordinary effort and work in therapy

_____
Date

Presenter

Certificate of Achievement

Awarded to

_____

For a job well done!

_____
Date

_____
Presenter

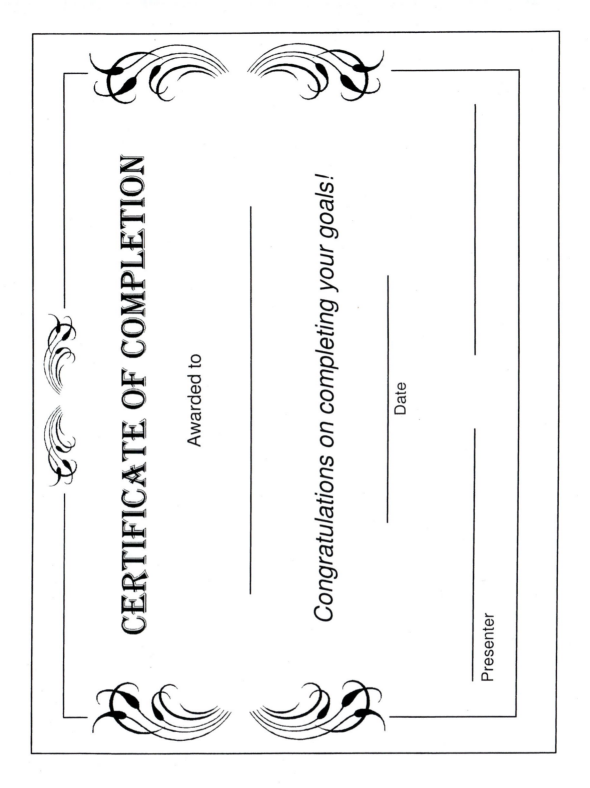

CERTIFICATE OF COMPLETION

Awarded to

_____

Congratulations on completing your goals!

_____
Date

_____
Presenter

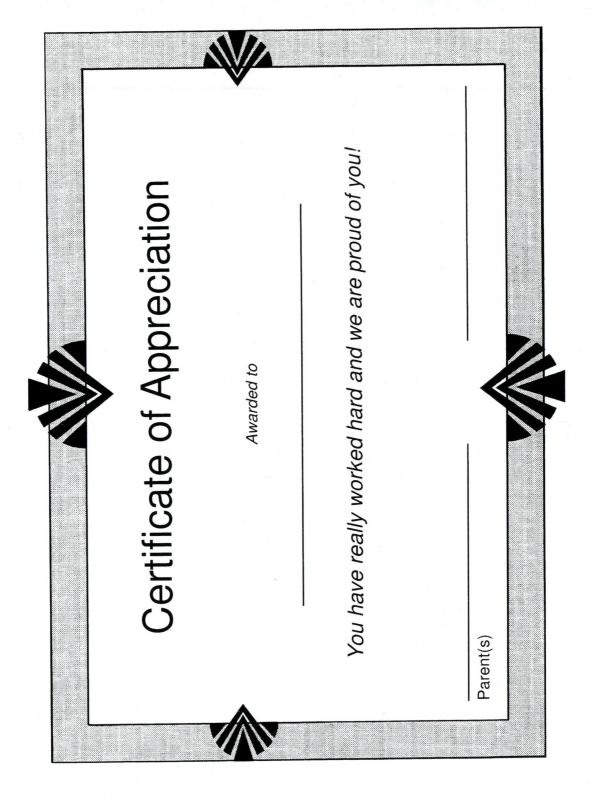

Certificate of Appreciation

Awarded to

_____

You have really worked hard and we are proud of you!

_____
Parent(s)

372

SECTION V:
HOMEWORK, HANDOUTS,
AND ACTIVITIES FOR ADOLESCENTS

74

Teenage Clients' Favorite Music
as an Aid in Therapy

Martin J. Erickson

Type of Contribution: *Activity*

Objective

This is an experiential, dialogue-instigating activity designed to encourage clients to discuss issues that are significant to them, but that they would not or may not be able to discuss directly. The activity can be used to uncover the client's feelings or thoughts, and/or as an assessment tool. This activity is primarily used in individual sessions, but is designed to uncover specific systemic issues, problems, or concerns. This activity could also be incorporated into family or group sessions.

Rationale for Use

Teenagers and young adults are often attracted to popular music. Popular music artists often try to speak of the problems and issues that their fans deal with in their daily lives. They speak directly about the political, philosophical, and relational issues of our society, with which teenagers and young adults can identify. Popular music often takes a very central position in the lives of teenagers. Popular music often has a very significant impact in the family, social, and individual systems of youth. Young people identify with the lyrics, or the general attitude of their favorite songs or artists. Young people may feel that a particular song is talking about the very same thing they are experiencing and/or that they feel or believe. Therefore, by having clients talk about some of their favorite songs, the therapist is afforded particular insight into what issues the clients may be dealing with, what their values are, what they think about their lives, and perhaps what their hopes and desires may be. Teenagers are notorious for complaining that no one understands them or knows what they are going through. This activity can be effective in helping the therapist join with clients, and be more "in their world."

Instructions

The therapist asks the client to pick a few songs that are very meaningful to the him/her; the lyrics of the song should be particularly meaningful to the client, not just the musical aspects of the song. Then the client can bring a recorded copy of each song, and/or a written copy of the lyrics of the songs to the therapy session. The therapist can choose to listen to the songs along with the client and/or read over the lyrics with the client. The therapist can then ask the client any of the following questions:

- What is it about this song that you really like?
- Why is this song particularly meaningful to you?
- What are some similar things in this song that you have (1) experienced or (2) felt?
- What are some ideas, positions, statements, philosophies, etc., in this song that you believe in?
- What ways does this song "speak" to you, or what does it say about who you are, your life, or life in general?

It is hoped that these questions can aid the therapeutic dialogue by helping clients to open up more to the therapist, and talk more about their feelings, thoughts, beliefs, hopes, and ambitions.

The therapist may then choose to address these new issues and new insights from the particular theoretical orientation that they are working from.

Suggestions for Follow-Up

Insight gained from the activity could be a focus of continuing individual or family therapy. The activity could be conducted in the future to observe what kind of changes or progress the client(s) have made.

Contraindications

Some clients will be much more receptive to this activity than others. Some teenagers and young adults simply are more attracted to, and invest more time in popular music than others. As with any intervention, a specific theoretical framework ought to guide the implementation of this intervention.

Readings and Resources for the Therapist

Hansen, C. H. and Hansen, R. D. (1991). Constructing personality and social reality through music: Individual differences among fans of punk and heavy metal music. *Journal of Broadcasting and Electronic Media, 35 (3)*, 335-350.

Singer, S., Levine, M., and Jou, S. (1993). Heavy metal music preference, delinquent friends, social control, and delinquency. *Journal of Research in Crime and Delinquency, 30 (3)*, 317-329.

Trzcinski, J. (1992). Heavy metal kids: Are they dancing with the devil? *Child and Youth Care Forum, 21 (1)*, 7-22.

van Wel, F. (1994). A culture gap between the generations? Social influences on youth cultural style. *International Journal of Adolescence and Youth, 4 (3-4)*, 211-228.

75

"I Am the Expert!"

Stacy Hernandez

Type of Contribution: *Activity*

Objective

This activity is designed to promote conversation regarding feelings. It can also be used as an assessment tool for identifying areas that should be addressed in therapy.

Rationale for Use

This activity is designed for use with clients who answer most questions with "I don't know." It is a fun way to promote conversation about feelings and emotions. This activity is also useful with clients who have trouble expressing their feelings and emotions with their family/partners.

Instructions

Beginning with the nonfeelings cards. Hand one person a card, and tell him/her to be the expert and answer that particular question. The first rule: when a person becomes the expert, he/she can no longer say "I don't know." Some people may say that they have never done the action on the card. In this situation, the therapist should repeat that the clients are the experts, and tell them to explain how they would handle the situation as experts on the subject. If the clients are having trouble, the therapist may want to take a card and model how the exercise is to be done. After one person has answered a question, it is another person's turn. If a blank card is drawn, that person is allowed to make up his/her own question and be the expert to answer it.

When the clients become comfortable with the activity, begin handing out cards that ask about feelings and emotions. The clients' responses to these cards will facilitate conversation amongst the group and/or with the therapist. One final rule is that no one is allowed to refute someone else's response. Remember . . . *he/she is the expert!*

Suggestions for Follow-Up

When the activity is completed, the therapist may want to revisit people's responses and discuss how their methods of doing things have been effective for them. If this activity is used in family or couples therapy, the therapist may want to highlight to the other members how each person displays his/her feelings and emotions. When the case is near termination, it can be fun and constructive to play the game again and evaluate the changes that have taken place.

Contraindications

This activity could be harmful in a crisis situation (e.g., rape, incest, etc.) where feelings and emotions that are kept in are serving a function of protection. In addition, this activity may not be appropriate for young children due to the developmental level of the activity.

Questions for the Expert

How do you plant a tree?	How do you wash the car?
How do you cook hamburgers?	How do you fix a flat tire?
How do you answer the telephone?	How do you clean the kitchen?
How does someone know you are happy?	What do you do when you are frustrated?
How does someone know you trust them?	How do you know when someone loves you?

Questions for the Expert

How do you show your sadness?	What do you do when you get angry?
How do you show affection?	How would you discipline a child who breaks curfew?
How do you maintain privacy in your home?	What do you do when you need affection?
What are the consequences for breaking rules?	How do you display control in your relationship?
How do you solve problems?	How do you have an argument?

Questions for the Expert

How does someone know you are proud of them?	What do you do when you are irritated?
How would someone know that you are stressed?	How do you decide who makes the decisions?
What do you do to relax?	How do you know that you are appreciated?
How do others know you are angry?	What do you do when you are disappointed?
How do you show respect to others?	What do you do when you are afraid?

Questions for the Expert

What do you do when you are lonely?	How do you show that you are grateful?
What do you do to show others you love them?	How do you show you care?

76

I Wish I Had the Cosby Family

Sharon A. Deacon

Type of Contribution: *Activity*

Objective

The purpose of this activity is to help teenagers verbalize how they feel about their families, what they feel is problematic with their families, and how they wish things to be different in their lives. This activity helps adolescents and their therapists to define what problems teenage clients experience in their families, and what means of discipline would be most fair and effective.

Rationale for Use

Adolescents are usually very familiar with sitcoms on television. They know the characters, various plots, and how TV families operate. It is not uncommon for a teenager to wish he/she had one of those "TV families." Teenagers often complain about their families and fantasize about what "cool parents" would be like. They are always comparing their family to others'.

In addition, it can be difficult for adolescents to verbalize exactly what they need and want from their families. They are adequate at verbalizing complaints and problems; however, they usually feel awkward about discussing what *realistic* changes need to be made in their lives. It can be difficult to express needs for attention, time alone with a parent, affection, guidance, or help. Yet, behavioral problems are often the result of a cry for attention, a request for more structure, or some other need the teen has.

Using fictional families as comparisons, teens have an easier time noticing what they like and do not like about families in general, and then transferring those feelings to their own families. Teens are able to clarify how they want to be treated and what changes they are requesting, without feeling awkward. It is easier for a teen to ask to "be more like the Cosbys" than it is to request "more love, more stability, discussions about events in their lives, or affection."

Instructions

This activity is best started in an individual meeting with the adolescent. The therapist can begin a discussion about television shows that are currently broadcasted. It is usually rather easy to engage a teenager in conversation about the television shows he/she likes. This is also a good method for joining.

Next, ask the adolescent what TV family his/her family most resembles. This can be humorous. Give the teen extreme examples such as the Munsters, the Flintstones, or the Urkels (from *Family Matters*). It really does not matter if the teen picks a show the therapist is unfamiliar with, as the teen can then be an "expert" and teach the therapist about that TV family. Once a TV family has been chosen, discuss with the teen how the qualities and interactions of the TV family resemble his/her own family. This is a great opportunity for the adolescent to clarify and verbalize what he/she does and does not like about the family, as well as provide information about his/her perceptions of his/her own family.

Following that discussion, ask the adolescent to choose a TV family that he/she wishes was his/her own family, or a TV family that he/she would most like to be a part of. Ask the teen to discuss what qualities that family has that his/hers does not. How is that family different from the adolescent's own? What is his/her own family missing? Be careful here, as adolescents may choose families with more money, fewer children, or who live somewhere exciting—all things that cannot realistically be changed. Therefore, the therapist may need to guide the teen in choosing a family for its qualities, rather than its context. Discuss what needs the adolescent has that are fulfilled by the TV family, and what needs his/her own family in not fulfilling. What changes is the teen requesting?

Suggestions for Follow-Up

The next step would be to include parents in the discussion about what needs the adolescent has and how the family can work together to see that everyone feels good about the family. The parents and teens can discuss what changes could realistically be made in the family that might make everyone happier.

Contraindications

It is important in staging this intervention that the adolescent be willing to take responsibility for his/her "character's" behavior; in other words, the teen must be willing to accept responsibility for his/her part in the family's problems. The adolescent is not in a place to make demands, but rather in a position to express needs and desires.

If the family's problems are of a more serious nature or the family is in crisis, the family may not yet be ready to discuss the adolescent's concerns. Parents and teenagers must first be willing to listen to each other and be motivated to change their problematic relationships and interactions with one another before any requests can be made. If the family is highly conflictual, other interventions may be more appropriate first.

Readings and Resources for the Professional

Haley, J. (1987). *Problem-solving therapy.* San Francisco, CA: Jossey-Bass Inc.

Bibliotherapy Sources for the Client

Harris, S. O. and Reynolds, E. N. (1990). *When growing up hurts too much.* Lexington, MA: D.C. Heath and Company.

77

Beliefs and Tactics
That Encourage Behavior Problems

Rudy Buckman

Type of Contribution: *Handout/Homework/Activity*

Objective

The objective of this contribution is to help parents recognize and manage the beliefs and tactics commonly used by adolescents with behavior problems diagnosable as oppositional defiant or conduct disorder.

Rationale for Use

Most of the parents and family members dealing with this type of behavior problem come to therapy feeling defeated, powerless, and bewildered by their adolescent's behavior. By externalizing (Durrant, 1984; White and Epston, 1990) the teen's beliefs and tactics, this handout and activity encourages the parents to view the beliefs and tactics as the problem, rather than their adolescent as the problem. This strategy helps parents take a tough stand against the teen's beliefs and tactics, and interrupt destructive interpersonal patterns.

Instructions

Once it is determined through interviews with the family that the adolescent is under the influence of these beliefs and tactics, the parents are asked to meet alone with the therapist. The therapist: (1) compliments the parents on how hard they have worked to help their child and keep their family together; (2) explains that he/she would love to draw up a treatment plan, but needs to know how far the parents are willing to go in helping their child/adolescent; (3) describes paths the parents can choose: (a) the parents do nothing, meaning the child/adolescent will probably get worse, (b) they can send the child to a treatment facility for behavior problems, which may not be financially feasible, and the adolescent will probably return home for them to deal with eventually or, (c) they turn their home into a treatment center knowing the adolescent will fight them every step of the way. If they choose path (c), the therapist offers to help them understand and manage the adolescent's beliefs and tactics by educating them with this handout and coaching them in behavioral interventions. Using the handout, parents are to rank how much influence the four core beliefs and their tactics have on their adolescent. This can be done on a scale from 0 to 10, with 0 meaning no influence and 10 meaning a great deal of influence. These numbers give the family and the therapist a way to evaluate therapeutic progress.

Suggestions for Follow-Up

Once the parents rate the influence of the beliefs and tactics on their family, the therapist can focus on teaching the parents how to manage the beliefs and tactics in future sessions. Sessions usually focus on helping parents recognize beliefs and tactics used by their adolescent to get his/her way, and how negative feelings and negative interactions in the family can encourage a continuation of the inappropriate behavior(s). Once these are identified, the therapist coaches parents in strategies that are effective in dealing with the beliefs and tactics influencing their adolescent. Gradually, behavioral interventions are introduced to the parents, giving them additional tools to aid them in their journey along path (c).

Contraindications

Families that do not seem to have really talked over the paths and/or have not considered how difficult path (c) is do not do as well with this approach.

Readings and Resources for the Professional

Patterson, G. (1975). *Families: Applications of social learning to family life.* Champaign, IL: Research Press.
White, M. and Epston, D. (1990). *Narrative means to therapeutic ends.* New York: Norton.

Bibliotherapy Sources for the Client

Durrant, D. (1989). *Temper taming: An approach to children's temper problems—revisited.* Adelaide, Australia: Dulwich Centre Publications.
Samenow, S. (1989). *Before it's too late.* New York: Random House.

Beliefs and Tactics That Encourage Behavior Problems

A child who exhibits behavior problems requires much love, patience, and compassion. However, parents of these children can feel bewildered and helpless as they talk themselves "blue in the face," only to see their child reject their guidance. Rather than branding themselves as failures and giving up, some courageous parents learn how to combine their love with what at times seem like pretty tough or stern measures.

Parents report that one of the things that is helpful to them is learning which beliefs and tactics encourage the misbehavior of their child. Similar to how a "Life Is Cheap" bumper sticker influences a person to drive recklessly, beliefs can guide or even command a person to behave certain ways. The good news is that just as a bumper sticker can be removed and a new one added, beliefs and tactics can be challenged and new ones can be learned. The following list is not complete, so feel free to add your own discoveries.

1. I Want Life One Way—My Way!

With this belief in the driver's seat of your adolescent's life, he/she begins to feel like a giant bulldozer, and sees rules and those who try to guide him/her as merely obstacles to be bulldozed over. If left unchallenged, this bulldozer driven by "My Way" can eventually convince your child that it is a waste of time to consider the needs, wishes, and desires of others. Consequently, relationships are damaged as others feel used, abused, and defeated by the "my way" approach to life. This belief and its tactics can be tricky too; it can get your adolescent to use tricky charm and politeness to get others to think he/she has learned his/her lesson and that it is safe to lower their guards. However, each time tricky charm and tricky politeness get their way, their influence on your adolescent not only gets stronger, but their twisted desire to turn your adolescent into a devious and false person is nurtured.

Faced with the "My Ways," many parents are coached into giving in to the demands of this belief/tactic. However, each time the "My Ways" feed on the fears of others by getting them to back down, the stronger and more confident they become in training others to get out of their way. Consequently, any peace gained by giving in is temporary, and eventually exacts a very high cost on the family.

The "My Ways" are good at getting adolescents to plead their case with statements such as "you're mean," "you don't love me," and "I don't want to live here any more." As you can see, these statements are cleverly designed to get you to feel sorry for your adolescent, and give in to the "My Ways." Many parents care enough about their adolescent's life, and are willing to learn to stand up to the "My Ways." They do this by learning to say "no," and meaning it and by imposing significant consequences for destructive behavior.

Being firm in challenging the "I want life one way—my way!" lifestyle does not mean being less loving to your child; it certainly does not mean being harsh and/or abusive. In fact, if you are not careful, the "My Way" style of life can train you to see your child as bad, and then you might get caught up in punishing him/her more and more severely. This negative cycle of parent seeing child as bad—parent treating child harshly or abusively—child feeling anger/resentment—child getting back at parent with more misbehavior—parent seeing child as bad and treating him/her harshly or abusively—and so on, only leads to a very unpleasant home life. Also, it becomes very difficult to influence your child if there is not anything positive in your relationship.

2. Excuses, Excuses, Excuses!

To add insult to injury, the twisted thinking of "Excuses, excuses, excuses!" will then try to convince you that it is your fault that the adolescent misbehaves. If you had not grounded her, she wouldn't have had to run away! If this does not work, the "Excuses, excuses, excuses!" do not give up, but will attempt to confuse you and gain sympathy by emphasizing that she "didn't mean to misbehave" or that her actions were justified. For example, "I just meant to give her a little tap!" or "It's her fault I hit her with the bat; she threw the first punch! What did you want me to do, just stand there and take it?" If a child is left in the clutches of the "My Ways" and the twisted thinking of "Excuses, excuses, excuses!" his/her life will not only be destroyed, but he/she will be cheated out of one of the most important things in life. The child will fail to learn compassion for other human beings, never understand how to put him- or herself in the place of another person, nor will the child ever be able to understand the wisdom of "Do unto others as you would have them do unto you."

In each of the previous examples, the excuses were quite convincing, twisting things so that it seems your child is a victim of circumstance. Beware! The way the excuses grow and come to claim your child's life is by others believing them. Once believed, the excuses grow and grow like a virus until they are able to contaminate a whole family and make them all sick.

Parents interested in helping their child fight against the excuses must be aware of two common mistakes: (1) letting the excuses convince you that your child's version of events is accurate; (2) being taken in by the tales of victimization, and not holding your child responsible for his/her behavior. One example is the child claiming she was arrested for shoplifting because she was bored and there was nothing else to do. It is very hard to avoid being taken in by these tales of victimization, but parents must develop the capacity to detach themselves, and to figure out whether their child has been treated unfairly or if the child is using a tactic to avoid responsibility.

3. Why Don't You Trust Me?

This tactic tries to play on parents' sense of fair play and our society's belief that a person is innocent until proven guilty. This tactic knows that most parents want to be trustworthy and want to trust their child; however, it blinds parents to the possibility of asking the question—"How trustworthy does my child *behave*?"

Many parents get caught up in trying to determine if their child is trustworthy when he/she claims to have "found" or "borrowed" certain items. This typically resembles a courtroom scene with statements by witnesses, cross examination of witnesses, and the introduction of evidence to determine the guilt or innocence of the accused. Usually in the ensuing chaos of the trial, this tactic, like a slick lawyer, will turn the tables on the parents with this question, "Don't you trust me?" Now the parents are on trial for abandoning their precious beliefs of fair play and "innocent until proven guilty." This tactic presses the parents—"How could you just toss aside your precious beliefs? What kind of person are you if you doubt your own flesh and blood?"

So how do you handle situations where this tactic has typically gotten you so defensive and confused that you have not held your child responsible for earning your trust? One way is to straightforwardly explain that trust is a two-way street, and rather than giving the child trust, he/she must earn your trust. Since trust has been destroyed between the two of you resulting in a trust rating of zero, you will assume the child is untrustworthy until he/she *proves* he/she can be trusted. In other words he/she is guilty until proven innocent! For example, if he/she claims to have been "given" a compact disc, he/she is assumed to be guilty unless he/she can produce the person's name, address, and phone number that gave the disc. If he/she cannot produce this information or if this information is inaccurate, the disc is assumed to be stolen and removed from his/her possession. This means the child will occasionally be punished for things he/she did not do, but that is a small price to pay for an opportunity to earn your trust.

4. Divide and Conquer!

Whether used by kings and queens, heads of governments, or parents, one of the great tactics of war is to divide and conquer. By dividing parents, this tactic disempowers the parents while empowering the child to get away with more and more. The divide and conquer tactic typically gets one parent to be more sympathetic to the child, while the other parent takes a tougher stance toward the child. As the sympathetic parent goes easier on the child, the tougher parent gets even tougher, which invites the sympathetic parent to go even easier, and so on. The feuding between the parents may become so intense that one parent gives up and withdraws, or both put up a wall of silence about how to handle the misbehavior of their child. In either case, the parents become divided, resulting in their being easier to conquer.

As you can see, the tail is wagging the dog in these situations. The divide and conquer tactic is basically in charge of the family. In order for things to get better in the family, the parents must serve notice that the family will not permit this tactic of divide and conquer to destroy the family. This will require the parents to: (1) recognize the divide and conquer tactic so they do not get caught up in feuding with each other; (2) calmly talk out their differences, presenting a united front to the tactic and the children; (3) help the rest of the family to recognize this tactic and develop ways to conquer the division among them; and (4) give extra time and support to the rest of the children in the family affected by this tactic.

Rewriting Youth Stories:
An Activity with Troubled Youth

Robert A. Bertolino

Type of Contribution: *Activity*

Objective

The following involves a postmodern exploration into the process of working with youth stories. The main purpose is to demonstrate how a *restorying* homework activity can be used to help youth move beyond the existing constraints and complaints that surround their lives. This particular activity can be helpful with youths who have fallen under the influence of truancy, curfew violation, running away, or what may otherwise be referred to as incorrigibility. It can also be of assistance to therapists who have become "stuck" in their work with youths. In order to conceptualize this youth restorying activity, several overarching concepts including *stories, problem saturation, multiple realities,* and *externalizing* the problem will be discussed.

The restorying homework task can be useful in helping youths to rewrite a new story that contradicts the problem narrative. When a new, less oppressive story begins to take the place of the old problem-saturated one, a future with possibilities can become more evident. The youth is not considered the problem; focus is instead placed on how he or she can overcome the problem behavior. As many youths are accustomed to being identified as chronic offenders or problem children, this can be a freeing experience. It is hopeful that given the chance to cocreate and reauthor a more satisfying story, youths can feel empowered to live their lives crime free, and with optimism about the future.

Rationale for Use

From a postmodern perspective (Gergen, 1991, 1994), *stories* are considered a way in which people come to describe lived experience. Stories or narratives can captivate others merely by the way they are communicated. They can take us on journeys that entail adventure, drama, comedy, and sometimes horror, all the while excapsulating the elements of a novel, poem, song, play, or movie. Stories are comprised of past experiences, interactions, and events which lend to the construction of meaning and understanding (Berger and Luckmann, 1966; Anderson and Goolishian, 1988). For any one event, there are no less than two views; hence, there are *multiple realities* (Anderson and Goolishian, 1988; Gergen, 1991, 1994). No one view is superior to another; all are relative to the person and his or her experiences.

Therapy becomes a consideration when the stories people live by have become *problem-saturated* (White and Epston, 1990). That is, the problematic stories adhered to tend to be dominating or impairing to some degree. For youths, problem-saturated stories can involve experiences with family life, drugs/alcohol, school, gangs, friends, other youth, and so on. In some instances, a youth may recognize the need for change with the life he/she has been leading. More often, a parent, family member, teacher, police officer, juvenile officer, judge, or other person's story about the youth leads to therapy. These stories often involve themes such as truancy, running away, curfew violation, fighting, stealing, bad grades, nonaccountability, or a host of others.

Instructions

The role of the therapist is to assist youths in cocreating and reauthoring alternatives—less oppressive stories—while holding each person accountable for his/her actions. To do this, the therapist must first inquire as to how a particular youth has become inhibited or dominated in regard to the problem, hence, the problem-saturated story. In cases where a youth sees no problem, this inquiry can be expanded to involve others such as parents, relatives, juvenile officers, teachers, etc. These individuals can relate how the youth has been tied up by misbehavior, and consequently, define its effects on others. Expanding the system helps to *determine what needs to change.*

A useful way of dialoguing about what needs to change is by *externalizing the problem* (White and Epston, 1990). From this perspective, the person is not seen as the problem, the problem is considered the problem. Thus, the idea is to determine the problem's influence over the youth. Externalizing the problem involves giving it a name, thereby forming a different type of relationship in respect to the youth and the problem. Questions to ask might include:

- *How has Mr. B. Truant come between you and your family?*
- *What kinds of tricks does the Temper Tantrum Monster play on your son that keep him from doing the things he likes?*
- *When has impulsiveness recruited you into something that you later got in trouble for?*

It is important to notice that the language used here is not deterministic. O'Hanlon (1994) stated, "The problem never *causes* or *makes* the family do anything, it only *influences, invites, tells, tries to convince, uses, tricks, tries to recruit,* etc." (p. 26, emphasis in original). Thus, the youth maintains accountability or *personal agency* in relation to his or her actions (White and Epston, 1990).

Externalizing the problem allows information to be gathered by the therapist in respect to how and in what ways the problem has been influential. The information attained helps to define what needs to change with a particular youth in a given situation. In addition, externalization can assist the clinician in understanding how the desired change can be defined in behavioral terms.

Once it has been agreed upon as to what needs to change, it is important to *determine what the change will look like when it happens* (if it has not already). A consideration here is, "If you do not know where you are going, you will probably end up somewhere else." Externalizing questions can also be useful here. For instance, a therapist might ask:

- *What will be different when Johnny is able to stand up to Mr. B. Truant, and is no longer recruited into his school-skipping program?*
- *When Mr. Nonsense is whispering into your son's ear, trying to convince him to fight, how will you know he is not listening anymore?*
- *How will you know when Lisa has got the upper hand with the "runaways?"*

The use of *video description* or *videotalk* (O'Hanlon and Wilk, 1987; Hudson and O'Hanlon, 1991) can also be helpful at this juncture. This involves asking the youth or significant others to define, in visual terms, what things will look like in the future when the youth is doing better. A therapist might inquire, "If we were to videotape Johnny three months down the road, and things were going better, what would we see happening on the videotape when we watched it?" Again, it is important to find out what will be happening behaviorally. That is, in realistic and attainable terms, what the youth will be *doing* (O'Hanlon and Weiner-Davis, 1989). When there is an agreed upon picture of what "better" is, change and the extent of it can be more easily recognized. At this point, the clinician should also explore with the youth or family identifiable *signs*, however small, that may indicate change. A therapist might inquire:

- *What might be a sign that Johnny is turning the corner?*
- *What will indicate to you that change is beginning to occur?*
- *When Kelly starts to get on track, how will you know?*

Once it has been determined what the desired change is and how it will look, the focus can be shifted to deconstructing the dominant, problem-saturated story. During this process of conversation and dialogue, the therapist, as would Sherlock Holmes or Columbo, explores with the youth (and family if possible) occasions when the problem has not been so dominating. An assumption here is that no problem exists all the time. This relates to glimpses, fleeting moments, and other times when the youth has had influence over the problem. These are considered *unique outcomes* (White, 1989) or *exceptions* (de Shazer, 1985, 1988; Freedman and Combs, 1993) which represent an alternative, less oppressive story.

Again, the idea of externalizing questions can be helpful during this process. Listed below are some examples of questions that can help therapists identify unique outcomes and exceptions:

- *When have you been able to stand up to Mr. B. Truant?*
- *When has the Temper Tantrum Monster whispered in your ear, but you didn't listen?*
- *How have you managed to get the upper hand with Impulsivity lurking near?*

The therapist, along with the youth and/or family, is also encouraged to search for competencies, strengths and abilities. Examples include such things as successes in school, ability in sports, music, art, or anything that the youth does well. These contradict the problem story, and can ultimately breathe new life into what may seem to be a difficult situation. The recognition of competencies, strengths, and abilities can also serve as significant building blocks for future endeavors.

To summarize, there are usually three things that have taken place by this point:

1. *It is understood how the "problem" has had influence over the youth, and how it has interfered with the life of youth and/or others.*
2. *It is understood, in behavioral terms, what the desired change may look like, and what kinds of actions might be signs or indicators that change has started.*
3. *Evidence relating to when the youth has had influence over the problem has been identified, and the evocation of exceptions, unique outcomes, competencies, strengths, and abilities has occurred. This evidence contradicts the dominant, problem-saturated story, and represents the evolvement of a new, less oppressive narrative.*

Most of the time, to simply know what needs to change is not enough. Saleeby (1994) stated that people should be encouraged to "begin to create a vision about what might be and to take steps to achieve it" (p. 357). Thus, the next step is to get youths *to take action* and *state their case*. Usually, the youth is asked something such as:

> *Down the road, others may be curious as to how you managed to get the upper hand with . . . (fill in the blank). I am wondering . . . sometimes kids or teenagers have scrap books, diaries, or other ways of keeping track of their accomplishments. I am curious as to how you will be keeping track of your struggle with . . . (fill in the blank). What are some ideas that might work for you?*

The youth is then asked to go home and collect evidence, data, or any information that supports his/her cause. This can be in the form of grades, completed assignments, teacher progress reports, pay stubs from a job, parental notes identifying improved behavior, juvenile officer reports, and so on. Initially, "hints" of change may be more of the norm. These tend to be smaller bits of evidence that are signs or part of a more significant future change (e.g., passing a test, not running away that week, etc.).

In addition, the youth is also asked to bring in a way of storing this information, and documenting the change. Some choose traditional enclosures, such as scrapbooks. Others may be more creative and design posters or put the evidence together in the form of a chart, diary, journal or book. For many youths, it is an opportunity to be artistic or inventive.

These collections can be an interesting forum for youths to display to a larger audience how some adversity in their past was overcome. For example, good news about youths (e.g., honor roll, sports successes, academic achievements, community efforts, etc.) appears in newspapers and other mediums every day. It is a means of spreading news of accomplishments. Similarly, for youth with new stories, the sharing of it with other audiences can be a way of *historicizing* the change.

Suggestions for Follow-Up

As the evidence begins to mount, in subsequent sessions and follow-up, the youth is encouraged to consider how his/her *self-story* has changed, and how others are perceiving his or her change. Questions might include:

- *What have others noticed that is different about you?*
- *How have others responded to your changes?*
- *Who has been most surprised?*
- *What is that like for you knowing that others' stories about you may be changing?*
- *How would you describe the new story that is happening with you?*

Many youths accept the challenge to "prove" that the problem behavior can be defeated. At the same time, some have the desire to show others what they are *really* about. Thus, a future task such as the youth "going public" with his or her new story can be helpful. This can occur in the form of talking with other youths about how the problem was defeated, public speaking engagements to encourage people to stand up to oppressive behaviors, or by simply sharing the experience with another audience. He or she will also have the documentation of their experience with the problem to share with others. This resource containing the youth's accomplishments can be an excellent guide for the future.

As it is a common ritual for youth to receive awards identifying accomplishments, youths may be given a certificate in recognition of escaping their problematic behavior (White and Epston, 1990). This documented evidence can serve as a reminder to the youth that things *can* be different. In turn, this difference may represent a new story as a symbol for the future—a future with possibilities.

Contraindications

As previously mentioned, externalization of the problem does not remove personal agency. Therefore, it is important for youths to be held accountable for their actions and behaviors. In addition, it is up to the therapist to use language that promotes responsibility. This also concerns the notion of multiple realities. Although it is important to respect a client's worldview, therapists must be aware of those that may be harmful to the client or others. This can be of particular concern when working with youths, as even though a situation may have serious implications, the choice may be to ignore the potential *physical realities*, such as incarceration, residential placement, injury, or in certain instances, the risk of death. Finally, some youths may have difficulty with the language associated with externalization. If this is the case, the activity can still be helpful, but without the use of externalization.

Readings and Resources for the Professional

Freedman, J. and Combs, G. (1996). *Narrative therapy: The social construction of preferred realities.* New York: Norton.

Friedman, S. (Ed.). (1993). *The new language of change: Constructive collaboration in psychotherapy.* New York: Guilford.

Hoyt, M. (Ed.). (1994). *Constructive therapies.* New York: Guilford.

Hoyt, M. (Ed.). (1996). *Constructive therapies 2.* New York: Guilford.

Metcalf, L. (1995). *Counseling toward solutions: A practical solution-focused program for working with students, teachers, and parents.* New York: Simon & Schuster.

O'Hanlon, B. and Beadle, S. (1994). *A field guide to possibility land: Possibility therapy methods.* Possibility Press: Omaha, NE.

Parry, A. and Doan, R. E. (1994). *Story re-visions: Narrative therapy in the postmodern world.* New York: Guilford.

Selekman, M. D. (1993). *Pathways to change: Brief therapy solutions with difficult adolescents.* New York: Guilford.

White, M. (1995). *Re-authoring lives: Interviews and essays.* Adelaide, Australia: Dulwich Centre Publications.

REFERENCES

Anderson, H. and Goolishian, H. (1988). Human systems as linguistic systems: Preliminary and evolving ideas about the implications for clinical theory. *Family Process, 27,* 371-393.

Berger, P. L. and Luckmann, T. (1966). *The social construction of reality: A treatise in the sociology of knowledge.* New York: Anchor Books.

deShazer, S. (1985). *Keys to solution in brief therapy.* New York: Norton.

deShazer, S. (1988). *Clues: Investigating solutions in brief therapy.* New York: Norton.

Freedman, J. and Combs, G. (1993). Invitations to new stories: Using questions to explore alternative possibilities. In S. Gilligan and R. Price (Eds.), *Therapeutic conversations* (pp. 291-308). New York: Norton.

Gergen, K. J. (1991). *The saturated self: Dilemmas of identity in contemporary life.* New York: Basic Books.

Gergen, K. J. (1994). *Realities and relationships: Soundings in social construction.* Cambridge, MA: Harvard University Press.

Hudson, P. O. and O'Hanlon, W. H. (1991). *Rewriting love stories: Brief marital therapy.* New York: Norton.

O'Hanlon, B. (1994). The third wave. *Family Therapy Networker, 18,* November/December, 18-26, 28-29.

O'Hanlon, B. and Wilk, J. (1987). *Shifting contexts: The generation of effective psychotherapy.* New York: Guilford.

O'Hanlon, W. H. and Weiner-Davis, M. (1989). *In search of solutions: A new direction in psychotherapy.* New York: Norton.

Saleeby, D. (1994). Culture, theory, and narrative: The intersection of meanings in practice. *Social Work, 39,* 351-359.

White, M. (1989). The process of questioning: A therapy of literary merit? In M. White (Ed.), *Selected papers* (pp. 37-46). Adelaide: Dulwich Centre Publications.

White, M. and Epston, D. (1990). *Narrative means to therapeutic ends.* New York: Norton.

My Evidence Log

Name: _____

Week of: _____

 1.

 2.

 3.

 4.

5.

Official

Letter of Evidence

Type of Evidence Reviewed:

_____

_____

_____

_____

_____

Dated: _____

Signed: _____

Certificate of Change

This certificate is awarded to: _____

for success at standing up to and opposing juvenile delinquency,

and getting his/her life back

Dated: _____

Signed: _____

79

Soap Talk

Lorna L. Hecker

Type of Contribution: *Activity*

Objective

The objective of this activity is to work with adolescent clients in "their world" by relating to them through the soap opera stars they admire.

Rationale for Use

Adolescents often watch soap operas. With the advent of the VCR, many female adolescents (and some male adolescents) are able to watch their "daily soaps" after school.

Instructions

The therapist must be, or make him- or herself familiar with, the adolescent's favorite soap opera. The therapist then uses the client's favorite same-sex soap opera character as an access point to talk about the client's life, including topics such as love relationships, sexual behavior, pregnancy and child rearing, values, relationships with parents, dating, and so on. The guiding questions below allow the therapist to use the soap opera star's life as a metaphor for the client's.

For example, a female client who has been sexually promiscuous, been involved in several romantic relationships, has a stormy relationship with her parent(s), and is very flagrant in her sexuality may have as her favorite soap opera character, Erica Kane, of *All My Children*. The therapist then queries the client about Erica, her views on Erica's life, the parts of Erica she really likes. The therapist can liken the client to the soap opera character in a supportive and complimentary way. The therapist can also ask the client about her views on Erica's romantic relationships with men (for example, Dimitri, Jonathan, Jack, Travis, Mike, Tom, etc.). She can query the client on Erica's relationship with her daughter. As the therapist engages the adolescent in a fun and lively discussion about her favorite character, the "Hollywood-esque" sides of Erica can be discussed, and the therapist can then query the client if she believes there are any downsides to Erica's behavior. Some examples include:

- What do you think are the pros and cons of Erica's many relationships with men? What do you think she gets from her relationship with Dimitri? Would you like that type of relationship? Why or why not?

- What did you think about Erica's affair with Jonathan?
- What do you think about Erica's many scrapes with the law?
- What do you think about the way Erica handles her sexual relationships? What do you like and dislike about her sexuality?
- How do you think Erica feels about herself as a woman?
- Do you think Erica practices safe sex? Why or why not?
- What type of relationship do you think Erica had with her mother? Was it the type of relationship you would have liked to have had?
- Do you think Erica is a good mother? Would you want to have her as a mother?
- Do you think Erica has any regrets in how she has lived her life?
- Why doesn't Erica ever mention her father?

This can be a completely lively, fun, and useful exercise with adolescents. Adolescents are often reluctant to talk about themselves, but can relate easily regarding their favorite soap character. It is a nonthreatening way for the therapist to assess the client's views, as well as to begin to intervene on a cognitive level with a client regarding his or her maladaptive behaviors. Unfortunately, soap opera characters often are great models for maladaptive behaviors!

Suggestions for Follow-Up

As events change in the client's life, the therapist can continue to integrate the soap opera character as a way to talk about the client. Questions such as "How do you think Erica would handle your situation? Would her actions be helpful or harmful to her?" may be asked. In addition, as the soap changes, new situations can be brought to therapy for discussions as they relate to the client.

Contraindications

There are none. This activity could be adapted for use with any television show, though soap operas are ripe with issues that adolescents face on a daily basis.

SECTION VI:
THERAPIST HELPERS

80

Assessing Client Risk of Violence

Lorna L. Hecker

Type of Contribution: *Activity*

Objective

The objective of this intervention is to facilitate therapist management of the risk of client violence. The attached assessment device and "no violence contract" can help therapists manage potentially violent clients.

Rationale for Use

Often, therapists have little information on a client's history of violence. When therapists ascertain that a client may potentially be violent, specific assessment procedures should be implemented to ensure that the risk has been managed as effectively and safely as possible. It is important that violence be addressed both to decrease the risk of violence, as well as to decrease therapist liability in potentially litigious issues such as those where injury or death could occur. When legal issues concerning duty to warn arise, therapists are advised to access legal counsel to further manage liability and risk when dealing with violent clients. This assessment does not replace legal advice when faced with complicated client issues.

Instructions

The "Violence Risk Assessment" is a tool for therapists to assess the potential for violence with clients. It can also be used in domestic violence situations. Therapists should complete the assessment, and then be sure that each risk marker has been addressed with a therapeutic plan. If therapists believe that a client is not capable or willing to carry out the therapeutic plan to manage the violence, outside authorities will likely need to be called in. In addition, a "No Violence Contract" can be utilized as part of a therapeutic plan. Therapists who deal with potentially violent clients should also take precautions in and before sessions, such as the following:

- Have a security plan in place (e.g., alert security guards of potential violence, have a route of escape, or an emergency alert button in your office; always think in terms of prevention of violence whenever possible).
- Learn basic self-defense.
- Alert others in your office to potential crises.

- Keep protective devices on your person (e.g., pepper spray, a body alarm).
- Stay calm with clients.
- Maintain a safe distance from clients.
- Never stop a potentially violent client from leaving the therapy room.
- Help the client to relax; do not further agitate an angry client.
- Avoid making demands on potentially violent clients.
- Do not point fingers or use threatening body language.
- Sit closest to the door, but do not block the door.
- Do not leave potential weapons (e.g., scissors, letter openers) out on your desk.
- Learn which of your client's hands is dominant, and keep to their weaker side.

Suggestions for Follow-Up

After working with a potentially violent client to secure a nonviolence treatment plan, the therapist should:

(a) Obtain commitment to the plan (be sure each step of the plan is something the client is willing and able to perform).
(b) Help the client implement the plan. For example, if the client needs time-out procedures in place, practice those procedures in session.
(c) Follow-up with the client. The more urgent the situation is, the sooner follow-up should occur to be sure that the client was able to implement the plan. With less urgent situations, the therapist may use the beginning of subsequent sessions to evaluate and refine the treatment plan.

Contraindications

In emergency situations, the "Violence Risk Assessment" is not appropriate. More immediate measures (e.g., hospitalization, notifying authorities, etc.) may need to be implemented. Also, when utilizing a "No Violence Contract," the contract is not legally binding. It is a good faith contract. If the therapist has reason to believe that the client cannot or will not implement the plan, other measures of intervention should be used.

Readings and Resources for the Professional

McCue, M. L. (1995). *Domestic violence: A reference handbook*. Santa Barbara, CA: ABC-CLIO.
Shupe, A. D. (1987). *Violent men, violent couples: The dynamics of domestic violence*. Lexington, MA: Lexington Books.

Bibliotherapy Sources for the Client

Fein, M. L. (1993). *I. A. M.: A common sense guide to coping with anger*. Westport, CT: Praeger.

Violence Risk Assessment

Case #: _____ Name of Client: _____

	YES	NO
Assessment Question #1: Has the client had violent thoughts in the past? If the client answers "Yes," what was the nature of the violent thoughts? Describe below.	YES	NO
Risk Marker #1: Does the client have present violent thoughts? If client answers "Yes," what is the nature of the violent thoughts? Describe below.	YES	NO
Assessment Question #2: Has the client acted in a violent manner in the past? If client answers "Yes," what was the nature of the violence and when did it occur? Describe below.	YES	NO
Assessment Question #3: Has the client ever been arrested for violent acts in the past? If client answers "Yes," what was the arrest for? Describe below.	YES	NO
Assessment Question #4: Has the client made any threats of violence in the past? If client answers "Yes," describe below.	YES	NO
Risk Marker #2: Is the client presently making any threats of violence? If client is making threats, describe the threat below.	YES	NO
Risk Marker #3: Does the client have a specific plan for violence? If client answers "Yes," describe below.	YES	NO

Risk Marker #4: Does the client have a weapon available? If client answers "Yes," describe below:	YES	NO
Risk Marker #5: Is there a foreseeable victim of the threat? If client answers "Yes," name intended victim(s):	YES	NO
Assessment Question #5: Is there a history of violence in the client's family? If clients answers "Yes," what was the nature of the violence? Describe below:	YES	NO
Assessment Question #6: Is there anyone who can act as a support person for the client? If client answers "Yes," list the person or persons below:	YES	NO

Note: If client answered "Yes" to Risk Marker Questions 2, 3, and 5, it is probable that you have a duty to warn an intended victim, contact authorities, or to hospitalize your client; seek immediate supervisory or legal counsel.

Address how each risk marker that client answered "Yes" to above has been managed.

Describe the therapeutic plan implemented to address potential violence.

NO VIOLENCE CONTRACT

I pledge never to allow my anger to reach the point that I forcefully touch another person, no matter how right or justified I feel I am.

I pledge to use the following tactics or procedures I have discussed with my therapist in order to avoid any potential for violence or harm to others.

In the event that I feel like I may hurt someone, I promise to:

1._____

_____

or

2._____

_____

or

3._____

_____.

_____   _____
Client Signature   Date

_____   _____
Witness Signature   Date

Case #_____

81

Assessing Client Risk of Suicide

Lorna L. Hecker

Type of Contribution: *Activity*

Objective

The objective of this intervention is to facilitate therapist management of the risk of client suicide. The attached assessment device and "No Harm Contract" can help therapists manage potentially suicidal clients.

Rationale for Use

When therapists ascertain that a client may potentially be suicidal, specific assessment procedures should be implemented to ensure that the risk has been managed as effectively and safely as possible. It is recommended that *all levels of suicide risk be thoroughly assessed;* it is always preferable to err on the side of caution when dealing with suicidal ideation. This assessment is designed to help the therapist ask questions to learn more about the suicide potential of a particular client. This assessment does not replace legal advice or good therapy skills when faced with complicated client issues.

Instructions

The "Suicide Risk Assessment" is a tool for therapists to assess the potential of client suicide. Therapists should complete the assessment, ensuring that each risk marker has been addressed with a therapeutic plan. If the therapist believes that a client is not capable of or willing to carry out the therapeutic plan to manage his or her suicidal thoughts, hospitalization or contacting outside authorities may need to occur prior to the client leaving the therapist's office. In addition, a "No Harm Contract" can be utilized as part of a therapeutic plan. Therapists who deal with potentially suicidal clients should look for warning signals from clients including, but not limited to, one or more of the following:

- depression
- sudden uplift in mood (while some suicidal clients are depressed, a sudden change in mood may indicate that they now have the energy to carry out the plan, and feel relieved at having made the decision to commit suicide)
- giving away possessions
- vague to clear threats of suicide (These may range from "I can't take it anymore" or "I don't care," to clearer threats, such as "I think about ending it all.")

- intense anger or despair
- feelings of hopelessnes; not being able to see any answer to their problems

Suggestions for Follow-Up

After working with a potentially suicidal client to secure a treatment plan which manages the threat of suicide, the therapist should:

(a) Obtain commitment to the plan. (Be sure each step of the plan is something the client is willing and able to perform.)

(b) Help the client implement the plan. For example, if the client has agreed to call suicide hotlines if feeling suicidal, the therapist should provide the client with hotline phone numbers so they are readily accessible. These numbers should be checked for accuracy prior to being given to a client, as suicide hotlines can be short-lived due to funding problems. A disconnected number can cause a crisis with these types of clients.

(c) Follow-up with the client. The more urgent the situation is, the sooner follow-up should occur to be sure that the client was able to implement the plan. With less urgent situations, the therapist may use the beginning of subsequent sessions to evaluate and refine the treatment plan.

Contraindications

In emergency situations, the "Suicide Risk Assessment" alone is not appropriate. More immediate measures (e.g., hospitalization, notifying authorities, etc.) may need to be implemented. Also, when utilizing a "No Harm Contract," the contract is not legally binding. It is a good faith contract. If the therapist has reason to believe that the client cannot or will not implement the plan, other measures of intervention should be utilized.

Readings and Resources for the Professional

Ackerman, D. (1997). *A slender thread*. New York: Random House.
Beckman, E. E. and Leber, W. R. (1995). *Handbook of depression*. New York: Guilford Press.
Chiles, J. and Strosah, K. (1995). *The suicidal patient: Priniciples of assessment, treatment, and case management*. Washington, DC: American Psychiatric Press.

Bibliotherapy Sources for the Client

Hauck, P. A. (1973). *Overcoming depression*. Philadelphia: Westminster Press.
Hazleton, L. (1984). *The right to feeling bad: Coming to terms with normal depression*. Garden City, NY: Doubleday.

Suicide Risk Assessment

Case #: _____ Name of Client: _____

	YES	NO
Assessment Question #1: Has the client had suicidal thoughts in the past? If the client answers "Yes," what was the nature of the suicidal thoughts? Describe below.	YES	NO
Risk Marker #1: Does the client presently have suicidal thoughts? If client answers "Yes," what is the nature of the suicidal thoughts? Describe below.	YES	NO
Assessment Question #2: Has the client attempted suicide in the past? If client answers "Yes," what was the nature of the attempt, and when did it occur? Describe below.	YES	NO
Assessment Question #3: Has the client ever been hospitalized for suicidal thoughts/acts in the past? If client answers "Yes," what was the precipitating event for the hospitalization? Describe below.	YES	NO
Assessment Question #4: Has the client made any suicidal threats in the past? If client answers "Yes," describe below.	YES	NO
Risk Marker #2: Is the client presently making any threats of suicide? If client is making threats, describe below.	YES	NO
Risk Marker #3: Does the client have a specific plan for suicide? If client answers "Yes," describe below.	YES	NO

Risk Marker #4: Does the client have the means of suicide described in Risk Marker #3 available to him/her? If client answers "Yes," describe below.	YES	NO
Risk Marker #5: Does the client live alone? If client answers "yes," who can we list as sources of support we can call in case of an emergency?	YES	NO
Assessment Question #5: Is there a history of suicide threats, attempts, or completed suicide in the client's family? If client answers "Yes," what was the nature of the threats, attempts, or action taken? Describe below.	YES	NO
Assessment Question #6: Is the client on any psychotropic medication?	YES	NO
Has there been a recent change in the medication?	YES	NO
Who administers the medication?		
Is the client willing to sign a release form for you to speak with the administrator of the medication?	YES	NO
Assessment Question #7: Is there anyone who can act as a support person for the client? If so, list the person(s) below:	YES	NO
Is the client willing to sign a release form so the therapist may enlist the support person(s) as aid(s) for the prevention of suicide?	YES	NO

Note: If client answered "Yes" to Risk Marker Questions 2, 3, and 4, you must take action to protect your client from suicide. This may include notifying authorities or hospitalizing your client; seek immediate supervisory counsel.

Address how each risk marker that client answered "Yes" to above has been managed.

Describe the therapeutic plan implemented to address potential violence.

NO HARM CONTRACT

I agree that I will not do anything that would cause harm to myself or anyone else, for the following length of time: _____.

I realize that I am responsible for my own actions, and that if I feel my life is becoming too difficult, I agree to do one or more of the following actions so that there is no harm to myself or others:

1._____

_____

or

2._____

_____

or

3._____

_____,

or I will go to a hospital emergency room.

_____   _____
Client Signature   Date

_____   _____
Witness Signature   Date

Case #_____

82

Client Assessment and Treatment Planning

Lorna L. Hecker

Type of Contribution: *Handout/Activity*

Objective

The purpose of this handout is to guide the therapist in helping individuals, couples, or families verbalize goals that are both attainable and measurable. Often when clients are asked what their goals are for therapy, they are unable to formulate clear reasons for being in therapy. The attached handout helps clients formulate goals, and asks clients to rate their goal attainment both at the beginning of therapy, and again at the end of therapy. The goal attainment scaling can also be used on a weekly basis in therapy as a way for the therapist to track client progress. In addition, the form and intervention are formulated to help therapists who wish to practice in solution-focused terms (deShazer, 1988, 1991). While the form does not have to be used from this theoretical orientation, goals that are formed in terms of what the client(s) wants to see happen, instead of what they do not want to have happen, can be more easily turned into treatment interventions and assignments. Clients often have an easier time of doing *more* of certain nonproblematic behaviors than doing *less* of certain problematic behaviors.

Rationale for Use

If you do not have a road map, you will not know where you are going. In therapy, both therapists and clients need to be guided by goals in order to ensure treatment efficacy. Often, simply formulating goals with clients can be therapeutic. The attached handout is for therapists to use with clients to help assess goals and track the progress of client goals. Scaling of goals is utilized so that progress can be measured. For therapists working with managed care or insurance companies, the scaling of goals can also be tangible proof of client progress, thereby increasing therapists' credibility with these outside sources.

Instructions

Step 1. Problem List Assessment

Ask the client(s) to state what the most important problem is for which they are coming to therapy. The therapist should help put the problem in behavioral terms, e.g., "We would like to fight less at home."

Assess whether the problem has become worse, remained the same, or become better since calling for services. Often, problems lessen between the time clients call for therapy and end up in the therapist's office. To work from a solution-focused framework (deShazer, 1985, 1991), the therapist may then find out what specific actions the client(s) took to make things better. If client(s) report that the situation has not changed, the therapist may inquire as to how the client(s) kept things from becoming worse. If client(s) respond that their situation is worse, the therapist may inquire how they kept their problem from becoming disastrous (e.g., "How is it you were still able to get to my office today, despite this crisis?").

Step 2. Treatment Plan

By the end of the third client session (or before), the therapist should be able to help the family attain a treatment plan with specific goals. It is suggested that these goals be in solution-focused terms that help the family focus on what they should be doing *instead* of the problem behaviors. For example, the family which would like to fight less might state that they would like to "have more peaceful meals together." The therapists then asks each family member to rate, on a scale of one to ten, where he/she believes the family is in attaining the goal *now*. The therapist may also query family members (or the couple or individual) where they would *like to be* on the scale. When there is more than one client, scores may be added together and averaged for a couple or family score for assessment and treatment purposes.

The therapist can then intervene with the client(s) by finding out specifically what needs to happen in order for the client(s) to meet his/her/their goals. These tasks can then become subgoals which can be monitored on a weekly basis (and may also be scaled). Once goals are established, the client(s) takes part in the treatment plan by reviewing the goals, and signing the agreement to the treatment goals. Signing the agreement can help give the client(s) more commitment to the process of therapy. It is also provides good case management for therapists.

Suggestions for Follow-Up

Therapists can check in each week on the goals or subgoals and ask the client(s) to scale his/her/their progress on each of the goals. In solution-focused modality, therapists may also continue to explore exceptions to problem behavior(s) and amplify changes the client(s) makes. Again, questions can be formulated in the following solution-focused (deShazer, 1988, 1991) manner:

- If the client(s) went up on the scale, the therapist may respond:
  "Wow, that's really great! Tell me specifically what you did this week to make the score go up."
- If the client(s) stayed the same on the scale, the therapist may respond:
  "That's interesting! Tell me what you did to keep from going down on the scale."
- If the client(s) states their score is worse on the scale, the therapist may respond:
  "You know, a lot of people in your position would have given up. What kept you going through the hard times of this week?" Or:
  "With the stress of this week, what kept you from going all the way down to a '1' on the scale, instead of a '3'?"

Contraindications

There are times when scaling of goals may be contraindicated. For example, grief or loss issues may supersede the need for goal attainment scaling. At times, people simply need to vent their loss or grief in order to be productive in therapy. Other times, people may come in with vague goals, or none at all, complaining of generic malaise. With these clients, while goals are important, it may serve the client better for the therapist to have several sessions to evaluate the client, with the initial goal being "to explore and refine my goals for therapy."

Readings and Resources for the Professional

deShazer, S. (1988). *Clues: Investigating solutions in brief therapy:* New York: Norton.
deShazer, S. (1991). *Putting difference to work.* New York: Norton.
deShazer, S. (1994). *Words were originally magic.* New York: Norton.
deShazer, S., Berg, I. K., Lipchik, E., Nunnally, E., Molnar, A., Gingerich, W., and Weiner-Davis, M. (1986). *Brief therapy: Focused solution development, Family Process, 25,* 207-222.

REFERENCES

deShazer, S. (1985). *Keys to solution in brief therapy.* New York: Norton.
deShazer, S. (1988). *Clues: Investigating solutions in brief therapy:* New York: Norton.
deShazer, S. (1991). *Putting difference to work.* New York: Norton.

CLIENT ASSESSMENT AND TREATMENT PLAN

Client Name(s): _____

Case #: _____   Date: _____

SECTION I: Problem List

The client(s) is seeking (circle):   Individual Therapy   Couple Therapy   Family Therapy

1. What does/do the client(s) report as the most important problem for which they are seeking therapy? (Describe clearly in behavioral terms):

2. Since the client(s) called for therapy services, this problem has become (circle):

much worse   somewhat worse   same   somewhat better   much better

SECTION II: Treatment Plan (to be filled out by therapist)

Goals agreed upon by therapist and family (couple or individual):
(outline specific, behavioral goals, in solution-focused terms—**have clients discuss what they would like to see happen INSTEAD of the problem**) Example of goal: "We would like to talk more together."

Goal #1: _____

_____

On a scale of 1 to 10, with 1 being "not at all" and 10 being "all the time," where are the clients presently on attaining their goal?

Pretest for Goal #1: Week #: _____   Date: _____

Perspective of: First name: _____ Age: _____
1   2   3   4   5   6   7   8   9   10

Perspective of: First name: _____ Age: _____
1   2   3   4   5   6   7   8   9   10

Perspective of: First name: _____ Age: _____
1   2   3   4   5   6   7   8   9   10

Perspective of: First name: _____ Age: _____
1   2   3   4   5   6   7   8   9   10

Score (add all family members' numbers together): _____

Posttest for Goal #1: Week #: _____ Date: _____

Perspective of: First name: _____ Age: _____
1   2   3   4   5   6   7   8   9   10

Perspective of: First name: _____ Age: _____
1   2   3   4   5   6   7   8   9   10

Perspective of: First name: _____ Age: _____
1   2   3   4   5   6   7   8   9   10

Perspective of: First name: _____ Age: _____
1   2   3   4   5   6   7   8   9   10

Score (Add all family members' numbers together): _____

Goal #2: _____

_____

On a scale of 1 to 10, with 1 being "not at all" and 10 being "all the time," where are the clients presently on attaining their goal?

Pretest for Goal #2: Week #: _____ Date: _____

Perspective of: First name: _____ Age: _____
1   2   3   4   5   6   7   8   9   10

Perspective of: First name: _____ Age: _____
1   2   3   4   5   6   7   8   9   10

Perspective of: First name: _____ Age: _____
1   2   3   4   5   6   7   8   9   10

Perspective of: First name: _____ Age: _____
1   2   3   4   5   6   7   8   9   10

Score (Add all family members' numbers together): _____

Posttest for Goal #2: Week #: _____ Date: _____

Perspective of: First name: _____ Age: _____
1   2   3   4   5   6   7   8   9   10

Perspective of: First name: _____ Age: _____
1   2   3   4   5   6   7   8   9   10

Perspective of: First name: _____ Age: _____
1   2   3   4   5   6   7   8   9   10

Perspective of: First name: _____ Age: _____
1   2   3   4   5   6   7   8   9   10

Score (add all family members' numbers together): _____

Goal #3: _____

_____

On a scale of 1 to 10, with 1 being "not at all" and 10 being "all the time," where are the clients presently on attaining their goal?

Pretest for Goal #3: Week #: _____ Date: _____

Perspective of: First name: _____ Age: _____
1   2   3   4   5   6   7   8   9   10

Perspective of: First name: _____ Age: _____
1   2   3   4   5   6   7   8   9   10

Perspective of: First name: _____ Age: _____
1   2   3   4   5   6   7   8   9   10

Perspective of: First name: _____ Age: _____
1   2   3   4   5   6   7   8   9   10

Score (add all family members' numbers together): _____

Posttest for Goal #3: Week #: _____ Date: _____

Perspective of: First name: _____ Age: _____
1   2   3   4   5   6   7   8   9   10

Perspective of: First name: _____ Age: _____
1   2   3   4   5   6   7   8   9   10

Perspective of: First name: _____ Age: _____
1   2   3   4   5   6   7   8   9   10

Perspective of: First name: _____ Age: _____
1   2   3   4   5   6   7   8   9   10

Score (add all family members' numbers together): _____

Signatures of family members (or individual or couple) agreeing to treatment goals listed above:

⇒ _____

⇒ _____

⇒ _____

⇒ _____

⇒ _____

83

Use of Disclosure Statements in Practice

Lorna L. Hecker

Type of Contribution: *Handout/Activity*

Objective

The purpose of using disclosure statements in therapy is to educate clients so that they may give informed consent to the therapeutic process. The disclosure statement: (1) helps the therapist maintain ethical practice by informing the client of procedures and expectations of therapy, and (2) protects both the therapist and client from misunderstandings that may arise from lack of education about therapy itself.

Rationale for Use

Disclosure statements are a tool that can be used on a regular basis with all clients. Within licensing or certification statutes, some states now require therapists to provide clients with disclosure statements. It is recommended that each therapist develop his or her own statement for use with clients, and that the statement be reviewed with clients so that they have the opportunity to ask questions regarding their treatment. Ironically, while the goal of disclosure statements is to educate the client, specificity within the statement can also increase therapist liability issues. That is, if you say you are providing x amount of services, you then need to provide x amount of services. In this litigious era, it is wise to have an attorney review one's disclosure statement to be sure it is in line with state statutes, and to decrease potential liability issues.

Instructions

Each therapist should develop his or her own disclosure statement based on one's qualifications and the unique needs and amenities of his or her office. Disclosure statements may include the following:

- The therapist's qualifications—the type of training the therapist has had and the types of degrees held. If the therapist is certified or licensed, the types of certification or licensure held, and in what states. If the therapist states a specialty area, proof that he/she has the training to justify this specialty area.
- Any applicable laws should be explained (duty to warn, child abuse reporting, etc.).
- The orientation of the therapist (e.g., behavioral, family systems, cognitive).

- The expectations the therapist has of clients.
- Office policies regarding cancellations, payment, missed appointments, and so on.
- Office policies and phone numbers regarding emergency procedures—things the client should do in the event of a crisis.
- Limitations of one's practice. For example, some clients will assume therapists can prescribe medication; this misconception can be cleared up by addressing therapist limitations.
- If the therapist is seeing more than one person in therapy (e.g., couples or families), the therapist may want to inform the clients of his/her view of secrets in therapy (see Karpel, 1980).

Additional information may be integrated as each therapist sees fit. A sample disclosure statement is provided below. It is recommended that therapists review the disclosure statement carefully with clients at the first session. Questions should be answered in their entirety.

Suggestions for Follow-Up

The therapist can follow-up in the next session by asking if the client(s) has any questions regarding the disclosure statement.

Readings and Resources for the Professional

Huber, C. H. (1994). *Ethical, legal, and professional issues in the practice of marriage and family therapy* (second ed.). New York: Macmillan College Publishing.
Schlossberger, E. and Baker, L. (1996). HIV and family therapists' duty to warn: A legal and ethical analysis. *Journal of Marital and Family Therapy, 22,* 27-40.

REFERENCE

Karpel, M. (1980). Family secrets I. Conceptual and ethical issues in the relational context. II. Ethical and practical considerations in therapeutic management. *Family Process, 19,* 295-306.

Sample Disclosure Statement

Corrine Baker, PhD
Marriage and Family Therapist
Seattle Center for Family Health
Seattle, WA
(865)555-2938

Some Things You Should Know
About Your Therapist and Therapy:

Since therapy is conducted in a number of different ways, depending upon the therapist and his or her orientation, this description has been prepared to inform you about Dr. Baker's qualifications, the therapeutic process, and general knowledge about what to expect from therapy.

Your Therapist's Qualifications:

Dr. Baker received her PhD in marriage and family therapy from Purdue University in West Lafayette, Indiana. In addition, she holds a master's degree in counseling from Washington State University, and a bachelor's degree in psychology from University of Washington. Dr. Baker has been with the Seattle Center for Family Health for five years. She has had over eighteen years experience as a therapist, is a Clinical Member of the American Association for Marriage and Family Therapy (AAMFT), and is an AAMFT-approved supervisor. She has been a licensed Marriage and Family Therapist in the state of Washington since 1988.

The majority of Dr. Baker's experience is working with individuals, couples, and families. Her theoretical orientation includes family systems theory, which focuses on the relationships people have, both within and outside their families. Dr. Baker tends to focus on family strengths, and within her work, she does not utilize blame, but rather helps people develop their strengths (individual, couple, and family) to overcome or manage their problems.

Dr. Baker is not a physician, and cannot prescribe or provide any medication. If medical treatment is indicated, she will recommend a physician or psychiatrist to you, depending upon the nature of your concerns.

The Therapeutic Process:

You have made the first step on your road to feeling better by contacting a therapist. Like every important decision you make in your life, you may want to talk to several therapists about their training, treatment approach, fees, and so on. "Shopping" for a therapist is often vital in getting the satisfaction you want from therapy. Before you decide on a therapist, be sure to get any questions you have answered to your satisfaction.

If you decide to enter therapy with Dr. Baker, she will initially spend time with you exploring the problems which brought you to therapy. Next, you will work with Dr. Baker to set specific goals which you wish to work toward in therapy. Your progress in therapy will be periodically reviewed. The length of therapy will vary depending upon the type and amount of concerns you bring to therapy. At times, changes brought about by your efforts in therapy may cause you discomfort or anxiety; your feelings should be discussed with Dr. Baker. These feelings often accompany behavioral change, and are often a sign of progress. Nevertheless, you may find it helpful to discuss these feelings in therapy.

Confidentiality:

As a client, one of your most important rights is that of confidentiality. Information obtained during therapy sessions will be held confidential, and will not be disclosed to anyone outside of therapy without your written consent. If you are attending therapy as part of a couple or family, you may at times see Dr. Baker without your partner or other family members present. In this instance, if information is divulged to Dr. Baker which she thinks is important for you to share with your partner or other family members, or if you present a situation which is blatantly harmful, unfair, or unethical, she may: (1) ask you to divulge this information before therapy continues, (2) ask your permission to divulge the information before therapy continues, or (3) discontinue therapy if options (1) or (2) are not met. There are also few exceptions to confidentiality as defined by law to which you should be aware. Dr. Baker will be required to break confidentiality if one or more of the following conditions exist:

1. If Dr. Baker has reason to think that you (clients involved in therapy) may be harmful to yourself or others.
2. If Dr. Baker suspects that child abuse or neglect has occurred.
3. If a court orders the release of information regarding your treatment.

Additional Considerations:

To insure quality control in therapy, Dr. Baker reserves the right to consult with therapist-colleagues regarding your treatment. This is similar to a physician "getting a second opinion," and can be very helpful in therapeutic treatment. If consultation occurs outside of the Center for Family Health, identifying information, such as your surname, will not be discussed during these consultations.

Because part of the goal of therapy is to protect confidentiality, Dr. Baker asks that you not have your attorney subpoena her testimony regarding divorce or child custody, in the event of such hearings.

Your Rights as a Client:

As a client you have the right to:
1. Ask questions at any point in time regarding therapeutic or office procedures.
2. Terminate therapy at any time; you may ask Dr. Baker for a list of possible referral sources.
3. Specify and negotiate therapeutic goals and be an active participant in therapy.
4. Confidentiality, as designated above.
5. Be apprised of fees and payment policies.
6. Ask about alternative procedures available for meeting your goals.

Office Procedures and Fees:

If you are unable to attend an appointment, it is your responsibility to cancel your session at least twenty-four hours in advance of the session. Failure to do so will result in you being fully charged a fee for the session. Certain exceptions will be made to this policy in the event of emergencies, provided that the therapist is informed prior to the time of the appointment.

In the event of a crisis, you may try to reach Dr. Baker by phone at 555-2938. If she is not available, you will be referred to the crisis worker for the Center for Family Health.

Telephone calls lasting longer than five minutes will be billed in quarter-hour increments at your set therapy rate. Therapeutic phone calls are not generally reimbursable by insurance.

Each session hour is fifty minutes in length. (This allows your therapist time to complete your case records, file insurance forms, etc.). Dr. Baker's fee is $95 per fifty-minute session. Payment is required at the end of each session. The Center for Family Health does not file insurance for clients. A receipt will be provided to you that you may file with your insurance company.

Informed Consent:

By signing below, I agree that I have read and understand the above information, and agree to the terms of therapy stated above. Dr. Baker has adequately answered any questions I have at this point in time.

I understand I have the right to terminate therapy at any time, and may ask for a list of referral sources. I understand that it is usually best for therapists and clients to make joint decisions about termination of treatment.

My signature indicates that I am giving my consent for Dr. Baker to treat me (us) in therapy. My signature also indicates that Dr. Baker has permission to treat any of my minor children whom I bring to therapy.

_____   _____
Client Signature   Date

_____   _____
Client Signature   Date

_____   _____
Client Signature   Date

_____   _____
Therapist Signature   Date

Index

429

SUPERVISION/TRAINING

TERMINATION
THERAPEUTIC IMPASSES/"RESISTANT" CLIENTS

VIOLENCE/ABUSE

 **easy ways to order!**

❏ **YES!** Please rush me the following book(s)

❶ ❏ The Therapist's Notebook
Homework, Handouts, and Activities for Use in Psychotherapy

❏ $49.95 soft. ISBN: 0-7890-0400-3 _____ Quantity

Order this book online at: www.HaworthPressInc.com/store/product.asp?sku=1567

❷ ❏ The Therapist's Notebook for Children and Adolescents
Homework, Handouts, and Activities for Use in Psychotherapy

❏ $39.95 soft. ISBN: 0-7890-1096-8 _____ Quantity

Order this book online at: www.HaworthPressInc.com/store/product.asp?sku=4742

❸ ❏ The Therapist's Notebook for Families
Solution-Oriented Exercises for Working with Parents, Children, and Adolescents

❏ $39.95 soft. ISBN: 0-7890-1244-8 _____ Quantity

Order this book online at: www.HaworthPressInc.com/store/product.asp?sku=4645

❹ ❏ The Therapist's Notebook for Lesbian, Gay, and Bisexual Clients
Homework, Handouts, and Activities for Use in Psychotherapy

❏ $39.95 soft. ISBN: 0-7890-1252-9 _____ Quantity

Order this book online at: www.HaworthPressInc.com/store/product.asp?sku=4743

Order Today!

PAYMENT OPTIONS

❏ BILL ME LATER. ($5.00 service charge will be added.) (Not available on individual orders outside US/Canada/Mexico. Minimum order: $15. Service charge is waived for jobbers/wholesalers/booksellers.)

P.O.# _____

Signature _____

❏ PAYMENT ENCLOSED. $ _____
Payment by check or money order must be in U.S. or Canadian dollars drawn on a U.S. or Canadian bank.

❏ PLEASE CHARGE TO MY CREDIT CARD:

❏ Visa ❏ MasterCard ❏ AmEx ❏ Discover ❏ Diners Club ❏ Eurocard ❏ JCB

Account _____

Exp. Date _____

Signature _____

May we open a confidential credit card account for you for possible future purchases? ❏ Yes ❏ No

FINAL TALLIES

COST OF BOOK(S)	
POSTAGE & HANDLING See chart at right.	
IN CANADA Please add 7% for GST. NFLD, NS, NB: Add 8% for province tax.	
State Tax NY, OH & MN add local sales tax.	
FINAL TOTAL	

POSTAGE AND HANDLING:

If your book total is:	Add this amount:
up to $29.95	$5.00
$30.00 – $49.99	$6.00
$50.00 – $69.99	$7.00
$70.00 – $89.99	$8.00
$90.00 – $109.99	$9.00
$110.00 – $129.99	$10.00
$130.00 – $149.99	$11.00
$150.00 – and up	$12.00

US orders will be shipped via UPS; Outside US orders will be shipped via Book Printed Matter. For shipments via other delivery services, contact Haworth for details. Allow 3–4 weeks for delivery after publication. Based on US dollars. Booksellers: Call for freight charges.

• If paying in Canadian funds, please use the current exchange rate. Payment in UNESCO coupons welcome.
• Individual orders outside the US/Canada/Mexico must be prepaid by check or credit card.
• Prices in US dollars and subject to change without notice.

ADDITIONAL INFORMATION

Please fill in the information below or **TAPE YOUR BUSINESS CARD IN THIS AREA.**

NAME _____

INSTITUTION _____

ADDRESS _____

_____

CITY _____

STATE/PROVINCE _____

ZIP/POSTAL CODE _____

COUNTY (NY Residents only) _____

COUNTRY _____

PHONE _____

FAX _____

E-MAIL _____

PLEASE PRINT OR TYPE CLEARLY.

May we use your e-mail address for confirmations and other types of information? ❏ Yes ❏ No

We appreciate receiving your e-mail address and fax number. Haworth would like to e-mail or fax special discount offers to you, as a preferred customer. We will **never share, rent, or exchange** your e-mail address or fax number. We regard such actions as an invasion of your privacy.

THIS FORM MAY BE PHOTOCOPIED FOR DISTRIBUTION.

Order from your local bookstore or directly from
The Haworth Press, Inc.
10 Alice Street • Binghamton, New York 13904–1580 • USA
Telephone: 1.800.429.6784 • Fax: 1.800.895.0582
Outside US/Canada: Telephone: 607.722.5857 • Fax: 607.771.0012
E-mail: orders@haworthpressinc.com

Visit our website at: www.HaworthPress.com

CODE: BOF02